THE NOBLE TRAVELLER

THE NOBLE TRAVELLER

O. V. de L. MILOSZ

INTRODUCTION BY CZESLAW MILOSZ
EDITED BY CHRISTOPHER BAMFORD

INNER TRADITIONS
LINDISFARNE PRESS

The French texts, upon which the translations in this edition are based, are published in France in O. V. de L. Milosz, Oeuvres Complètes, Vols I, II, VII, VIII © 1960, 1961, 1948
Éditions André Silvaire, Paris.

This edition © The Lindisfarne Press 1985

All individual translations etc. are © the translators or authors:

Foreword, "Mists," "Lullaby," "Egeia," "The Sea," "Earth," "Muse," "September Symphony," "November Symphony," "Sunday, 14 March, 1915," "The Cart," "The Scale," "Canticle of Knowledge," Bio-chronology © Christopher Bamford.

"Unfinished Symphony," "Insomnia," "The Bridge," "The Hooded Carriage Halted in the Night," "The Confession of Lemuel," "Canticle of Spring," "Psalm of the Morning Star" © David Gascoyne.

Introduction, Ars Magna, The Arcana, Notes © Czeslaw Milosz.

"King don Luis," "When she comes," "Bridge on the Rhine," "A Few Words on Poetry" © John Peck.

"To the sounds," "We need," "Especially," "Monkey Dance" (all from 14 Poems by O. V. de L. Milosz), "Nihumim" (from 100 French Poems), "Vacant Lots" (from New Directions 15) © the Kenneth Rexroth Trust, reprinted by permission.

"Karomama," "All the dead are drunk," "The soft and rusty creaking," "Talita Cumi," "1922: The Initiate's Christmas Eve," "Psalm of the King of Beauty," "Psalm of Ripening," "Psalm of Reintegration," "A Note" © Edouard Roditi.

"Milosz and Symbolism" © Mortimer Guiney.

Portions of this book have previously appeared in Ironwood 18 and Temenos 3.

All rights reserved.

No part of this book may be reproduced or used in any manner whatsoever without written permission except in the case of brief quotations embodied in critical articles and reviews. For information address The Lindisfarne Press.

An Inner Traditions/Lindisfarne Press Book

Published by The Lindisfarne Press, Box 127, West Stockbridge, MA 01266
Distributed to the book trade by Inner Traditions International. All inquiries regarding distribution should be addressed to Inner Traditions International, 377 Park Avenue South, New York, N.Y. 10016.

Designed by Judith Lerner

ISBN 0-89281-064-5   trade paperback
ISBN 0-89281-066-1   cloth

LIBRARY OF CONGRESS CATALOGING IN PUBLICATION DATA
Milosz, O. V. de L. (Oscar Vladislas de Lubicz), 1877–1939.
The noble traveller.

English and French.
Bibliography: p.
1. Milosz, O. V. de L. (Oscar Vladislas de Lubicz), 1877–1939—Translations, English. 2. Mysticism—Poetry. 3. Metaphysics—Addresses, essays, lectures. I. Bamford, Christopher. II. Title.
PQ2625.I558A2   1984   841'.912   84-25029
ISBN 0-89281-066-1
ISBN 0-89281-064-5 (pbk.)

TRANSMITTED by oral tradition to initiates of the Middle Ages and of modern times, Noble Traveller is the secret name of initiates of antiquity. The last time that it was pronounced in public was on May 30, 1786, in Paris, at a session of Parliament devoted to the cross-examination of a famous defendant*, victim of a pamphleteer, Theveneau de Morande. Initiates' wanderings did not differ from ordinary travels for study except that their itinerary, though apparently haphazard, rigorously coincided with the adept's most secret aspirations and gifts . . .

O.V. de L. Milosz, *Exegetic Note, verse 46*
THE ARCANA

* Cagliostro.

CONTENTS

LIST OF ILLUSTRATIONS   11
ACKNOWLEDGMENTS   13
INTRODUCTION BY CZESLAW MILOSZ   15
FOREWORD BY CHRISTOPHER BAMFORD   49

PART ONE
The Poems
TRANSLATED BY CHRISTOPHER BAMFORD, DAVID GASCOYNE, JOHN PECK, KENNETH REXROTH AND EDOUARD RODITI

from *Le Poème des Décadences*
The Poem of Decadences (1899)
Brumes, 66   Mists, 67
Berceuse, 68   Lullaby, 69
Egeia, 70   Egeia, 71

from *Les Sept Solitudes*
The Seven Solitudes (1906)
Karomama, 72   Karomama, 73
Aux Sons d'une Musique . . . , 76   To the sound . . . , 77
Tous les Morts sont ivres . . . , 78
    All the dead are drunk . . . , 79

Grincement doux . . . , 80
    The soft and rusty creaking . . . , 81
Il nous faut . . . , 82   We need . . . , 83
Et surtout que . . . , 84   Especially . . . , 85
Le roi don Luis . . . , 86   King don Luis . . . , 87
Quand elle viendra . . . , 88   When she comes . . . , 89
Danse de Singe, 90   Monkey Dance, 91

    from *Les Éléments*
    The Elements (1911)
Le Mer, 92   The Sea, 93
La Terre, 96   Earth, 97
La Muse, 100   Muse, 101

    from *Poèmes*
    Poems (1915)
Le pont sur le Rhin, 106   Bridge on the Rhine, 107
Symphonie de Septembre, 108   September Symphony, 109
Symphonie de Novembre, 116   November Symphony, 117
Symphonie Inachevée, 120   Unfinished Symphony, 121
Insomnie, 128   Insomnia, 129
Nihumim, 132   Nihumim, 133

    Uncollected (1915)
Dimanche, 14 Mars 1915, 140   Sunday, 14 March 1915, 141

    from *Adramandoni*
    Adramandoni (1918)
H, 142   H 143
La Charrette, 146   The Cart, 147
La Gamme, 150   The Scale, 151
Les Terrains vagues, 154   Vacant Lots, 155
Le Pont, 158   The Bridge, 159

from *La Confession de Lemuel*
    The Confession of Lemuel (1922)
La Berline arrêtée dans la nuit, 160
    The Hooded Carriage Halted in the Night, 161
Talita Cumi, 166   Talita Cumi, 167
Cantique de la Connaissance, 170
    Canticle of Knowledge, 171
La Confession de Lemuel, 184
    The Confession of Lemuel, 185

from *Poèmes (1895-1927)*
    Poems (1895-1927) (1929)
Cantique du Printemps, 198   Canticle of Spring, 199
La Nuit de Noël de 1922 de l'Adepte, 204
    1922: The Initiate's Christmas Eve, 205
Psaume du Roi de Beauté, 212
    Psalm of the King of Beauty, 213
Psaume de la Maturation, 216   Psalm of Ripening, 217
Psaume de la Réintégration, 220   Psalm of Reintegration, 221

The Last Poem (1936)
Psaume de l'Étoile du Matin, 224
    Psalm of the Morning Star, 225

PART TWO
The Metaphysical Works
TRANSLATED BY CZESLAW MILOSZ

Ars Magna, 1924

1   Epistle to Storge   233
2   Memoria   248

3 Numbers   257
4 Turba Magna   264
5 Lumen   269

The Arcana, 1927

The Poem of the Arcana   277
Hiram's Prayer   289
Exegetic Notes   291
The Author's Prayer   399
A Few Notes   401

APPENDICES

A FEW WORDS ON POETRY, *translated by John Peck*	414
MILOSZ AND SYMBOLISM, *by Mortimer Guiney*	419
A NOTE, *by Edouard Roditi*	428
BIO-CHRONOLOGY WITH PHOTOGRAPHS	432
BIBLIOGRAPHY	479
NOTES ON THE TRANSLATORS	482

LIST OF ILLUSTRATIONS

FRONTISPIECE
Milosz at 44, December 1921

FOLLOWING PAGE 448

Milosz, aged 4, with his mother
Milosz, aged 12, with his mother
Milosz, aged 19
Manuscript page of "September Symphony," 1913
Manuscript page of *Epistle to Storge*, 1916
Milosz by Henry de Groux, 1917
Milosz at the League of Nations, September 1921
Manuscript of *Memoria*, c.1922
Manuscript of "Psalm of the King of Beauty," 1923
Lithuanian Diplomatic Representatives, Kaunas, 1923
Manuscript page of the "Poem of the Arcana," 1926
Milosz by Aron Bilis, Paris, 1930
Milosz on vacation, c.1930
Staff of the Lithuanian Legation, Paris, 1931
Milosz and Jean de Boschère, Fontainebleau, c.1935
Milosz and the Baronne de Tinan, Maggie de Lauris and
    Renée de Brimont, by the feeder, Fontainebleau, 1938
Milosz on his deathbed

ACKNOWLEDGMENTS

The Lindisfarne Press and the editor wish to thank the following for their help and support during the four years that it has taken to bring *The Noble Traveller* to fruition (many others must remain nameless, but our thanks go to all):

first, the translators—who gave of themselves freely, with enthusiasm, for the sake of the work alone—David Gascoyne, John Peck, Edouard Roditi and, above all, Czeslaw Milosz, whose courtesy and patience have been unfailing; thanks in this regard are due also to Carol Tinker and Bradford Morrow for poems from the Kenneth Rexroth Estate; and to M. Georges Junosza-Zdrojewski in Paris;

next, those whose committedness and cooperation aided the project in innumerable and different ways: S. A. Backis (Lithuanian Chargé d'Affaires in Washington), Eva Balamuth, Maribeth Bunn, François Chapon (of the Bibliothèque littéraire J. Doucet), June Cobb, Mr. and Mrs. Jonas Dovydenas, Elise Frick, Joscelyn Godwin, Mortimer Guiney, George Mills Harper, Robert and Deborah Lawlor, Margaret Lloyd, Darrel Ruhl, Kathleen Raine, André Silvaire, Mr. and Mrs. Kazys Varnelis, Vytautas Virkau;

and finally all those institutions who have helped financially: the Association for the Advancement of Baltic Studies, the Lithuanian Foundation, the Alfred Jurzykowsky Foundation, the Mayer Family Fund and especially the Barbara H. Culver Foundation and the Swedenborg Foundation.

INTRODUCTION

The Man and His Work

In 1939, not quite twenty years ago, an unknown man was buried in the cemetery of Fontainebleau: one of the truest, loftiest poets of our tongue or of any tongue. One of the most demanding artists and one of the most notable failures. But he failed as Nerval and Baudelaire failed, as Rimbaud and Verlaine failed, as Van Gogh failed. Forgive us, Milosz. You are one of those whom France ignores even unto their last breaths—only to pride herself afterward on their destinies, as moving as they were tragically unrecognized—one of those whom France never hears while they are living but to whom, afterward, she does not cease to listen.

When the French critic André Blanchet wrote those words in 1958, they were only partly true. Milosz had had a few staunch admirers both in France and abroad, and first studies of his works had already appeared during his lifetime. Among poets of other countries his poetry had found translators sensitive to its unique tone. Blanchet's remarks expressed correctly, however, a change, noticeable at that moment, in the French reading public's attitude toward Milosz's poetry. In fact, the year 1958 may be considered a turning point. That year Milosz's mystery play *Miguel Mañara* was successfully staged by Le Théâtre des Champs-Élysées, and the first volumes of a new edition of his collected works (following a previous incomplete Swiss one of 1944-1946) began to appear at the publishing house of André Silvaire. The number of books and essays devoted to his poetry has been increasing ever since.

In 1966, an association, "Les Amis de Milosz," was founded in Paris; it placed a commemorative plaque on his house in Fontainebleau, and its members gather every year on the anniversary of his death. The association also publishes a journal, *Cahiers de L'Association des Amis de Milosz*, which reproduces biographical documents and records new scholarly publications on his writings. His manuscripts, letters and the first editions of his works are preserved in the "Collection Doucet," a division of the Bibliothèque de St. Geneviève in the Latin Quarter.

Yet, although some poems of Milosz became anthology pieces, and the literary press and television made the French public familiar with his name, only a part of his oeuvre profits from this belated fame. Quite often a distinction is made between Milosz the poet and Milosz the metaphysician, the latter still being accused of utter obscurity if not of outright madness. It is true that after his early cynical-melancholy-ironic verse he moved steadily toward a vision of the world and a concept of poetry, both of which were completely alien to his contemporaries. At a given moment he relegated everything he had written to the lowly category of preparatory labor and undertook what he regarded as the culmination of his work, an exposition of his doctrine in two, as he calls them, "metaphysical poems," *Ars Magna* and *The Arcana*. But even many of his poems of the earlier period would hardly be comprehensible to anyone who would like simply to put aside his illuminism and his prophecy as to the future of mankind. Inasmuch as a continuous search led the writer to his final work, nothing authorizes us to divide his oeuvre into two halves. Yet only by attaching special importance to his later phase when, as he was convinced, he had fulfilled his destiny on earth, may we grasp the incomparable strangeness of such a voice in our century.

INTRODUCTION

O. V. de L. Milosz was a Frenchman by education, by language, by choice and by his profound attachment to France, but in his origin there was nothing French. A newcomer from Northeastern Europe, from that Septentrion which has always remained for the French imagination a mythical realm inhabited by bears and bearlike human creatures or part-time beasts, he has confronted his French biographers with puzzles. The solutions they offer have often made me smile. After all, belonging to the same family, though a distant cousin, I know a great deal about its past and about all the tangle of nationalities, religions and divided loyalties of the area from which it comes. Moreover, in 1931, when as a very young man I met him for the first time in Paris, I was privileged to receive his friendship, or rather the touching solicitude of an elder poet for a beginner and puppy, and this persisted till his death. Through our conversations I had an opportunity to learn some details of his life. Even so, although in one of his letters (published in *Soixante-quinze lettres inédites*, Paris: André Silvaire, 1969) he wrote, "I consider him a bit as my son," he did not expect that one day I would be one of the translators of his work into English.

Oskar Wladyslaw Milosz (if we keep to the original spelling of his name) was born May 28, 1877, on the estate of Czereïa, in the eastern outskirts of a vast country once known (before it was swallowed up by Russia) as the Grand Duchy of Lithuania. Today this district belongs to the Byelorussian S.S.R. His father was a Polish-Lithuanian nobleman, but his paternal grandmother was an Italian cantatrice from an old Genoan family and his mother was Jewish. His ancestors were not natives of the region; they had migrated there, in or shortly before 1802, from the very heart of ethnic Lithuania, on the Baltic peninsula, and thus from a non-Slavic land where too, according to a family legend, the Miloszes had been only settlers. Several centuries earlier, fleeing German pressure, they had left behind their estates in the country of the Slavic Lusatian Sorbs, near Frankfurt on the Oder; hence, in Milosz's writings the allusions to his lineage going back to the sovereigns of Lusatia. Such data are enough to bring biographers to grief. Even the way he signed his books, O.V. de L. Milosz (for Oscar Vladislas de Lubicz Milosz), disturbs them with the superfluous "Lubicz." Not, as they suppose, another family name, "Lubicz" refers to a complex system of heraldry, common in the Middle Ages, whereby every coat of arms, sign of several families belonging to a clan, bore a name of its own.

Everything related to his origin and his national options conspires to turn any sketch into the indefiniteness of a legend. Above all, his "Lithuanianness." For, though he died a naturalized Frenchman, he had also stressed that he was a Lithuanian. He was the author of charming adaptations of Lithuanian fairy tales and folk songs. However, at the time of his birth, Lithuania meant no more than a vaguely delineated area with several tongues and dialects. After World War I the meaning of the word Lithuania changed and began to designate a small Baltic country speaking one non-Slavic language (imagine Ireland returning completely to Gaelic) which Milosz had never heard in his childhood. The truth is that he was a Lithuanian by choice as he was a Frenchman by choice. His fate was to be a wanderer and a life-long seeker for a place, both in a terrestrial and in a metaphysical sense. Aristocratic, because he believed in the ancestral memory preserved in blood, he wanted to remain faithful to his double, noble and Jewish, parentage; in this also he took issue with the spirit of uniformity of his age.

In scandalous chronicles of Nineteenth Century high society his father, Wladyslaw Milosz, figures as an atheist and anarchist, a wealthy man of unrestrained temperament. Taken with the beauty of a young girl, Miriam Rosenthal, the daughter of a Warsaw teacher of Hebrew, he carried her off to his estate in the Byelorussian forests. Maria Rosalia Milosz proved generous to the few Roman Catholic churches of the region but, according to rumors, the Sabbath candles were lit every Friday in Czereïa. Whether this is true or not, it was with rapture that her son discovered Jewish mystical writings and integrated many of their elements into his Christian cosmology.

Few other examples of poetry return, as obstinately as his does, to a remembrance of childhood. Yet he was not a happy child. "Coldness and insanity roamed in the house," as he confesses in one of his poems. His parents were distant, and their only child was left in the care of nurses and tutors. Early in life he began to bear the stigma of loneliness, of unappeased craving for love. A sensitive, delicate boy wandering alone in the immense parks of an estate: this was perhaps enough to predestine him for a life of contemplation. Northern landscapes seen through the eyes of a pensive child constantly return in his imagery, striking French critics as exotic. In what language then did he think? The language spoken at home was Polish, but very early he learned German and French from his Alsatian governess; by the age of twelve he was trilingual.

Exactly at that age he was transferred by his parents to Paris and placed as a boarder at the Lycée Janson-de-Sally. To deposit him like a bundle in alien surroundings was perhaps not a very loving act, and yet by so doing they bound his fate to the whole artistic and intellectual heritage of France. The French educational system of that time was rigid, severe and marked by a Republican zeal for promoting a Nineteenth Century scientific *Weltanschauung*; a struggle with the flatly rationalistic upbringing which he received at the Lycée was to fill many years of his life. A choice he made after he had finished high school—he was then already writing poetry—is characteristic: he turned not to science, literature or philosophy but to the study of the pre-Greek and pre-Roman origins of Mediterranean civilization, e.g., Egyptian, Assyrian and Hebrew antiquities. From 1896 to 1899, he was a student at the École du Louvre and at the École des Langues Orientales, where, under the guidance of Professor Eugène Ledrain, translator of the Bible, he learned to read Hebrew texts.

During the time he was emerging from adolescence, French literature was resounding with quarrels about symbolism and the so-called decadence. His first volume of poems, published in 1899, has a title too literary and thus not well chosen: *Le Poème des Décadences,* which does not do justice to the contents. Already his early poetry, the influence of Baudelaire and of Heine notwithstanding, has a recognizable quality of its own. Its desperate-sarcastic lyricism reminds us of Jules Laforgue. Yet as a very young man Milosz had a sense of direction which led him away from his elders and contemporaries. He felt that something wrong had befallen the whole of European art. His article "A Few Words on Poetry" written at the end of his life, in the 1930's, is revealing in this respect, as in it he reminisces on his first literary steps. Already, by then, the tendency toward "purity" of art for art's sake seemed to him to complete the estrangement of poetry from "the great human family," an estrangement which had gradually set in during the Nineteenth Century. Let me quote: "In essence, that pursuit of pure poetry derives directly from the mannerisms of the so-called 'esthetic' schools. This, under various names, we made a subject of our discussions, around 1895, in Kalissaya, the first American bar in Paris, which counted among its regular customers my friends Oscar Wilde and Moréas. And I will never forget the horrified look that I attracted from the Irish poet when, one day, in the midst of a conversation on Shelley, great ancestor of estheticism, I voiced my preference for the rhymster Byron, disciple of classical Pope...."

Milosz's English and American connections merit mention here. He spoke fluent English. Margins of books from his library are covered with notes in four languages: French, English, German and Polish. Not only did he frequent Kalissaya, but later he also used to visit Raymond Duncan, brother of Isadora Duncan (whose adventures he knew of first hand) in his so-called Academy. A close friendship developed between him and Natalie Clifford Barney, of whose famous literary salon he was one of the regular guests. A no less lasting friendship bound him to Christian Gauss of Princeton and his wife. And lest bilingual poets, active both in France and in America, should be omitted here, let me name Jean de Boschère, his faithful friend, and young Edouard Roditi, whom he befriended in the 1930's. From all this one should not draw the conclusion that he was especially pro-American, for he feared America as an Apocalyptic beast of the future and his words of compassion for Edgar Allen Poe "who found the worst of hells in his native American land" convey his ambivalent feelings.

By his formative years, he belonged to the Paris and Europe of "La Belle Époque." Judging from the torment and despair which pervade the poetry written in his youth, the epoch did not seem to him so joyful after all. But at least in those days travel was quite a different thing from the tourism of today. The itinerary of the young poet's voyages (initiatory, he would say later) covered England, Germany, Italy, Austria, Poland, Spain and North Africa, as well as his native land where he witnessed the revolutionary upheaval of 1905; there, mother and son (his father was no longer alive) sold in 1906 the fabulously vast forest estate of Czereïa to a government-sponsored company which was parcelling out land among the peasants. Because of the scarcity of extant letters, his stays in various European capitals would be difficult to trace to definite dates. Likewise, his amorous involvements elude his biographers, as the names of women are known only by initials. What can be said is that behind the poems collected in his first volume, as well as those in *Les Sept Solitudes*, 1906, and many included in *Les Éléments*, 1911, stands a sensuous, violent and unhappy man. An attempted suicide; Don Juanism; paganism; tones of hatred both for the Hebrew heritage and for "the Nazarene"; outbursts of derision at the absurdity of existence—all this seems, in retrospect, the stormy maturation which led by degrees to a breakthrough opening upon his most creative period.

To be brief in explaining his internal journey, perhaps it is enough to recall once again his homelessness. He had no home in space, but neither had he a home in his time. By his "elective affinities" he was a man of the end of the Eighteenth Century, a century much too complex to be defined as the Age of Reason. We can imagine him as an acquaintance of Cagliostro, as a member of one of the "mystical lodges" or as one of the characters in Goethe's *Wilhelm Meister*. His admiration for Goethe verged on worship; his translation of the prologue and of the first act of *Faust* is probably the best among many attempts to render Goethe's verse into French. If we succeed in picturing Milosz in the garb of that epoch—as he did himself in his strongly autobiographical novel *L'Amoureuse Initiation* (1910), its action set in Venice of the Eighteenth Century—we would also have an indication of his literary tastes. He liked poets from the turn of the century; Byron, Hölderlin, Chamisso; he was attracted by the fantastic and the bizarre. And though he was well read in philosophy, he would have assigned a higher rank to "the Anonymous Philosopher," Claude de Saint-Martin, than to Kant. Thus he was a spiritual brother of those who a hundred years before him had looked for a way out of the trap constructed by presumptuous Reason.

L'Amoureuse Initiation is a story about the last love of comic, pathetic Sassolo Sinibaldo, Count Pinamonte, the thirteenth duke of Brettinoro, for a beautiful and perfidious Venetian courtesan, Clarissa Annalena. Or, to put it another way, it is a story of the ascent from a sensual love to a celestial love. A passion for a woman initiates poor Sassolo into an all-embracing love for the Creator and the Creation. A similar theme, with changed scenery, is given dramatic form in *Miguel Mañara*, first printed in the September and October 1912 issues of *La Nouvelle Revue Française*. The hero is the true, historical Don Juan (as distinct from the fictitious character created by Tirso de Molina): Don Miguel Mañara Vicentelo de Leca, born in 1626, a debauchee in his youth, then a monk in Seville, where soon after his death the process of his canonization as a saint began. Milosz faithfully followed historical documents, even as to Don Miguel's marriage to the young and pure Girolama, whose death after a few months of happiness caused him to enter a monastery. Here, too, love for a creature acquires a meaning of providential initiation into love which "surpasseth all understanding." *Miguel Mañara* is the most accessible and the most acclaimed work of Milosz (two composers have written music to it).

But *Miguel Mañara* is only one of three mystery plays. *Méphiboseth*, 1913, continues the exploration of the bond uniting sin and saintliness, this time the plot being taken from the Bible. King David, in love with Bathsheba, wife of Uriah, sends a letter to Joab, commander of the army: "Set ye Uriah in the forefront of the hottest battle, and retire from him, that he may be smitten, and die." A child of David and Bathsheba dies too, as punishment for David's deed, but through their next child, Solomon, David's line will survive to bring forth, many generations later, Jesus the Saviour, son of the sinful human race. *Saul de Tarse* (written probably in 1913-1914, but published only in 1970) takes us to Palestine under Roman rule, when a hard, fanatical defender of the Law, Saul, does not hesitate to sentence his friends to death for sympathizing with the Christians—till a vision on the road to Damascus changes him into Paul the Apostle. Because of the dates the plays were written, their religious topics and the very genre of poetic drama, readers familiar with the French literary scene may be tempted to associate them with those of Paul Claudel, but this would be an obvious error. Milosz was not indebted to Claudel, nor did he rate Claudel's poetry very highly. Neither the latter's verse nor his treatment of religious themes would justify analogies. Claudel's plays bear the imprint of a personality well established in Roman Catholic beliefs, while Milosz's plays are a religious quest.

His poems of maturity begin with *Symphonies*, 1915, composed in 1913-14, and are contained in a few slim volumes: *Nihumim*, 1915; *Adramandoni*, 1918; *La Confession de*

Lemuel, 1922. He was completely impervious to the literary fashions of the day and his free verse is unlike that of his contemporaries. In terms of English poetry, T.S. Eliot sometimes reminds us of Milosz, who was obsessed with the solitude of man in a big city. As in Eliot, there are images of desolation, of "terrains vagues" (wastelands), of "railway track deserts," of empty lots overgrown with nettles. The basic difference is that from December, 1914, on, Milosz was an initiate and his poetry became hermetic. Not always perceivable, this change grows more apparent every year, up to his abandonment of verse altogether.

When French scholars speak of Milosz's moment of illumination, they invoke Pascal's "night of fire." What Blaise Pascal saw that night we will never learn. After his death, on a piece of paper covered with his handwriting and sewn into his jacket was found this constant reminder: "The year of grace 1654. Monday 23, November, day of Saint Clement, pope and martyr, and of others in martyrdom/ Eve of Saint Chrysogonus, martyr, and others./ From half past ten in the evening until about half past twelve./ FIRE/ God of Abraham, God of Isaac, God of Jacob,/ not of the philosophers and savants./ Certitude. Certitude. Feeling. Joy. Peace./ God of Jesus Christ."

In *Ars Magna*, Milosz's detailed account of what happened to him on the night of December 14, 1914 is an attempt to convey his visual and auditory perceptions. It seems that only after that experience did he extend his reading to a field which would strangely agree with his nature—that of a man from around 1800, which he was by personal inclination—treatises on alchemy; the Kabbalah; Jakob Boehme; Paracelsus; the history of secret esoteric orders; and Emanuel Swedenborg (though, let me stress this in advance, he cannot be called a Swedenborgian in a strict sense). He made use of what he read but kept his distance, discovering, nevertheless, a continuity of "the hermetic doctrine" throughout the ages and finding it present, under a cipher, in monumental achievements of the

Western mind: in the architecture of Gothic cathedrals, in Dante—and in René Descartes.

His studies and meditations left their imprint upon his poetry and culminated in two treatise-poems: *Ars Magna*, the first chapter of which was published in 1917 and the work in its entirety in 1924, and *Les Arcanes (The Arcana)*, published in 1927. As Milosz says of himself, the completion of those two messages addressed to readers of the future brought to an end his vocation as a poet. Only several years later, in 1936, did he write one more hermetic poem, "Psaume de L'Étoile du Matin" ("Psalm of the Morning Star").

Nothing would be more mistaken than to imagine Milosz the metaphysician as a man withdrawing from the world. *Ars Magna* and *The Arcana* were written in the midst of intense political and diplomatic activity, from which he had previously kept himself as distant as possible. At the outbreak of World War I he held a Russian passport; drafted in 1916 into the Russian units in France, he was assigned as a press officer to the Bureau of Diplomatic Studies at the French Ministry of Foreign Affairs.

Soon afterward came the Russian Revolution and its definitive change of his social status. A wealthy man before, he was now ruined, though not, as his French biographers maintain, because of the expropriation of his land by the revolutionary authorities. His estate had been sold long before, but the money had been invested in Tsarist government bonds. From one day to the next, of course, those bonds lost their value. Diplomacy, to which Milosz seemed predestined by his knowledge of several languages and by his connections, then became his profession; with zeal and fervor he threw himself into international politics. Paris, in the days when the war was drawing to its end, was host to delegations from many countries and was the scene of innumerable maneuvers, in expectation of a new order of things. That new order was announced by President Wilson's Fourteen Points and was subsequently implemented in part by the Peace Conference of

Versailles. National states were emerging from the chaos of war in the territories controlled, prior to 1914, by the Hapsburg Empire, Germany and Russia: Czechoslovakia, Poland, and, on the Baltic Peninsula, Lithuania, Latvia and Estonia, as well as, in the north, Independent Finland. Because of his family background Milosz now had to choose between Poland and Lithuania, a predicament not rare among people of that area, where sometimes even brothers chose opposite sides. He chose Lithuania, although he did not speak the language of the new republic. (My branch of the family opted for Poland, and thus I was to go to Polish schools.)

Beginning with the crucial year 1918, he devoted much energy to defending the new State's interests, which clashed with those of Poland. In 1919, he was a member of the Lithuanian delegation to the Peace Conference, then the Representative to the French government, and, between 1920 and 1925, as Chargé d'Affaires, organized the Legations of Lithuania in Paris and Brussels. His official functions are not irrelevant to the purpose of this introduction, inasmuch as *The Arcana* tells of his acquaintance with the work of the League of Nations: in fact, in Geneva he acted as a Lithuanian delegate, and he took part in the international conferences of Brussels and of Genoa. His many speeches, political studies, contributions to *La Revue Baltique* and pamphlets *(L'Alliance des États Baltiques*, 1919) coincide with his creative labors as a poet-metaphysician.

Simultaneously he was re-creating in the French language Lithuanian folk songs, *dainos*, very old, some dating from pagan times *(Dainos*, 1928), and fairy tales *(Contes et fabliaux de la vieille Lithuanie*, 1930; *Contes Lithuaniens de ma Mère L'Oye*, 1933). These can hardly be termed translations, as they play brilliantly with the style of Old French and are seasoned with an exquisite humor, an ingredient not always found in the originals. Even the words used in the titles: *fabliaux*, Mère L'Oye (Mother Goose), with their antiquated spelling, betray the author's intent to embed his stories in the French literary tradition. Perhaps, while having reached a limit as a poet so that any verse seemed to him pale and insufficient, his earthy and wryly compassionate nature looked for an outlet in those tales of leprechauns, talking animals and trees.

In sharp contrast to the alleged "madness" of his metaphysical works, his way of life in no way resembled that of the *"poètes maudits."* As a Counsellor at the Lithuanian Legation in Paris he performed his diplomatic functions until his retirement in 1938. Decorated with the French *Legion d'Honneur*, he also received a title of doctor *honoris causa* from the Theology-Philosophy Department of the University of Kaunas, Lithuania. In the 1930's his Biblical studies exposed him, it is true, to reproach for extravagance, especially his Kabbalistic deciphering of the Apocalypse and his forecast of "the year of the Great Conflagration," 1944, *(L'Apocalypse de Saint Jean Déchifrée*, 1933), as well as his hypothesis as to the native land of the Jewish people. According to Milosz, in prehistoric times the Iberian Peninsula was the original Eden of the Bible *(Les Origines Ibériques du Peuple Juif*, 1933). However, even this kind of venture one should not see as a complete break of communication with others. In the year he finished and published *The Arcana*, 1927, he returned to the faith in which he had been baptized and from that time on was a practicing Roman Catholic, obediently following the counsel of his confessor. Whatever theologians might have thought of his cosmology, he himself firmly believed that it did not depart by even an iota from Catholic dogma, and that opinion was shared, it seems, by his confessor, Father Huriet. The priest, perhaps familiar with the prominent role played by alchemy and the Christianized Kabbalah in Roman Catholicism of the late Middle Ages and the Renaissance, not only did not discourage his pupil and friend from pursuing his Biblical exegesis (a Bible in Hebrew was Milosz's bedside book), but rather encouraged his pursuits in that direction.

All those who met O. Milosz in the last decade of his life had the impression of finding themselves in the presence of an extraordinary personality. Courteous, with a sense of humor devoid of malice, capable of outbursts of rage at human stupidity, proud, melancholy, aristocratic and respectful of the French working-class, he emanated benevolence and compassion, having truly learned to love people, as he says in one of his poems, "with an old love exhausted by loneliness, pity and anger." His love embraced not only human beings: he used to spend his vacations in Fontainebleau, mostly because of the park, full of birds, surrounding the royal castle. Hard as it may be to believe, O. Milosz spoke the language of birds, of various species, which arrived at his call, alighting on his shoulders and hands. Of all the park's regular visitors, this solitary man was the only one whom the birds admitted into such intimacy.

During World War II, the outbreak of which he foresaw as early as the 1920's, an important collection of his unpublished texts and of essays about him appeared in Lyon: *Milosz—Cahier Spécial de Poésie 42* (today a rare find). (The first monograph, a doctoral dissertation by J. Grinius, in Lithuanian, dates from 1930.) A book by Armand Godoy—*Milosz, le poète de l'amour*, 1944—was published in Switzerland where also an edition of his collected works was started by Les Éditions Egloff. After the war, several studies and doctoral dissertations were dedicated to his works, among them Geneviève-Irène Zidonis: *O.V. de L. Milosz, sa vie, son oeuvre, son rayonnement*, 1951; André Lebois: *L'oeuvre de Milosz*, 1960; Jacques Buge: *Milosz en quête du divin*, 1966; Jean Bellemin-Noel: *La Poésie-philosophie de Milosz*, 1975.

It was in Fontainebleau that he settled after his retirement. He died there suddenly on March 2, 1939. His funeral was attended by the staff of the Legation of Lithuania in Paris and by a few friends. Yet even at the time when his name meant little to the reading public, on the granite slab of his tomb, not far from the entrance to the cemetery of Fontainebleau, anonymous admirers would place fresh flowers.

On his philosophy

O. Milosz's "philosophical poems"—*Ars Magna* and *The Arcana*—are very difficult to understand and fit no literary genre. In order to identify them as poetry we must first recognize a specific concept of poetic creation, as professed by the author in his mature phase. Contrary to opinions prevalent in the Twentieth Century, for him a poem was not a linguistic structure whose meaning originates in, and is inseparable from, the structure, but rather was the by-product of a spiritual attainment which must precede a poet's struggle with the insufficiency of language. Two poets who, in his view, approached to some extent the unrivaled perfection of the Bible—Dante the alchemist and Goethe the sage—left works which are cryptic. A great poem is not limited to a pursuit of the ineffable created if not revealed by the very act of writing; it is a contour around the core of a more or less precise knowledge. One would be tempted to call this knowledge *gnosis*, but with some misgivings, as the word lost its original connotations after the struggle between the early Christian communities and the Gnostics, and has since been associated with the dualistic bent of the Greek philosophic mind. The author often voiced his dislike of theosophy and in general of all purely "spiritual" doctrines because of their concern with spirit at the expense of matter; he regarded himself as a disciple of the alchemists, in whose teachings "the regeneration of matter" went together with the spiritual regeneration of the man who practiced the alchemic art. Thus the epithet "theosophic" does not apply here, and I would also avoid another epithet, "occult," inasmuch as this word may mean anything.

The task of an introduction is to open access to a work which at first sight seems inaccessible. In the case of O. Milosz this may be done by placing him in the context of a certain European tradition, so that many of his ideas and images will be seen as inherited from those writers of the past whom he considered his masters and guides.

Both *Ars Magna* and *The Arcana* deal with the central enigma of our civilization (at least since the time of the Renaissance): namely, how a scientific vision of the world has influenced the inner life of man. Let us recall here that the evolution of scientific method did not follow a strictly linear pattern. At first several options seemed to offer themselves to the European mind engaged in the exploration of Nature; a purely quantitative approach was only one of them. Many eminent figures in the history of science, for instance Paracelsus (1493-1541), stand at the crossroads, and while, according to a popular view, they represent mere gropings towards a truly scientific thinking, one may also see in their work much more: an attempt both to explore the world of matter and to interpret it symbolically, thus trying to preserve the unity of various levels of existence.

After the investigations of C. G. Jung and Mircea Eliade it would be frivolous to dismiss as mere immaturity and pseudo-science the Sixteenth Century thought strongly marked by hermetic writings and alchemy. Symbolic interpretation of natural phenomena shows its depth and fecundity, especially in the painting of that time. The greatness of many works of art created then is due to a mysterious web of meanings hidden beneath a representation of external reality.

Be that as it may, the evolution of science took a course that in retrospect seems to us inevitable. The new image of the universe, which, since Copernicus, had dislodged man from his central position, found its implementation in the Eighteenth Century, when Newton's physics and deism in religion assigned to the earth and to man a very small place in a terrifying, self-perpetuating mechanism. That century boasted of its *Lumières*, its Enlightenment, which was equated with a triumph of Reason. Through a curious combination of diminishment and aggrandizement of man, the Age of Reason embarked upon a great adventure of faith in a better humanity. Voltaire and Rousseau were optimistic standard-bearers, indeed. At the same time, though, some sensitive thinkers intuited a dangerous dichotomy in the modern vision, a split into, on the one hand, an external reality submitted to blind immutable laws alien to any notion of value, and, on the other hand, an inner realm of human subjectivity which is value-oriented but to whose values nothing in an indifferent universe corresponds.

Erich Heller, in his seminal book on the great split, *The Disinherited Mind*, describes the anxieties of one of those thinkers, Goethe. In a way, Goethe, through his active interest in alchemy, botany and physics, represented the ideal of a humanist, living in the time before knowledge was divided into science and literature. He sensed that this parting of the ways could still be avoided and that the imagination of a poet like himself could no less effectively penetrate the secrets of matter than would the instruments of a scientist.

In his treatises *The Metamorphosis of Plants* and *A Theory Of Colors*, Goethe intended to provide an alternative to the "empirico-mechanico-dogmatic torture chamber" (to use his expression) of quantitative knowledge, and thus to go back to the Renaissance, when options were still possible. To quote Heller: "It was Goethe's ambition to play, in the history of thought, the role of another Francis Bacon, insisting on not merely pragmatic, but what he understood to be objective, dealings with Nature; or that of an Immanuel Kant of the Objective Reason. He [Goethe] said, in a review of a scientific work: 'A man born and bred in the so-called exact sciences will, on the height of his analytical reason, not easily comprehend that there is also something like an exact concrete imagination.' This exact concrete imagination is the glory of Goethe's poetry, and he knew that it was the great instrument of truth."

According to Heller, Goethe had an ally of whose existence he was unaware: William Blake. Heller does not mention, though, that in his rebellion against the spirit of the age Blake owed his basic orientation to Emanuel Swedenborg. These names—Goethe, Swedenborg, Blake—are important for anyone who confronts O. Milosz's philosophical poems.

Emanuel Swedenborg (1688-1772) influenced not only Blake. Throughout the Nineteenth Century Swedenborg's theory of correspondences is present in European poetry and prose. A famous sonnet of Baudelaire, "Correspondances," makes use of a basic Swedenborgian idea and thus introduces it into French symbolism. Quite a number of poems in various languages were inspired by the great Swede, as if poets were intuitively looking to him for a protection against civilization's dominant trend, which was hostile to them.

Another part of Swedenborg's heritage is purely religious, preserved by the Swedenborgian church. But in spite of a vague notoriety and praise by eminent writers (in France, by Balzac; in America, by Henry James, Sr. and Emerson), the man has remained till today a mystery not unravelled by several books on his life and works. Swedenborg describes in a pedantic, dry, placid Latin prose his travels through the three zones of the posthumous life of man, the world of spirits, Heaven and Hell. An interpreter hesitates between taking the author for a madman and imputing to him a nearly Swiftian taste for a fantastic parable, while the truth is, he senses, somewhere else, but where?

Probably the future interpreters of Swedenborg will have to start with what he was by his training and his profession, a scientist, one of the most brilliant discoverers in a century of discoveries, and, according to historians of science, a genius. At a given moment in his career he experienced a mystical illumination and from that time turned against the science of his contemporaries. The crisis he lived through, whatever its character, marks his opening to a new vision of the world. That vision cannot be isolated from his previous preoccupations; on the contrary, it seems to draw its strength from his desire to turn science back from what he suddenly discerned as a wrong track. No less was involved than the recovery of a broken unity of the internal and the external, spirit and matter, religion and science.

Swedenborg's voluminous oeuvre was meant to serve that purpose. In it he presented the inner vocabulary of a Nature bound to the central figure of the universe, man. Christianity is the most anthropocentric of religions, and Swedenborgian Christianity accentuates that aspect even more strongly. He says that God is man, i.e., the human likeness is a part of the divine likeness. Jehovah's incarnation as Christ means that the God-man is one. In the three "persons" of the Trinity as in Catholicism, Swedenborg saw vestiges of polytheism. Readers of William Blake would immediately recognize here his insistence on the all-forgiving force of one true God-man, Jesus or the Imagination. It is this that relates Blake to Swedenborg.

If man is so important, then his inner life cannot be just a kind of vapor, of no consequence when compared to tangible physical phenomena, but must have a cosmic meaning. Swedenborg turns upside down the relation between data of sensory perceptions and human thinking, as presented by John Locke, and assigns to the human mind the priority. In his system sensory perception provides information of a low degree, which, however, hides layers of meaning that need to be deciphered. For Goethe too (who read Swedenborg) the whole natural world was an image, an external representation of the spiritual world. Let us consider what derives from such a premise. I see a tree; it is, however, not only a tree, but also a sign. In a way Swedenborg's world is all language. Material objects have their real existence not here but in eternity where there is no time and no space. There, they function as components of an immense vocabulary of attractions and repulsions felt by immortal men and corresponding to their most intimate inclinations. Similarly, on the earth every object is emotionally charged in either a positive or a negative way. For instance, fruits, bread, wine, precious stones, flowers on one side; toads, snakes, thorny plants on the other. Swedenborg had no understanding of poetry, yet in fact created what O. Milosz, his attentive reader, called "metaesthetics," because the Swedenborgian doctrine grounds poetic metaphors in a pre-established divine order.

Swedenborg's detailed descriptions of beautiful gardens, their trees and their flowers in Heaven, and of slums, dirt and ruins in Hell do not mean that he believed they existed other than in imagination, which was for him the most real existence. In fact, they correspond to the states of mind of eternal men living after their death as spiritual bodies: as you are, so you see. Nobody is "admitted" to Heaven or "sentenced" to Hell, for Heaven and Hell signify his or her inner orientation and consist of visual, as we are tempted today to say, projections. Thus Swedenborg introduces a new dimension of human interiority, paralleling what his contemporary Kant established as categories within the mind.

An incomparable oddity of Swedenborg's system is to a large extent due to his rationalistic habits. In this he is a man of his century. He was of the opinion that man cannot believe what he does not understand. How then can we explain the following passage from Swedenborg's *Arcana Caelestia:*

> The worldly and corporeal man says in his heart: if I am not instructed concerning the faith, and everything relating to it, by means of the things of sense, so that I may see, or by means of scientifics, so that I may understand, I will not believe.

Of course, for Swedenborg that way of understanding was worthless, for such a man "is desirous of being instructed from things of sense, in what is celestial and Divine, which is as impossible as it is for a camel to go through the eye of a needle!" He was deciphering meticulously and explaining God's message contained—here he followed medieval theology—both in the book of Nature and in the Bible. Swedenborg distinguished three levels of meaning: the natural or, in the case of the Holy Writ, literal; the spiritual; the celestial.

Read with such a key, the Book of Genesis, for instance, loses its contradictions that are offensive to reason. Adam and Eve mean then not the first couple but the first, as Swedenborg calls it, "church," i.e., the most ancient civilization, and the garden of Eden was "the wisdom of the men of that church." Eating from the tree of the knowledge of good and evil means a victory of man's *proprium* or selfhood and a break from the state of harmony in which man did not ascribe anything to himself but lived submerged in God. Thus we may place Swedenborg on the pole opposite to that of those philosophers who have attempted to defend religion from the assaults of its detractors by assigning to it a specific sphere in which tenets of faith need not be submitted to verification by reason. On the other hand, his specific "reasonableness of Christianity" does not resemble John Locke's; it rather consists in an antireductionist attempt to move both religion and science to another level, universal symbolism.

Any brief discussion of Swedenborg's system will hardly touch its intricate structure, and in fact his reader has constantly a feeling of grasping at something that eludes him at the last moment. William Blake, both as an engraver and painter and as a poet, makes Swedenborg's thought more tangible; also, Blake cannot be understood without referring his oeuvre to the main source of his intellectual inspiration—certainly not after the convincing studies of Kathleen Raine. Forms in Blake's art, including personifications of forces, angelic or diabolic, are gigantic and human, confirming a cosmic dimension of man as opposed to his diminutive size in the Newtonian universe. Also God-man in Blake—Jesus, the Imagination—is the opposite of the Creator-demiurge, a lawgiver and a severe moralist of the Eighteenth Century scientist-deists and of the Anglican Church. Swedenborg considered that scientists, while paying lip-service to God, worshiped, under that name, Nature, i.e., remained on the lowest level of interpretation of phenomena, not reaching to the spiritual and celestial levels.

When Blake occasionally engaged in a polemic with his

master Swedenborg, it was about how the idea of Nature as a huge mechanism was linked to conventional morality—that link, according to him, being insufficiently stressed by Swedenborg. For Blake, a vision of a mechanistic universe was terrifying, destructive, and contrary to a true vocation of the human imagination. Bacon, Locke and Newton, responsible for implementing and perpetuating that vision, were evildoers, for man under its impact isolates himself from his fellow men and becomes a Spectre (Swedenborg's *proprium*, selfhood), an inhabitant of the desolate land of cold and despair, Ulro. He is then a worshipper of a cruel God-demiurge whom Blake calls Urizen and who, if invoked by the churches, serves as a prop of a "spectral" morality based upon the law of retaliation.

In the England of his time Blake observed at first hand the consequences of the victory of science. After all, England was the first country in Europe to embark upon an industrial revolution. Decades before Darwin's "survival of the fittest," the struggle of an isolated individual against another isolated individual became a common feature of economic practice. And not only of practice. Blake's contemporary, Thomas Robert Malthus, provided that struggle with a justifying theory according to which growth of workers' population was self-regulating: if they grow too numerous, some of them simply will starve to death and equilibrium will be restored. Blake's London was already a city of misery, of prostitution, of rigid morality imposed by the clergy with its system of posthumous rewards and punishments. No wonder that Blake's indignation was directed against all those things as a whole and that he searched for their interdependence. Were Bacon, Locke and Newton really guilty of what was for Blake a spiritual sleep of Albion? His answer was a categorical yes. They represented science as the Reasoning Power, an abstract objectifying power, that negates everything. "This is the Spectre of Man, the Holy Reasoning Power, and in its Holiness is closed the Abomination of Desolation" *(Jerusalem)*. The

Spectre, the Selfhood, is Satan, called by Blake the Prince of Starry Wheels. Why "Starry Wheels"? Blake denounced as a delusion of the spectral mind the unimaginable concept of absolute space and absolute time. To live with such a concept meant to inhabit Ulro. The delusion of absolute space and absolute time deprives the individual's life of any meaning as it contrasts his insignificance with the immensity of infinite space filled with galaxies. The galaxies revolve in infinite time in which the whole adventure of humanity is like an instant, while the universe follows its meaningless cycles. To quote one Blake scholar, Northrop Frye:

> Such an idea, Blake insists, is a mental cancer: man is not capable of accepting it purely as an objective fact; its moral and emotional implications must accompany it into the mind, and breed there into cynical indifference, short-range vision, selfish pursuit of expediency, and all the other diseases of Selfhood, ending in horror and despair.

The social equivalent and consequence of such a cosmology are "dark Satanic mills."

Thus, at the turn of the Eighteenth Century an early warning against the direction taken by science and technology was sounded by poets and visionaries: Goethe, Swedenborg, Blake. Too bizarre to be understood, as it attempted to undermine the premises that seemed obvious, their warning did not succeed in turning the tide. European romanticism signified just the opposite solution: once the authority of reason and its quantitative methods were recognized as the only certain source of truth—but of a truth impersonal, cold, severed from man's aspirations and longings—human subjectivity was left to itself as a sort of outcast in the world of iron laws. A poet, an artist, would protect his "truth of the heart" from that world of causes and effects, of universal necessity, conceding at the same time that his inner fortress was made with a fabric of dreams—while only the external, the domain of the scientist, was real. Throughout all the Nineteenth Century and until today the complaint against a reality alien to man's desires has underlain poetry of various schools. All of them may be traced back to the romantic heritage. One such mutation was French symbolism in which Swedenborgian "correspondences" performed a rather modest function, cut off, as they were, from their philosophical implications.

O. Milosz as a young poet was ranked with the late wave of symbolists. But, as I already said, his "elective affinities" directed him towards poetry of the turn of the Eighteenth Century. That was due to the estrangement he felt wherever he lived, to the situation of an exile from his epoch, which he called "the age of jeering ugliness," and also to both his multilingual education and the German literature he had read. From the beginning, the influence of Goethe, as well as that of Heine, is strong. In summer, 1913, while in Munich, he discovered Hölderlin, whose works had just been published. Milosz remained, however, primarily a man of letters and he was not acquainted with the hermetic tradition before his mystical experience on the night of December 14, 1914. The extreme vividness of things he saw and heard that night induced him to search for testimonies of similar states known to others. This he himself confesses to James Chauvet, in his letter of July 5, 1926, which I quote in my translation:

> Sir,
>
> Allow me to thank you for your kind letter which I have read with most vivid pleasure. What you say of *Ars Magna* does not leave in my mind any doubt as to the attraction you must feel for certain doctrines that are all too forsaken in these times. I was deeply moved by an allusion to the Rosicrucians, suggested to you by the five poems of my little book. I have given myself the pleasure of mailing to you a more recent work, "The Arcana," and soon you shall receive a study, both literary and biographic, which *La Revue Euro-*

péene dedicated to me last year. I would have great difficulty in trying to indicate for you the Sources of my doctrine. At the risk of being accused (by others, not you) of charlatanism and megalomania, I am compelled by the spirit of truth to confide to you that the knowledge came to me by way of a revelation after twenty years devoted to uninterrupted and passionate meditations, the subject of which was provided by space, time and movement. It was only after I felt an inner sight opening within me, a sight which I call mnemonic, that I yielded to my curiosity in learning about the doctrines of my predecessors in sacred science. Those studies taught me the only thing they could, namely that *the truth is one* and that some *respect* and *love* are enough to discover it in the depths of our consciousness. There are only two kinds of men: the negators who profess irreconcilable systems and the modest affirmers who, from Pythagoras to Plato, through the initiates of Alexandria and Christian mystics, to Claude de Saint-Martin and Swedenborg, etc.— all say the same things to anyone who knows how to listen.

Thank you, again.

Milosz called Goethe his spiritual master and Swedenborg his celestial master. He made revealing annotations* on the margins of Swedenborg's *The True Christian Religion* and *Conjugial Love*, both of which he read in English in 1915. In Swedenborg he saw a "Faust without human tragedy, a celestial Faust, free from torment and doubt." As to Goethe, in his scientific tentatives he probably borrowed from Swedenborg (his morphological theory of plants). In one of his notes O. Milosz says: "By *intuition* Swedenborg *sensed* the future science, till the day it will fuse with the true spiritual religion." Identical in their strivings, though on two different levels—

---

*They are reproduced in a doctoral thesis of Stanley M. Guise, *La sensibilité esoterique de Milosz*, 1964, unpublished. In the library of the Sorbonne.

spiritual and celestial—Goethe and Swedenborg stand as two avowed comforters of Milosz, transmitters of "the truth which is one."

There are no traces of his ever having read Blake, probably because in the years O. Milosz spent in England, roughly 1908-1910, Blake's name still did not belong to the canon of English poetry. Yet his affinities with Blake are obvious and go beyond their common share of Swedenborgian inspirations, but with a basic difference: Blake lived in the period of a victorious Newtonian concept of a mechanistic universe and rebelled against it, while O. Milosz, in his mature years, witnessed the ascent of Einsteinian physics (unheard of by him before his "inner sight" was opened) in which he found a confirmation of his new idea of time and space. In Blake's era two ways of thinking opposed each other, as the Age of Reason had its counterpart in visionaries and in some "mystical lodges" of freemasonry. Similarly, O. Milosz distinguished two currents in his century and he regarded this as a reason for hope. "As in the Eighteenth Century, we find in all spiritual manifestations of our epoch a disintegrating negation on the surface, a creative affirmation in the depth," Milosz says in one of his political articles.* There is no doubt that, for him, Einstein's theory of relativity belonged to "creative affirmation." It liberated man from the terrifying presence of infinite space and infinite time. Space conceived as a limitless void, as a limitless container of whirling lumps of matter, is basic to Newtonian physics no less than linear time extending infinitely backwards and forward. That was probably Blake's horror of "Starry Wheels." For O. Milosz the question: *"Where is space?"* in the sense *"Where is it situated?"* was *the* question central to all his search. His own, intuitive discovery of the relativity of space and time, corroborated by the physics of Einstein, was loaded, according to him, with implications abolishing all mental habits of his contemporaries and open-

---

* "La vraie question de Vilna," "L'Europe Nouvelle" 24.XII.1921.

ing a new era. Had O. Milosz read Jung, perhaps he would have said that, astrologically, the new era would correspond to the sign of Aquarius after two thousand years under the sign of Pisces. In any case, like Swedenborg and Blake, he assigned to himself the role of a forerunner and a prophet, addressing his philosophical poems to man of the future.

Thus, Milosz's work was a new effort to go back in the history of Western thought to that moment when exploration of Nature did not as yet lead to a separation of the inner from the outer, a separation of human interiority from matter measured quantitatively. His dedication to *Ars Magna*, "To Renaissance," and his expression, "my spouse the Renaissance," undoubtedly denote deep faith in an approaching renewal, an era of reborn humanity. Even so, the word Renaissance cannot be isolated from associations sending us back to a historical period of that name—different, however, from that presented in the textbooks: an age of humanism, of the Latin and Greek poets imitated by the literati, an age of classical beauty in fine arts. Such a picture is, of course, superficial. The study of Greek made Plato accessible to the learned. Yet he remains quite a mysterious, not to say a hermetic, writer. But Hebrew was also studied then as the language of the Bible, and the migration of Sephardic Jews from Spain, the main seat of Jewish mysticism, facilitated the contact of scholars with the Kabbalah. This other side of the Renaissance, where Platonism, the Christianized Kabbalah, alchemy and the formation of Rosa Crucis fraternities paralleled each other, is epitomized by the names of Giovanni Pico della Mirandola (1463-1494) in Italy; Johananes Reuchlin (1455-1522) in Germany; Paracelsus (1493-1541) in Switzerland; and, in France, Guillaume Postel (1510-1581), to mention only a few of numerous writers.

In *Ars Magna*, O. Milosz invokes the whole line of hermetic thought as represented by "Boehme, Sendivogius and Paracelsus." It is curious to note that Jakob Boehme (1575-1624) was, together with Swedenborg, a major influence upon Blake.

Sendivogius is a latinized name of a Polish alchemist, Michal Sędziwój (1556-1636). The true name of Paracelsus was Theophrast Bombast von Hohenheim. O. Milosz sometimes refers to him as the "divine Hohenheim."

Why, then, does *The Arcana* open with a quotation from Descartes? After all, he is known as the originator of modern philosophy and as a force in the scientific revolution; "the Cartesian spirit" became synonymous with rationalism. Yet for Milosz Descartes was somebody else. And, in fact, it would be difficult to prove that Milosz was mistaken in his assessment of that epitome of methodical doubt. After all, to this day, various schools of philosophy, each drawing Descartes to its own side, have failed to reach agreement as to the consequences of his reasoning. Neither has the rich amount of literature on Descartes elucidated certain aspects of his life, for instance his night of "enthusiasm," his constant travels while he lived in Holland, his Protestant connections and the way he combined his "method" with an exemplary Roman Catholic piety. He remained "a man walking in a mask," but what the man was and what the mask was is a matter of conjecture. According to some of his biographers, during his short stay in Germany he was admitted to a secret Rosicrucian confraternity. Upon his return to Paris persistent rumors caused him to deny his affiliation, but seemingly he is the author of a work entitled *Polybii Cosmopolitani thesaurus mathematicus* which is sympathetic to the Rosicrucian brethren. Because of Descartes' striving for the unity of science and religion, Milosz linked him to the hermetic Renaissance movement and even called him "father of modern intuitionism." His own doctrine identifies thought with "awareness and love of movement" and thus Descartes' *cogito ergo sum*. "I think, therefore I am" becomes identified with "I love, therefore I am." He applied to Descartes what he believed to be his name as an initiate: Polybius the Cosmopolitan. Milosz spoke of himself as "son of the Cosmopolitan" which meant: son of Descartes.

La Poésie-philosophie de Milosz, Jean Bellemin-Noel's voluminous dissertation on *Ars Magna* and *The Arcana*, presented at the Sorbonne in 1975, is a curious example of breath-taking erudition and analytical brilliance combined with what is, I feel, a subservience to intellectual fashions of today—a combination that must lead to preconceived false conclusions. When Bellemin-Noel applies a Freudian-Lacanian psychoanalysis to a work of a fundamentally anti-reductionist tendency, he changes it into a text safe at last, with a message to be taken no more seriously than confessions of a patient. It seems to me that even if we are free to treat prophecies of Blake or of O. Milosz with a dose of scepticism, we are obliged to show them respect. This attitude is what Milosz recommended when he summarized, in Goethe's words, a lesson learned by the hero of *Wilhelm Meister* after many trials: "respect, respect, respect." Bellemin-Noel's book had to be mentioned here, though, for it is an illustration of the Milosz oeuvre's strange adventures several decades after its appearance.

Just as Swedenborg remains today an unexplained phenomenon, substantially the same can be said of O. Milosz. However, some of the questions we ask when reading Swedenborg were not alien to his student. Milosz explains in one marginal note: "What a curious mixture of puerility of images, of nobility and profundity of feeling and of architectonic skill!" Another note on the margin of *True Christian Religion*: "The work is comprised of two parts: one, revealed in *the spiritual world*, another constructed as a theological-philosophical system in the natural world. Which of the two preceded the other? Are *memorabilia* from before the system, or did the system precede them? Was the work born out of a vision or out of an idea? For those 'reports' look like compositions aimed at a *proof* by *allegory*."

The respect and admiration he felt for the Swedish sage did not prevent Milosz from criticizing him. He considered that his own philosophy did not depart even by an iota from the teaching of the Roman Catholic Church and, of course, realized in what ways his and Swedenborg's views differed. In one particular O. Milosz is very close to Swedenborg, whose doctrine has for its center the idea of angelic sexuality. A key book of the Bible for Milosz was the Song of Songs, because love is its subject. It is, on one level, a sexual love between man and woman; on another, a spiritual or angelic love between the two; on the third, love between God and Creation. Milosz speaks of *"La Feminité de la Manifestation*—"Manifestation" being God's act of creation analogous to the birth of Eve out of Adam's rib in Genesis. I have stressed already the cosmic importance that Swedenborg and Blake attributed to man. So did O. Milosz, for whom relativity of time and space performs a liberating function because it makes our vision of the world depend upon our blood, i.e., rhythm (pulsebeat). ("For every Space larger than a red Globule of Man's blood is visionary," says Blake.) And for Milosz thought is love of Movement. At the core of his system is love, for the rhythm of blood rules everything and, as we remember, "God is man." Milosz's philosophical poems are, in this sense, a natural sequence to two of his works written before the experience of 1914, *Miguel Mañara* and *L'Amoureuse Initiation*. Both deal with a link between sensual and celestial love; Miguel accedes to love of God through his love for Girolama, Sinibaldo through his love for Clarissa Annalena. A supreme *arcanum* is that of a union between man and woman. Because of universal analogy, i.e., correspondences, the whole Creation, which is feminine and fecundated by the divine light, is drawn to God as woman is drawn to man. God looks at Creation with a *"folie d'amour,"* madness of love. Incarnation is called by Milosz "conjunction" and signifies a marriage between God and the created universe.

The relationship between Adam and Eve is therefore decisive—as, obviously, is the interpretation of the Fall. For a reader of O. Milosz this is also one of the most difficult points.

The Fall due to "Adam's prevarication" entailed a transformation of the First Nature into the Second Nature. Of that change O. Milosz says to Ernest Gegenbach in a letter dated August 10, 1938: "Nature (so beautiful in the eyes of the majority of people) is a kind of absolute of ugliness and infamy. We bear it only because, inside ourselves, there survives a memory of the First Nature which is divine and true. . . . A true Revolution will be the one which will transmute the Second Nature, all stench, lie, ugliness and ferocity, and will give back to it the angelic face of God's daughter, of the First Nature."

Man's relation to God is not the same as woman's. "Man is a harsh Law by which he is movement, action and nothing more—it is in the beauty and charity of woman that the Law is transmuted into Love." In other words, man is thought; woman, love of thought. "Adam's prevarication" consisted in breaking a union binding him to God (a victory of *proprium* in Swedenborg, of the Spectre-Selfhood in Blake). This break was prompted by Eve, who "materialized love." What does it mean? Neither in Swedenborg, Blake nor Milosz is a sexual taboo involved. Using a slightly paradoxical expression we can say that Eve was responsible for Adam's embracing a purely materialistic philosophy, for his start down the road taken by Blake's diabolical triumvirate, Bacon, Locke and Newton. For in fact Eve questioned Adam, asking him whether it was not true that nothing separated her from him and therefore whether she was not him. But nothing separated Adam from God either, then was it not true that he himself was a god? In that manner she accepted the temptation of the serpent: "your eyes shall be opened, and ye shall be as gods, knowing good and evil."

I do not pretend to understand O. Milosz's doctrine of the Fall, except that it involves a transformation of the First Nature into the Second Nature through a different *vision*, much as in Blake. The role of Eve in Adam's descent into a purely sensual perception of space cannot endear Blake or

Milosz to the feminist movement. Neither can the place of Adam as a kind of priest bringing offerings to God in his and Eve's name. Besides, O. Milosz openly expressed his dislike of the feminists in whose program he saw an attempt to depersonalize woman by forcing her to compete with man.

From the doctrine of the Fall we move with increasing difficulty to the world of archetypes and the first fall, before creation of the universe. Here we are in the realm of the Kabbalah, and O. Milosz appears to follow the path of the Kabbalists: this kinship can be explained in various ways, primarily, though, by the roots of the Kabbalah in Neoplatonic and Gnostic thought. A detailed discussion of that part of his work would go beyond the limits imposed by the form of an introduction.

Perhaps the most attractive feature of Swedenborg's Heaven is an incessant activity of its inhabitants, who are grouped into "societies" according to their most profound desires and who engage in constant joyous labors ("uses"). Blake's Eternity is boundless energy, a land of incessant intellectual hunting, of "the great Wars of Eternity, in fury of Poetic Inspiration." For O. Milosz art is a supreme "use" and for an artist life eternal consists in knowing for whom he labored—and, we may surmise, continues to labor. "The archetypes of art reside in the Celestial sphere," he notes, "and this explains emotion provoked by their reflections in this world. . . . All our arts are vestiges of a Golden initiation." Which means that the very essence of art, rhythm, and consequently our blood, has a celestial origin, in the non-physical light where the archetypes dwell.

By comparing Swedenborg, Blake and O. Milosz I may be guilty of creating a false impression as to their resemblance; they differ in their ideas as much as in their languages and styles. Moreover, O. Milosz, in spite of his "elective affinities" with the turn of the Eighteenth Century, is a son of his own epoch and reacts to it. What I wanted to achieve by making this comparison was to make the reader aware that there is a history of what may be called a visionary science opposed to the scientific *Weltanschauung* and that certain names are links in an impressive chain. The predecessors of O. Milosz taught him that "the truth is one, and some respect and love suffice to discover truth in the depths of our consciousness." How surprised and delighted he would have been had he read the words of Blake. There he would have found, formulated in nearly the same words, an account of perceptions like his own on December 14, 1914. For Blake told Crabb Robinson once that he had seen "the spiritual sun." "I have. I saw him on Primrose Hill." And whatever be the interpretation of initiatory states lived through by exceptional individuals, we have no right whatsoever to doubt the veracity of their testimonies.

O. Milosz until now has been virtually unknown in the United States, with the exception of a few literati. Ezra Pound published in *The Dial* in 1921 an adaptation of "Symphonie de Novembre"; a translation of *Miguel Mañara* never appeared in book form.* The only book publication, *Fourteen Poems by O. V. de L. Milosz*, Translated and with Introduction by Kenneth Rexroth, The Peregrine Press, 1955, San Francisco, has recently been reprinted (Copper Canyon Press, 1983, Port Townsend, Washington). I am inclined to believe that a long delay in O. Milosz's reaching the American public was not without advantages and that the present volume appears at a more propitious moment, if he is to find at least a few attentive readers. The decades which have elapsed since the year of "conflagration universelle," 1944, have brought home a growing awareness of dangerous potentialities hidden in science and technology during their formative period, the Sixteenth to Eighteenth Centuries. Those potentialities have revealed their finished form not only in the means of massive physical destruction, but also in their ability to pollute the mind. Can we switch tracks, when we have been speeding on

---

* Translated by Edward J. O'Brien.

one for so long? In other words, can there be possible another, new, science that would heal the rift between scientific reason and imagination? Swedenborg, Goethe and Blake did not change the course taken by their contemporaries. Will O. Milosz be a more convincing witness? He believed in a new image of the universe, one which would reconcile science, religion, art and philosophy. He prophesied an inevitable unification of our "small planet earth" and the triumph of one universal church. But all predictions of the future are no more than those of events seen in a mirror, darkly, and the time of fulfillment must remain unknown.

CZESLAW MILOSZ

FOREWORD

The Amorous Initiate

HERMOGENES ... but what is the meaning of the word *hero?*

SOCRATES I think that there is no difficulty in explaining it, for the name is not much altered, and signifies that they were born of love.

HERMOGENES What do you mean?

SOCRATES Do you not know that the heroes are demigods?

HERMOGENES What then?

SOCRATES All of them sprang either from the love of a god for a mortal woman, or of a mortal man for a goddess. Think of the word in the old Attic, and you will see better that the name *heros* is only a slight alteration of Eros, from whom the heros sprang ...

Plato, CRATYLUS, 398c

This is what it is to love, this is what it is to love: to seek love with love.   *O. Milosz,* CANTICLE OF KNOWLEDGE

Oscar Milosz is one of those extraordinary figures, anciently called heroes, now and then produced by literature, whose powers and seriousness are such as to call into question all our preconceptions, thereby allowing us to reconsider, as it were *ab initio,* our culture's meaning and value. In a certain sense Oscar Milosz is the last flower of Romanticism; a neo-Romantic, if you will. But Milosz is a neo-Romantic only as Plotinus is a neo-Platonist. In other words, he is a Romantic purely, essentially, and *originally*, beyond all national and chronological particularity. Describing himself as "a Lithuanian poet in the French language," Milosz is that almost impossible creature, not so much a 'European,' as a fully realized Occidental, a true son and heir of the West as such. We need only to note, for instance, in ever-expanding circles: his translations, published and unpublished, of Shelley, Coleridge, Byron, Rosetti, Goethe, Schiller, Hölderlin, Lenau, Chamisso, Brentano, Mickiewicz, Slowacki, Norwid, Pushkin, Lermontov, as well as of those Lithuanian folksongs called *Dainos*; his deep love for, and his familiarity with, medieval literature; and his prolonged study of the "modest affirmers" which allowed him to propose himself to his friend Christian Gauss as a lecturer in "Hermetic doctrines and metaphysics, from Egypt to today, passing through the Pre-Socratics, Plato, the School of Alexandria, the Neo-Platonists of the Middle Ages, Swedenborg and the mystical eighteenth century. . . ." To this list should be added Milosz's love of alchemists such as Flamel, Boehme, Sendivogius and Paracelsus, whom he read to clear his mind of "the endless negotiations at the *Quai (d'Orsay)*"; and his knowledge of Spinoza, Kant, Schopenhauer and Nietszche; not to mention his lifelong reading of the Bible, his knowledge of Hebrew, and his more than passing acquaintance with Jewish mystical tradition and Kabbalah. Add to this again his astonishing literacy in science, anthropology, archeology, folklore and history, and one realizes that here is a poet—a prophet and visionary—who must be measured, as he measured himself, against the giants (Dante, Cervantes, Shakespeare, Goethe): a poet who, passing beyond all boundaries, causes us to reconsider boundaries as such.

Obviously, therefore, there are many ways of approaching the hero of this tale. Czeslaw Milosz, in his Introduction, places him in the counter-scientific lineage of Swedenborg, Blake and Goethe. But that by no means exhausts the field. It would be equally appropriate to consider O. Milosz from the hermetic or alchemical point of view as an esoteric or even initiated poet. After all, it is the fact that Milosz underwent a profound initiatory illumination or inner transformation, comparable to Pascal's "night of fire," that distinguishes him from other contemporaries such as Yeats or Eliot, who share certain broadly religious concerns. As Milosz himself confesses:

> I have seen. He who has seen stops thinking and feeling. He can only describe what he has seen.
> CANTICLE OF KNOWLEDGE

Nor is that all. Too often treated as a French symbolist or neo-Romantic poet, Milosz has deep affinities with his natal cultures—Baltic, Slavic and Lithuanian. Hence there is an explanation that would place him in that context and reveal his connections with such contemporaries and near-contemporaries as Vladimir Solovyov, Andrei Bely, and Alexander Blok, Ciurlionis and Kandinsky, Pavel Florensky and Sergei Bulgakov. Whatever the approach chosen, however, the language and frame of reference will always be as much theological as literary, for O. Milosz was a poet-philosopher who felt himself called, in his own words, to revitalize Christian metaphysics. Any argument concerning him will in the end inevitably hinge, therefore, upon the primacy of love—*eros, storge* and *agape*—for these are the essential premises of any poetic Christianity. As always, that is, implicitly or explicitly, one will begin with Plato, the Orphic Plato of the *Symposium*, the *Phaedrus* and the *Timaeus*, dialogues in which the Master transmits a poetic, cosmogenic philosophy of love, linking it to the deepest mysteries of the human soul in its kinship with the cosmos and the divine.

Oscar Milosz, who called himself "Love's Knight," and whose work is a continuous deepening and revealing of love's mystery, is Platonic in this sense—which is perhaps to say that he is a Christian Platonist or even a Platonist transformed and inverted. But simply to say so is no longer sufficient, for with the erosion of the context that once sustained them these words have lost their power and meaning. As Milosz himself says:

> To this word, love, the ignorance and coarseness of the epochs which separate us from the Middle Ages have given many puerile or irreverent meanings, and even those minds which are the least false in these horrible times—times of expiation in which we have the misfortune to love—do not seem to wish to express with it anything other than passion, pleasure, or curiosity. But such is not the meaning that I attach to this august, enchanting, and terrifying word, I who take pride in writing with the soul of words. For me, love always means the eternal feminine-divine of Alighieri and Goethe, angelic sentiment and sexuality, virginal maternity, wherein are blended, as in a fiery crucible, the adramandonic of Swedenborg, the hesperic of Hölderlin, the elysian of Schiller: the perfect human harmony formed by the attracting wisdom of the bridegroom and the amorous gravitation of the bride, the true spiritual situation of the one with respect to the other, an essential arcanum so terrible and so beautiful that since I have penetrated it I have been unable to speak of it without shedding a torrent of tears. . . .
> EPISTLE TO STORGE

Plato's philosophy begins with the soul-movement inspired by the beauty of sensible things, "our mother, the world's beauty," which as late as Hölderlin still held the promise of eternal peace. Pursuing this beauty, the Platonist dies to the world, passing from sensible to supersensible phenomena, ending, beyond beauty—beyond this world, even—in love's very sanctuary, Unity or the One. As Plutarch writes: "Love entering through the body, becomes a guide to lead the soul from the world below to truth and the fields of truth, where full, pure, deceitless beauty dwells. . . ." Platonic *eros* intensifies desire into a single, heavenly desire, whereby human, earthly desire is raised up and cancelled out in the death of desire's body, its limitation, this earth. Platonic love, unlike Christian, thus proposes as its end not marriage or adoration, but identity-as-union.

Earthly beauty, the earth herself of our habitation, is for the Platonist a memory, an image spurring recollection; and the soul's yearning for it is a token of an ideal kinship, existing beyond space and time, out of body and out of mind. Platonic lovers love beauty for ideal beauty's sake alone, and that exists no-where. Laying aside the flesh, they seek to be "alone with the alone." For them, true love aims at engendering only mystical, not natural, fruits.

Nevertheless, even Plato felt, though dimly, that love was of necessity twofold, angelic-supersensible and natural-human. Therefore he spoke of love as ascending and descending, of celestial Aphrodite *Ourania* and of common Aphrodite *Pandemos*; and precisely because he knew that these two were destined to be one—as the human was with the divine—he made love the fundamental mediator, the universal medicine. In Diotima's words: "God does not mingle with man; it is uniquely by means of love, or the *daimon*, that there is intercourse between the gods and men." Love for Plato is the vehicle between desire and what is desired, between the knower and the known. It is the interpreter and the interpretation: the interpreter interpreted. Therefore it is the revelation—the knowing or *gnosis*—that binds: the fundamental *re-ligio*. And so love is by definition visionary and prophetic. Plotinus, too, knew this and spoke of love as the eye of the desirer, by whose power a lover beholds the beloved: "There is a strenuous activity of contemplation in the soul; there is an emanation towards it from the object contemplated; and *Eros* is born, the love which is an eye filled with its vision, a meeting which bears its image with it."

In the *Symposium*, Aristophanes attributes to humanity an originally spherical nature, forfeited as a result of overweening yearning and pride. This is commonplace. In the words of

Novalis: "The need for love betrays a prior disunity within us." But for Plato and the Greeks this love, if it is to be true, must be transcendent. Love is love of God exclusively. Woman in her beauty may serve to remind Plutarch of a first beauty but, having served that function, she must drop away without a trace. The return to sphericity is an inner, spiritual good, only incidentally, if at all, transformative of human, social, earthly relations, which betoken only suffering. And yet, for Plato, love is deeply present in creation. Wherever there is harmony, beauty, or order, it is the power of love that has imposed restraint. As Simone Weil, another inverted (Christian) Platonist observes: "If one gives oneself up to love, if for the sake of love one accepts to have within one a never-fulfilled yearning, one has the perfection of restraint." To achieve such a "lifetime's death in love" is not easy. In Oscar Milosz's words: "In order to understand such things, one has to give oneself up to the madness of love, which happens precisely at the moment when, either out of pity or out of passion, man speaks to the four walls," and thereby pays "the prescribed tribute of tears."

Yet with Plato and Platonism, however much these foreshadow the fully risen visionary poetry of Dante, Shakespeare, Swedenborg, and Goethe, we are still in the pre-dawn era. The change comes about with Christianity, viewed as the incarnation—fulfillment and inversion—at once of Platonism (the *Symposium*, the *Timaeus*) and of Judaism (*Genesis, The Song of Songs*), of poetry and of love: of *eros*. *Eros* incarnated = *agape*. In the old erotic religion, according to de Rougemont, death was the last term, a release symbolizing union, but in the new *re-ligio* of Christianity, *agape* or charity *(caritas)*, death is the beginning of a new life. Love, which was death, returns to life, to particularity: to one's neighbor and spouse. *Caritas est passio.* Love is passion, in the full meaning of both senses. Therefore God is passionate love also. As God's love—"He first loved us"—is individualized, how much more must human love too be individual and particular. Each so-called earthly thing now demands we restitute its love, raped and desecrated since the fall. Such, too, is the teaching of Milosz's Storge:

> I, who could never watch a pebble, taken from the road, drop from my hand without something secret in myself breaking, as if two hearts had split apart, I was the first, I, Storge, to have understood this: that the holy pebble of the road is the indivisible and unfathomable unity of space, time and Movement. For matter, space, time and Movement have fallen from the situated Place in a single stone of testimony. This is the fundamental arcanum, understand it well; because each initial reality asks for the humility of a body and the trial of a life, and this for the purpose of adoration; because the goal of all things is in the act of adoration. . . .
> MEMORIA

Thus, in place of Eros' infinite yearning, *agape* proposes marriage, the conjugal arcanum of neighbors: of man and woman, God and creation, Christ and the church. Not union, but marriage, affirmation, adoration: not identity, but blessing. This is Patmos, the path of the Muses, whereby redemption (charity) is identical with the self-sacrifice of creation from the beginning, "the lamb slain from the foundation of the world," and true love is prayer. It is to this primordial act—Faust's *Im Anfang war die Tat*—that Milosz refers repeatedly, as, for example, when he writes that the first sacrifice—"the one which raised Being above its own necessity"—made it free, so that beauty might appear and love be exalted above the law, an exaltation which was the first relationship—first love—between God and his creation as between Adam and Eve.

The key to this is St. John's Gospel, particularly its Prologue, which Milosz rememorated at the close of every Mass. The Word in the beginning, the eternal *Logos*, to whose inhumation St. John testifies, proclaims the redemptive value—

goodness, truth, beauty and love—of creative suffering and divine self-sacrifice. The *Logos*, as *ratio*, is the creative love—"eternal Word and first of all cries"—that, sacrificing Unity, distinguishes and reveals Identity—Particularity—the I AM, identity. This Word (Love) therefore is none other than the Divine Imagination *(vide* Blake and Coleridge) that, uttering aloud, binds together while holding apart, thus constituting the mystical body, now the earth's material body. As Milosz says, "It would be folly to look for proofs of the earthly reality of our life other than in the recognition that the matter which clothes us and surrounds us is absolutely identical with that in which all-powerful Love humbled Himself during the years of the Incarnation." The home of all things, its Logos—"the absolute place of Affirmation"—is love. Not for nothing does the ancient Presbyter of Ephesus enjoin his children to love one another, for God *is* love. God speaks, giving himself eternally in a single sacrifice—movement and expression, polarity and union, communication and relation—so that what He is, pure Spirit, may take form and rejoice in Him.

In the *Timaeus*, Plato wrote: "It is impossible for the determination or arrangement of two of anything, so long as there are only two, to be beautiful without a third. There must come between them, in the middle, a bond which brings them into union." But Jesus says, "When two or more are gathered together in my name, I am there"; and, more explicitly, he prays "that they may all be one; as thou, Father, art in me, and I in thee, that they may also be one in us. . . ." Such a bond of union transcending duality, such to-gatheredness and identity, is possible only and through love. Love is that bond. Therefore Milosz writes: "Spiritual beings find their ideal place in a gravitation we call love. The latter is our only reality, and when it transports us into the incorporeal light which it makes visible, the whole universe is restored to its place." For this reason, he adds, "the conjugal arcanum has remained the daily bread and also the wine of poetry and of science." In a word: "It is to love that we owe all things of value."

Confirming this, Peter Dronke, in *Medieval Latin and the Rise of the European Love Lyric,* demonstrates that the mystical and metaphysical origins of the Troubadour impulse, as those of St. Bernard and the School of Chartres, lie in the conscious effort to unite, in art as in science and in life, divine and human loves. Dronke shows how the more deeply *religious* the language of mystics and theologians becomes, the more closely it approximates the language of the highest states of *courtoisie* or courtly love: how the virtues acquired by the soul as it is illuminated by divine grace are exactly those that a lover acquires by virtue of his lady's grace. As Dronke puts it: "these are not two kinds of grace and two kinds of virtue, but one. It is divine grace itself that the beloved sheds upon the lover's soul." Thus the paths of the mystic and the lover are the same, that outlined by the poet Goethe in his poem "Holy Yearning," namely, "die and become." Without this act of renunciation, the poet or his lover remains "but a dismal guest upon this dark earth." Unilluminated by the light of sacrifice—"the free sacrifice of love," in Milosz's phrase—the earth remains forever dark. The earth, the duality of inner and outer, calls out to be redeemed by the sacrificial deed of love—that re-enactment of the primordial creative gesture whose secret also resides in the mystical relation between the sexes. There is therefore but a single love, a single union, the same as that ideally manifest between the sexes, as St. Hildegard of Bingen affirms in words uncannily like those of Oscar Milosz: "God gave an embodiment to the man's love, and thus the woman is the man's love. . . . Therefore there will be but a single love, and thus and thus only should it be in the love between man and woman." Nor is this all. She who thus embodies a lover's love is Love herself. St. Hildegard writes: "I seemed to see a girl of surpassing beauty. . . . On her breast she had an ivory tablet on which appeared in shades of sapphire the image of a man. And all creation called this girl 'sovereign lady.' The girl began to speak to the image on her breast: 'I was with you in the beginning, in the dawn of your strength and in the brightness of all that is holy I bore you from the womb before the star of day!' And I heard a voice saying to me, 'The girl whom you behold is Love; she has her dwelling in eternity.'"

This girl is Sophia, Divine Wisdom in its form of Love. Called by Milosz "our mother, the world's beauty," she is none other than creation itself. By union with her in conjoint, "ingrafted," prayer to the Father of Wisdom and Love, *gnosis* or non-dual, supersensible, imaginal knowledge is achieved. By such a path of praise and affirmation the many and the one are reconciled and poetry is made. Thereby the world is made poetic and revealed in its glory as the heavenly bride. And thereby, too, the higher purpose of love is revealed: to heal the rift between inner and outer by revealing what is within as without and what is without as within. Metaphysically, as Dronke says, the problem was to envisage a simultaneous fulfilment of earthly-human and heavenly-divine loves: to incarnate in a single deed a single love—and so a single, unifying knowledge. This cognitive deed, the union of wisdom and love, inner and outer, male and female, in a single soul is Imagination, the divine androgyne. It is the blessed mediator: love-surrender through love-service. By it, the lover is spiritually reborn in the beloved. Dronke concludes: "The mediation of the divine through love is necessarily individual and unique—the Beloved embodies Revelation for her devotee, and all he could know of the Divine on earth is in and through her. Thus, in this way, the union, which is supernatural, implies in its turn the winning of a new, personal individuation, an individual revealing of knowledge." Such, as Oscar Milosz knew from his own experience, is the fiery crucible wherein Swedenborg's Adramandoni, Hölderlin's Hesperides, Schiller's Elysium are blended:

> Here the true spouse the lost beloved regains,
> And on the enamelled couch of summer plains
>   Mingles sweet kisses with the zephyr's breath;

> Here, crowned at last, love never knows decay,
> Living through the ages its one bridal day,
>   Safe from the stroke of death!
> Schiller, ELYSIUM

This is why Beatrice, awaited with faith, leads Dante into the earthly Paradise; Dante, who feels "all the mighty power of ancient love" surging through him and recognizes thereby "the tokens of the ancient flame," now purified; Dante who can only write:

> Count of me but as of one
> Who am but the scribe of love; that when she breathes
> Take up my pen and, as she dictates, write . . .
> Dante, PURGATORIA XXIV, 52

The "Initiate" of Weimar, as Milosz called him, is particularly instructive here, for he associates sexuality and knowledge—*eros* and *agape*—in an almost biblical sense. Consider, out of many possible, the moment during Walpurgis Night when Faust meets Lilith. Dancing with her, he sings:

> A lovely dream once came to me;
> Then I beheld an apple tree,
> Two fairest apples on it shone:
> They lured me so, I climbed thereon.

Lilith replies:

> Apples have been desired by you,
> Since in Paradise first they grew;
> Now I am moved with joy to know
> That such within my garden grow.
> FAUST I, 4128-35

Powerfully attracted to her, Faust is recalled to his 'higher purpose' by a momentary vision of Gretchen, his conscience and his destiny. The point is twofold. In desire is knowledge, but this knowledge, this desire, must be infinitely extended, stretched. It must transcend all limits of time and space. The poet must die and become. Therefore Goethe names as the key lines in Faust's salvation those which state:

> He whose strivings never cease
> Is ours for his redeeming.
> If touched by celestial love,
> His soul has sacred leaven,
> There comes to greet him, from above
> The company of heaven . . .
>   FAUST II, 11936-41

Thus Faust strives unceasingly, ever drawn up by the eternal feminine, an ability granted him above all by a key. This key occurs in *Wilhelm Meister,* and on its occurrence there Milosz comments in his exegetic notes to *The Arcana.*

> Man, the creature, is as free as God. The only thing of importance in this world—this total universe—is prayer. It is prayer which gives knowledge and charity. Here is the reason why it was of the utmost necessity that man be free to pray or not to pray. Prayer was given him as a golden key and the universe as a box full of diamonds and rubies. The key was unique. Your pride rebelled against the idea of using a key invented by someone other than you. You threw the key into a well and kept the indestructible box, a night-colored box, hermetically closed forever. But the golden key has been found; its image—the only image in the whole book, drawn by Master Wolfgang Goethe himself—decorates page 883 of *Wilhelm Meister . . .*

What has prayer to do with this mysticism of love and poetry that we are proposing? Prayer for Oscar Milosz is synonymous with renunciation and sacrifice—renunciation, above all, of possession, "the compulsion to situate all things," i.e., of the desire for an object by a subject. Renunciation, prayer = the key, then: divine self-sacrifice enacted on the personal level. This was the key that Rilke, too, like Kabir, taught so fervently. He knew that "singing . . . isn't desiring,/ nor luring something conquered in the end./ Singing is Being. . . ."

> Young man,
> your loving isn't it, even if your mouth
> is pried open by your voice—learn
>
> to forget your impulsive song. Soon it will end.
> True singing is a different kind of breath.
> A breath about nothing. A gust in the god. A wind.
> SONNETS TO ORPHEUS, I, 3.

Goodness, Truth, Beauty—Love—given by heaven, incarnated in creation, must be returned to their origin, spoken, that all things may be made new and God be all in all. This is the Orphic intuition. *Apocatastasis.* Traditionally, there is a hierarchy of loves: first, Divine Love, the Holy Spirit, uncreated and creating, Sophia; then, love of parents for children *(Storge)*; and finally, conjugal love of men and women: of the human other. These three must be made one love, one movement, one rhythm—this is the problem of the *Eins und Alles*, the core of XIXth century Romantic philosophy. As in *Faust*, the Romantic troubadour-poet-philosopher must ascend from carnal desire—Gretchen, Beatrice—through the realm of the Mothers, the Nothing, Helen, Storge, to a mystical-spiritual finale in which a Gretchen, now transfigured, once more leads the poet on, as Beatrice led Dante on. In this way, Gretchen, like Beatrice, interiorized, becomes what she always was: the "woman in the heart." Thus mortal beauty reveals immortal beauty, mortal desire immortal love. The world is overcome. Outward sensuality, duality, sexuality are transformed; the heart becomes the gnostic key to the world. It knows no limits. In the words of Hölderlin's Hyperion: "The dissonances of the world are like lovers' quarrels. Reconciliation lies in the midst of strife, and all things separated come together again. The veins separate and return in the heart, and everything is one, unified, eternal, glowing Life."

Of this interiorization, which is resurrection, renaissance in immortality, Milosz writes explicitly in *Memoria:*

> I was alone in the silence of the total light of the world; for Renaissance, my spouse, slept at the feet of the throne on terraces suspended between two immense sheets of dew, one above and one below, the stellar and the terrestrial. And as I contemplated her, the Sleeper enveloped in the fire of night, she appeared to me, across the distance of sleep, remote as a constellation. And yet I felt her in myself, more sweetly and more terribly in myself than ever. With the ray of a sun that had set long ago, she was descending into the most silent depths of my life, into that abyss where recollection and premonition are one. And suddenly I felt her completely inside me and my own, and as if transmuted into the beauty of the universe. What compassion then took hold of me at the sight of the entire cosmos below! I lost even the notion of what was external—love became charity again, and I felt my own blood running through all creation, and the manifestation of Being appeared to me in its feminine form and light. Thus the Conjugal Arcanum was revealed to me. . . .

Extraordinary though this is, it is very similar to that experience recounted by Novalis in the third section of the *Hymns to the Night.*

Milosz's poetical career may, in short, be viewed as the process of the interiorization of the divine feminine, the divinization of the male by the interiorization of the female. In his early poems, Milosz is haunted by the memory of the eternal woman, and of his union with her in the Conjugal Arcanum:

Take my heart, O sister dear, and rock it!
Gardens, rivers, mountains in your eyes I see,
A whole landscape disappearing, growing distant,
A whole kingdom sinking in blue silence.
Take my heart, O sister dear, and rock it!

O Lilia, mist of the garden of thought, you are sweet
As music heard in half-sleep!
LULLABY

Haunted by this presence, the poet searches for her wherever he can. Thrown into the objectified, fallen, physical world of time and space, he seeks her desperately, physically, like Baudelaire, among 'real' women who turn out to be not so real and yet act as guides to a reality beyond: a passion called "Donjuanism." This is the phase that culminates in *The Amorous Initiation*, in which the poet's alter ego, Pinamonte, drunk, howling with desire, dies in love eternally. Pinamonte confesses: "My childhood never knew love; my youth failed to taste passion's sweet fruit; and, at the gates of age, the prime of life left me without the memory of a friendship. I have never known any care other than that of filling (with a thousand follies) the empty place that love left in my heart, for the places where gentleness deigns to pause are visited by the sores of deceit, madness and horror. My sensual delight has been nothing but a derangement of the imagination. . . ."

His love dies. Having sought it in the flesh, carnally, he finds that what he has sought is of the spirit; it is spiritual. His love is reborn, but outside space and time; it transcends the objectified frame of the ordinary material universe. Now the time of apprenticeship is over; now the hour of renunciation has come. "Your years of apprenticeship are over; nature has absolved you," the Abbé tells Wilhelm Meister. Milosz annotates his copy: "Sublime! Sublime! Sublime! And therewith the loves of Lothario. Apprenticeship, obviously. A great spirit's education requires cruel sacrifices: in this matter, woman, the being of feeling, must be sacrificed. She is indispensable for our education, but pity must not stop Me." Such is the way of the Noble Traveller: renunciation, yearning, suffering, sacrifice, interiorization. It is the universal path of *amor ascendens* marked out by the Troubadours: desire, prayer, service, the kiss, the deed. Such is the revelation of "the supreme absolute number and immutable ending of every poem . . .," the "superhuman fulfillment of the final rhythm." Milosz speaks truly when he says:

> I have visited the two worlds. Love led me to the very depth of being.   CANTICLE OF KNOWLEDGE

CHRISTOPHER BAMFORD

PART ONE
The Poems

BRUMES

Je suis un grand jardin de novembre, un jardin éploré
Où grelottent les abandonnés du vieux faubourg;
Où la couleur misérable des brumes dit: Toujours!
Où le battement des fontaines est let mot: Jamais . . .
—Autour d'un buste ridicule qui médite,
(Marie, tu dors, ton moulin va trop vite),
Tourne la ronde des désespoirs du vieux faubourg.

Entendez-vous la ronde qui pleure, dans le jardin noyé
De brume aveugle, au fond du vieux faubourg?
Pauvres amitiés mortes, burlesques amours oubliées,
O vous les mensonges d'un soir, ô vous les illusions d'un jour,
Autour du buste ridicule qui médite,
(Marie, tu dors, ton moulin va trop vite),
Venez danser la ronde noire du vieux faubourg.

La brume a tout mangé, rien n'est gai, rien n'irrite,
Le rêve est aussi creux que la réalité.
Mais dans le parc où vous avez connu l'été
La ronde, la ronde immense tourne, tourne toujours,
Amis que l'on remplace, amantes que l'on quitte . . .
(Marie, tu dors, ton moulin va trop vite . . .)

Je suis un grand jardin de novembre, au fond d'un vieux faubourg.

from *Le Poème des Décadences*
The Poem of Decadences
1899

MISTS

I am a great November garden, a weeping garden
Where the forsaken of the old suburb shiver;
Where the miserable color of the mists says: Always!
Where the fountains' beating is the word: Never . . .
—Around an absurd bust in meditation
(Mary, you're asleep, your mill goes too fast),
Turns the wheel of the old suburb's despairs.

Do you hear the wheel weeping in the garden
Drowned in blind mist in the old suburb's heart?
Poor dead friendships, burlesque forgotten loves,
O you lies of an evening, O you illusions of a day,
Around an absurd bust in meditation
(Mary, you're asleep, your mill goes too fast),
Come dance the old suburb's black roundel.

The mist has eaten everything, nothing is gay, nothing happens,
The dream is as hollow as the reality.
But in the park where you knew the summer
The wheel, the immense wheel, turns, still turns,
Friends whom one replaces, lovers whom one leaves . . .
(Mary, you're asleep, your mill turns too fast . . .)

I am a great November garden, in the heart of an old suburb.

translated by Christopher Bamford

BERCEUSE

Vos yeux sont un demi-jour bleu-gris, ô ma Lilia,
Un demi-jour bleu-gris sur la contrée des joies lointaines . . .
Au pays de vos yeux la somnolence est reine.
Les fontaines chantent doucement aux parcs d'autrefois . . .
Vos yeux sont un demi-jour bleu-gris, ô ma Lilia!

Prenez mon cœur, ô sœur chérie, et bercez-le!
Je vois, dans vos yeux, des jardins, des rivières, des montagnes,
Tout un paysage qui s'efface et s'éloigne,
Tout un royaume qui sombre dans le silence bleu.
Prenez mon cœur, ô sœur chérie, et bercez-le!

Comme une musique entendue dans le demi-sommeil,
O Lilia, brume du jardin des Songes, vous êtes douce!
—Le réveil sera beau, demain, des fleurs des bois parmi les mousses,
Et dans le soleil jeune sonneront les abeilles!
—O Lilia, musique entendue dans le demi-sommeil!

Nous reverrons, en rêve, les grands arbres lourds de fleurs,
O ma pensive,—les grands arbres de la vallée,
Et votre regard sur mon âme sera la couleur
De la lune penchée sur les pierres des mausolées . . .
Nous reverrons, en rêve, les grands arbres lourds de fleurs.

Notre bonheur connaît le jardin des Mélancolies.
Ah! Lilia, qui sait si, demain, le mensonge de nos pensées
Ne sera pas la réalité de l'oubli?
La douceur ne se mire qu'aux lagunes du passé . . .
Notre bonheur connaît le jardin des Mélancolies.

Dormons . . . Les ombres des chemins se font fondues dans l'Ombre.
Qu'importe Demain? Je suis sûr qu'Aujourd'hui existe,
Et que la brise du jour clair n'est pas morte sur les fleurs sombres,
Et que mon âme vibre encore sur vos lèvres tristes . . .
Dormons, dormons . . . Les ombres des chemins se sont fondues dans
  l'Ombre.

from THE POEM OF DECADENCES

LULLABY

Your eyes are a twilight blue-grey, O my Lilia,
A twilight blue-grey on the land of far joys . . .
Somnolence is queen in the country of your eyes.
And fountains sing sweetly in the parks of old . . .
Your eyes are a twilight blue-grey, O my Lilia!

Take my heart, O sister dear, and rock it!
Gardens, rivers, mountains in your eyes I see,
A whole landscape disappearing, growing distant,
A whole kingdom sinking in blue silence.
Take my heart, O sister dear, and rock it!

O Lilia, mist of the garden of Thoughts, you are sweet
As music heard in half sleep!
—Beautiful tomorrow will be the waking of woodflowers amid mosses
And in the young sun bees will hum!
O Lilia, music heard in half sleep.

We shall meet again in dreams great trees heavy with flowers,
O my pensive one,—great trees of the valley,
And your gaze upon my soul will be the color
Of the moon bent over sepulchral stones . . .
We shall meet again in dreams great trees heavy with flowers.

Our happiness knew the garden of Melancholies.
Ah! Lilia, who knows if tomorrow our thoughts' lie
Will not be oblivion's reality?
Sweetness reflects only in lagoons of the past . . .
Our happiness knew the garden of Melancholies.

Let us sleep . . . The paths' shadows have melted in Shadow.
What matters Tomorrow? That today exists I am sure
And that the breeze of bright daylight has not died upon dark flowers,
And that my soul still sings on your sad lips . . .
Let us sleep, let us sleep . . . The paths' shadows have melted in
  Shadow.

translated by Christopher Bamford

EGEIA

Pourquoi ce front si triste, Egeia, forme de mon âme,
Pourquoi ces larmes dans les yeux de ma bien-chère?
Le sourire de mon amie est comme un blâme,
Ses yeux sont comme un grand silence sur la mer . . .

Egeia, Egeia! C'est l'atroce insomnie
De la Vie, ô ma douce, qui psalmodie en vous
Sa berceuse sans fin, dont la monotonie
N'endort ni les regrets, ni les frayeurs, ni les dégoûts!

Je me penche sur mon mirage en l'eau grise de vos pensées
Et ma tristesse est un vertige de parfums fades,
Et les doux flots lents sont un troupeau bêlant d'agnelles malades,
Là-bas, sur la plage nocturne où nos pas se sont effacés . . .

Nos âmes sont la mort de la mer sur les sables
Où tremble le vieux clair-de-lune des regrets,
Et les jours que nous regrettons sont misérables,
Et les jours que nous espérons sont des désespérés . . .

Adieu les mots chanteurs, adieu les nobles attitudes,
Adieu l'amour de la Douleur, adieu le mépris de la Gloire!
—Ecoutons sangloter, dans les lointaines solitudes,
L'eau faible et résignée où défaille le Soir . . .

EGEIA

Why this sad face, Egeia, form of my soul,
Why these tears in the eyes of my dearest?
My friend's smile is like a reproach,
Her eyes are like a great silence on the sea.

Egeia, Egeia! It is the awful sleeplessness
Of life, my sweet, that sings in you
The endless lullaby whose monotones
Anesthetize neither fears, nor disgusts, nor regrets!

I bend over my image in the grey water of your thoughts
And my sadness is a dizziness of stale perfume,
And the sweet slow billows on the beach at night
Are a flock of sick ewe lambs bleating where our steps have washed away.

Our souls are the death of the sea on the sand
Where the old moonlight trembles with regrets,
And the days we regret are full of misery
And the days we hope for are hopeless . . .

Farewell singing words, farewell noble attitudes,
Farewell love of suffering, farewell contempt of glory!
—Let us listen to the sobbing in the distant solitude
Of the weak and passive water where Evening decays . . .

translated by Christopher Bamford

KAROMAMA

Mes pensées sont à toi, reine Karomama du très vieux temps,
Enfant dolente aux jambes trop longues, aux mains si faibles
Karomama, fille de Thèbes,
Qui buvais du blé rouge et mangeais du blé blanc
Comme les justes, dans le soir des tamaris.
Petite reine Karomama du temps jadis.

Mes pensées sont à toi, reine Karomama
Dont le nom oublié chante comme un chœur de plaintes
Dans le demi-rire et le demi-sanglot de ma voix;
Car il est ridicule et triste d'aimer la reine Karomama
Qui vécut environnée d'étranges figures peintes
Dans un palais ouvert, tellement autrefois,
Petite reine Karomama.

Que faisais-tu de tes matins perdus, Dame Karomama?
Vers la raideur de quelque dieu chétif à tête d'animal
Tu allongeais gravement tes bras maigres et maladroits
Tandis que des feux doux couraient sur le fleuve matinal.
O Karomama aux yeux las, aux longs pieds alignés,
Aux cheveux torturés, morte du berceau des années . . .
Ma pauvre, pauvre reine Karomama.

Et de tes journées, qu'en faisais-tu, prêtresse savante?
Tu taquinais sans doute tes petites servantes
Dociles comme les couleuvres, mais comme elles indolentes;
Tu comptais les bijoux, tu rêvais de fils de rois
Sinistres et parfumés, arrivant de très loin,

from *Les Sept Solitudes*
The Seven Solitudes
1906

KAROMAMA

My thoughts go to you, Queen Karomama of the very old times,
Sickly child whose legs are too long, whose hands are too weak,
Karomama, daughter of Thebes,
Who drank teas of red wheat and ate white wheat,
Like the Just, in the evening beneath the tamarinds,
Little Queen Karomama of so long ago.

My thoughts are all yours, Queen Karomama,
Whose forgotten name sings like a choir of complaints
In the half-laughter and the half-sobbing of my voice;
For it is absurd and sad to love Queen Karomama,
Who lived surrounded by strange painted figures,
In an open palace, so very long ago,
Little Queen Karomama.

What did you do with your wasted mornings, Lady Karomama?
Towards the rigidity of some weakly animal-headed god,
You gravely extended your own thin and clumsy arms
While soft and fast lights floated by on the stream in the morn.
Oh, Karomama, weary-eyed, with your long feet aligned,
Your tortured locks, you who died in history's infancy,
My poor, oh so poor Queen Karomama!

And with your days, what did you do, so wise as a priestess?
You probably teased your little hand-maidens
That were as docile, and lazy too, as grass-snakes,
And you counted your jewels and dreamed of sons of kings,
Sinister and perfumed, who came from afar,

De par delà les mers couleur de toujours et de loin
Pour dire: "Salut à la glorieuse Karomama."

Et les soirs d'éternel été tu chantais sous les sycomores
Sacrés, Karomama, fleur bleue des lunes consumées;
Tu chantais la vieille histoire des pauvres morts
Qui se nourrissaient en cachette de choses prohibées
Et tu sentais monter dans les grands soupirs tes seins bas
D'enfant noire et ton âme chancelait d'effroi.
Les soirs d'éternel été, n'est-ce pas, Karomama?

—Un jour (a-t-elle vraiment existé, Karomama?),
On entoura ton corps de jaunes bandelettes,
On l'enferma dans un cercueil grotesque et doux en bois de cèdre.
La saison du silence effeuilla la fleur de ta voix.
Les scribes confièrent ton nom aux papyrus
Et c'est si triste et c'est si vieux et c'est si perdu . . .
C'est comme l'infini des eaux dans la nuit et dans le froid.

Tu sais sans doute, ô légendaire Karomama!
Que mon âme est vieille comme le chant de la mer
Et solitaire comme un sphinx dans le désert,
Mon âme malade de jamais et d'autrefois.
Et tu sais mieux encor, princesse initiée,
Que la destinée a gravé un signe étrange dans mon cœur,
Symbole de joie idéale et de réel malheur.

Oui, tu sais tout cela, lointaine Karomama,
Malgré tes airs d'enfant que sut éterniser
L'auteur de la statue polie par les baisers
Des siècles étrangers qui languirent loin de toi.
Je te sens près de moi, j'entends ton long sourire
Chuchoter dans la nuit: "Frère, il ne faut pas rire."
—Mes pensées sont à toi, reine Karomama.

from THE SEVEN SOLITUDES

From beyond the seas of the color of Always and of Very Far,
To say: "Greetings to glorious Karomama!"

And on evenings of eternal summer beneath the sacred
Sycamores, Karomama, blue flower of burned-out moons,
You sang the ancient tale of the poor dead
Who feed in secret on forbidden foods,
And you felt your low breasts rise with the heavy sighs
Of a black child whose soul is tottering in terror,
On those eyes of eternal summer, I'm sure, Karomama.

One day—did she really exist, Karomama?—
They wound yellow strips round your corpse
And enclosed it in a grotesque and sweet-smelling cedar-wood coffin.
The season of silence then scattered the petals of your voice
And the scribes entrusted your name to papyrus-leaves.
But all this is so sad and ancient and so lost
That it's like the infinite of waters in the night and the cold.

You may well know, legendary Karomama,
That my soul too is as old as the song of the sea
And as lonely as a Sphinx in the desert sands,
My soul that is sick of Nevermore and Yesteryear.
You know even better, Princess initiated in mysteries,
That Fate has engraved a strange sign in my heart,
A symbol of ideal joy and of real despair.

Yes, all this you know, Karomama from afar,
In spite of your childlike appearance immortalized
So well by the author of your statue now polished by the kisses
Of alien centuries that languished far away from you.
Yet I feel you close by me, I can hear your long smile
As you whisper in the night: "Brother, refrain from laughter!"
—My thoughts are all yours, Queen Karomama.

translated by Edouard Roditi

AUX SONS D'UNE MUSIQUE...

Aux sons d'une musique endormie et molle
Comme le glouglou des marais de la lune,
Enfant au sang d'été, à la bouche de prune
Mûre;
Aux sons de miel de tes chevrotantes paroles
Ici, dans l'ombre humide et chaude du vieux mur
Que s'endorme la bête paresseuse Infortune.

Aux son de ta chanson de harpe rouillée,
Tiède fille qui luis comme une pomme mouillée,
—(Ma tête est si lourde d'éternité vide,
Les mouches d'or font un bruit doux et stupide
Qui prennent tes grands yeux de vache pour des fenêtres),
Aux sons de ta dormante et rousse voix d'été
Fais que je rêve à ce qui aurait pu être
Et n'a pas été ...

Quels beaux yeux de n'importe quel animal tu as,
Blanche fille de juin, grande dormeuse!
Mon âme, mon âme est pluvieuse,
D'être et de n'être pas je suis tout las.
Tandis que ta voix d'eau coule comme du sable
Que je m'endorme loin de tout et loin de moi
Entre les trois bouteilles vides sur la table.

—Noyé voluptueux du fleuve de ta voix ...

from THE SEVEN SOLITUDES

TO THE SOUND . . .

To the sound of soft sleepy music
Like the gurgling of the marshes of the moon,
Child with the blood of summer, with a mulberry
Mouth . . .
To the honeyed sound of your quivering words,
Here, in the damp warm shadow of the old wall
The stupid tramp Misfortune falls asleep.

To the sound of a song on your rusty harp,
Languid girl who shines like a wet apple,
—(My head is heavy with vacant eternity,
The golden flies buzz, sweet and dull,
And mistake your great cowlike eyes for windows.)
To the sound of the drowsy, russet voice of summer
Make me dream of what might have been
And was not . . .

It doesn't matter what animal your eyes are like,
White girl of June, deep sleeper!
My soul, my soul is rainy,
I am tired of to be and not to be.
And yet your voice of water running like sand
Which puts me to sleep far from everything and far from myself
Between three empty bottles under the table . . .

—Drowned voluptuously in the river of your voice.

translated by Kenneth Rexroth

TOUS LES MORTS SONT IVRES...

Tous les morts sont ivres de pluie vieille et sale
Au cimetière étrange de Lofoten.
L'horloge du dégel tictaque lointaine
Au cœur des cercueils pauvres de Lofoten.

Et grâce aux trous creusés par le noir printemps
Les corbeaux sont gras de froide chair humaine;
Et grâce au maigre vent à la voix d'enfant
Le sommeil est doux aux morts de Lofoten.

Je ne verrai très probablement jaimais
Ni la mer ni les tombes de Lofoten
Et pourtant c'est en moi comme si j'amais
Ce lointain coin de terre et toute sa peine.

Vous disparus, vous suicidés, vous lointaines
Au cimetière étranger de Lofoten
—Le nom sonne à mon oreille étrange et doux,
Vraiment, dites-moi, dormez-vous, dormez-vous?

—Tu pourrais me conter des choses plus drôles
Beau claret dont ma coupe d'argent est pleine,
Des histoires plus charmantes ou moins folles;
Laisse-moi tranquille avec ton Lofoten.

Il fait bon. Dans le foyer doucement traîne
La voix du plus mélancolique des mois.
—Ah! les morts, y compris ceux de Lofoten—
Les morts, les morts sont au fond moins morts que moi...

from THE SEVEN SOLITUDES

ALL THE DEAD ARE DRUNK...

All the dead are drunk beneath the rain that's grey and old
As it falls on Lofoten's cemetery that's so strange
While the distant clock of the thaw is ticking
Inside the coffins of the paupers of Lofoten.

And thanks to the holes that the dark spring digs
The crows grow fat on cold human flesh;
And thanks to the thin wind with its childish voice
The sleep of Lofoten's dead is still sweet.

Most likely I'll never see those seas
That surround Lofoten, nor see its tombs;
And yet I feel as if I loved
Those distant isles and all their grief.

All of you who are gone, who have taken your own lives,
All so far away in Lofoten's strange graveyard,
Its name sounds so soft and strange in my ears,
Tell me truly, tell me, are you all asleep?

—You might well be telling me brighter tales,
My fine claret that fills my silver goblet,
Tales that are more charming or less mad.
Leave me in peace. I'll have none of your Lofoten.

This room is warm. In the hearth we hear softly
The voice of the most melancholy of all months.
Well, the dead, including those of Lofoten,
Yes, the dead, all the dead, after all are more live than I.

translated by Edouard Roditi

GRINCEMENT DOUX...

Grincement doux et rouillé d'une berline...
Le crépuscule pleure de vieille joie...
—Il faudrait pourtant aller voir qui est là.
—"Bonsoir, comment vous portez-vous, Mylord Spleen?"

Les chevaux, les chevaux du passé hennissent
Le soir, le soir, aux fenêtres de l'oubli.
—"La diva que vos sentiments applaudissent,
Mylord, l'avez-vous revue en Italie?"

Il pleut, il pleut doux de la pluie ancienne
Sur les toits, sur les toits rouges d'autrefois.
—"Merci pour votre aimable lettre de Sienne;
Et Noël, se souvient-il encor de moi?"

Ton coq, ton coq, girouette, dit jamais plus,
J'ai mal, j'ai mal, ô grand-père soir, à l'âme.
—"Ces maudites routes d'automne, goddam!
A propos... Godwin et Percy vous saluent."

Soir de jadis naïf, doux comme un qui cuve
Son vieux vin de l'an vingt près d'un feu léger.
—"Et puis vous savez, je suis si distrait!—J'ai
Oublié de jeter moi dans le Vésuve."

from THE SEVEN SOLITUDES

THE SOFT AND RUSTY CREAKING...

The soft and rusty creaking of a horse-drawn coach,
While the dusk is weeping of its age-old joy....
—One should really go and see who's there...
—"Welcome, and how have you fared, my Lord Spleen?"

The horses, those horses of yesteryear are whinnying
In the evening, in the dusk, beyond the windows of oblivion.
—"The diva whom you still applaud in your sentiments,
My Lord, did you see her again in Italy?"

It's raining, gently raining with an ancient rain
On the roofs, the red roofs of yesteryear.
—"Thank you for your kind letter from Sienna.
And Noel, does she still remember me?"

Weathervane, weathervane, your cock crows Nevermore,
My soul, my soul, Grandfather Dusk, is in pain.
—"Those wretched autumn roads, Goddam!
By the way, greetings from Godwin and Percy."

Simple-minded evenings of the past, gentle as one who digests
His good old wine of the year Twenty by a light fire.
—"Besides, you know how absent-minded I can be:
I even forgot to throw me into the crater of Vesuvius!"

translated by Edouard Roditi

IL NOUS FAUT...

Il nous faut un aubergiste bien rond,
Sautillant, au bonnet saluant preste,
Aux boutons de métal doux sur sa veste.
Il nous faut, il nous faut, mon cœur profond.

Une vallée un peu de vieille estampe,
Des Peterborough aux habits de plaids,
Les amours de Newstead au gris des lampes,
Un grand vent qui déclame du Manfred.

Il nous faut l'oubli le plus implacable,
(C'est comme si nous n'avions pas été)
Des noms de jadis gravés dans les tables;
Voilà ce qu'il nous faut, en vérité.

—Comme plus haut: un aubergiste rond
Et des chambres discrètement baignées
De demi-jour de toiles d'araignée.
—Il nous faut, il nous faut, mon cœur profond.

from THE SEVEN SOLITUDES

WE NEED . . .

We need a good round innkeeper,
Frisky, always tipping his hat,
With bright metal buttons on his vest.
We need him, we need him, my deep heart.

A valley something like an old print
Of Peterborough where they wear kilts,
The loves of Newstead in the grey lamplight,
The great wind declaiming Manfred.

We need the most implacable forgetfulness,
(To be as though we had never been)
The names of old carved on the tables;
Yes, that's what we really need.

—Like on high: a round innkeeper
And rooms discreetly bathed
In a twilight of cobwebs
—That's what we need, that's it, my deep heart.

translated by Kenneth Rexroth

ET SURTOUT QUE...

—Et surtout que Demain n'apprenne pas où je suis—
Les bois, les bois sont pleins de baies noires—
Ta voix est comme un son de lune dans le vieux puits
Où l'écho, l'écho de juin vient boire.

Et que nul ne prononce mon nom là-bas, en rêve,
Les temps, les temps sont bien accomplis—
Comme un tout petit arbre souffrant de prime sève
Est ta blancheur en robe sans pli.

Et que les ronces se referment derrière nous,
Car j'ai peur, car j'ai peur du retour.
Les grandes fleurs blanches caressent tes doux genoux
Et l'ombre, et l'ombre est pâle d'amour.

Et ne dis pas à l'eau de la forêt qui je suis;
Mon nom, mon nom est tellement mort.
Tes yeux ont la couleur des jeunes pluies,
Des jeunes pluies sur l'étang qui dort.

Et ne raconte rien au vent du vieux cimetière.
Il pourrait m'ordonner de le suivre.
Ta chevelure sent l'été, la lune et la terre.
Il faut vivre, vivre, rien que vivre...

from THE SEVEN SOLITUDES

ESPECIALLY . . .

—Especially tomorrow mustn't find out where I am—
The woods, the woods are full of blackberries—
Your voice is like the sound of the moon in an old well
Where the echo, the echo of June comes to drink.

And nobody must pronounce my name down there, in dream,
The times, the times are well fulfilled—
Your whiteness in its simple dress
Is like a tree, suffering, too young for its first sap.

And the briars must close behind us,
For I am afraid, I am afraid to go back.
The great white flowers caress your sweet knees,
The shadow, the shadow is pale with love.

You mustn't tell the water of the forest who I am;
My name, my name is utterly dead.
Your eyes are the happy color of young showers,
Of young showers on a drowsy lagoon.

Don't say anything to the wind of the old cemetery.
It could order me to follow it.
Your hair is like the summer, the moon and the earth.
We must live, live, nothing but live . . .

translated by Kenneth Rexroth

LE ROI DON LUIS...

Le roi don Luis voulut revoir
Le château des Douces Années.

Manteau de deuil et cheval noir.

Jamais heure au vide du soir
N'a si lugubrement sonné.

C'est pire que le bruit du vent
Dans les maisons abandonnées.

Ah c'est un son, un son vraiment
Qui vient de plus loin que le temps.

C'est pire que le bruit des portes
Alors qu'on songe aux morts, aux mortes.

Ce son félon me vient, m'arrive
De quels rêves, de quelles rives.

Il se couche sur ma raison
En lueurs fausses de poison.

Le long mendiant de la route
Est la chair de ce son sans doute.

Rencontre de chemin d'exil.
O le sinistre qui s'arrête!

Je vois deux yeux presque sans tête,
Deux yeux sur deux jambes de fil.

De plus loin que les oubliés
De plus profond que les noyés.

Le cheval noir dresse l'oreille.

Le sang du roi voudrait crier
L'odeur du silence est si vieille.

from THE SEVEN SOLITUDES

KING DON LUIS . . .

King don Luis wanted to see again
The palace called Sweet Years.

Cloak of grief and a black horse.

Bell in the blank of evening:
Never so ominous as this—

Harsh as the wind's hurry
Through abandoned houses.

Indeed, it is a sound
Travelling farther than time.

Doors swinging into reveries
Over men dead, and women.

Treacherous advent, entering
From what dreams, what shores.

Over my mind it sleeps
In false glimmers of poison

And the tall beggar, most certainly,
Is that sound's body.

On the road into exile.
Sinister, self-encountering!

I see two eyes nearly headless,
Two eyes on two legs of thread.

Farther than the forgotten,
Deeper than the drowned.

The black horse pricks its ears.

The king's blood would cry out,
The smell of silence is so old.

translated by John Peck

QUAND ELLE VIENDRA...

Quand elle viendra—fera-t-il gris ou vert dans ses yeux,
Vert ou gris dans le fleuve?
L'heure sera nouvelle dans cet avenir si vieux,
Nouvelle, mais si peu neuve...
Vieilles heures où l'on a tout dit, tout vu, tout rêvé!
Je vous plains si vous le savez...

Il y aura de l'aujourd'hui et des bruits de la ville
Tout comme aujourd'hui et toujours—dures épreuves!—
Et des odeurs,—selon la saison—de septembre ou d'avril
Et du ciel faux et des nuages dans le fleuve;

Et des mots—selon le moment—gais ou sanglotants
Sous des cieux qui se réjouissent ou qui pleuvent,
Car nous aurons vécu et simulé, ah! tant et tant,
Quand elle viendra avec ses yeux de pluie sur le fleuve.

Il y aura (voix de l'ennui, rire de l'impuissance)
Le vieux, le stérile, le sec moment présent,
Pulsation, d'une éternité sœur du silence;
Le moment présent, tout comme à présent.

Hier, il y a dix ans, aujourd'hui, dans un mois,
Horribles mots, pensées mortes, mais qu'importe.
Bois, dors, meurs,—il faut bien qu'on se sauve de soi
De telle ou d'autre sorte...

from THE SEVEN SOLITUDES

WHEN SHE COMES . . .

When she comes—will her eyes go green, gray,
Gray or green in the river?
The hour will be new in that archaic future,
New, but hardly novel—
Old hours: one has seen, dreamed, spoken them all!
I pity you the knowledge . . .

There will be something of the present and its street-sounds
Just as today and always—firm ordeals—
And odors, depending on the season, September's, April's,
And the false sky, and clouds in the river;

And words, depending on the moment, spirited, broken,
Under skies arranged correspondingly,
For we shall have lived a great deal, shall have pretended to live such a great deal
When she comes with her eyes of rain over that river.

There will be (weary voice, impotent smile)
The moment we now have, senile, sterile, dry,
The pulsing of eternity, sister of silence;
The moment we now have, just as we have it now.

Yesterday, ten years ago, today, in a month—
Frightful words, clichés, but what does it matter.
Drink, sleep, die—one must escape from himself
In some way or another . . .

translated by John Peck

DANSE DE SINGE

Aux sons d'une petite musique narquoise, sautillante,
Essoufflée,—tandis qu'il pleut, tandis qu'il pleut de la pluie pourrie,
Saute, saute, mon âme, vieux singe d'orgue de Barbarie,
Petit vieillard pelé, sournois, animal romantique et tendre.

Avec ta queue l'automne effeuillée, prétentieusement tordue
En point d'interrogation sur le vide ciel du crépuscule,
Essuie tes pleurs, singe galant, mélancolique et ridicule,
Singe galeux de l'amour mort, singe édenté des jours perdus.

Encore un air, encore un air! Celui qui sent les tabagies,
Le faubourg lépreux, la foire d'automne et les fritures aigres
Pour faire rire les filles mal nourries,—ô sale, affreux, maigre,
Piteux, épileptique singe, animal pur des nostalgies!

Encore un air, hélas! le dernier!—Et que ce soit cette sourde
Valse de jamais, requiem des voleurs morts, musique en échos
Qui dit: adieu les souvenirs, l'amour et la noix de coco . . .
—Tandis qui la pluie pauvre fait glouglou dans la boue vieille et
    lourde.

from THE SEVEN SOLITUDES

MONKEY DANCE

To the tune of a little mocking music, frisking
Breathlessly, and weeping, weeping like the pouring rain,
Jump, jump, my soul, old monkey, to the Barbary organ,
Little old ragamuffin, sly, romantic and tender animal.

With your tail like leafless autumn, pretentiously twisted
In a question mark against the empty twilight sky,
Wipe your tears, gallant monkey, melancholy and ridiculous,
Monkey scabby with dead love, monkey toothless with lost days.

Another tune, give us another tune! You know the low dives,
The leprous slums, the autumn street fairs, the sour fish and chips.
You make the malnourished girls laugh,—o dirty, frightful, skinny,
Piteous, epileptic monkey, animal of pure homesickness.

Give us another tune, too bad it's the last!—And let it be that sordid
Last waltz, the requiem of dead thieves, echoing music
Which says, "Goodby memory, love and coconuts . . ."
While the poor rain gurgles in the old and heavy mud.

translated by Kenneth Rexroth

LA MER

Salut, belle Thétis, mère des destinées!
Ce n'est point pour me plaindre ou pour pleurer mes morts
Que le front ceint de fleurs je reviens sur tes bords;
Je n'ai plus rien à dire aux rapides années
Qui m'ont fui dans les vents toutes voiles dehors.
Comme tes profondeurs mes regards sont tranquilles:
Ils se sont délivrés du stérile souci
De scruter longuement l'horizon obscurci
Afin d'y découvrir ces merveilleuses îles
Où la joie et l'amour sont mortels comme ici.
La vie en nous quittant nous apprend qui nous sommes:
Il se fait tard, Thétis, dans le ciel de mon jour;
J'ai perdu ma jeunesse; elle a fui sans retour;
Je suis trop grand aussi pour les filles des hommes;
Elles ne peuvent pas comprendre mon amour.
Mon amour est si grand que nulle créature
N'oserait l'approcher, ne saurait le nourrir;
Il lui faut tout l'espoir et tout le souvenir,
Tout ce qui pleure et rit, la profonde Nature,
La mère au large sein qui ne sait pas mourir.
Heureux qui s'abandonne à la tendresse humaine
Et qui reçoit du monde autant qu'il a donné!
J'ai semé le grain d'or et n'ai pas moissonné;
Mais je porte en mon âme indulgente et hautaine
La consolation d'avoir tout pardonné.

from *Les Éléments*
The Elements
1911

THE SEA

Hail, beautiful Thetis, mother of destinies!
It is not to complain or to weep for my dead
That I return to your shores my brow bound with flowers;
I have nothing more to say to the rapid years
Which have fled me in winds far from all sail.
My gazes are as tranquil as your depths:
They are freed of the useless worry
Of searching forever the darkened horizon
To find those marvellous islands
Where joy and love are mortal like here.
Life in leaving us teaches us who we are:
It is late, Thetis, in the heaven of my day;
I have lost my youth; it has gone never to return;
I am too great for the daughters of men;
They cannot understand my love.
My love is so great no creature
Would dare approach it, or know how to feel it;
It needs all hope, all memory,
All that weeps and laughs, deep Nature,
The great-breasted mother who does not know how to die.
Happy he who abandons himself to human tenderness,
Who receives from the world as much as he has given.
I have sown the golden germ and have not harvested;
But within my proud and noble soul I carry
The consolation of having forgiven all.

C'est pourquoi j'ose aimer la plus belle de toutes,
Celle qui sous le joug d'un labeur incessant
Porta toute la vie en son sein frémissant,
A l'homme aventureux ouvrit ses larges routes.
Et je veux seulement que soit pure de brume
Des horizons d'été la sainte profondeur
Et qu'au large des mers quelque oiseau migrateur
S'attachant aux longs plis de mon linceul d'écume
Puisse se rassasier de l'amour de mon cœur.

That is why I dare to love her who is most beautiful of all,
Who beneath the yoke of incessant labor
Carries all life in her quivering breasts,
Opening her broad ways to the adventuring man.
I desire only that her holy depths
Should be pure and without the haze of summer horizons
And that far out to sea some migrating bird
Attaching itself to the long folds of my spumy shroud
Should gather again the heart of my love.

translated by Christopher Bamford

LA TERRE

Je t'aime d'un amour si joyeux et si tendre
O toi qui me créas pour exalter le Beau
Que lorsqu'il sera temps d'éteindre le flambeau
Et de choisir la place où doit dormir la cendre
Je dirai seulement: la Terre est mon tombeau.
J'ai laissé de mon cœur dans toutes ses contrées;
Ici j'aimais les jours, là-bas j'aimais les nuits;
Et dans mon souvenir, comme au secret d'un puits,
Les faces aux beaux yeux autrefois rencontrées
Se mirent longuement pour tromper mes ennuis.
Des paysages purs rêvent dans ma mémoire
Comme un mirage étrange au sein des brumes d'or;
Penchez-vous vers mon cœur: vous entendrez encor
Dans ce monde lointain une rumeur de foire
Des bruits de va-et-vient et des sanglots de cor.
Ce cœur tantôt bruyant et tantôt solitaire
Fut comme une cité fière de son jardin;
Non, amis, approchez; donnez-moi votre main;
Et surtout dites-moi: "Toute la douce terre
Sûrement tu l'auras pour sépulcre demain.
Elle n'a point d'amant qui te soit comparable;
C'est toi qui nous appris la douceur de l'aimer;
Tu fus d'abord la graine; elle te fit germer
Et tu devins un lis. Sur ta fleur lamentable
Avec quelle douceur elle se va fermer!"
—Certes, certes, amis, bien avant ma venue
D'autres s'étaient nourris de la même ferveur;
Mais il n'est point d'esprit, mais il n'est point de cœur
Qui sache mieux que moi chérir la mer, la nue,
L'orage, le soleil, la joie et la douleur.
Si j'élevais un temple à mon idôlatrie
Afin d'y réunir tout ce qui me fut cher
Son ombre couvrirait et la terre et la mer.
Je n'ai point de maison; je n'ai point de patrie;
L'univers seul a su combler mon cœur amer.

EARTH

I love you with so joyful and tender a love
O you who created me to exalt the Beautiful
That when the time comes to put out the torch
And choose the place where my ashes should rest
I shall only say: the Earth is my tomb.
I have left a piece of my heart in all its regions;
Here I loved the days, there I loved the nights;
And in my memory, as in the secret depths of a well,
Once-encountered faces with beautiful eyes
Cast long reflections to deceive my cares.
Pure landscapes dream in my memory
Like a strange mirage in the midst of golden mists;
Lean towards my heart: you will still hear
In this far world a din of market,
Of the noise of coming and going, of horns' sobs.
This heart sometimes noisy sometimes solitary
Was like a city proud of its garden;
No, friends, come close; give me your hand;
And above all tell me: "The whole gentle earth
Surely you will have it for your burial tomorrow.
She has no lover to compare with you;
It was you who taught us the sweetness of loving her;
First you were seed; she germinated you
And you became a lily. Upon your sad flower
With what gentleness will she close!"
Surely, surely, friends, before my coming
Others were fed with the selfsame ardour;
But there is no spirit, there is no heart
Who knows better than I to cherish the sea, the cloud,
Storm, sun, joy and pain.
Were I to raise a temple to my idolatry
To unite there all that was dear to me
Its shadow would cover earth and sea.
I have no home; I have no mother country;
The universe alone knew to fill my bitter heart.

J'amais également toutes les créatures
Et jamais je n'ai su morceler mon amour;
J'ai vécu solitaire au sommet de ma tour
Les yeux illuminés de visions futures.
Humble ami de la nuit et confident du jour
J'écoutais battre au cœur compatissant des choses
L'écho mystérieux de cet émoi divin
Qui me dévorait l'âme et déchirait le sein
Et quand je m'endormais, sour mes paupières closes
Le monde triste et beau ressuscitait soudain.

All creatures I loved equally
And never did I know to divide my love;
I have lived alone at the top of my tower
My eyes lit up with future visions.
Humble friend of the night and confidant of the day
In the compassionate heart of things I have heard beating
The mysterious echo of the divine emotion
Which consumed my soul and pierced my breast
And when I fell asleep, beneath closed lids,
This sad and beautiful world suddenly came back to life again.

translated by Christopher Bamford

LA MUSE

Tandis que sur les yeux riants du paysage
Une lointaine ondée agite un voile d'or
Quel vol de souvenirs migrateurs prend l'essor
Dans la pâleur de fin d'été de ton visage
Où l'alcyon Espoir tantôt planait encor?
Quelle est donc l'île heureuse où ton soupir les porte
Ces gris oiseaux d'adieux, messagers sans retour
Que suit de loin l'Oubli, silencieux vautour,
Et pourquoi donc m'es-tu comme une douceur morte
Et comme un ciel d'enfance et comme un dernier jour?
De ton souci muet la cendreuse phalène
Pantelle sur le miel assoupi de ton cœur
Toi qui de la rosée as l'étrange pâleur;
Et mon ennui penché sur ta forme lointaine
Respire tout l'automne en une seule fleur.
De tes lèvres d'écho, de tes yeux de mirage
Mon cœur à jamais las pénètre le secret:
La vieillesse a soufflé sur ton front; le regret
Se déploie en silence au ciel de ton visage
Ainsi que l'arc-en-ciel flétri sur la forêt.
Hélas! Je sais, je sens, sœur inquiète et tendre
Ce que voudrait en vain me taire ta bonté:
Dans le vent blanc qui fuit vêtu de ta clarté
L'effeuillaison sur nos chemins répand la cendre
De ce qui fut jeunesse, illusion, beauté.
Ce rayon dont l'encens s'élargit par la chambre
Plonge au fond de tes yeux son regard d'étranger
Et bien que dans ton cœur rien ne veuille changer
Septembre dans tes yeux a reconnu Septembre
Et le désir plane plus bas dans l'air léger
Et devant la pâleur de tes grâces nouvelles
Que l'amour abandonne aux bras de l'amitié
Sur la route de deuil parcourue à moitié
J'ai senti sous mes pas les pierres fraternelles
Frémir comme des cœurs étouffés de pitié.

MUSE

While on the landscape's laughing eyes
A distant shower wimples a golden sail,
What flight of migrant memories takes off
In the summer's end paleness of your face,
Where a moment ago calm hope still soared?
To what happy isle does your sigh bear
Those grey birds of parting, messengers unreturning,
Following Forgetfulness, the silent vulture, from afar.
And why are you so sweet but dead for me
Like a childhood sky, like a last day?
You who have the dew's strange paleness,
The ashen moth of your inquietude
Mutely pants on the drowsing honey of your heart;
And my boredom brooding on your distant figure
Breathes all of Autumn in a single flower.
Forever tired my heart penetrates the secret
Of your echoing lips, of your mirage eyes:
Old age has blown upon your brow; regret
Rises in silence to your face's heaven
Like the rainbow over the forest.
Alas! I know, I feel, O gentle, anxious sister
What your goodness vainly tries to silence in me:
In the white wind fleeing clad in your brightness
The leaves as they fall on our paths spread the ashes
Of what was youth, illusion, beauty.
This beam whose incense widens room by room
Plunges its stranger's gaze into your eyes' depths
And although nothing in your heart could change
In your eyes September has recognized September
And desire soars lower in the gentle air
And before the paleness of your new graces,
Which love abandons to friendship's arms
Halfway down the road of mourning,
Beneath my feet I felt the fraternal stones
Shudder like hearts choking with pity.

Tu chantes comme en rêve: et l'écho des vallées
Se soulève à demi, soupire et se rendort;
Et le vent reconnaît à tes mûrs cheveux d'or
Les lambeaux de soleil arrachés aux allées
Et tout ce qui t'aima veut mourir de ta mort.
Ame de ce qui tombe et de ce qui décline,
Sœur de ce qui sourit sous la douleur courbé,
Un voile de soupirs sur ta face est tombé
Comme choit sur un front ébloui de colline
Le demi-jour soudain du nuage plombé.
Tes yeux lourds comme l'heure où sur les mers lointaines
Les éternels chercheurs se sentent las d'errer,
Tes yeux tristes et purs ont l'air de soupirer:
"Le mirage d'Amour s'éteint dans nos fontaines;
Le pouvoir qui nous reste est celui de pleurer.
O terre de douleur! L'espoir nous abandonne;
Ton ciel s'est obscurci; l'azur se voile en nous;
Et les jours ne sont plus qui nous furent si doux;
Voici notre vieillesse et voici ton automne
Qui se parlent tout bas se touchant des genoux!"
—Cesse de feindre, ô Muse, et permets que je pleure
Et pose dans tes mains ainsi qu'en un cercueil
Mon cœur que trop longtemps a torturé l'orgueil!
Comme le rythme au rythme et comme l'heure à l'heure
Dans mon affreux destin le deuil succède au deuil.
Mon sang est de la pluie en un creux de ténèbres;
Pour les autels du noble et du pur et du beau
J'ai cultivé des fleurs sous un soleil nouveau;
Et me voici semblable à ces jardins funèbres
Qui n'abreuvent leur soif qu'aux sèves du tombeau.
Toi que le temps trahit et que la mort menace
Pardonne à mon silence, accueille l'insensé,
Berce en tes pauvres mains mon cœur d'aigle blessé.
Dis-moi qu'Amour survit, dis-moi que si tout passe
Ton rêve au moins subsiste à mon rêve enlacé.

You sing as in a dream: and the echo of the valleys
Half-rises, sighs and falls asleep once more;
In your ripe golden hair the winds recognize
Shreds of sun torn from leafy lanes
And everything that loved you wants to die your death.
Soul of what falls, of what declines,
Sister of what smiles beneath bent suffering,
A veil of sighs fell over your face
As a leaden cloud's half-light
Drops on the dazzled brow of a hill.
Your eyes, heavy as the hour on distant seas
When eternal seekers tire of wandering,
Your sad, pure eyes seem to sigh:
"Love's illusion dies out in our fountains;
Weeping is the power left us;
O painful earth! Hope deserts us;
Your sky is darkened; veiled for us is your blue;
And days which were so sweet for us are gone;
Look, our old age and your Autumn
Speak gently to each other, knees touching!"
Stop pretending, Muse, O let me weep
And place in your hands as in a coffin
My heart too long wracked with pride!
As rhythm follows rhythm, and hour follows hour
Mourning follows mourning in my fearful destiny.
My blood is rain in a hollowed darkness;
I have grown flowers for altars beneath a new sun
For the noble, the pure and the beautiful;
And here I am, like those cemetery gardens
Quenching their thirst with the sap of the tomb.
You whom time betrays and death threatens,
Forgive my silence, welcome the madman,
Cradle my wounded eagle's heart in your poor hands.
Tell me love survives, tell me if all passes
Your dream at least remains inwoven with mine.

Et laisse-moi vieillir tout baigné de tendresse
Ainsi qu'un noble lis au soleil pâlissant,
Et laisse dans le feu farouche de mon sang
Doucement crépiter l'encens de ta caresse
Et parle à ma douleur comme on chante à l'enfant.
Et toi-même vieillis lentement dans mon songe
Et fais de mon grand cœur un lit pour ton repos
Et soupire tout bas à travers les sanglots:
"Hormis le tendre Amour tout est mort et mensonge"
O sœur de mes secrets, soleil de mes yeux clos!

Let me grow old bathed in gentleness
Like a noble lily in the paling sun;
Leave the incense of your caresses gently crackling
In my blood's fierce fire;
Speak to my suffering as you sing to a child.
Grow old slowly in my mind
And make my great heart a bed for your rest
And sigh softly through sobbing tears:
"Except sweet love, all, all is death and lying"
O sister of my secrets, O sun of my closed eyes.

translated by Christopher Bamford

LE PONT SUR LE RHIN

Douce, chantante averse blonde d'été sur le Rhin,
Lianes d'or somnolent aux balcons fleuris de rouille.
La musique d'un nom étrange et des pleurs dans du vin
—Toutes choses qui furent et ne furent pas—
Et des adieux d'enfants en deuil, dans le matin . . .

Cherches-tu ton mirage mort dans l'eau grise du Rhin?
—Dans l'eau vieille du Rhin, qui trouve son mirage éteint?
Yeux d'enfant-reine, lèvres de fée et printemps de voix,
—Toutes choses qui furent et ne furent pas—
Et le même goût, et plus le même, ah, dans ce vin . . .

Espérer? qui te défend d'espérer? Songe aux années
De te revoir tout autre, tellement autre, étonnées!
Ah, plus de rêves, ni de demains ni d'amours pour toi.
—Toutes choses qui furent et ne furent pas—
Songe, ami, à tes grandes solitudes effeuillées!

Je te donnerai—mais ne le dis pas—la pauvre clef
Du caveau de ton passé, là-bas, loin dans la vallée
Où l'on voit jour et nuit la neige neiger sur le Rhin;
—Et toutes choses qui furent et ne furent pas
Luiront comme des villes dans les lacs d'or de ton vin,
Dans les lacs d'or—songe aux années—de ton cher vin du Rhin.

from *Poèmes*
Poems
1915

BRIDGE ON THE RHINE

Melodious sweet summer-tawny downpour along the Rhine,
golden creepers drowse on balconies petalled with rust.
Music of a strange name and crying gluts the wine—
everything that has been and not been—
and goodbyes from grieving children, through the morning.

Do you look for your perished mirage in grey Rhine-waters,
in the ancient flood of Rhine that finds its own quenched?
Eyes of a child queen, lips of fairies and voices in their springtime—
everything that has been and not been—
and the same savor, the same and more, in this wine . . .

Hope? Who will keep you from hoping? Dream upon them,
yourself changed, wholly altered, the shaken years!
No more reveries, neither tomorrows nor loves for you.
Everything that has been and not been—
muse, friend, on your vast leafless solitudes.

I shall give you—but don't speak of it—the thin key
to the vault of your past, far down there in the valley
where day and night one sees snow flurrying the Rhine;
and everything that has been and not been
gleams like the towns in the tawny lakes of your wine,
in the golden lakes—the years, the years—of your dear Rhine wine.

translated by John Peck

SYMPHONIE DE SEPTEMBRE

1

Soyez la bienvenue, vous qui venez à ma rencontre
Dans l'écho de mes propres pas, du fond du corridor obscur et froid du temps.
Soyez la bienvenue, solitude, ma mère.
Quand la joie marchait dans mon ombre, quand les oiseaux

Du rire se heurtaient aux miroirs de la nuit, quand les fleurs,
Quand les terribles fleurs de la jeune pitié étouffaient mon amour
Et quand la jalousie baissait la tête et se regardait dans le vin
Je pensais à vous, solitude, je pensais à vous, délaissée.

Vous m'avez nourri d'humble pain noir et de lait et de miel sauvage;
Il était doux de manger dans votre main, comme le passereau,
Car je n'ai jamais eu, ô Nourrice, ni père ni mère
Et la folie et la froideur erraient sans but dans la maison.

Quelquefois, vous m'apparaissiez sous les traits d'une femme
Dans la belle clarté menteuse du sommeil. Votre robe
Avait la couleur des semailles; et dans mon cœur perdu,
Muet, hostile et froid comme le caillou du chemin,

Une belle tendresse se réveille aujourd'hui encore
A la vue d'une femme vêtue de ce brun pauvre,
Chagrin et pardonnant: la première hirondelle
Vole, vole sur les labours, dans le soleil clair de l'enfance.

Je savais que vous n'aimiez pas le lieu où vous étiez
Et que, si loin de moi, vous n'étiez plus ma belle solitude.
Le roc vêtu de temps, l'île folle au milieu de la mer
Sont de tendres séjours; et je sais maint tombeau dont la porte est de rouille et de fleurs.

Mais votre maison ne peut être là-bas où le ciel et la mer
Dorment sur les violettes du lointain, comme les amants.
Non, votre vraie maison n'est pas derrière les collines.
Ainsi, vous avez pensé à mon cœur. Car c'est là que vous êtes née.

SEPTEMBER SYMPHONY

1

Welcome, you who come to meet me
In the echo of my footsteps, from the bottom of the cold, dark corridor of time,
Welcome, solitude, my mother.
When joy walked in my shadow, when the birds

Of laughter knocked against the mirrors of the night, when the flowers,
When the terrible flowers of youthful pity choked my love
And when jealousy lowered its head and looked at itself in the wine
I thought of you, solitude, abandoned.

You suckled me with homely black bread and milk and wild honey;
Sweet it was to eat from your hand, like the sparrow,
For I have never had, O Wet-Nurse, mother or father
And madness and coldness wandered endlessly in the house.

Sometimes, you appeared to me with the features of a woman
In the beautiful lying clarity of sleep. Your dress
Was the color of fields at sowing-time; and in my lost heart,
Dumb, hostile, cold as the pebble in the road,

A beautiful tenderness still awakens today
At the sight of a woman dressed in this poor brown,
Sad and forgiving: the first swallow
Flies, flies over the tillage in the bright sun of childhood.

I knew that you did not like the place where you were
And that, far from me, you were my beautiful solitude no longer.
The rock clad with time, the wild isle in the midst of the sea
Are gentle resting places; and I know many a tomb whose door is rust and flowers.

But your home cannot be where sky and sea
Sleep on the violets of the distance, like lovers.
No, your true home is not behind the hills.
Hence, you thought of my heart. For there you were born.

C'est là que vous avez écrit votre nom d'enfant sur les murs
Et, telle une femme qui a vu mourir l'époux terrestre,
Vous revenez avec un goût de sel et de vent sur vous joues blanches
Et cette vieille, vieille odeur de givre de Noël dans vos cheveux.

Comme d'un charbon balancé autour d'un cercueil
De mon cœur où bruit ce rythme mystérieux
Je sens monter l'odeur des midis de l'enfance. Je n'ai pas oublié
Le beau jardin complice où m'appelait Echo, votre second fils, solitude.

Et je reconnaîtrais la place où je dormais jadis
A vos pieds. N'est-ce pas que la moire du vent y court encore
Sur l'herbe triste et belle des ruines, et du bourdon velu
Le son de miel ne s'attarderait plus dans la belle chaleur

Et si du saule tremblant et fier vous écartiez
La chevelure d'orphelin: le visage de l'eau
M'apparaîtrait si clair, si pur! Aussi pur, aussi clair
Que la Lointaine revue dans le beau songe du matin!

Et la serre incrustée d'arc-en-ciel du vieux temps
Sans doute abrite encore le cactus nain et le faible figuier
Venus jadis de quel pays de bonheur? Et de l'héliotrope mourant
L'odeur délire encore dans les fièvres d'après-midi!

O pays de l'enfance! ô seigneurie ombreuse des ancêtres!
Beau tilleul somnolent cher aux graves abeilles
Es-tu heureux comme autrefois? et toi, carillon des fleurs d'or,
Charmes-tu l'ombre des collines pour les fiançailles

De la Dormeuse blanche dans le livre moisi
Si doux à feuilleter quand le rayon du soir
Descend sur la poussière du grenier: et autour de nous le silence
Des rouets arrêtés de l'araignée fileuse.—Cœur!

Triste cœur! le berger vêtu de bure
Souffle dans le long cor d'écorce. Dans le verger
Le doux pivert cloue le cercueil de son amour
Et la grenouille prie dans les roseaux muets. O triste cœur!

from POEMS

There you wrote your childhood name upon the walls
And, like a woman who has seen her earthly bridegroom die,
You come back with a taste of salt and wind upon white cheeks
And that old, old scent of Christmas hoar-frost in your hair.

As from a censer swung around a coffin
From my heart where this mysterious rhythm beats
I feel the scent of childhood middays rise. I have not forgotten
The beautiful complicitous garden whither Echo, your second son, solitude, called me.

And I would recognize the place where I once slept
At your feet. Doesn't the rippling wind still run there
Over the ruins' sad, beautiful grass, and doesn't the honey sound
Of the shaggy bumblebee still linger in the beautiful heat?

And if of the proud, trembling willow
One were to spread the orphan hair: the water's face
Would appear to me so clear, so pure! As pure, as clear
As the Distant One glimpsed anew in a beautiful morning daydream!

And the greenhouse incrusted with a rainbow from the old days
Doubtless still shelters dwarf cactus and feeble fig
Come once from who knows what country of happiness? And the odour of the dying heliotrope
Still raves in the fevers of the afternoon!

O country of childhood! O shadowy ancestral manor!
Beautiful somnolent lime tree, dear to the heavy bees,
Are you happy as of old? And you, carillon of golden flowers,
Do you charm the hills' shadow for the betrothal

Of the White Sleeper in the musty book
So sweet to leaf through when the evening ray
Descends upon the attic dust; and around us the silence
Of the spinning spider's halted wheels—Heart!

Sad heart! The shepherd dressed in fustian
Blows into the long horn of bark. In the orchard
The gentle green woodpecker nails the coffin of his love
And the frog prays in the dumb reeds. O sad heart!

Tendre églantier malade au pied de la colline, te reverrai-je
Quelque jour? et sais-tu que ta fleur où riait la rosée
Etait le cœur si lourd de larmes de mon enfance? ô ami!
D'autres épines que les tiennes m'ont blessé!

Et toi, sage fontaine au regard si calme et si beau,
Où se réfugiait, par les chaleurs sonnantes
Tout ce qui restait d'ombre et de silence sur la terre!
Une eau moins pure coule aujourd'hui sur mon visage.

Mais le soir, de mon lit d'enfant qui sent les fleurs, je vois
La lune follement parée des fins d'été. Elle regarde
A travers la vigne amère, et dans la nuit de senteurs
La meute de la Mélancolie aboie en rêve!

Puis, l'Automne venait avec ses bruits d'essieux, de haches et de puits.
   Comme la fuite
Du lièvre au ventre blanc sur la première neige, le jour rapide
D'étonnement muet frappait nos tristes cœurs.—Tout cela, tout cela
Quand l'amour qui n'est plus n'était pas né encore.

   2
Solitude, ma mère, redites-moi vie! voici
Le mur sans crucifix et la table et le livre
Fermé! si l'impossible attendu si longtemps
Frappait à la fenêtre, comme le rouge-gorge au cœur gelé,

Qui donc se lèverait ici pour lui ouvrir? Appel
Du chasseur attardé dans les marais livides,
Le dernier cri de la jeunesse faiblit et meurt: la chute d'une seule
   feuille
Remplit d'effroi le cœur muet de la forêt.

Qu'es-tu donc, triste cœur? une chambre assoupie
Où, les coudes sur le livre fermé, le fils prodigue
Ecoute sonner la vieille mouche bleue de l'enfance?
Ou un miroir qui se souvient? ou un tombeau que le voleur a réveillé?

Lointains heureux portés par le soupir du soir, nuages d'or,
Beaux navires chargés de manne par les anges! est-ce vrai
Que tous, tous vous avez cessé de m'aimer, que jamais,
Jamais je ne vous verrai plus à travers le cristal

from POEMS

Tender wild rose briar sick at the foot of the hill, will I see you again
Some day? And do you know that your flower where dew smiled
Was my childhood's heart so heavy with tears? O friend!
Other thorns than yours have wounded me!

And you, wise fountain, with look so calm and fine,
Where, amidst the sounding heat, all that remained
Of the earth's shade and silence sought refuge!
A water less pure flows upon my face today.

But in the evening, from my childhood bed smelling of flowers, I see
The crazily trimmed moon of the end of summer. She watches
Through the bitter vine, and in the perfumed night
Melancholy's pack barks in a dream!

Then autumn came, with its sounds of axles, axes and wells. Like the
   flight
Of the white-bellied hare over the first snow, the unexpected day
Struck our sad hearts with dumb astonishment.—All this, all this
When love which is no longer was not yet born.

2
Solitude, my mother, tell me my life again! Here is
The wall without crucifix and the table and the book,
Closed! If the impossible so long awaited
Knocked at the window, like the redbreast with the frozen heart,

Then who would rise to open for her? The call
Of the hunter delayed in the ghastly fens,
The last cry of youth grows faint and dies: the fall of a single leaf
Fills the forest's dumb heart with dread.

What are you then, sad heart? A drowsy room
Where, elbows upon the closed book, the prodigal son
Hears the old blue fly of childhood buzz?
Or a mirror which remembers? Or a tomb the robber has awoken?

Happy distances born by evening's sigh, golden clouds,
Fine ships by angels loaded down with manna! Is it true
That all, all of you, have ceased to love me, that never,
Never, will I see you again through the crystal

De l'enfance? que vos couleurs, vos voix et mon amour,
Que tout cela fut moins que l'éclair de la guêpe
Dans le vent, que le son de la larme tombée sur le cercueil,
Un pur mensonge, un battement de mon cœur entendu en rêve?

Seul devant les glaciers muets de la vieillesse! seul
Avec l'écho d'un nom! et la peur du jour et la peur de la nuit
Comme deux sœurs réconciliées dans la malheur
Debout sur le pont du sommeil se font signe, se font signe!

Et comme au fond du lac obscur la pauvre pierre
Des mains d'un bel enfant cruel jadis tombée:
Ainsi repose au plus triste du cœur,
Dans le limon dormant du souvenir, le lourd amour.

Of childhood? That your colors, your voices and my love,
That all of this was less than the flash of the wasp
In the wind, than the sound of the tear fallen on the coffin,
A pure lie, my heart's beat heard in a dream?

Alone before the silent glaciers of age! Alone
With the echo of a name! And fear of the day and fear of the night
Like two sisters reconciled in misfortune
Standing on the bridge of sleep, signing to each other, signing to each other!

And like the poor stone at the bottom of the dark lake
Fallen once from the hands of a beautiful cruel child:
So rests in uttermost sadness of heart,
In sleeping silt of memory, heavy love.

translated by Christopher Bamford

SYMPHONIE DE NOVEMBRE

Ce sera tout à fait comme dans cette vie. La même chambre.
—Oui, mon enfant, la même. Au petit jour, l'oiseau des temps dans la
   feuillée
Pâle comme une morte: alors les servantes se lèvent
Et l'on entend le bruit glacé et creux des seaux

A la fontaine. O terrible, terrible jeunesse! Cœur vide!
Ce sera tout à fait comme dans cette vie. Il y aura
Les voix pauvres, les voix d'hiver des vieux faubourgs,
Le vitrier avec sa chanson alternée,

Le grand-mère cassée qui sous le bonnet sale
Crie des noms de poissons, l'homme au tablier bleu
Qui crache dans sa main usée par le brancard
Et hurle on ne sait quoi, comme l'Ange du jugement.

Ce sera tout à fait comme dans cette vie. La même table,
La Bible, Gœthe, l'encre et son odeur de temps,
Le papier, femme blanche qui lit dans la pensée,
La plume, le portrait. Mon enfant, mon enfant!

Ce sera tout à fait comme dans cette vie!—Le même jardin,
Profond, profond, touffu, obscur. Et vers midi
Des gens se réjouiront d'être réunis là
Qui ne se sont jamais connus et qui ne savent

Les uns des autres que ceci: qu'il faudra s'habiller
Comme pour une fête et aller dans la nuit
Des disparus, tout seul, sans amour et sans lampe.
Ce sera tout à fait comme dans cette vie. La même allée:

Et (dans l'après-midi d'automne), au détour de l'allée,
Là où le beau chemin descend peureusement, comme la femme
Qui va cueillir les fleurs de la convalescence—écoute, mon enfant,—
Nous nous recncontrerons, comme jadis ici;

Et tu as oublié, toi, la couleur d'alors de ta robe;
Mais moi, je n'ai connu que peu d'instants heureux.
Tu seras vêtu de violet pâle, beau chagrin!
Et les fleurs de ton chapeau seront tristes et petites

NOVEMBER SYMPHONY

It will be exactly as in this life. The same room.
—Yes, my child, the same. At daybreak, time's bird in the foliage
Pale as a corpse: then the servants rise
And you hear the frozen, hollow noise of buckets

At the fountain. O terrible, terrible youth! Empty heart!
It will be exactly as in this life. There will be
Poor voices, wintry voices of old neighborhoods,
The glazier with his singsong call,

The bent grandmother who beneath a dirty bonnet
Calls out the names of fishes, and the man in the blue apron
Who spits into his barrow-worn hand
And roars who knows what, like the Angel of Judgement.

It will be exactly as in this life. The same table,
The Bible, Goethe, the ink and its odour of time,
Paper, the white woman who reads thought,
The pen, the portrait. My child, my child!

It will be exactly as in this life! The same garden,
Deep, deep, thick, dark. And towards midday
People will delight to be united there
Who never knew each other and who knew

Only this: that they must dress
As for a celebration and go, without love, without light,
Alone into the night of those who have disappeared.
It will be exactly as in this life. The same avenue:

And (in the autumn afternoon) at the bend of the avenue,
Where the beautiful path descends timidly like a woman
Going to gather flowers of convalescence—listen, my child,—
We shall meet each other, as we once did here.

And you, you have forgotten the color your dress was then;
But I have only known a few moments of happiness.
You will be clothed in pale violet, beautiful sorrow!
And the flowers in your hat will be sad and small

Et je ne saurai pas leur nom: car je n'ai connu dans la vie
Que le nom d'une seule fleur petite et triste, le myosotis,
Vieux dormeur des ravins au pays Cache-Cache, fleur
Orpheline. Oui, oui, cœur profond! comme dans cette vie.

Et le sentier obscur sera là, tout humide
D'un écho de cascades. Et je te parlerai
De la cité sur l'eau et du Rabbi de Bacharach
Et des Nuits de Florence. Il y aura aussi

Le mur croulant et bas où somnolait l'odeur
Des vieilles, vieilles pluies, et une herbe lépreuse,
Froide et grasse secouera là ses fleurs creuses
Dans le ruisseau muet.

And I won't know their name: because I have known the name
Of only a single, small, sad flower in my life, the forget-me-not,
The orphan flower, the old sleeper in ravines of the land
Of Hide-and-Seek. Yes, yes, deep heart! as in this life.

And the dark path will be there, damp
With an echo of waterfalls. And I shall speak to you
Of the city on the water and of the Rabbi of Bacharach
And of Florentine Nights. The low, crumbling wall

Will also be there, where the odour drowsed
Of old, old rains, and a leprous herb,
Cold and oily, will shake its hollow flowers there
In the silent stream.

translated by Christopher Bamford

SYMPHONIE INACHEVÉE

1

Tu m'as très peu connu là-bas, sous le soleil du châtiment
Qui marie les ombres des hommes, jamais leurs âmes,
Sur la terre où le cœur des hommes endormis
Voyage seul dans les ténèbres et les terreurs, et ne sait pas vers quel pays.

C'était il y a très longtemps—écoute, amer amour de l'autre monde—
C'était très loin, très loin—écoute bien, ma sœur d'ici—
Dans le Septentrion natal où des grands nymphéas des lacs
Monte une odeur des premiers temps, une vapeur de pommeraies de légende englouties.

Loin de nos archipels de ruines, de lianes, de harpes,
Loin de nos montagnes heureuses.
—Il y avait la lampe et un bruit de haches dans la brume,
Je me souviens,

Et j'étais seul dans la maison que tu n'as pas connue,
La maison de l'enfance, la muette, la sombre,
Au fond des parcs touffus où l'oiseau transi du matin
Chantait bas pour l'amour des morts très anciens, dans l'obscure rosée.

C'est là, dans ces chambres profondes aux fenêtres ensommeillées
Que l'ancêtre de notre race avait vécu
Et c'est là que mon père après ses longs voyages
Etait venu mourir.

J'étais seul et, je me souviens,
C'était la saison où le vent de nos pays
Souffle une odeur de loup, d'herbe de marécage et de lin pourrissant
Et chante de vieux airs de voleuse d'enfants dans les ruines de la nuit.

2

Le dernier soir était venu et avec lui la fièvre
L'insomnie et la peur. Et je ne pouvais pas me rappeler ton mon.
La garde était sans doute allée au presbytère
Car la lanterne n'était plus sur l'escabeau.

UNFINISHED SYMPHONY

1

You scarcely knew me down there, under the sun of chastisement
That unites men's shadows, never their souls,
On the earth where the hearts of benumbed men
Travel alone through the darks and terrors, without knowing their
   destined land.

It was long ago—listen, bitter love of the other world—
It was far, far away—hearken to me, sister of this present world—
In the North of our birth, where scent from the primal past ascends
From the large water-lilies of the lakes, a waft of fabulous engulfed
   orchards.

Far from our archipelagoes of ruins, lianas and harps,
Far from our fortunate mountains.
—There was a lamp and a sound of hatchets in the haze
I remember,

And I was alone in the house you never knew,
The house of childhood, the dumb, dark house,
Deep in the leafy parks wherein the chill bird of morning
Softly sang for the love of the long-since dead, in the sombre dew.

It was there, in those vast drowsily windowed rooms
That the ancestor of our family line once lived,
And it was there that my father, his long journeys done,
Went back to die.

I was alone and, I remember,
It was the season when the wind of our native lands
Bears with it a breath of wolves, sedges and rotting flax
And sings old child-snatcher's lays in the ruins of the night.

2

The last evening had come and with it fever,
Sleeplessness and fear. And I could not recall my name.
The guard had no doubt gone to the priest's house
For the lantern no longer stood on the footstool.

Tous nos anciens serviteurs étaient morts; leurs enfants
Avaient émigré; j'étais un étranger
Dans la maison penchée
De mon enfance.

L'odeur de ce silence était celle du blé
Trouvé dans un tombeau; et tu connais sans doute
Cette mousse des lieux muets, sœur des ensevelis
Couleur de lune mûre et basse sur Memphis.

J'avais longtemps couru le monde avec mon frère
Sans repos; j'avais veillé avec l'angoisse
Dans toutes les auberges de ce monde. Maintenant, j'étais là,
Tête blanche déjà comme le frère nuage. Et il n'y avait plus personne.

L'echo d'un pas, le trot de la vieille souris m'eût été doux,
Car ce qui me mangeait le cœur ne faisait pas de bruit.
J'étais comme la lampe de la mansarde au petit jour,
Comme le portrait dans l'album de la prostituée.

Parents et amis étaient morts. Toi, ma sœur, tu étais plus loin
Que le halo dont se couronne en janvier clair
La mère de la neige. Et tu me connaissais à peine.
Quand tu parlais, je tressaillais d'entendre la voix de mon cœur,

Mais tu ne m'avais rencontré qu'une fois, une seule,
Dans la lumière étrange des lampes d'apparat
Entre les fleurs de nuit, et il y avait là des courtisans dorés
Et je ne dis adieu qu'à ton reflet dans le miroir.

La solitude m'attendait avec l'écho
Dans l'obscure galerie. Un enfant était là
Avec une lanterne et une clef
De cimetière. L'hiver des rues

Me souffla une odeur miséarable au visage.
Je me croyais suivi par ma jeunesse en pleurs;
Mais sous la lampe et mon Hypérion sur les genoux,
La vieillesse était assise: et elle ne leva pas la tête.

All our old servants were dead; their children
Had emigrated; I was a stranger
In the slanting house
Of my childhood.

The smell of that silence was just like that of corn
Found in a tomb; and no doubt you know
That moss of the mute places, sister of the buried
And colored like a full moon low over Memphis.

For a long while I had travelled the world with my restless
Brother: and had lain awake with anguish
In all the inns of this world. Now, there I was,
Whiteheaded as our brother cloud. And there was no-one left.

A footstep's echo, the old mouse's scuttering would have been sweet to me,
For what was eating my heart out made no sound.
I was like the garret's lamp at daybreak,
Like the portrait in the album of the prostitute.

Family and friends were dead. You, my sister, you were further
Away than the halo with which in bright January
The snow's mother crowns herself. And you scarcely knew me.
When you spoke, you trembled to hear the voice of my heart,

But you had met me only one single time,
In the strange light of the gaudy lamps
Among the night flowers, and there were gilded courtiers there
And I bade farewell only to your reflection in the mirror.

Solitude was awaiting me with the echo
In the sombre gallery. A child was there
With a lantern and the key
To a graveyard. The winter of the streets

Breathed a wretched odor into my face.
I believed myself followed by my weeping youth;
But beneath the lamp with my Hyperion on her knees
Old age was seated; and she did not raise her head.

3

Ecoute bien, ma sœur d'ici. C'était la vieille chambre bleue
De la maison de mon enfance.
J'étais né là.
C'est là aussi.

Que m'apparut jadis, dans le recueillement de la vigile,
Mon premier arbre de Noël, cet arbre mort devenu ange
Qui sort de la profonde et amère forêt,
Qui sort tout allumé des vieilles profondeurs

De la forêt glacée et chemine tout seul,
Roi des marais neigeux, avec ses feux follets
Repentis et sanctifiés, dans la belle campagne silencieuse et blanche:
Et voici les fenêtres d'or de la maison de l'enfant sage.

Vieux, très vieux jours! si beaux, si purs! c'était la même chambre
Mais froide pour toujours, mais muette, mais grise.
Elle semblait avoir à jamais oublié
Le feu et le grillon des anciennes veillées.

Il n'y avait plus de parents, plus d'amis, plus de serviteurs!
Il n'y avait que la vieillesse, le silence et la lampe.
La vieillesse berçait mon cœur comme une folle un enfant mort,
Le silence ne m'aimait plus. La lampe s'éteignit.

Mais sous le poids de la Montagne des ténèbres
Je sentis que l'Amour comme un soleil intérieur
Se levait sur les vieux pays de la mémoire et que je m'envolais
Bien loin, bien loin, comme jadis, dans mes voyages de dormeur.

4

—"C'est le troisième jour."—Et je tressaillis, car la voix
Me venait de mon cœur. Elle était la voix de ma vie.
—"C'est le troissième jour."—Et je ne dormais plus, et je savais que l'heure
De la prière du matin était venue. Mais j'étais las

3
Hearken to me, my earthly sister. It was the old blue room
Of the house of my childhood.
There was I born.
It was also there

That long ago I beheld, at the festal Eve gathering,
My first Christmas tree, that dead tree turned into an angel
Emerged from the deep, harsh forest,
Emerged all lit up from the ancient depths

Of the frozen forest and proceeding all by itself,
King of the snowy swamps, with its repentant and sanctified
Will-o'-the-wisps, in the beautiful silent and white countryside:
And behold the refulgent windows of the house of the well-behaved
   child.

Such olden far-off days! so beautiful, so pure! it was the same
Room, but forever cold, but dumb and gray.
It seemed to have lost all recollection
Of the hearth and the cricket of long-ago evenings.

There were no relatives, friends or servants there any more!
There were only old age, silence and the lamp.
Old age lulled my heart as a maddened mother would a dead child,
Silence no longer loved me. The lamp went out.

But under the weight of the Mountain of darkness
I felt that Love was rising like an inner sun
Over the olden lands of memory and that I was flying
Far, far away, as I used to once in my sleeper's travels.

4
—"This is the third day."—And I suddenly shivered, for the voice
Came from my heart. It was the voice of my life.
—"This is the third day."—And I slept no more but knew that the
   time
Had come for the morning prayer. But I was tired

Et je pensais aux choses que je devais revoir; car c'était là
L'archipel séduisant et l'île du Milieu,
La vaporeuse, la pure qui disparut jadis
Avec le tombeau de corail de ma jeunesse

Et s'assoupit aux pieds du cyclope de lave. Et devant moi,
Sur la colline, il y avait le château d'eau avec
Les lianes d'Eden et les velours de vétusté
Sur les degrés usés par les pieds de la lune; et là, à droite,

Dans la belle éclaircie au mitan du bocage,
Les ruines couleur de soleil! et là, point de passage
Secret! car j'ai erré dans cette thébaïde
Avec l'amour muet, sous le nuage de minuit. Je sais

Où sont les mûres les plus sombres; l'herbe haute
Où la statue frappée a caché son visage
Est mon amie et les lézards savent depuis longtemps
Que je suis messager de paix, qu'il ne tonne jamais

Dans le nuage de mon ombre. Ici tout m'aime
Car tout m'a vu souffrir.—"C'est le troisième jour.
Lève-toi, je suis ta dormeuse de Memphis,
Ta mort au pays de la mort, ta vie au pays de la vie.

La très-sage, la méritée" . . .

And I thought of the things I should see once more; for there
Was the alluring archipelago and the isle of the Center,
The misty, the pure, that vanished long ago
With the coral tomb of my youth

And fell half-asleep at the feet of the lava cyclops. And before me
On the hill, there was the ornamental fountain with
The lianas of Eden and the velvets of decay
On the steps worn by the moon's feet, and there, on the right,

In the glorious glade in the midst of the grove
The ruins colored like the sun! and there, not a single secret
Passage! for in this desert solitude I have strayed
With speechless love, beneath the midnight snow. I know

Where to find the darkest mulberries; the tall grass
In which the stricken statue has hidden its face
Is my friend and the lizards have long known
That I am a messenger of peace, that it never thunders

In the cloud of my shadow. Everything here loves me
For everything has seen me suffer.—"This is the third day.
Arise, I am thy sleeper of Memphis,
Thy death in the land of death, thy life in the land of life.

The most wise, the well-deserved" . . .

translated by David Gascoyne

INSOMNIE

Je dis: ma Mère. Et c'est à vous que je pense, ô Maison!
Maison des beaux étés obscurs de mon enfance, à vous
Qui n'avez jamais grondé ma mélancolie, à vous
Qui saviez si bien me cacher aux regards cruels, ô
Complice, douce complice! Que n'ai-je rencontré
Jadis, en ma jeune saison murmurante, une fille
A l'âme étrange, ombragée et fraîche comme la vôtre,
Aux yeux transparents, amoureux de lointains de cristal,
Beaux, consolants à voir dans le demi-jour de l'été!
Ah! j'ai respiré bien des âmes, mais nulle n'avait
Cette bonne odeur de nappe froide et de pain doré
Et de vieille fenêtre ouverte aux abeilles de juin!
Ni cette sainte voix de midi sonnant dans les fleurs!
Ah ces visages follement baisés! ils n'étaient pas
Comme le vôtre, ô femme de jadis sur la colline!
Leurs yeux n'étaient pas la belle rosée ardente et sombre
Qui rêve en vos jardins et me regarde jusqu'au cœur
Là-bas, au paradis perdu de ma pleureuse allée
Où d'une voix voilée l'oiseau de l'enfance m'appelle,
Où l'obscurcissement du matin d'été sent la neige.
Mère, pourquoi m'avez-vous mis dans l'âme ce terrible,
Cet insatiable amour de l'homme, oh! dites, pourquoi
Ne m'avez-vous pas enveloppé de poussière tendre
Comme ces très vieux livres bruissants qui sentent le vent
Et le soleil des souvenirs et pourquoi n'ai-je pas
Vécu solitaire et sans désir sous vos plafonds bas,
Les yeux vers la fenêtre irisée où le taon, l'ami
Des jours d'enfance, sonne dans l'azur de la vieillesse?
Beaux jours! limpides jours! quand la colline était en fleur,
Quand dans l'océan d'or de la chaleur les grandes orgues
Des ruches en travail chantaient pour les dieux du sommeil,
Quand le nuage au beau visage ténébreux versait
La fraîche pitié de son cœur sur les blés haletants
Et la pierre altérée et ma sœur la rose des ruines!
Où êtes-vous, beaux jours? où êtes-vous, belle pleureuse,

INSOMNIA

I say: my Mother. And it is of you that I'm thinking, O House!
House of the lovely murky Summers of my childhood, of you
Who never chided my melancholy, of you
Who knew so well how to protect me from unkind eyes, O
Accomplice, sweet accomplice! Did I not encounter
Once upon a time, during the murmurous season of my youth, a lass
Whose soul was as strange, as shadowed and fresh as your own,
With transparent eyes, enamoured of crystalline distances,
Beauteous and comforting to see in the half-light of Summer!
Ah! I have inhaled many a soul, but not one possessed
That wholesome odour of cold linen, gold-crusted bread
And ancient window open to the bees of June!
Nor this blest voice of noon vibrant amidst the flowers!
Ah, those crazily kissed countenances! they were not
Like yours, O woman of yore upon the hill!
Their eyes were not in the beauteous ardent and dark dew
That daydreams in your gardens and sees into my heart's depths
Down there, in the paradise lost of my weeping walk
Whence with veiled voice the bird of childhood hails me,
Where the Summer morning's dimness smells of snow.
Mother, why did you implant in my soul this terrible,
This insatiable love of man, oh! tell me why
You did not enshroud me in delicate dust
Like those very old muttering books that smell of the wind
And the sun of memories, and why have I not
Lived lone and devoid of desire beneath your low ceilings,
Eyes turned to the iridescent windows where the gadfly, the friend
Of childhood days, can be heard in the calm blue sky of old age?
Fine days! limpid days! when the hill was in bloom,
When in the heat's golden ocean the toiling hives'
Great organs sang for the gods of sleep,
When the cloud with the fine overcast face poured down
The cool pity of its heart on the panting corn
And the thirsting stone and my sister the ruins' rose!
Where are you, fine days? Where are you, beautiful weeper,

Tranquille allée? aujourd'hui vos troncs creux me feraient peur
Car le jeune Amour qui savait de si belles histoires
S'est caché là, et Souvenir a attendu trente ans,
Et personne n'a appelé: Amour s'est endormi.
—O Maison, Maison! pourquoi m'avez-vous laissé partir,
Pourquoi n'avez-vous pas voulu me garder, pourquoi, Mère,
Avez-vous permis, jadis, au vent menteur de l'automne,
Au feu de la longue veillée, à ces magiciens,
O vous qui connaissiez mon cœur, de me tenter ainsi
Avec leurs contes fous, pleins d'une odeur de vieilles îles
Et de voiliers perdus dans le grand bleu silencieux
Du temps, et de rives du Sud où des vierges attendent?
Si sage vous saviez pourtant que les vrais voyageurs,
Ceux qui cherchent la Baie du Sincère et l'Ile des Harpes
Et le Château Dormant ne reviennent jamais, jamais!
—Mon cœur est tout seul dans la froide auberge et l'insomnie
Debout dans le vieux rayon contemple mon vieux visage
Et nul, nul avant moi n'avait compris de quelles morts
Sourdes, irrémédiables, sont faits ces jours de la vie!

Peaceful walk? Today I'd be scared by your hollow trunks
For the young Cupid that knew such precious tales
Hid himself there, and Memory waited thirty years,
And nobody has called: Cupid has fallen asleep.
—O House, House! why did you let me leave,
Why did you not want to keep me, why, Mother,
Did you once allow that liar the Autumn wind
And the long evening's hearthfire, those magicians,
O you who knew my heart, to tempt me as they did
With their mad tales full of a smell of old islands
And of sailships lost in the vast and soundless blue
Of time, and of Southern strands where virgins wait?
Being so wise, you must have known that the true travellers,
Those in search of the Bay of the Sincere and the Isle of Harps
And the Sleeping Castle, never, never return!
—My heart is all alone in the cold inn and insomnia
Standing in the old beam contemplates my old face
And nobody, nobody before me ever understood how many unhearing,
Irremediable dead go to make up the days of this life!

translated by David Gascoyne

NIHUMIM

Quarante ans.
Je connais peu ma vie. Je ne l'ai jamais vue
S'éclairer dans les yeux d'un enfant né de moi.
Pourtant j'ai pénétré le secret de mon corps. O mon corps!
Toute la joie, toute l'angoisse des bêtes de la solitude
Est en toi, esprit de la terre, ô frère du rocher et de l'ortie.
Comme les blès et les nuages dans le vent,
Comme la pluie et les abeilles dans la lumière,
Quarante ans, quarante ans, mon corps, tu as nourri
De ton être secret le feu divin du Mouvement:
Tu ne passeras pas avant le mouvement de l'univers.
Que le son de ton nom inutile et obscur
Se perde avec le cri du dormeur dans la nuit;
Rien ne saurait te séparer de ta mère la terre,
De ton ami le vent, de ton épouse la lumière.
Mon corps! tant que deux cœurs séparés, égarés,
Se chercheront dans les vapeurs des cascades du matin,
Tant qu'un douzième appel de midi vibrera pour réjouir
La bête qui a soif et l'homme qui a faim; tant que le loriot,
L'hôte des sources cachées, renversera sa pauvre tête
Pour chanter les louanges du Père des forêts; tant qu'une touffe
De myrtil noir élèvera ses baies pour leur faire respirer
L'air de ce monde, quand l'eau de soleil est tombée,
O errante poussière! ô mon corps, tu vivras pour aimer et souffrir.

Quarante ans.
Pour apprendre à aimer la noblesse de l'Action. O action!
Quarante ans, quarante ans la vanité des solitaires
M'a tourmenté. Je demandais sa mort dans mes prières.
Elle a quité mon cœur. O triomphe!—ô tristesse . . .
Elle a emmené ma jeunesse,
Ma cruelle jeunesse, la seule femme aimée.
Mais qu'importe! déjà, mes mains, déjà la pierre vous attire.
Mains aux veines gonflées, la fureur de bâtir
Vous saisit, vous possède déjá!

NIHUMIM

Forty years.
I know little about life. I have never seen it
Light up in the eyes of an infant born of me.
Yet I have penetrated the secret of my body. O my body!
All the joy, all the anguish of the beasts of solitude
Are in you, spirit of earth, brother of rocks and nettles.
Like wheat and clouds in the wind
Like rain and bees in the light,
Forty years, forty years, my body, you have fed
In your secret being the divine fire of Movement:
You will not pass away before the movement of the universe.
Let the sound of your useless, obscure name
Be lost with the cry of the sleeper in the night:
Nothing could separate you from your mother the earth,
Your lover, the wind, your bride the light.
My body! As long as two separate, bewildered hearts
Seek themselves in the spray of the cascades of morning,
As long as the twelfth call of noon vibrates to rejoice
Hungry beasts and thirsty men, as long as the oriole,
The guest of hidden springs, turns her poor head
To sing the praises of the Father of Forests, as long as a spray
Of black myrtle lights its berries to breathe
The air of this world, when the water of the sun has fallen,
O wandering dust! O my body! You live to love and suffer.

Forty years
To learn to love nobility of Action. O action!
Forty years, forty years, the vanity of the solitary
Has tormented me. I asked its death in my prayers.
It left my heart. O triumph!—O sorrow!
It lead away my youth
My cruel youth, the only woman I loved.
But what difference does it make?
Already, my hands, already the stone attracts you.
Hands with swollen veins, the fury of building
Seizes you, possesses you already!

Quand le midi des forts sonnera sur la mer
Nous irons saluer les constructeurs de môles.
Debout dans le soleil, en face de la mer
Ils mangent lentement leur pauvre et noble pain
Et leur sage regard va plus loin que le mien.
Honneur à toi, honneur à toi qui es né dans les pleurs
Comme l'Amen, et qui mourras dans l'abandon au pied du temple de l'amour
Ou du palais d'orgueil, ouvrages de tes mains!
Bientôt, demain, mon frère, je pourrai te parler
Face à face, sans rougir, comme parlent les hommes, car
Moi aussi, moi aussi je ferai la maison
Large, puissante et calme comme une femme assise
Dans un cercle d'enfants sous le pommier en fleur.
J'ouvrirai les fenêtres de la joyeuse église
Toutes grandes aux anges du soleil et du vent.
J'y bénirai le pain de l'Affirmation,
De ce oui éternel qui est une saveur
De feu, de blé et d'eau à la bouche des purs;
Et quand la laideur dira: non!
Et quand la femme et la mort crieront: non!
Frère, nous saluerons l'espace ivre de vie
Et le mot appris des Héros,
Le Oui universel montera à nos lèvres.

Quarante ans.
Pour apprendre à parler sans mépris de la femme. O Amour!
Quarante ans je vous ai cherché parmi les femmes
Mais ce n'est point parmi les femmes que je vois ai trouvé.
O Femme! La pitié des pierres me saisit!
Mère! Mère! tu ne sais plus, tu ne sais pas encore qui tu es.
Toi, blanche renversée dans les fleurs! si longtemps
Tu as dormi au plus obscur, au plus muet du beau jardin abandonné!
Et te voici debout dans ce temps de laideur rieuse,
Au milieu de ces fils qui ont perdu leur dieu et n'ont pas trouvé la nature.
O Mère! Mère! et cette belle épaule tombante de porteuse d'eau fraîche,
Et cet air rentré de servante réveillée avant l'heure.

When the noon of the strong sounds on the sea
We will go to salute the builders of piers.
Standing in the sun, beside the sea
They slowly munch their poor and noble bread
And their wise looks go far beyond wine.
All honor to you, all honor to you, born in tears
Like an Amen, dying abandoned at the foot of the temple of love
Or the palace of pride, the work of your own hands!
Soon, tomorrow, my brother, I will be able to speak to you
Face to face, without blushing, like men talk, for
I too, I too will build a house,
Large, powerful, calm, like a woman seated
In the midst of her children, under the flowering apple tree.
I will open the windows of a joyous church
Glorious with angels of sun and wind.
I will bless the bread of affirmation,
The eternal yes, which tastes
Of fire, of wheat, and of water in the mouth of the pure;
And when ugliness cries out: "No!"
And when woman and death cry out: "No!"
Brother, we will hail space drunk with life
And the word we have learned from the Heroes,
The universal Yes will rise to our lips.

Forty years
To learn to speak without contempt of woman, O love!
Forty years I have sought you among women
But it was not among women I found you.
O woman! The pity of stones seizes me!
Mother! Mother! You no longer, you still, do not know who you are.
You, turned while among the flowers! For you slept
So long in the dark, still, abandoned garden.
And here you are, standing in this time of laughing ugliness,
In the midst of your sons who have lost their god
And have yet to find nature.
O Mother! Mother! And the beautiful falling shoulder
Of this girl carrying fresh water,
And the air brought in by this servant who woke up early.

Quelle sagesse et quelle connaissance, ô femme, dans la paume de tes mains!
Que je ne les puisse contempler sans qu'une colombe s'en échappe!
Et ta sainte blancheur apprivoise le cygne!
Lorsque l'époux mourra, tu suivras, tu mourras:
Non pas de la tristesse de la chair, mais de la joie
Profonde de l'esprit!
Pour te parler et être compris, ô Mère, il faut redevenir enfant.
Car que peux-tu comprendre à ce monde du Mouvement,
O belle, grave et pure colonne du foyer!
Mère! les sources voilées du Mouvement sont en un lieu obscur et défendu
Dont le nom est Vallée de la Séparation. Là,
Les mondes et les cœurs soupirent l'un vers l'autre en vain.
Et tout ce que l'on touche est la distance et la durée
De la Séparation.
Qui cherche mal ne trouve rien nulle part.
Qui cherche bien ne trouve rien ici;
Qui trouve ici se heurte ailleurs aux portes closes.
Car il est un pays où l'être unique est seul
En face de soi-même.
Là il s'aime
Et s'épouse
Et se crée.
Là, il se glorifie.
Et le lieu est nommé par ceux qui te ressemblent, Lieu
De la Conjonction,
De la Féminité Eternelle et de la
Vie.

Quarante ans.
Pour apprendre à chercher la Cité. O Jérusalem!
Tu n'es pas un désert de pierres liées de chaux, de sable et d'eau
Comme les villes des hommes,
Mais, au sein du Réel, dans le silence de la tête,
Le planement muet de l'or intérieur.
Ma vie! ma vie! je sais que les six jours du monde
Sont là pour révéler ce que l'on doit connaître
Du septième, ennemi de tout étonnement.

What wisdom and what knowledge, O woman, in the palm of your hands!
Which I can only see when a dove escapes from them.
And your holy whiteness which tames the swan!
When your husband dies, you will follow, you will die.
Not for sadness of flesh, but for the
Profound joy of the spirit!
To speak to you and be understood, O Mother, one must become a child.
For what can you understand of this World of Movement,
O Beautiful, grave and pure column of the hearth!
Mother! The veiled springs of Movement are in a dark protected place
Whose name is the Valley of Separation. There
All the worlds, all the hearts, sigh vainly against each other
And nothing can be felt but distance and hardness
Of Separation.
Who seeks evil will find nothing, nowhere.
Who seeks good will find nothing, here.
Who finds here will beat elsewhere on closed doors.
For this is a land where unique being is all alone
Face to face with itself.
There it loves itself.
And weds itself.
And creates itself.
There it glorifies itself
And the place is named by those who are like you, Place
Of Conjunction,
Of the Eternal Feminine and of
Life.

Forty years
To learn to find the City. O Jerusalem!
You are not a desert of stones cemented with lime, sand and water,
Like the towns of men.
But in the bosom of the Real, in the silence of the head
The still soaring of the interior gold.
My life! My life! I know that the six days of the world
Are to reveal what ought to be known
Of the seventh, enemy of all wonder.

Car dans la déchirure du nuage gardien
Arrêté sur Pathmos (le lieu universel
Contemplé par les yeux renversés de l'Amour)
J'ai vu dans un grand vent d'influx, l'ellipse du sabbat
Prendre feu et dorer ma naissance sans cri.
O mon frère! ô mon corps! ne crains pas. Je connais le chemin.
Entrons dans les profondes vapeurs de la Montagne
Qui prend son essor et s'élève
Avec le confiant qui la gravit,
Jusqu'à la nuée longue, jusqu'à la couleur-mère,
La blancheur bleue, l'annonciation de l'or.
L'aube paraît derrière nous!
Au-dessus de mon front se lève
Et fuit vers les contrées qui sont derrière nous
Le Soleil.
Le couchant est loin devant nous!
Maintenant, le profond, terrible et beau murmure
Des sages abeilles du pays
T'enseigne la langue oubliée (aux lourdes et tremblantes syllabes de miel sombre)
Des livres noyés de Yasher.

For in the gap of the guardian cloud
Fixed on Patmos (the universal place
Seen by the inward eye of Love)
I have seen the great whirlwind, the ellipse of the Sabbath
Take fire and gild my unweeping birth.
O my brother! O my body! Fear no more! I know the road.
Let us enter the deep mists of the Mountain,
Which takes life and rises
With the one who climbs it confidently
As far as the long cloud, as far as the mother color,
The blue white annunciation of gold.
Dawn rises behind us!
Above my forehead lift and
Fly the lands behind us
The Sun.
The sunset is far ahead of us!
Now the deep, terrible, beautiful murmur
Of the wise bees of this land
Teach you the forgotten tongue, (in heavy
Trembling syllables of sombre honey)
Of the drowned books of Yasher.

translated by Kenneth Rexroth

DIMANCHE, 14 MARS 1915

C'était vers le déclin du premier des sept jours; et le plus pauvre
Avait son moment de la nuit qu'il appelait le veilleur d'or;
Car la prière de cet âge était visible, et elle était
Plus profondément douce et belle que toi, enfant,
Avec son grand visage d'or levé dans les vapeurs de l'Est.
Tous ces sages autour de nous qui n'ont jamais vu le Soleil!
O mon enfant! c'est à pleurer! ô mon enfant!
Car, une nuit, l'homme ne reconnut pas sa voix, en priant;
Et il lui sembla qu'une étrangère était là,
Qu'une femme qu'il ne connaissait pas était venue
Apporter un vêtement pour un mort.
Alors l'homme cria: Iegueodah, Iegueodah!
Vers Iehovah d'avant Iasher; mais le beau chemin bleu
Ne s'ouvrit pas, le cri ne souleva pas la montagne,
Rien ne parut à l'Est: l'Age d'Or n'était plus.

C'était donc vers le soir du premier des sept jours;

Et nous vivons dans le cinquième jour, ma sœur,
Celui dont traite l'Apocalypse, le jour de la Conjonction.
Le sixième jour approche!

Uncollected
1915

SUNDAY, 14 MARCH 1915

It was towards the close of the first of the seven days; and the poorest
Had his moment of the night which he called the golden watcher;
For prayer in that age was visible, and it was
More profoundly sweet and beautiful than you, child,
With its great golden face risen in the vapors of the East.
All these wise men around us who have never seen the sun!
O my child! One can but weep! O my child!
For one night, praying, man did not recognize his voice;
And it seemed to him that a stranger was there,
That a woman whom he did not know was come
To bring a garment for a corpse.
Then man cried: Jegodah, Jegodah!
To Jehovah before Jasher; but the beautiful blue road
Did not open, the cry did not raise the mountain,
Nothing appeared in the East; the Golden Age was no more.

It was therefore towards the evening of the first of the seven days;

—And we live in the fifth day, my sister,
That of which the Apocalypse treats, the day of CONJUNCTION.
The sixth day approaches!

translated by Christopher Bamford

H

Le jardin descend vers la mer. Jardin pauvre, jardin sans fleurs, jardin
Aveugle. De son banc, une vieille vêtue
De deuil lustré, jauni avec le souvenir et le portrait,
Regarde s'effacer les navires du temps. L'ortie, dans le grand vide

De deux heures, velue et noire de soif, veille.
Comme du fond du cœur du plus perdu des jours, l'oiseau
De la contrée sourde pépie dans le buisson de cendre.
C'est la terrible paix des hommes sans amour. Et moi,

Moi je suis là aussi, car ceci est mon ombre; et dans la triste et basse
Chaleur elle a laissé retomber sa tête vide sur
Le sein de la lumière; mais
Moi, corps et esprit, je suis comme l'ammare

Prête à rompre. Qu'est-ce donc qui vibre ainsi en moi,
Mais qu'est-ce donc qui vibre ainsi et geint je ne sais où
En moi, comme la corde autour du cabestan
Des voiliers en partance? Mère

Trop sage, éternité, ah laissez-moi vivre mon jour!
Et ne m'appelez plus Lémuel; car là-bas
Dans une nuit de soleil, les paresseuses
Hèlent, les îles de jeunesse chantantes et voilées! Le doux

from *Adramandoni*
Adramandoni
1918

H

The garden descends towards the sea. Poor garden, garden without
   flowers, blind
Garden. On her bench, an old woman clad
In glossy mourning, yellowed like the memento and the portrait,
Watches the vessels of time departing. The nettle, in the great
   emptiness

Of two-o'clock, hairy and black with thirst, keeps watch.
As though from the depths of the heart of the most lost of days, the
   bird
Of the dull district chirps in the bush of slag.
The peace is the same as the terrible stillness of men devoid of love.
   And I,

I too am there, for this is my shadow; and in the sad and vile
Heat she has let her empty head fall back upon
The bosom of the light; but I,
Body and soul, myself am like the hawser

About to break. What is it then that's throbbing so in me,
But what is it that's throbbing so, groaning I know not where
In me, like the rope about the capstan
Of sailing-vessels ready to depart? Too wise

Mother, eternity, ah! let me live my day!
And no longer call me Lemuel; because down there
In a sunlit night, the lazy girls
Hail the islands of their singing and veiled youth! The sweet

Lourd murmure de deuil des guêpes de midi
Vole bas sur le vin et il y a de la folie
Dans le regard de la rosée sur les collines mes chères
Ombreuses. Dans l'obscurité religieuse les ronces

Ont saisi le sommeil par ses cheveux de fille. Jaune dans l'ombre
L'eau respire mal sous le ciel lourd et bas des myosotis.
Cet autre souffre aussi, blessé comme le roi
Du monde, au côté; et de sa blessure d'arbre

S'écoule le plus pur désaltérant du cœur.
Et il y a l'oiseau de cristal qui dit mlî d'une gorge douce
Dans le vieux jasmin somnambule de l'enfance.
J'entrerai là en soulevant doucement l'arc-en-ciel

Et j'irai droit à l'arbre l'épouse éternelle
Attend dans les vapeurs de la patrie. Et dans les feux du temps
   apparaîtront
Les archhipels soudains, les galères sonnantes—
Paix, paix. Tout cela n'est plus. Tout cela n'est plus ici, mon fils
   Lémuel.

Les voix que tu entends ne viennent plus des choses.
Celle qui a longtemps vécu en toi obscure
T'appelle du jardin sur la montagne! Du royaume
De l'autre soleil! Et ici, c'est la sage quarantième

Année, Lémuel.
Le temps pauvre et long.
Une eau chaude et grise.
Un jardin brûlé.

from ADRAMANDONI

And heavy mourning murmur of the wasps of noon
Floats low above the wine and there is a kind of craziness
About the look of the dew upon the hills of my beloved
Shady ones. In the religious gloom the brambles

Have seized hold of the girl's hair of sleep. Yellow in the shade
The water difficultly breathes beneath the heavy, low sky of
    forget-me-nots.
That other suffers too, bearing like the king
Of the world, a wounded side: and from his scarred-tree wound

There flows the purest stream ever to quench the thirsty heart.
And there is the crystal bird that sweetly trills
In the old somnambulistic jasmine-tree of childhood.
I will enter in there gently raising the rainbow

And I will go straight to the tree where the eternal bride
Awaits amidst the mists of the native land. And in the fires of time
    there will appear
The sudden archipelagoes, the sonorous hulks—
Peace, peace. All that is no more. All that is no longer here, my son
    Lemuel.

The voices you hear no longer come from things.
That which has long lived so darkly in you
Calls you from the garden on the mountain! From the kingdom
Of the other sun! And here, it is the disillusioned fortieth

Year, Lemuel.
The poor long time.
A water warm and grey.
A garden burnt.

                                        translated by David Gascoyne

LA CHARRETTE

L'esprit purifié par les nombres du temple,
La pensée ressaisie à peine par la chair, déjà,
Déjà ce vieux bruit sourd, hivernal de la vie
Du cœur froid de la terre monte, monte vers le mien.

C'est le premier tombereau du matin, le premier tombereau
Du matin. Il tourne le coin de la rue et dans ma conscience
La toux du vieux boueur, fils de l'aube déguenillée,
M'ouvre comme une clef la porte de mon jour.

Et c'est vous et c'est moi. Vous et moi de nouveau, ma vie. Et je me
  lève et j'interroge
Les mains d'hôpital de la poussière du matin
Sur les choses que je ne voulais pas revoir.
La sirène au loin crie, crie et crie sur le fleuve.

Mettez-vous à genoux, vie orpheline
Et faites semblant de prier pendant que je compte et recompte
Ces fleurages qui n'ont ni frères ni sœurs dans les jardins,
Tristes, sales, comme on en voit dans les faubourgs

Aux tentures des murs en démolition, sous la pluie. Plus tard,
Dans le terrible après-midi, vous lèverez les yeux du livre vide et je
  verrai
Les chalands amarrés, les barils, le charbon dormir
Et dans le linge dur des mariniers le vent courir.

Que faire? Fuir? Mais où? Et à quoi bon? La joie
Elle-même n'est plus qu'un beau temps de pays d'exil;
Mon ombre n'est ni aimée ni haïe du soleil; c'est comme un mot
Qui en tombant sur le papier perd son sens; et voilà,

O vie si longue! pourquoi mon âme est transpercée
Quand cet enfant trouvé, quand frère petit-jour
Par l'entrebâillement des rideaux me regarde, quand au cœur de la ville
Résonne un triste, triste, triste pas d'épouse chassée.

Te voici donc, ami d'enfance! Premier hennissement si pur,
Si clair! Ah, pauvre et sainte voix du premier cheval sous la pluie!
J'entends aussi le pas merveilleux de mon frère;
Less outils sur l'épaule et le pain sous le bras,

from ADRAMANDONI

THE CART

The spirit purified by temple numbers,
The thinking scarcely recaptured by the flesh, and already,
Already the old dull wintry sound of the life
Of the earth's old heart rises, rises towards mine.

It's the first tipcart of the morning, the first tipcart
Of the morning. It turns the corner of the street and in my
    consciousness
The cough of the old street cleaner, son of the tattered dawn,
Opens the gate of my day for me like a key.

And it's you and I. You and I again, my life. And I rise and I question
The hospice hands of the morning dust
About things I did not wish to see again.
The siren in the distance cries, cries, cries upon the river.

Set yourself upon your knees, orphan life,
And pretend to pray while I count and count again
These flowers which have neither brothers nor sisters
In the sad, dirty gardens one sees in suburbs

Hanging on walls under demolition, in the rain. Later
In the awful afternoon, you will lift your eyes from the empty book
And I will see moored barges, casks, slumbering coals
And the wind running in the bargemen's rough linen.

What to do? Flee? But whither? For what? Joy
Itself is no more than fine weather in a country of exile;
My shadow is neither hated nor loved by the sun; it is like a word
Which falling on paper loses its meaning; and that—

O life so long!—that is why my soul is pierced through
When this child is found, when brother daybreak
Watches me through the blind's chink, when in the heart of town
Resounds the sad, sad, sad step of a rejected wife.

Here you are then, childhood friend! The first whinny, so pure,
So clear! Ah, poor holy voice of the first horse in the rain!
I hear too my brother's wonderful step;
Tools upon his shoulders, bread beneath his arm,

C'est lui! c'est l'homme! Il s'est levé! Et l'éternel devoir
L'ayant pris par la main calleuse, il va au-devant de son jour. Moi,
Mes jours sont comme les poèmes oubliés dans les armoires
Qui sentent le tombeau; et le cœur se déchire

Quand sur la table étroite où les muets voyages
Des veilles de jadis ont, comme ceux d'Ulysse,
Heurté toutes les îles des vieux archipels d'encre,
Entre la Bible et Faust apparaît le pain du matin.

Je ne le romprai pas pour l'épouse terrestre,
Et pourtant, ma vie, tu sais comme je l'ai cherchée
Cette mère du cœur! Cette ombre que j'imaginais
Petite et faible, avec de belles saintes mains

Doucement descendues sur le pain endormi
A l'instant éternellement enfant du Bénédicité
De l'aube; les épaules étaient épaules d'orpheline
Un peu tombantes, étroites, d'enfant qui a souffert, et les genoux

De la pieuse tiraient l'étoffe de la robe
Et dans le mouvement des joues et de la gorge
Pendant qu'elle mangeait, une claire innocence,
Une gratitude, une pureté qui faisait mal—ô

Vie! O amour sans visage! Toute cette argile
A été remuée, hersée, déchiquetée
Jusqu'aux tissus où la douleur elle-même trouve un sommeil dans la plaie
Et je ne peux plus, non, je nen peux plus, je ne peux plus!

from ADRAMANDONI

It is he! Man! He is risen! And eternal duty
Having taken him by the callused hand, he walks before his day. I,
My days are like poems forgotten in wardrobes
Savoring of the tomb; and my heart is torn

When upon the narrow table where dumb voyages
Of former vigils, like those of Ulysses,
Have struck all the islands of old ink archipelagoes,
Between the Bible and Faust, the bread of morning appears.

I shall not break it for an earthly bride,
And yet, my life, you know how I have searched for her,
This heart's mother! This shadow whom I imagined
Small and feeble, with beautiful holy hands

Softly descended upon the sleeping bread
In an instant and eternally made the Child
Of Dawn's Grace; her shoulders were the orphan shoulders,
A little sloping, narrow, of a child who has suffered, and the knees

Of this pious child pulled the stuff of her dress
And in the movement of the cheeks and of the throat
While she ate, a bright innocence,
A gratitude, a purity which hurt—O

Life! O faceless love! All this clay
Has been shaken, harrowed, slashed
To the very tissues where suffering itself finds sleep in the wound
And I can bear no more, no, I can bear no more, I can bear no more!

translated by Christopher Bamford

LA GAMME

Dans ce jardinet d'église
Où le vieux soleil des pauvres
Réussit parfois, vers juin
A faire éclore à demi
Deux ou trois fleurs de faubourg
Qui font pousser de grands ah!
Le jeudi et le dimanche
Aux blancs et sages forçats
Du voisin orphelinat,
Tantôt (et je connais là
Une vierge sans visage
Qui dans sa niche effritée
Berce un vieux Jésus moussu),
Dans le silence moisi
J'ai senti mon cœur saisi
Par un son de clavecin
Sourd, jauni, quasi défunt,
Trouble comme le parfum
De pluie et de parchemin
Des in-folio latins
Et proche et pourtant éteint
Comme un moi-même indistinct
Au fond d'un miroir sans tain,
Etrange, secret tintouin
Intérieur et lointain,
Une de ces pauvres gammes
De bémols couverts, chagrins,
Qui réveillent dans les âmes
La sainte odeur des matins
De la claire adolescence
Et du profond des jardins
Et de l'eau dans le silence
Et du soleil sur le pain
Et du miel dans les faïences
Lourdes de mil huit cent vingt.

from ADRAMANDONI

THE SCALE

In this small church garden
Where the poor people's old sun
Sometimes succeeds, around June,
In half-opening
Two or three city flowers
Which put forth great sighs
On Thursdays and Sundays
To the pale, wise convicts
Of the neighboring orphanage,
Just a moment ago (and I know
A faceless virgin there
Who in her crumbling niche
Cradles an old, mossy Jesus)
In the mildewed silence
I felt my heart touched
By the sound of a harpsichord
Muffled, sickly, almost defunct
Turbid as the odor
Of rain and Latin
Parchment folios
Clear and yet faint
As an indistinct image of myself
In the depths of an unsilvered mirror,
A strange, secret moan
Interior and distant,
One of those poor, melancholy scales
Filled with flats
Rousing in souls
The holy scent
Of bright adolescent mornings
And garden deeps
And silent water
And sun on bread
And honey in heavy
Earthenware pots of eighteen twenty.

Et soudain, comme l'enfant
Ferme ses mains étrangleuses
Sur le moineau grelottant
Trop tôt envolé du nid,
Oui,—qui le croirait?—soudain
Comme quand j'avais vingt ans
(Enfant épris d'une enfant)
J'ai dans mes deux vieilles mains
Serré ce cœur irritant
Qui s'était pris, tout-à-coup,
A battre, mais follement,
Mais affreusement, mon Dieu!—pour vous—

Then suddenly, as a child
Closes his strangler's hands
About a trembling sparrow
Flown too soon from its nest,
Yes—who would believe it?—suddenly
As when I was twenty
(A child infatuated with a child)
I clasped in my two old hands
This exasperating heart
Which had begun, suddenly,
To beat, but madly,
But horribly, my God!—for you—

translated by Christopher Bamford

LES TERRAINS VAGUES

Comment m'es-tu venu, ô toi si humble, si chagrin? Je ne sais plus.
Sans doute comme la pensée de la mort, avec la vie même.
Mais de ma Lithuanie cendreuse aux gorges d'enfer du Rummel,
De Bow-Street au Marais et de l'enfance à la vieillesse

J'aime (comme j'aime les hommes, d'un vieil amour
Usé par la pitié, la colère et la solitude) ces terrains oubliés
Où pousse, ici trop lentement et là trop vite,
Comme les enfants blancs dans les rues sans soleil, une herbe

De ville, froide et sale, sans sommeil, comme l'idée fixe,
Venu avec le vent du cimetière, peut-être
Dans un de ces ballots d'étoffe noire, lisse et lustrée, oreillers
Des vieilles dormeuses des berges, dans les terribles crépuscules.

De toute ma jeunesse consumée dans le sud
Et dans le nord, j'ai surtout retenu ceci: mon âme
Est malade, passante, comme l'herbe altérée des murs,
Et on l'a oubliée, et on la laisse ici.

J'en sais un qu'obscurcit un cèdre du Liban! Vestige
De quelque beau jardin de l'amour virginal. Et je sais, moi que le saint arbre
Fut planté là, jadis, en son doux temps, afin
De porter témoignage; et le serment tomba dans la muette éternité,

Et l'homme et la femme sans nom sont morts, et leur amour
Est mort, et qui donc se souvient? Qui? Toi peut-être,
Toi, triste, triste bruit de la pluie sur la pluie,
Ou vous, mon âme. Mais bientôt vous oublierez cela et le reste.

Et l'autre, où le grand vent, la pluie et le brouillard ont leur église.
Quand venait l'hiver des faubourgs; quand le chaland
Voyageait dans la brume de France, qu'il m'était doux,
Saint-Julien-le-Pauvre, de faire le tour

De ton jardin! Je vivais dans la dissipation
La plus amère; mais le cœur de la terre m'attirait
Déjà; et je savais qu'il bat non sous la roseraie
Choyée, mais là où croît ma sœur ortie, obscure, délaissée.

VACANT LOTS

How did you come to me, o you so humble, so sad? I no longer know.
Probably like the thought of death, in the midst of life.
But, from my ashen Lithuania to the hellgate of Rummel,
From Bow Street to the Marais, and from childhood to old age,

I love (like I love mankind, with an old love,
Worn with pity, anger and solitude) these forgotten places
Where sprouts, here too slowly, here too quickly,
Like white children in sunless streets, a weed

Of the city, cold and soiled, sleepless as an obsession,
Come with the wind from the cemetery perhaps
In one of those bolts of black cloth, smooth and shiny, pillows
For the old Sleepers of the Rocks, in the terrible twilights.

From my whole youth, wasted in the south
And the north, I have kept only this—my soul
Is sick, passing, like a thirsty wallflower
Which has been picked and forgotten and left here.

I know one more shadowy than a cedar of Lebanon! The vestige
Of a beautiful garden of virginal love. And I myself know that holy tree
Was planted there, long ago, one balmy day, at last
To bear witness; and the word fell into mute eternity;

And the nameless man and woman are dead, and their love
Is dead, and who remembers them now? Who? You, perhaps,
You, sad, sad, sound of rain on rain—
Or you, my soul. But soon you will forget this and everything else.

And the other, where the great wind and rain and mist are their church.
When winter comes to the slums, when the barge
Travels through the fogs of France, how good it was,
St. Julian the Poor, to walk

In your garden. I have lived in the bitterest
Dissipation. But already the heart of the earth
Was drawing me, and I knew that it beat, not under
The carefully tended rose bushes, but where my sister the nettle
flourished, obscure and broken.

Ainsi donc, si tu veux me plaire—après! loin d'ici! toi
Murmurant, ruisselant de fleurs ressuscitées, toi jardin
Où toute solitude aura un visage et un nom
Et sera une épouse,

Réserve au pied du mur moussu dont les lézardes
Montrent la ville Ariel dans les chastes vapeurs,
Pour mon amour amer un coin ami du froid et de la moisissure
Et du silence; et quand la vierge au sein de Thummîm et d'Urîm

Me prendra par la main et me conduira là, que les tristes terrestres
Se ressouviennent, me reconnaissent, me saluent: le chardon et la haute
Ortie et l'ennemie d'enfance belladone.
Eux, ils savent, ils savent.

from ADRAMANDONI

And so, if you wish to please me, afterward, far away! You
Murmuring, streaming with reborn flowers, you, garden
Where all loneliness has a face and a name
And will be a mate,

Do not walk on the mossy wall where crevices
Reveal the city, Ariel, in the pure clouds,
For my bitter love, a friendly corner of cold, mildew
And silence, and when the Virgin with Thummim and Urim on her
   breasts

Takes me by the hand, and leads me there, how the sad earthly people
Will remember, will recognize me, will welcome me, the thistle and
   the high
Nettle, and belladonna the enemy of childhood.
Those, they know, they know.

translated by Kenneth Rexroth

LE PONT

Les feuilles mortes tombent dans l'air dormant.
Vois, mon cœur, ce que l'automne a fait à ta chère île:
Comme elle est pâle!
Quelle orpheline au cœur tranquille!
Les cloches sonnent, sonnent à Saint-Louis-en-l'Isle
Pour le fuchsia mort de la patronne du chaland.

Tête basse, deux vieux chevaux très humbles, somnolents, prennent
    leur dernier bain.
Un gros chien noir aboie et menace de loin.
Sur le pont, il n'y a que moi et mon enfant:
Robe fanée, faibles épaules, visage blanc,
Un bouquet dans les mains.
O mon enfant! Ce temps qui vient!
Pour eux! Pour nous! O mon enfant!
Ce temps qui vient!

THE BRIDGE

The dead leaves are dropping in the dormant air.
My heart, see what autumn has done to your dear isle:
How wan it looks!
An orphan with how hushed a heart!
The bells are tolling, tolling at Saint-Louis-en-l'Isle
For the dead fuschia of the barge-skipper's wife.

With bowed heads, two most humble old hacks are sleepily taking their last dip.
A big black dog is barking threats from afar.
On the bridge stand only myself and my child:
Faded dress, frail shoulders, white face,
A bunch of flowers in her hands.
O my child! The time to come!
For them! For us! O child!
The time to come!

translated by David Gascoyne

LA BERLINE ARRÊTÉE DANS LA NUIT

En attendants les clefs
—Il les cherche sans doute
Parmi les vêtements
De Thècle morte il y a trente ans-
Ecoutez, Madame, écoutez le vieux, le sourd murmure
Nocturne de l'allée . . .
Si petite et si faible, deux fois enveloppée dans mon manteau
Je te porterai à travers les ronces et l'ortie des ruines jusqu'à la haute et
    noire porte
Du château.
C'est ainsi que l'aïeul, jadis, revint
De Vercelli avec la morte.
Quelle maison muette et méfiante et noire
Pour mon enfant!
Vous le savez jéjà, Madame, c'est une triste histoire.
Ils dorment dispersés dans les pays lointains.
Depuis cent ans
Leur place les attend
Au cœur de la colline.
Avec moi leur race s'étient.
O Dame de ces ruines!
Nous allons voir la belle chambre de l'enfance: là,
La profondeur surnaturelle du silence
Est la voix des portraits obscurs.

from *La Confession de Lemuel*
The Confession of Lemuel
1922

THE HOODED CARRIAGE HALTED IN THE NIGHT

While waiting for the keys
—No doubt he is searching for them
Among the clothes
Of Theclia dead now for thirty years past—
Hark, Madame, hark to the ancient muffled murmur
Of the avenue by night . . .
I'm going to carry you, so small, so weak,
Doubly bundled in my coat, through the brambles and nettles to the
   high black door
Of the castle.
Thus was it once, long ago, that grandfather came back
From Vercelli with the dead woman.
What a mute and mistrustful black mansion
For my child!
As you already know, Madame, it is a sorrowful tale.
For a hundred years they have been sleeping
Scattered in distant lands.
Their place awaits them
At the heart of the hill.
With me their lineage ends.
O Lady of these ruins!
We are going to see childhood's beautiful room: there,
The supernatural depth of the silence
Is the voice of the dim portraits.

Ramassé sur ma couche, la nuit,
J'entendais comme au creux d'une armure,
Dans le bruit du dégel derrière le mur,
Battre leur cœur.
Pour mon enfant peureux quelle patrie sauvage!
La lanterne s'étient, la lune s'est voilée,
L'effraie appelle ses filles dans le bocage.
En attendant les clefs
Dormez un peu, Madame.—Dors, mon pauvre enfant, dors
Tout pâle, la tête sur mon épaule.
Tu verras comme l'anxieuse forêt
Est belle dans les insomnies de juin, parée
De fleurs, ô mon enfant, comme la fille préférée
De la reine folle.
Enveloppez-vous dans mon manteau de voyage:
La grande neige d'automne fond sur votre visage
Et vous avez sommeil.
(Dans le rayon de la lanterne elle tourne, tourne avec le vent
Comme dans mes songes d'enfant
La vieille,—vous savez,—la vieille.)
Non, Madame, je n'entends rien.
Il est fort âgé,
Sa tête est dérangée.
Je gage qu'il est allé boire.
Pour mon enfant craintive une maison si noire!
Tout au fond, tout au fond du pays lithuanien.
Non, Madame, je n'entends rien.
Maison noire, noire.
Serrures rouillées,
Sarment mort,
Portes verrouillées,
Volets clos,
Feuilles sur feuilles depuis cent ans dans les allées.
Tous les serviteurs sont morts.
Moi, j'ai perdu la mémoire.
Pour l'enfant confiant une maison si noire!

from THE CONFESSION OF LEMUEL

Huddled on my bed, at night,
I heard as if I were inside armour
In the sound of the thaw outside the wall
Their beating hearts.
What a barbarous birthplace for my timid child!
The lantern's gone out, the moon's become veiled,
The barn-owl in the boscage calls to her female young.
While waiting for the keys
Sleep for a while, Madame.—Sleep, my poor child, sleep,
Quite pale, with your head upon my shoulder.
You will see how beautiful the restless forest
Can be during the sleepless nights of June, adorned
With flowers, O my child, like the mad queen's
Dearest daughter.
Wrap yourself in my travelling-coat:
Autumn's abundant snow is melting on your face
And you are sleepy.
(In the lantern's beam she is twirling, twirling in the wind
As in my childhood's dreams,
The old woman,—you know who,—the old one.)
No, Madame, I hear nothing.
He is very aged,
He is a crackpot.
I bet he's gone drinking.
Such a black mansion for my timorous child!
Right in the depths, in the depths of the Lithuanian land.
No, Madame, I hear nothing.
Black mansion, black,
Rusty locks,
Dead vine-branch,
Bolted doors,
Shutters closed,
In the avenues leaves piled on leaves for a hundred years.
All the servants are dead.
As for me, my memory's gone.
Such a black mansion for the trustful child!

Je ne me souviens plus que de l'orangerie
Du trisaïeul et du théâtre:
Les petits du hibou y mangeaient dans ma main.
La lune regardait à travers le jasmin.
C'était jadis.
J'entends un pas au fond de l'allée,
Ombre. Voici Witold avec les clefs.

All I can remember are the orangery,
The great-great-grandfather and the theatre
Where the owl's fledgelings fed from my hand.
The moon looked down through the jasmine.
That was once upon a time.
I hear a footfall at the far end of the avenue,
Phantom shade. Here is Witold with the keys.

translated by David Gascoyne

TALITA CUMI

Je te connais déjà depuis quelque dix ans, sur la terre suspendue dans le silence,
Enfant du destin; et c'est ta pauvre image qui toujours m'apparaît la première
Dans la lucidité de mes réveils du déclin de la nuit,
Quand, suivant en esprit le Cosmos dans son vol muet,
Tout à coup je sens l'univers s'engouffrer en moi comme aspiré par le vide de tous ces jours.
Je suis alors comme une chose en feu sur le fleuve dans la nuit d'été
Et la clef de soleil est sous ma main, qui ouvre les Réels miroitants d'un brouillard de vie.
Et certe, un seul mot, et, dans ce pays vrai où j'ai maint serviteur éblouissant
M'apparaîtraient des formes tout autres que la tienne, caillou ramassé ici pour le souvenir.
Mais ne t'ai-je pas aimé d'humilité dans cette toute petite succession de jours?
Je partirai bientôt. O moitié de cœur, moitié de cœur jetée
Dans la boue et le froid et la pluie et la nuit de la ville!
O mon apprivoisé menacé par l'hiver!
Ecoute-moi. Ouvre tout grand ce quelque chose en toi que tu ne connais pas,
Et tâche, quoi qu'il advienne, tâche de retenir en ta minuscule mémoire
Ce conseil d'un qui a mûri avec l'ortie dans le long et torride été de l'amertume:
Travaille!
Ne tente pas le roi terrible de la vie, le dieu dans le mouvement
Impitoyable des routes du monde, l'idole dans le chariot aux roues broyeuses.
Travaille, enfant! Car tu es condamnée, frêle, à vivre longtemps
Et je ne voudrais pas m'enfuir de ces assourdissantes galères
Avec la pauvre image de ce que tu seras un jour:
Une petite enfant tout à coup devenue petit vieille,
Avec d'amers cheveux blancs sous la châle, je ne sais dans quel aigre et noir faubourg
Et seule sur la berge avec le fleuve, un ballot de terreur
Sur le dos, sœur des humides pierres et des grands, grands arbres nus.

from THE CONFESSION OF LEMUEL

TALITA CUMI

I've already known you some ten years on this earth that's suspended in silence,
My child of fate, and it's always your poor image that's the first to haunt me
In those lucid moments of my awakenings, when night begins to decline,
And when, as my spirit follows the Cosmos in its speechless flight,
I suddenly feel that the whole universe is vanishing within me, as if engulfed by the void of all these days.
I'm then like something that's afire on the river in the summer night,
And the sun's key is beneath my hand, ready to unlock realities that shimmer with a mist of life.
A mere word, of course, and also, in that real land where I've many a dazzling retainer,
Forms would appear which are anything but yours that I've gathered here like a pebble to be kept as a memento.
But haven't I loved you very humbly in this tiny succession of days?
Soon I'll go away. Oh, half of a heart, half of a heart cast out
In the mud and the cold and the rain and the night of the city!
Oh, my tamed one that winter threatens,
Listen to me, open up wide whatever within yourself you still fail to know,
And try, come what may, but try to retain in your midget memory
This advice from one who has ripened with the nettles in the long and torrid summer of bitterness:
And toil!
Don't tempt the terrible King of life, the God in the pitiless
Movement of the world's roads, the idol in the cart with the wheels that crush.
Toil, my child, for you are condemned, however frail, to live long,
And I would never want to flee from these deafening galleys
With the poor image of what you must one day become:
A small child suddenly turned into a tiny old woman
With bitter white locks beneath her shawl, in some acrid and dark suburb
And alone on the embankment by the river with a heavy load of fear
On her back, a sister of the damp cobbles and the tall leafless trees.

Epargne-moi cela. Car je serai affreusement absent, réveillé pour toujours
Dans l'un des deux Royaumes, je ne sais lequel, le ténébreux,
Je le crains, car il y a en moi quelque chose qui brûle d'un feu bas et jugé.
Et je te le dis bien, passereau de misère, tu seras seule dans cette vie atroce
Comme vers le petit jour avare et blême de la Seine
De tous abandonné, le signal rouge et vert.
Je ne sais plus qui a tué mon cœur; mais n'a-t-il pas en mourant, le mauvais,
Légué toute sa royauté funèbre de compassion à mes os? Enfant!
C'est une douleur que l'on n'exprime pas. L'homme atteint de ce nocturne mal
Souffre, omniscient et muet, avec les pierres des fondements dans la moississure des ténèbres.
Je sais bien que c'est Lui, Lui dont le nom secret est: le Séparé-de-Lui-même
Qui souffre en nous: et que lorsque sera enfin passée
La nuit sans fleurs et sans miroirs et sans harpes de cette vie, un chant
Vengeur, un chant de toutes les aurores de l'enfance
Se brisera en nous ainsi que le cristal immense du matin
Au cri des ailés, dans la vallée de rosée.
Eh oui, je le sais. Mais cette pauvre image de ta vie dans le solitaire avenir, cela
Je ne peux pas le supporter. C'est une véritable frayeur d'insecte en moi,
Un cri d'insecte au fond de moi
Sous les cendres du cœur.

from THE CONFESSION OF LEMUEL

Spare me this, for I shall be terribly absent, awakened for all times to come,
In one of the two kingdoms, I know not which one, but the darker one,
I fear, for I bear within me something that burns with a low fire like a condemnation.
And I warn you, pitiful sparrow, you'll be alone in that dreadful life,
Like the red and green lights abandoned
By all in the miserly pale dawn of the Seine.
Who killed my heart? I no longer know, but as it died, did it not, like a curse,
Bequeath all its funereal royalty of compassion to my bones? Oh, child,
It's a pain that one cannot express, and a man afflicted with this nocturnal ill
Suffers, omniscient and speechless, with the foundation-stones in the rotting darkness.
I know, of course, that it's He, He whose secret name is The-one-who-is-divided-from-Himself,
Who suffers in us: and when at long last
This life's night without flowers or mirrors or harps has gone by, a vengeful
Song, a song of all the dawns of childhood,
Will be shattered within us like the huge crystal of morning
When the winged ones cry in the valley of dew.
And yes, I know it. But that poor image of your life in the lonely future,
That's what I find unbearable. It's really the panic of an insect within me,
And an insect's cry deep within me,
Beneath the heart's ashes.

translated by Edouard Roditi

CANTIQUE DE LA CONNAISSANCE

L'enseignement de l'heure ensoleillée des nuits du Divin.

A ceux, qui, ayant demandé, ont reçu et savent déjà.

A ceux que la prière a conduits à la méditation sur l'origine du langage.

Les autres, les voleurs de douleur et de joie, de science et d'amour, n'entendront rien à ces choses.

Pour les entendre, il est nécessaire de connaître les objets désignés par certains mots essentiels

Tels que pain, sel, sang, soleil, terre, eau, lumière, ténèbres, ainsi que par tous les noms de métaux.

Car ces noms ne sont ni les frères, ni les fils, mais bien les pères des objets sensibles.

Avec ces objets et le prince de leur substance, ils ont été précipités du monde immobile des archétypes dans l'abîme de tourmente du temps.

L'esprit seul des choses a un nom. Leur substance est innomée.

Le pouvoir de nommer des objets sensibles absolument impénétrables à l'être spirituel

Nous vient de la connaissance des archétypes qui, étant de la nature de notre esprit, sont comme lui situés dans la conscience de l'œuf solaire.

Tout ce qui se décrit par le moyen des antiques métaphores existe en un lieu situé; de tous les lieux de l'infini le seul situé.

Ces métaphores que le langage aujourd'hui encore nous impose dès que nous interrogeons le mystère de notre esprit,

Sont des vestiges du langage pur des temps de fidélité et de connaissance.

Les poètes de Dieu voyaient le monde des archétypes et le décrivaient pieusement par le moyen des termes précis et lumineux du langage de la connaissance.

Le déclin de la foi se manifeste dans le monde de la science et de l'art par un obscurcissement du langage.

Les poètes de la nature chantent la beauté imparfaite du monde sensible selon l'ancien mode sacré.

Toutefois, frappés de la discordance secrète entre le mode d'expression et le sujet,

Et impuissants à s'élever jusqu'au lieu seul situé, j'entends Pathmos, terre de la vision des archétypes,

from THE CONFESSION OF LEMUEL

CANTICLE OF KNOWLEDGE

The teaching of the sunlit hour of the nights of the Divine.
For those, who, having asked, have received and know already.
For those whom prayer has led to meditation on the origin of language.
Others, thieves of joy and pain, knowledge and love, will understand nothing of these things.
To understand them, it is needful to know the objects designated by certain essential words
Such as bread, salt, blood, sun, earth, water, light, darkness, as well as the names of metals.
For these names are neither brothers, nor sons, but truly fathers of sensible objects.
With these objects and the prince of their substance they were hurled from the motionless world of archetypes into the abyss of the turmoil of time.
Only the spirit of things has a name. Their substance is nameless.
The power to name sensible objects absolutely impenetrable to spiritual being
Comes to us from knowledge of archetypes which, being of the same nature as our spirit, is like it situated in the consciousness of the solar egg.
Everything described by means of ancient metaphors exists in a situated place; of all places of the infinite the only one situated.
These metaphors which language still imposes on us today as soon as we question our spirit's mystery
Are vestiges of the pure language of times of faith and knowledge.
God's poets saw the world of archetypes and described it reverently by means of the precise and luminous terms of the language of knowledge.
The decline of faith shows itself in the world of art and science by a coarsening of language.
Nature poets sing the sensible world's beauty in the old sacred mode.
Yet, struck by the secret discord between the mode of expression and its object,
And powerless to lift themselves up to the only situated place, I mean Patmos, earth of the vision of archetypes,

Ils ont imaginé, dans la nuit de leur ignorance, un monde intermédiaire, flottant et stérile, le monde des symboles.
Tous les mots dont l'assemblage magique a formé ce chant sont des noms de substances visibles
Que l'auteur, par la grâce de l'Amour, a contemplées dans les deux mondes de la béatitude et de la désolation.
Je ne m'adresse qu'aux esprits qui ont reconnu le prière comme le premier entre tous les devoirs de l'homme.
Les plus hautes vertus, la charité, la chasteté, le sacrifice, la science, l'amour même du Père,
Ne seront comptées qu'aux esprits qui, de leur propre mouvement, ont reconnu la nécessité absolue de l'humiliation dans la prière.
Toutefois, je ne dirai de l'arcane du langage que ce que l'infamie et la démence de ce temps me permettent d'en révéler.
Maintenant, je peux chanter librement le cantique de l'heure ensoleillée des nuits de Dieu
Et, proclamant la sagesse des deux mondes qui furent ouverts à ma vue,
Parler, selon la mesure imposée par le compagnon de service
De la connaissance perdue de l'or et du sang.
J'ai vu. Celui qui a vu cesse de penser et de sentir. Il ne sait plus que décrire ce qu'il a vu.
Voici la clef du monde de lumière. De la magie des mots que j'assemble ici
L'or du monde sensible tire sa secrète valeur.
Car ce ne sont pas ses vertus physiques qui l'ont fait roi des esprits.
La vérité est cela par rapport à quoi l'Illimité est situé.
Mais la vérité ne fait pas mentir le langage sacré: car elle est aussi le soleil visible du monde substantiel, de l'univers immobile.
De ce soleil, l'or terrestre tire sa substance et sa couleur; l'homme la lumière de sa connaissance.
Le langage retrouvé de la vérité n'a rien de nouveau à offrir. Il réveille seulement le souvenir dans la mémoire de l'homme qui prie.
Sens-tu se réveiller en toi le plus ancien de tes souvenirs?
Je te révèle ici origines saintes de ton amour de l'or.
La folie a soufflé sept fois sur le chandelier d'or de la connaissance.
Les mots du langage des Aaronites sont profanés par les enfants menteurs et les poètes ignorants

They imagined in the night of their ignorance an intermediary world, floating and sterile, the world of symbols.
All the words whose magical gathering has formed this song are names of visible substances
Which, by grace of Love, the author has seen in the two worlds of blessedness and desolation.
I speak only to those who have recognized prayer as the first of man's duties.
The highest virtues, charity, chastity, sacrifice, knowledge, the Father's love itself,
Will be granted only to those who, by their own movement, have recognized the absolute necessity of humility in prayer.
Yet concerning the arcana of language I shall only reveal what the infamy and madness of this time allow me to reveal.
Now I can freely sing the canticle of the sunlit hour of the nights of God
And, proclaiming the wisdom of the two worlds opened to my sight,
Speak of the lost knowledge of blood and gold
Within limits imposed by the companion in service.
I have seen. He who has seen stops thinking and feeling. He can only describe what he has seen.
Here is the key to the world of light. From the magic of the words I gather here
The sensible world's gold draws its secret value.
For it is not its physical virtues that have made it king of spirits.
Truth is that in relation to which the Limitless is situated.
But truth does not make sacred language lie: for it is also the visible sun of the substantial world, of the motionless universe.
From this sun, earthly gold draws its substance and color; the man of light his knowledge.
Truth's language regained has nothing new to offer. It only awakens remembrance in the memory of the one who prays.
Do you feel the most ancient of your memories awakening in you?
I reveal to you here the holy origins of your love of gold.
Seven times has madness blown upon knowledge's golden candlestick.
The words of the Aaronites' language are profaned by lying children and ignorant poets

Et l'or du chandelier, saisi par les ténèbres de l'ignorance, est devenu le père de la négation, du vol, de l'adultère et du massacre.
Ceci est la clef des deux mondes de la lumière et des ténèbres. O compagnon de service!
Pour l'amour de cette heure ensoleillée de nos nuits,
Pour la sécurité de ce secret entre toi et moi,
Souffle-moi la parole enveloppée de soleil, le mot chargé de foudre de ce temps dangereux.
Je t'ai nommé! te voici dans le rayon avant-coureur au sein du nuage figé, muet comme le plomb,
Dans le bond et le vent de la masse de feu,
Dans l'apparition de l'esprit virginal de l'or,
Dans le passage de l'ove à la sphère,
Dans l'arrêt merveilleux et dans la sainte descente, quand tu regardes l'homme entre les deux sourcils,
Dans l'immobilité de la nuée infinie, d'une seule prière, ouvrage des orfèvres du Royaume,
Dans le retour à la désolation mariée au Temps,
Dans le chuchotement de compassion qui l'accompagne.
Mais la clef d'or de la sainte science est demeurée dans mon cœur.
Elle m'ouvrira encore le monde de lumière. Gravir les degrés jusqu'à se sentir pénétré de la matière même de l'espace pur,
Ce n'est pas connaître; c'est enregistrer encore des phénomènes de manifestation.
Le chemin qui mène du peu au beaucoup n'est pas celui de la sainte science.
Je viens de décrire l'ascension vers la connaissance. Il faut s'élever jusqu'à ce lieu solaire
Où l'on devient par la toute-puissance de l'affirmation—quoi donc?— cela même que l'on affirme.
C'est ainsi que les mille corps de l'esprit se révèlent aux sens vertueux.
Monter d'abord! sacrilègement! jusqu'à la plus démente des affirmations!
Et puis descendre, d'échelon en échelon, sans regret, sans larme, avec une joyeuse confiance, avec une royale patience,
Jusqu'à cette boue où tout est déjà contenu avec une évidence si terrible et par une nécessité si sainte! Par une nécessité sainte, sainte, sainte en vérité! Alleluia!

from THE CONFESSION OF LEMUEL

And the candlestick's gold, seized by the darkness of ignorance, has become the father of negation, theft, adultery, and massacre.
This is the key to the two worlds of darkness and light. O companion in service!
For love of this sunlit hour of our nights,
For the safety of the secret between you and me,
Whisper to me the sun-enveloped word, the thunder-charged word of this dangerous time.
I have named you! Here you are in the first ray in the womb of the fixed cloud, mute as lead.
In the leap and wind of the fiery mass,
In the appearance of the virginal spirit of gold,
In the passage from the egg to the sphere,
In the tremendous halt and the holy descent, when you look at a man between his two eyebrows,
In the immobility of the infinite cloud, of a single prayer, the work of the jewellers of the kingdom,
In the return to desolation wedded to Time,
In the compassionate whispering accompanying it.
But holy knowledge's golden key has stayed in my heart.
It will still re-open the world of light for me. By degrees to climb until you feel yourself penetrated by the very matter of pure space
Is not to know; it is still to record phenomena of manifestation.
The path leading from little to much is not holy science's.
I have just described the ascent towards knowledge. You must rise to the solar Place
Where by omnipotence of affirmation you become—what?—what you affirm.
Thus myriad spiritual bodies reveal themselves to virtuous senses.
First climb up! Sacrilegiously! To the craziest affirmations!
Then descend, rung by rung, regretless, tearless, with a joyous confidence, a regal patience,
To that mud which already contains everything with such terrible obviousness and by a necessity so holy! By a necessity so holy, holy, truly holy! Alleluia!

Et qui parle ici de surprise? il est encore une surprise dans l'apparition inattendue à travers les ombres d'une porte d'antique cité
D'un lointain de mer avec sa sainte lumière et ses voiles heureuses.
Mais dans la naissance d'un sens nouveau et d'un sens qui servira l'esprit de la science vraie, de la science amoureuse, il n'est plus de surprise.
C'est la coutume dans nos hauteurs d'accueillir toute nouveauté comme une épouse retrouvée après le temps et pour toujours.
Ainsi me fut révélée la relation de l'œuf solaire à l'âme de l'or terrestre.
Et ceci est la prière efficace où doit s'abîmer l'opérateur:
Entretiens en moi l'amour de ce métal que colore ton regard, la connaissance de cet or qui est un miroir du monde des archétypes
Afin que je dépense sans mesure tout mon cœur à ce jeu solaire de l'affirmation et du sacrifice.
Reçois-moi dans cette lumière archangélique qui sommeille mille ans dans le blé funéraire et y entretient le feu caché de la vie.
Car le blé des antiques tombeaux, versé dans le sillon, s'illumine comme un cœur de sa propre charité
Et ce n'est pas le soleil mortel qui donne à la moisson sa couleur invariable de sagesse
Telle est la clef du monde de lumière. A qui la manie d'une main pieuse et sûre elle ouvre aussi—l'autre région.
J'ai visité les deux mondes. L'amour m'a conduit tout au fond de l'être.
J'ai porté sur ma poitrine le poids de la nuit, mon front a distillé une sueur de mur.
J'ai tourné la roue d'épouvante de ceux qui partent et reviennent. Il ne reste de moi en maint endroit qu'un cercle d'or tombé dans une poignée de poussière.
J'ai exploré à tâtons les labyrinthes hideux du monde de fureur et sous les grandes eaux sommeillent mes patries étranges.
Je me taisais. J'attendais que la folie de mon roi me saisît à la gorge. Ta main, ô mon roi! est sur ma gorge. C est là le signe, voici l'instant. Je parlerai.
Tu m'as fait naître dans un monde qui ne te connaît plus, sur une planète de fer et d'argile, nue et froide.
Au milieu d'un grouillement de voleurs abîmés dans la contemplation de leur sexe.
Là, à la puanteur du massacre succède l'encensement imbècile des trompeurs de peuples.

from THE CONFESSION OF LEMUEL

Who speaks here of surprise? There is still surprise in the unexpected sight, through shadows of an ancient city gate,
Of a far view of the sea with its holy lights and blessed sails.
But in the birth of a new sense, a sense which will serve the spirit of true science, there are no more surprises.
It is the custom on our heights to embrace every novelty like a spouse regained after time and forever.
In this manner the relation of the solar egg to the soul of earthly gold was revealed to me.
And this is the efficacious prayer into which the operative must plunge himself:
Sustain in me love of this metal that colors your gaze, knowledge of this gold that is the world of archetype's mirror
So that I might measurelessly expend my whole heart in this solar game of affirmation and sacrifice.
Receive me in the archangelic light that slumbers thousands of years in funerary wheat, there sustaining life's hidden fire.
For the grain of ancient tombs, split in the furrow, lights up like a heart with its own charity
And it is no mortal sun that gives to the harvest its immutable hue of wisdom.
Such is the key to the world of light. To whoever handles it with a sure and pious hand it also opens—the other region.
I have visited the two worlds. Love led me to being's utter depth.
I have carried the weight of the night on my chest, my brow has distilled the walls' sweat.
I have turned the wheel of horror of those who go and return. In many places all that remains of me is a circle of gold in a handful of dust.
I have explored gropingly the raging world's hideous labyrinths and my strange homelands slumber beneath great waters.
I said nothing. I waited only for my king's madness to seize me by the throat. Your hand, O my king, is on my throat! That is the sign, this is the moment. I shall speak.
You had me born in a world that no longer knew you, on a naked, cold planet of iron and clay.
Amid a murmer of thieves sunk in contemplation of their sex.
The stench of massacre there is followed by the idiotic flattery of the deceivers of peoples.

Et pourtant, fils de la boue et de la cécité, je n'ai pas de mots pour décrire
Les précipices d'iniquité de cet autre Tout, de cet autre Illimité
Créé par ta propre toute-puissance de négation.
Ce lieu séparé, différent, hideux, cet immense cerveau délirant de Lucifer
Où j'ai subi durant l'èternité l'épreuve de la multiplication des grands fulgurants, des systèmes déserts.
Le plus atroce était au zénith et je le voyais comme d'un précipice de soleil noir.
Ah! sacrilège infini auprès duquel le saint cosmos développé devant notre monde infime
Est comme un carré de givre illuminé pour la Nativité et prêt à fondre au souffle de l'Enfant.
Car tu es Celui qui est. Toutefois, tu es au-dessus de toi-même et de cette nécessité absolue par laquelle tu es.
Voilá pourquoi, Affirmateur, la totale négation est en toi, liberté de prier ou de ne pas prier. Voilà pourquoi aussi tu fais passer les affirmateurs par les grandes épreuves de la négation.
Car tu m'as jeté dans la chaleur la plus noire de cette éternité d'épouvante où l'on se sent saisi
A la mâchoire par le harpon de feu et suspendu dans la folie du vide parfait,
Dans cette éternité où les ténèbres sont l'absence de l'autre soleil, l'extinction de la joyeuse ellipse d'or;
Où les lumières sont fureur. Où toute chose est moelle de l'iniquité.
Où l'opération de la pensée est unique et sans fin, partant du doute pour aboutir au rien.
Où l'on n'est pas solitaire mais solitude, ni abandonné mais abandon, ni damné mais damnation.
Je fus voyageur en ces terres du nocturne fracas
Où, seuls parmi les choses physiques,
L'amour furieux et la lèpre du visage baignent leurs maudites racines.
J'y ai mesuré, ver aveugle, les sinuosités d'une ligne de ta main. Ce pays de la nuit dense comme pierre,
Ce monde de l'autre étoile du matin, de l'autre fils, de l'autre prince, c'était ta main fermée. Cette main s'est ouverte et me voici dans la lumière.

from THE CONFESSION OF LEMUEL

And yet, son of mud and blindness, I have no words to describe
The iniquitous precipices of this other All, this other Limitlessness
Created by your own omnipotent negation.
This separated place, different, hideous, this immense, delirious, Luciferic brain
Where for eternity I suffered trials of the multiplication of great lightning-flashes, those barren systems.
At the zenith was the worst, and I saw it as from a black sun's precipice.
Ah! Infinite sacrilege, beside which the holy cosmos, the one revealed before our lowly world,
Is like a square of hoarfrost lit up for the Nativity and ready to melt at the Child's breath.
For you are He who is. You are both above yourself and the absolute necessity by which you are.
That is why, Affirmer, total negation is in you, the freedom to pray and not to pray. It is also why you make affirmers pass great trials of negation.
For you tossed me into the blackest heat of this eternity of horror where one feels seized
By the jaw by the fiery harpoon and hung in the folly of perfect emptiness,
In this eternity where darkness is absence of the other sun, extinction of the joyous golden ellipse;
Where lights are fury. Where all is marrow of iniquity.
Where thinking's operation is one and endless, beginning in doubt and ending in nothing.
Where a person is not solitary but solitude, not destitute but destitution, not damned but damnation.
I was a traveller in these lands of nocturnal din
Where, among physical things, only
Mad love and the lepra of the face bathe their damned roots.
There like a blind worm I measured the meanderings of a line of your hand. That country of night, thick as a stone,
That world of the other morning star, of the other sun, the other prince, was your closed hand. The hand opened and here I am in the light.

Il faut l'avoir vu, Lui, l'Autre, pour comprendre pourquoi il est écrit qu'il vient comme le voleur. Il est plus loin que le cri de la naissance, il est à peine, il n'est pas. L'espace d'un grain de sable, le voici tout entier en toi, lui, l'autre, le prince assis muet dans la cécité éternelle.

Toi dans l'œuf solaire, toi, immense, innocent, tu te connais. Mais les deux infinis de ton affirmation et de ta négation ne se connaissent pas, ne se connaîtront jamais, car l'éternité n'est que fuite de l'un devant l'autre.

Et toute la hideuse, la mortelle mélancolie de l'espace et du temps n'est que la distance d'un oui à un non et la mesure de leur séparation irrémédiable.

C'est ici la clef du monde des ténèbres.

L'homme en qui ce chant a réveillé non pas une pensée, non pas une émotion, mais un souvenir, et un souvenir très ancien, cherchera, dorénavant, l'amour avec amour.

Car c'est cela aimer, car c'est cela amour: quand on cherche avec amour l'amour.

J'ai cherché comme la femme stérile, avec angoisse, avec fureur. J'ai trouvé. Mais quoi? mais qui? le dominateur, le possesseur, le dispensateur des deux lèpres.

Et je suis revenu, afin de communiquer ma connaissance. Mais malheur à qui part et ne revient pas.

Et ne me plains pas d'y être allé et d'avoir vu. Ne pleure pas sur moi:

Noyé dans la béatitude de l'ascension, ébloui par l'œuf solaire, précipité dans la démence de l'éternité noire d'à côté, les membres liés par l'algue des ténèbres, moi je suis toujours dans le même lieu, étant dans le lieu même, le seul situé.

Apprends de moi que toute maladie est une confession par le corps.

Le vrai mal est un mal caché; mais quand le corps s'est confessé, il suffit de bien peu pour amener à soumission l'esprit même, le préparateur des poisons secrets.

Comme toutes les maladies du corps, la lèpre présage donc la fin d'une captivité de l'esprit.

L'esprit et le corps luttent quarante ans: c'est là le fameux âge critique dont parle leur pauvre science, la femme stérile.

Le mal a-t-il ouvert une porte dans ton visage? le messager de paix, Melchisedech entrera par cette porte et elle se refermera sur lui et sur son beau manteau de larmes. Mais répète après moi: *Pater noster*.

from THE CONFESSION OF LEMUEL

One must have seen Him, the Other, to understand why it is written that he comes like a thief. He is farther away than the first cry at birth, he hardly is, he is not. The space of a grain of sand, here he is, whole in you, he, the other, the prince seated mutely in eternal blindness.
You in the solar egg, you, immense, innocent, you know yourself. But the two infinites of your affirmation and your negation do not know each other, will never know each other, for eternity is but the flight of the one before the other.
All the hideous, mortal melancholy of space and time is only the distance from a yes to a no and the measure of their irremediable separation.
This is the key to the world of darkness.
The man in whom this song has awakened not a thought, not an emotion, but a memory, a most ancient memory, from now on will seek love with love.
For this is what it is to love, this is what it is to love: to seek love with love.
I sought like a sterile woman, furiously, with anguish. I found. What? Who? The dominator, the possessor, the dispensor of the two lepras.
I have returned to communicate my knowledge. Woe unto him who goes and does not return.
Do not pity me for having gone and seen. Do not weep for me:
Drowned in the blessedness of ascension, dazzled by the solar egg, hurled into the madness of the black eternity beside me, limbs bound about with algae of darkness, I am always in the same place, being in place itself, the only one situated.
Learn from me that all sickness is a confession of the body.
True evil is hidden evil; but once the body has confessed it takes very little to bring the spirit itself, the preparer of secret poisons, into submission.
Like all sicknesses of the body, lepra portends the end of spiritual captivity
Spirit and body struggle for forty years: this is the famous critical age of which their science, that sterile woman, speaks.
Has evil opened a door in your face? Melchizedek, the messenger of peace, will enter by this door and it will close behind him again and his beautiful coat of tears. But repeat after me: *Pater Noster*.

Vois-tu, le Père des Anciens, de ceux qui parlaient le langage pur, a joué avec moi comme un père avec son enfant. Nous, nous seuls, qui sommes ses petits enfants nous connaissons ce jeu sacré, cette danse sainte, ce flottement heureux entre la pire obscurité et la meilleure lumière.

Il faut se prosterner plein de doutes, et prier. Je me plaignais de ne le point connaître; une pierre où il était tout entier m'est descendue dans la main et j'ai reçu au même instant la couronne de lumière.

Et regarde-moi! environné d'embûches je ne redoute plus rien.

Des ténèbres de la conception à celles de la mort, un fil de catacombes court entre mes doigts dans la vie obscure.

Et pourtant, qu'étais-je? Un ver de cloaque, aveugle et gras, à queue aiguë, voilà ce que j'étais. Un homme créé par Dieu et révolté contre son créateur.

"Quelles qu'en soient l'excellence et la beauté, aucun avenir n'égalera jamais en perfection le non-être." Telle était ma certitude unique, telle était ma pensée secrète: une pauvre, pauvre pensée de femme stérile.

Comme tous les poètes de la nature, j'étais plongé dans une profonde ignorance. Car je croyais aimer les belles fleurs, les beaux lointains et mêmes les beaux visages pour leur seule beauté.

J'interrogeais les yeux et le visage des aveugles: comme tous les courtisans de la sensualité, j'étais menacé de cécité physique. Ceci est encore un enseignement de l'heure ensoleillée des nuits du Divin.

Jusqu'au jour où, m'apercevant que j'étais arrêté devant un miroir, je regardai derrière moi. La source des lumières et des formes était là, le monde des profonds, sages, chastes archétypes.

Alors cette femme qui était en moi mourut. Je lui donnai pour tombeau tout son royaume, la nature. Je l'ensevelis au plus secret du jardin décevant, là où le regard de la lune, de la prometteuse éternelle se divise dans le feuillage et descend sur les endormies par les mille degrés de la suavité.

C'est ainsi que j'appris que le corps de l'homme renferme dans ses profondeurs un remède à tous les maux et que la connaissance de l'or est aussi celle de la lumière et du sang.

O Unique! ne m'ôte pas le souvenir de ces souffrances, le jour où tu me laveras de mon mal et aussi de mon bien et me feras habiller de soleil par les tiens, par les souriants. *Amen.*

from THE CONFESSION OF LEMUEL

See, the Father of the Ancients, of those who speak pure language, played with me as a father with his child. Only we, who are his little children, know this sacred game, this holy dance, this happy floating between worst darkness and best light.

You must prostrate yourself, full of doubt, and pray. I complained I did not know him at all; a stone came down into my hand in which he was utterly and at the same instant I was given the crown of light.

Look at me! Surrounded by snares I no longer fear anything.

From the dark of conception to the dark of death a thread of catacombs runs through my fingers in dark life.

And yet, who was I? A cloacal worm, blind and fat, with a pointed tail. A man created by God and in revolt against his Creator.

"Whatever its excellence and beauty, the future will never equal non-being in perfection." Such was my sole certainty, my secret thought: a sterile woman's poor, poor thought.

Like all nature poets I was sunk in profound ignorance. For I believed that I loved beautiful flowers, beautiful views and even beautiful faces for their beauty alone.

I was questioning the eyes and faces of the blind: like all courtesans of sensuality I was threatened by physical blindness. This too is a teaching from the sunlit hours of the Divine.

Until the day when, noticing I had stopped before a mirror, I looked behind me. The source of lights and forms was there, the world of profound, wise, chaste archetypes.

Then this woman who was in me died. For a tomb I gave her all her kingdom, nature. I buried her in the most secret spot in the deceitful garden, where the gaze of the moon, the eternal promiser, divides in the leafage and descends upon the sleeping woman in myriad degrees of sweetness.

Thus I learned that in its depths man's body encloses a remedy for all ills and that the knowledge of gold is also knowledge of light and blood.

O unique One! Do not take from me the memory of these sufferings on that day when you cleanse me of my evil as of my good and have me clothed in the sun by your own, the smiling ones. *Amen.*

translated by Christopher Bamford

LA CONFESSION DE LEMUEL

L'HOMME
Quand je mesure ce chemin parcouru, moi, ver sous le plancher,
Quel amour et quelle pitié me saisissent le cœur pour les frères soleils
   dans la nuit!
Et pourtant, eux aussi ils sont de ce monde-ci, d'ici. Oh!
Permets que je regarde enfin plus loin, bien plus loin—en moi-même.
Ah! je le sais bien, toi, toi tu sais ce qu'il y a là, et comment n'aurais-je
   pas honte?
D'abord, une ferveur de réunir les Séparés.
Une angoisse de marier le feu et l'eau,
Plus tard, l'immense adieu de l'Epoux à l'Epouse,
Une division des deux belles clartés
Du jour et de la nuit . . . Certes, c'est peu; mais, réponds-moi,
Qui, parmi tes enfants, qui donc, depuis l'instant
Où tu te reconnus dans les traits d'une vierge
Comme en un sommeil d'eau, a jamais eu besoin
Comme moi, pour lire en son esprit, de la lumière de la femme?
Qui, ô heureux! qui veux que l'on pardonne, qui?
Et cela de toi, mauvais, qui ne venait pas, ma colère
L'a pourchassé avec les maigres chiens courants
Du gémissement de luxure. Mais,
Là encore, une pitié de père, ô Père!
Se déchirant en moi, obscure s'abattait
Comme glace d'été sur ma noire chaleur.
De sorte que dans cette vie, la mienne, comme dans le labour
Océanique, parmi les sillons de montagnes,
Tout, tout ne fut que tourment, amertume et stérilité.
Mais, toi qui sais, comment pouvais-je savoir moi
Qui étais comme le frémissement sacré
Du paon douloureux et beau de Midi
Que cela que j'attendais du dehors
Me viendrait de moi-même, et, feu conscient de sa route,
Pur, joyeux et puissant comme l'âme de l'or,
Soudain, s'arrêterait comme sur Josué,
Pour toucher d'un regard omniscient d'épouse
La vue intérieure, là, entre les sourcils . . .

THE CONFESSION OF LEMUEL

THE MAN

When I consider the path that I, worm beneath floorboards, have travelled,
With what love and pity my heart is assailed for the fraternal suns in the night!
And yet they too are of this world, this here below. Oh!
Allow me to see at last farther, much farther—into myself.
Ah! Well do I know that you, you know what is there and how should I not be ashamed?
First, a fervour to reconcile the Divided,
An anxious desire to join fire and water in wedlock,
And later, the boundless farewell of the Groom to the Bride,
A division of the two lovely lights
Of the day and the night . . . indeed that's not much; but answer me,
Which of your children, which then, from the instant
When you recognized yourself in a virgin's features
As in a liquid sleep, had ever such need
As I have of the wisdom of woman to read what there is in my spirit?
Who, O blessed one, who wishes that one should grant pardon, who?
And from you, recreant who never came, my wrath
Chased it away with the lean racing dogs
Of the moaning of lust. But,
There again, a father's pity, O Father!
Tearing itself apart in me, darkly shattered
Like Summer ice upon my black hotness.
So that in this life, in my own life, as in oceanic
Ploughing among the mountains' furrows,
There was nothing, nothing, but torment, grief and sterility.
But, you who know, how was I to know, I
Who was like the rapturous quivering
Of the mournful and handsome peacock of Noon,
That what I was awaiting from without
Would come to me from myself and, fire conscious of its way,
Pure, joyful and strong as the soul of gold,
Would suddenly pause as on Joshua
To touch with a bride's omniscient gaze
The inner prospect, there, between the brows . . .

(*Silence*)

Ce fut là le jeunesse avec ses jours, et puis
Vint l'âge mûr avec ses nuits;
Derrière le rideau de l'assoupissement
Ces terrasses, tu sais, hautes, hautes, qu'on balayait, ces pierres
Aussi qui, trois par trois, quatre par quatre
Tombaient tristement, d'où? dans le puits du sommeil.
Et certaine nuit . . . Mais ce sont là choses
Dont le nom n'est ni son, ni silence.

CHŒUR
(*Un chuchotement nombreux*)
Parle. Dis
Impitoyablement ce que ton âme a vu
Dans le cosmos aveugle, égaré et abandonné.
Parle, et imite l'éternité quand elle dit: non.
Dans ces déserts où jamais Oui n'a résonné.
Dis-nous comment des pieds à la tête, le corps
Devient pensée, dans ces pays plus insensibles que la lèpre.
Quel cri des ténèbres imparfaites
D'ici contient le nom de cette nuit totale
Vide des deux soleils?
Parle. Que t'advint-il dans cet infini AUTRE
Vu comme par des yeux de race disparue?
AUTRE. N'est-ce point là l'unique mot?
AUTRE. Non pas seulement différent,
N'est-il pas vrai mais AUTRE,
Et défendu, fermé,—mais ne veux-tu pas dire:
Même à la toute-puissance d'ici?
Dans cet infini AUTRE
Où celui-là qui nous contient est inconnu,
Où l'espace est la nuit au dedans de la pierre.

L'HOMME
Je me séparai d'elle—qui, par l'œuvre de mainte année
Etait devenue mon enfant, dans ce long corridor d'hôtel,
Et maintenant—quel froid coupe mon âme en deux!—

from THE CONFESSION OF LEMUEL

(silence)
That was all youth with its days, and then
Came mature age with its nights;
Behind the curtain of somnolence
Those terraces, you know, high, high up, swept clean, those stones
Also that, three by three, four by four,
Fell sadly, from whence? into the well of sleep.
And one night . . . But those are all things
Of which the name is neither sound nor silence.

CHOIR
(A multitudinous whispering)
Speak. Tell
Unsparingly what your soul has seen
In the blind, wandering and forsaken cosmos.
Speak, and copy eternity when it says: no.
In those deserts where Yes has never resounded.
Tell us how from head to foot the body
Becomes thought, in those lands with less feeling than leprosy.
What cry of this defective hither
Dark contains the name of that total night,
Devoid of the two suns?
Speak. What becomes of you in that OTHER infinity
Seen as through the eyes of a vanished race?
OTHER. Is that not the one and only word?
OTHER. Not only different,
Is it not true to say, but OTHER,
And forbidden, sealed up,—but do you not mean:
Even to the omnipotence reigning down here?
In that OTHER infinity
Where that which contains us is unknown,
Where space is the night in the midst of the stone.

THE MAN
I separated myself from her—who through the effort of many a year
Had become my child, in that long hotel corridor,
And now—what cold cuts my soul in twain!—

J'étais seul dans ma chambre allemande et je savais
Que de l'autre côté du mur, cette chose dormait
Pour la dernière fois à trois pas de ma vie
Et que, sans me revoir, au petit jour
Elle s'en irait—si enfant, si enfant
Vers la vaste, froide, vide vie.

  (Silence)

En moi, l'obéissance envers moi-même
Etait plus forte que tout.

  (Silence)

Et il vint un moment où je sentis Ceci:
Une soudaine immensité
Inexprimable, différente, séparée,
M'aspira dans un univers où le Oui n'avait plus de sens.
Pays fermé à nos vivants et à nos morts:
Tout était pénétré d'une autre éternité,
D'une autre nécessité,—d'un autre Dieu . . .
La toute-puissance de là-bas
N'était même plus l'ennemie de celle d'ici.
Séparation.
Oh! séparation.
Les deux omnisciences ne se connaissaient pas.

Tout, tout m'était déchirement. Comme les entrailles
Brusquement ramassées sous la main du boucher, tout
M'était déchirement.
                            Et pourtant, je gardais
Un sens, un toucher sûr pour cette sainte chose
Où cesse le lieu. Et le souvenir
D'un merveilleux passé m'éclairait. Même
Il advint qu'un Temple—

  CHŒUR
  (Même chuchotement)
Est-ce vrai? Tu te souviens?—Une arche d'immobilité
Sur l'espace créé, dans le lieu
Seul situé. Le mot unique ici: Surface.

from THE CONFESSION OF LEMUEL

I was alone in my German room and I knew
That on the other side of the wall, that being was sleeping
For the last time only three feet away from my life
And that at daybreak, without having seen me again,
She would go away,—such a child, such a child
Towards immense, cold, empty life.

  (silence)

Within me, obedience towards myself
Was stronger than aught else.

  (silence)

And there came a moment when I knew THIS:
A sudden boundlessness
Ineffable, different, set apart,
Drew me into a universe in which the Yes made no more sense.
Land closed to our living and to our dead:
All was pervaded by another eternity,
By another necessity,—another God . . .
The omnipotence reigning below
Was no longer even the enemy of that obtaining here.
Separation.
Oh! separation.
The two omnisciences knew each other not.

All, all was heart-rending to me. Like the guts
Roughly bunched in the butcher's hand, all
Was heart-rending to me.
                        And yet, I retained
  A feeling, a sure touch for this holy thing
That brings place to a halt. And the memory
Of a marvellous past enlightened me. It even
Befell that a Temple—

  CHOIR
  (same whispering)
Is it true? You remember?—An arch of stability
Across created space, in the sole
Situated place. The only word here is: SURFACE.

Les cimes d'or de la méditation
Pour cette nef ne sont point écueils.
Là, plus d'espace d'ascension:
Tout n'est que Salutation.
Et puis, c'est le retour—cherche en tes souvenirs—
La chute—la Ligne Droite, première.

   L'HOMME
              —tout en pierre de compassion,
Porté par un nuage de voix, je ne sais où;
Suspendu tout en haut, dans le Rien désiré,
Inaccessible au vol immobile, cruel, muet
Des noirs, vides, féroces espaces.
                             Et je tombai
Et oubliai; puis, tout à coup, me ressouvins.

   CHŒUR
   (Même chuchotement)
De la vie à la vie, quel chemin!

   L'HOMME
Je crois bien que c'est tout.

   CHŒUR
Non,—il y a les hommes.

   L'HOMME
Tout le drame du peuple élu
S'est joué dans ce cœur profond.
Ils ne savent pas ce qu'ils font.
Ils ne le savent plus.

   CHŒUR
Tu les hais donc?

   L'HOMME
Je les ai fort longtemps haïs,
Vieux cœur de voyageur; et dans tous les pays.

  (Silence)

Cependant, certain jour—

from THE CONFESSION OF LEMUEL

The golden peaks of meditation
Represent no perilous reefs for this ship.
There, no more place of ascent:
Only Greeting exists.
And then comes the return—search through your memories—
The fall—the Straight Line, the first.

   THE MAN
              —all built of compassion's stone,
  Borne on a cloud of voices, I know not where;
Suspended on high, in the longed-for Nought,
Out of reach of the motionless, cruel, dumb theft
Of the black, void, ferocious expanses.
                        And I fell
  And forgot; then, all of a sudden, remembered.

   CHOIR
   (same whispering)
From life to life, what a way!

   THE MAN
I really believe that is all.

   CHOIR
No, there are other men.

   THE MAN
The whole drama of the chosen people
Has been enacted in this sunken heart.
They know not what they do.
They no longer know it.

   CHOIR
So you hate them?

   THE MAN
For a very long while I hated them,
Old traveller's heart; and in all lands.

  (silence)

Nevertheless, one day—

Et c'est là un de ces souvenirs
Qui ne sont plus mesure du temps
Et que l'on aime
Non point pour leur trésor de jours, mais pour eux-mêmes,
Je me laissai porter par une vague humaine
Au sommet d'une tour.
C'était Juillet, c'était Midi. Midi, Juillet.
Il faisait chaud comme aux sources du sang.
Vivre était comme un très vieux vin
De sucre au chevet d'un convalescent.
Dans l'immobilité de l'air
Le feu laissait tomber l'or de sa lourde haleine.
Jamais je n'avais vu si pleine
La coupe de sanglots de l'univers.
L'esprit, la chair,
Le mal et le bien,
La tristesse et la joie,
Le grand et le petit, oh! comme tout était humain
En moi!

(Silence)

CHŒUR
Roi,
Parle.

L'HOMME
Et ma vue descendit vers cette chose grise
Dans la vibrante profondeur:
Maisons, usines,
Gares, églises,
—Partout, partout,
Aux bords du fleuve, aux flancs de la colline,
Entassés, dispersés, amoureux et hostiles,
Ces nids de boue
Trempés d'une salive d'insectes bâtisseurs.
Et là-bas, oh! là-bas . . .

CHŒUR
Tes frères, tes sœurs.

from THE CONFESSION OF LEMUEL

And this is one of those memories
That are no more a gauge of time
And that one does not love
At all for their treasure of days, but for themselves,
I let myself be carried by a human surge
Up to the top of a tower.
It was in July, it was Noon. Noon, July.
It was as warm as at the blood's very founts.
Living was like a very old sugared wine
At a convalescing invalid's bedside.
Into the stillness of the air
The fire dropped the gold of its heavy breath.
Never have I seen the cup
Of sobs of the universe so full.
Spirit, the flesh,
Evil and good,
Sorrow and joy,
The great and the small, oh! how human was all
That in me!

  (silence)

  CHOIR
King,
Speak.

  THE MAN
And my sight moved towards that grey thing
In the vibrant depths:
Houses, factories,
Stations, churches,
—Here there and everywhere,
On the riverbanks, on the hillsides,
Packed together, spread around, loving and hostile,
Those nests of mud
Moistened by a saliva of builder insects.
And down there, oh! down there . . .

  CHOIR
Your brothers, your sisters.

(Très long silence)

L'HOMME
Alors, dans un éclair
De lance dans le flanc percé
Je compris tout,
L'Annonciation et le Verbe fait chair,
Oui, dans un éclair de pensée
Je compris, je sentis, je vis
—COMMENT LES CHOSES S'ÉTAIENT PASSÉES.

(Silence)

Maintenant, les trois années de renoncement après les quarante ans d'attente tirent à leur fin. Je comprends.—je sens enfin que je sais, que j'ai toujours su, et qu'il est ici même une certaine manière de tout connaître.

J'ai fermé ma vue et mon cœur. Les voici réconfortés. Que je les ouvre maintenant. A toute cette chose dans la lumière. A ce blé de soleils. Avec quel bruissement de vision il coule dans le tamis de la pensée.

Immense, éternelle, effrayante Réalité. C'était toi, de toutes les possibilités, toi la plus extraordinaire. Car tu n'es pas en moi, et cependant je suis ton lieu; je passerai, et tu demeureras; et pourtant, nous deux, nous sommes inséparables; mon amour t'embrasse, et c'est là ton unique borne, ô Illimité!

Et que serais-tu sans cette attestation intérieure, sans ce Oui en moi jeté comme un pont de montagne entre les deux massifs de nuit d'avant et d'après.

CHŒUR
(Un peu plus haut)
La plus humble chose a sa vérité silencieuse.
Mais aux fils des artificieuses
Il faut de sacrilèges merveilles—nous le savons.
Et où est parmi vous celui qui ici même
Sur cette terre, goûte dans sa plénitude, la sainteté
Dont le ciel que nous respirons
Pénètre à tout instant votre pain, votre vin?

from THE CONFESSION OF LEMUEL

(very long silence)

THE MAN
Then, in a flash
Of the lance in the pierced side,
I understood all,
The Annunciation and the Word made flesh,
Yes, in a flash of thought
I understood, I felt, I saw
—HOW THINGS HAD HAPPENED.

(silence)

Now, the three years of renunciation after the forty-year waiting-period are drawing to a close. I understand,—at last I feel that I know, that I have always known and that even here there is a certain way of knowing everything.

I shut my eyes and my heart. Behold them consoled. Let me open them now. On all things in the light. On this wheat of suns. With what rustle of vision it flows through the sieve of thought.

Vast, eternal, appalling Reality. You, of all possibilities, were the most extraordinary. For you are not within me, and yet I am your place; I shall pass and you will remain; and we two however, we two are inseparable; my love embraces you and therein is your unique limit, O Boundlessness!

And what would you be without this inner affirmation, without this Yes within me flung like a mountain bridge between the two massive ranges of previous and following night.

CHOIR
(a little louder)
The humblest of things has its silent truth.
But the sons born of cunning
Require blasphemous wonders—we know it.
And where is there among you the one who here
On this very earth tastes in its wholeness the sanctity
With which the sky that we breathe in
Pervades at each instant your bread and your wine?

Homme, homme, quel chemin tu as fait
Pour arriver à nous qui étions en toi.

(Ils pleurent)

L'HOMME
O merveilleux, merveilleux
Penchés sur moi, car je sais, je sens
Que vous vous inclinez vers moi pour chuchoter,
Votre chuchotement est celui
De merveilleux tendrement penchés—
Tandis que sur moi vous vous penchez
Dans un chuchotement merveilleux,
Tandis qu'autour de moi vous chuchotez
De la sorte, dans un frémissement d'èlytres
O merveilleux (et quoi donc prédomine en vous,
Chuchoteurs, l'homme ou la femme?)
Laissez-moi, innombrables que j'aime comme un seul,
Beaux à faire mal, insupportablement gracieux
Vous demander une grâce.

CHŒUR
Elle est accordée.

(Ils rient)

L'HOMME
De longues, longues, puissantes années,
Et un immense amour, semblable au vôtre,
Ici-même déjà comme vous autres,
Et une Action, une noble, une haute Action,
Pacificatrice, purificatrice, comme la vôtre,
Ici-même, ici-même, rieurs-pleureurs, comme la vôtre.

Man, man, what a path you have trod
At last to reach us who were in you.

(they weep)

THE MAN
O marvellous, marvels
Bent over me, for I know, for I feel
That you are leaning towards me to whisper,
Your whispering is that
Of the marvellous tenderly bent—
While you are bending over me
In a marvellous whispering,
While around me you whisper
In such a way, in a shivering of wing-cases
O marvels (and which then in you predominates,
Whispering ones, the man or the woman?)
Allow me, myriad that I love as I would only one,
Painfully lovely, unbearably graceful,
To ask you a favour.

CHOIR
It is granted.

(they laugh)

THE MAN
Long, long, powerful years
And a vast love, similar to your own,
Already in the selfsame place as you others,
And an action, a noble, a lofty Action,
Peace-making, purifying, like yours,
Right here where we are, laughers-weepers, like yours.

translated by David Gascoyne

CANTIQUE DU PRINTEMPS

Le printemps est revenu de ses lointains voyages,
Il nous apporte la paix du cœur.
Lève-toi, chère tête! Regarde, beau visage!
La montagne est une île au milieu des vapeurs: elle a repris sa riante
　　couleur.
O jeunesse! ô viorne de la maison penchée!
O saison de la guêpe prodigue!
La vierge folle de l'été
Chante dans la chaleur.
Tout est confiance, charme, repos.
Que le monde est beau, bien-aimée, que le monde est beau!
Un grave et pur nuage est venu d'un royaume obscur.
Un silence d'amour est tombé sur l'or de midi.
L'ortie ensommeillée courbe sa tête mûre.
Sous sa belle couronne de reine de Judée.
Entends-tu? Voici l'ondée.
Elle vient . . . elle est tombée.
Tout le royaume de l'amour sent la fleur d'eau.
La jeune abeille,
Fille du soleil,
Vole à la découverte dans le mystère du verger;
J'entends bêler les troupeaux;
L'écho répond au berger.
Que le monde est beau, bien-aimée, que le monde est beau!
Nous suivrons la musette aux lieux abandonnés.
Là-bas, dans l'ombre du nuage, au pied de la tour,

from *Poèmes (1895-1927)*
Poems (1895-1927)
1929

CANTICLE OF SPRING

Spring has returned from its distant travels,
Bringing peace to our hearts.
Raise your fair head! Behold, fair countenance!
The mountain is an isle in the midst of the mists: it has recovered its cheerful color.
O youth! O viburnum of the leaning house!
O season of the prodigal wasp!
Summer's foolish virgin
Sings in the heat.
All is trust, enchantment and peace.
How fair the world is, beloved, how fair is the world!
A grave and pure cloud has come from a shady realm.
An amorous silence has overtaken the gold of noon.
The drowsy nettle inclines its ripe head
Beneath its fair queen of Judea's crown.
Do you hear? The shower is at hand.
Here it comes . . . it has fallen.
The whole realm of love has the odour of water's bloom.
The young bee,
Daughter of the sun,
Flies about exploring the murk of the orchard;
I can hear the flocks bleating;
Echo answers the shepherd.
How fair the world is, beloved, how fair is the world!
We will follow the bagpipe to the forsaken places.
Down there, in the cloud's shadow, at the foot of the tower,

Le romarin conseille de dormir; et rien n'est beau
Comme l'enfant de la brebis couleur de jour.
Le tendre instant nous fait signe de la colline voilée.
Levez-vous, amour fier, appuyez-vous sur mon épaule;
J'écarterai la chevelure du saule,
Nous regarderons dans la vallée.
La fleur se penche, l'arbre frissonne: ils sont ivres d'odeur.
Déjà, déjà le blé
Lève en silence, comme dans les songes des dormeurs.
Amour puissant, ma grande sœur,
Courons où nous appelle l'oiseau caché des jardins.
Viens, cruel cœur,
Viens, doux visage;
La brise aux joues d'enfant souffle sur le nuage
De jasmin.
La colombe aux beaux pieds vient boire à la fontaine;
Qu'elle s'apparît blanche dans l'eau nouvelle!
Que dit-elle? où est-elle?
On dirait qu'elle chante dans mon cœur nouveau.
La voici lointaine . . .
Que le monde est beau, bien-aimée, que le monde est beau!
La femme des ruines m'appelle de la fenêtre haute:
Vois comme sa chevelure de fleurs folles et de vent
S'est répandue sur le chéneau croulant
Et j'entends le bourdon strié,
Vieux sonneur des jours innocents.
Le temps est venu pour nous, folle tête,
De nous parer des baies qui respirent dans l'ombre.
Le loriot chante dans l'allée la plus secrète.
O sœur de ma pensée! quel est donc ce mystère?
Eclaire-moi, réveille-moi, car ce sont choses vues en songe.
Oh! très certainement je dors.
Comme la vie est belle! plus de mensonge, plus de remords
Et des fleurs se lèvent de terre
Qui sont comme le pardon des morts.
O mois d'amour, ô voyageur, ô jour de joie!
Sois notre hôte; arrête-toi;
Tu te reposeras sous notre toit.
Tes graves projets s'assoupiront au murmure ailé de l'allée.

The rosemary recommends sleep; and there's nothing so fair
As the dawn-coloured child of the ewe.
The muted moment makes signs to us from the shrouded hill.
Rise up, proud love, lean on my shoulder;
I will thrust aside the willow's tresses,
We will gaze into the valley.
The flower bends, the tree shivers, they are drunk with scent.
Already, already the corn
Is arising in silence, as in the dreams of sleepers.
Powerful love, my supreme sister,
Let us run whence the garden's hidden bird calls us.
Come, cruel heart,
Come, sweet countenance;
The baby-cheeked breeze is blowing on the cloud
Of jasmine.
The fine-toed dove comes to drink at the fountain;
How white she appears in the recent water!
What is she saying? where is she?
You could say she is singing in my heart.
Now she's far off . . .
How fair the world is, beloved, how fair is the world!
The woman of the ruins calls me from the high window:
See how her tresses of wild flowers and wind
Are spread out over the crumbling eaves-trough
And I hear the striped bumble-bee,
Old bell-ringer of innocent days.
The time has come, madcap, for us
To deck ourselves with the berries that breathe in the shade.
The oriole sings in the most hidden avenue.
So what, O sister of my musing!, is this mystery?
Enlighten me, awaken me, for these are things seen in a dream.
Oh! most certainly I sleep.
How lovely life is! no more lies, no more remorse
And flowers are rising from the earth
That are like the pardon of the dead.
O month of love, O traveller, O day of joy!
Be our guest; stay a while;
You will rest under our roof.
Your serious plans will be lulled by the avenue's winged murmur.

Nous te nourrirons de pain, de miel et de lait.
Ne fuis pas.
Qu'as-tu à faire là-bas?
N'es-tu pas bien ici?
Nous te cacherons aux soucis.
Il y a une belle chambre secrète
Dans notre maison de repos;
Là, les ombres vertes entrent par la fenêtre ouverte
Sur un jardin de charme, de solitude et d'eau.
Il écoute . . . il s'arrête . . .
Que le monde est beau, bien-aimée, que le monde est beau!

We will feed you on bread, milk and honey.
Do not flee.
What have you got to do yonder?
Are you not comfortable here?
We will hide you from your cares.
There is a beautiful secret room
In our house of repose;
There, green shadows enter through the window that opens
On a garden of enchantment, solitude and water.
It listens . . . it lingers . . .
How fair the world is, beloved, how fair is the world!

translated by David Gascoyne

LA NUIT DE NOËL DE 1922 DE L'ADEPTE

L'ADEPTE

Faisons,—sept fois pour le passé, et pour nos trois jours à venir, trois fois—le signe, le signe! le signe nourrissant, désaltérant, refraîchissant,—nos mains, nos fronts, nos cœurs,—le signe vainqueur, le signe vainqueur de la Croix. Et vous, Béatrix, paix à vous, reposez-vous! Faites silence dans ce corps, le mien, terrestre demeure. Car vous remuez trop, car vous faites un bruit comme de pas dans ma tête et dans mon cœur. O sept années déshéritées! Ma robe de patience m'a quitté lambeau par lambeau.

BÉATRIX

Tu dis vrai, maître. Oui, c'est bien la septième année de l'œuvre candide et secret. Sept années, maître! Mais, cette nuit, ils vont naître d'une miraculeuse et semblable merci, l'un à Bethléem, l'autre ici.

L'ADEPTE

Les parents dorment là, tendres métaux époux, dans cet œuf appuyé sur le feu nuptial. Qu'ils sont beaux, innocents!

BÉATRIX

Tu les vois donc? Comment? Dans cet œuf hermétique? Avec quels yeux?

L'ADEPTE

Chère enfant, par la grâce de la vue du milieu. Et puisque nous nous connaissons depuis sept ans, je te touche le front.

BÉATRIX
Adieu, espace, temps.

L'ADEPTE

Le clocher va bientôt sonner ses douze coups. Devant le cher fourneau, adorons à genoux.

(Silence)

1922: THE INITIATE'S CHRISTMAS EVE

THE INITIATE

Seven times for the past and, for our three days to come, again three times, let us make the sign, the sign that nourishes, quenches thirst, refreshes—our hands, our brows, our hearts—the victorious sign, the victorious sign of the Cross. And you, Beatrix, peace be with you, and may you rest! Bring silence within this body that is mine, my earthly abode. For you are moving too much, with a sound as of footsteps in my head and my heart. Oh, seven years of deprivation. My robe of patience has fallen away from me in strips.

BEATRIX

Master, you speak the truth. Yes, this is indeed the seventh year of the candid and secret task. Seven years, Master! But tonight they must both be born of a miraculous and similar mercy, the one in Bethlehem and the other one here.

THE INITIATE

The parents are sleeping there, tender metal partners in marriage, in this egg that rests on the nuptial flame. How beautiful and innocent they are!

BEATRIX

So you can see them? But how? In this hermetic egg? With what eyes?

THE INITIATE

Dear child, by virtue of median vision, and since we have now known each other seven years, I touch your brow.

BEATRIX

Farewell, space and time!

THE INITIATE

The bell-tower will soon toll the twelve strokes. Before this dear furnace, let us kneel in adoration.

(silence)

O divin Maître, souviens-toi qu'il est, même pour toi, une Hauteur. Implore, implore pour moi ta sainte épouse la Blancheur.

(Silence)

Je regarde. Et que vois-je? La pureté surnage, le blanc et le bleuté surnagent. L'esprit de jalousie, la maître de pollution, l'huile de rongement aveugle, lacrymale, plombée, dans la région basse est tombée. Lumière de l'or, charitée, tu te délivres. Viens, épouse, venez, enfant, nous allons vivre!

BÉATRIX
Cher époux, prends garde! Ecoute, regarde. Il siffle encore, il rampe encore quelque chose d'attroce au fond. Penche-toi, sainte face. Je ne sais ce qui se passe: ce que tu fais, ils le défont. Ils sont légions, obscurité, masse, menace . . .

L'ADEPTE
Je n'en vois qu'un. Il danse en rond dans la rigueur du rouge et du jaune et du noir, tout au fond du muet caveau. Chère dame, entre deux tombeaux, en vérité: celui d'Amour, celui d'Espoir. Ecoute, il crie . . . nul ne l'entend. Il voudrait, en dansant, sortir de l'espace et du temps. Jadis, dans mes tentations, que ne suis-je mort en rêvant! Tout, comme ici, était noir. Là-haut, plus loin que ma vraie vie, au bord du hideux entonnoir, hurlaient et geignaient les Harpies. Les eaux de Jupiter, de Vénus et de Mars se déversaient avec fracas sur les assises de l'infini.

BÉATRIX
J'en vois mille, dix mille! Montjoie Saint-Denis, maître! les nôtres, rapides, rapides, ensoleillés! Au maître des obscurs on fera rendre gorge. Vous, Georges, Michel, claires têtes, saintes tempêtes d'ailes éployées, et toi, si blanc d'amour sous l'argent et le lin . . .

L'ADEPTE
Ici encore, je n'en vois qu'un.

Oh, divine Master, remember that, even for you, there exists a Height. Implore, implore for me your holy spouse that is Whiteness.

(silence)

I watch, and what do I see? Purity rises to the surface, white and pale blue float on the surface. The spirit of jealousy, the master of pollution, the oil of blind corruption, leaden and lachrymal, is fallen to the lower region. Light of gold, charity, you liberate yourself. Come, my wife, come, my child, we are destined to live.

BEATRIX
Beware, dear husband, listen and watch. Something atrocious is still hissing and crawling below. Holy face, lean forward. I know not what is happening, but they destroy whatever you create, and they are legions, darkness, mass and menace. . . .

THE INITIATE
I see only one, dancing in a circle in the rigor of red, yellow and black, in the very depths of the silent vault. Dear lady, between the tombs in truth, that of Love and that of Hope, listen, he calls, but none barks. He would wish to escape, while dancing, from space and time. Formerly, in my temptations, why didn't I die while still dreaming? Everything, as here, was black. Up there, beyond my real life, on the brink of the hideous funnel, the Harpies were howling and moaning. The waters of Jupiter, Venus and Mars were crashing onto the foundations of the Infinite.

BEATRIX
I see a thousand of them, ten thousand! Mount Joy, Saint Denis, Master! Fast, fast, bathed in sunlight, ours to the rescue! We must force the master of darkness to disgorge. You, George, Michael, clear heads, holy storms of outspread wings, and you, so white with love beneath the silver and the linen. . . .

THE INITIATE
Here too, I see only one.

BÉATRIX

Troupe maudite! ricaneurs! spoliateurs! calomniateurs! Avec leurs froides, pâles épées atroces, dentelées, dans les larmes trempées, ils s'élancent . . . Ils l'ont saisi, ils l'entraînent . . . Tout est silence . . .

L'ADEPTE

Sept cris terribles dans la nuit: tout est fini, tout est fini. Fini terrestrement, fini petitement, fini, fini, irréparablement fini. Non. Il se soulève à demi: la blancheur de l'incandescence lui prend à deux mains, en silence, la tête. Elle le cajole ainsi. Souffle, soufflet, mais souffle donc! il est tout transi . . .

Un cri nouveau, par sept fois, résonne. Est-ce un nom? Je le crois. Le Maître me pardonne! Il ouvre les yeux, il renaît. Il renaît, te dis-je. Il renaît, renaît, renaît, renaît, renaît! O prodige! regarde bien, penche-toi, jeune mère! Le feu paternel rit, il n'est plus en colère. Quelle nuit! mais c'est la dernière.

BÉATRIX

Le voici à nos pieds. O chose de lumière! sainteté! charité! santé!

L'ADEPTE

Je renais, et cependant, je meurs. C'est comme il y a très longtemps, avant, avant, bien avant la dernière sortie du Semeur. Jeune mère, qu'arrive-t-il? Où sommes-nous, moi homme et toi femme, à genoux? Que signifie cela, ma chère, chère tête? Dehors, la sainte nuit est réelle, pourtant. Sur tout le corps du firmament en fête ruisselle une eau lustrale de beauté.

BÉATRIX

La lune, la grande diamantée, dans la saulaie muette du nuage, tisse en toute tranquillité son arentèle de miroitante cécité. Moi aussi, je renais, et cependant je meurs. Oui, c'est tout à fait comme avant la dernière sortie du Semeur.

BEATRIX

Infernal host! Sneerers, despoilers, slanderers! With their cold, pale and ghastly swords like teeth, tempered in tears, they leap ahead and have seized it and carried it off . . . All is silence now.

THE INITIATE

Seven deadly cries in the night, and all is finished, finished in earthly terms and pettily, finished, finished, irretrievably finished. No, he rises and the whiteness of incandescence silently holds his head in both hands while she coaxes him. Blow, bellows, blow, I beseech you! He is still benumbed. . . .

A new cry sounds seven times. Is it a name? I believe it is. The Master forgives me. He opens his eyes and is reborn, I tell you, he comes back to life, is reborn, reborn, reborn, reborn, reborn! A miracle! Young mother, lean forward and watch carefully: the paternal fire laughs, no longer angry. What a night! But it is the last.

BEATRIX

Here he is at our feet. Oh, thing of sheer light! Holiness, charity and health!

THE INITIATE

I am reborn, and yet I die. It is as it was long ago, before, before, long before the last time the Sower of Seed came forth. Young mother, what is happening? Where are we, I, a man, and you, a woman, both here on our knees? What does this mean, my dear, dear head? Yet the holy night outside is real enough. Over all the body of the firmament that celebrates the event the waters that cleanse in beauty are flowing.

BEATRIX

The moon, huge and diamond-studded, quietly weaves in the speechless clouded willows its web of glistening blindness. I too am reborn and am yet dying. Yes, it is all as it was before the Sower of Seed last came forth.

L'ADEPTE

Comme tout ton être secret respire en moi, femme, eau sourde et salutaire sous la crypte. Oh! ton visage comme l'Egypte! O visage, visage de fuite en Egypte! O mains comme un pain céleste rompu en deux! Oh! tes yeux si ... tes yeux! tes yeux! C'est comme si mon âme avait déjà quitté la terrestre livrée. Qui donc a dit cela: Heureux, heureux amants. Le Rien dans son souffle inspiré me retient suspendu sur la montagne des Dormans. Mes chaines de constellations sont rompues.

BÉATRIX

C'est la vie délivrée.

THE INITIATE
How all your secret being breathes within me, woman, deaf waters that give health beneath the crypt! Oh, your face that is like Egypt, oh, face of a flight into Egypt and hands like a heavenly loaf that is broken in two halves! Oh, your eyes that are so . . . your eyes, your eyes! It is as if my soul had already abandoned its earthly livery. Who pronounced those words: happy, happy lovers? The Nothing in its inspired breath holds me back in suspense on the hill of the Sleepers. My chains of constellations are broken.

BEATRIX
It is life now liberated.

translated by Edouard Roditi

PSAUME DU ROI DE BEAUTÉ

Des îles de la Séparation, de l'empire des profondeurs entends monter la voix des harpes de soleils. Sur nos têtes coule la paix. Le lieu où nous sommes, Malchut, est le milieu de la Hauteur.

Les pleurs féconds versés dans une pensée à mon Père, les mondes d'or éclairent de beauté l'abîme. Royale tête qui pourtant reposes sur mon cœur, quel effroi de nombres tu lis dans la mémoire de la nuit! Reine, sois femme vraiment par la compassion suprême. Toute blanche d'une pitié de la grandeur, songe au plus abandonné, au Créateur. Le lieu où nous sommes, Malchut, est le milieu de la Hauteur.

Devant le saint labeur des constellations, ne sens-tu pas ton cœur se déchirer? Malchut, Malchut, épouse! mère des générations! L'espace, essaim d'abeilles sacrées, vole vers l'Adramand d'extatiques odeurs. Le lieu où nous sommes, Malchut, est le milieu de la Hauteur.

Car de la chose en mouvement l'immobile Absolu est le secret désir. Régent solaire, pieux semeur de ce qui doit naître et mourir, je n'aime que ce qui demeure. Moi-même, moi Microprosope! je brûle de me transmuer. Ici ou dans la profondeur, rien n'est situé! rien n'est situé! Toute réalité est dans l'amour du Père. Le lieu où nous sommes, Malchut, est le milieu de la Hauteur.

Paix sur la terre, ô mon épouse, ô femme! paix dans tout l'empire irréel, aux âmes de douceur pur qui tu fais chanter les sept cordes de l'arc-en-ciel! Quand je contemple, ô Reine, ta face renversée, j'ai le cher sentiment que toutes mes pensées naissent dans ton suave cœur! Le lieu où nous sommes, Malchut, est le milieu de la Hauteur.

PSALM OF THE KING OF BEAUTY

From the Isles of Separation and the Empire of the Depths, hear the rising voice of the harps of the suns. Peace flows over our heads. The place where we now stand, Malchut, is the heart of Height.

The fruitful tears pour forth as I think of my Father and the worlds of gold shed a light of beauty on the depths. Royal head yet resting on my heart, what a fear of numbers you decipher in the memory of night! Queen, be truly a woman in supreme compassion. All white with pity for greatness, think of the Creator, most abandoned of all. The spot where we now stand, Malchut, is the heart of Height.

Facing the saintly toil of the constellations, can you not feel your heart torn asunder, Malchut, Malchut, wife, mother too of generations? Space, a swarm of sacred bees, flies towards the Adramand of ecstatic perfumes. The spot where we now stand, Malchut, is the heart of Height.

For the motionless Absolute is the secret desire of that which moves. A solar regent and pious Sower of seed destined to be born and die, I love only what is permanent. I myself, I who am but a small personification, I desire ardently to become transmuted. Here in the abyss, nothing is situated, nothing is situated! All reality exists only in the love of the Father. The place where we now stand, Malchut, is the heart of Height.

Peace on earth, oh my spouse, oh woman! Peace in all the unreal empire, peace for the gentle souls for which you make the seven strings of the rainbow sing! When I contemplate, oh Queen, your overturned face, I have the deep feeling that all my thoughts are born in your sweet heart. The place where we now stand, Malchut, is the heart of Height.

Et pourtant,—et pourtant je voudrais m'endormir sur ce trône du Temps! Tomber de bas en haut dans l'abîme divin! M'asseoir à jamais immobile parmi les sages. Oublier que le mot "ici" était absent de mon langage: Car moi qui crée sans cesse pour mériter le Rien, je suis le désir de la fin, Malchut, de la fin, de la fin des fins! Oh! te coucher, épouse morte, dans mon cœur, et te ressusciter pour le jour éternel du Père! Le lieu où nous sommes, Malchut, est le milieu de la Hauteur.

And yet, and yet I would wish to fall asleep on this throne of Time and to fall from the depths to the heights in the divine abyss! To be seated forever motionless among the sages. To forget that the word HERE was lacking in my language. For I, who constantly create in order to deserve the Nothing, I am the desire of the end, Malchut, of the end and of the end of all ends. Oh, to retire to rest, dead spouse, in my heart, and then to be reborn for the Father's eternal day! The place where we now stand, Malchut, is the heart of Height.

translated by Edouard Roditi

PSAUME DE LA MATURATION

Je n'ai pas trouvé la paix, dans ma jeunesse, auprès de celle qui s'offre sans angoisse, obéissant à un destin qui veut qu'elle se donne tout entière.

Sans doute l'ai-je blessée, en lui demandant cela seulement qui à ses yeux est si pauvre chose: l'intelligence et l'amour des esprits inférieurs.

Mais cette chose, je l'obtins; et alors, terriblement armé pour la solitude, je pris congé de celle qui m'avait tout appris et qui ne pouvait plus me comprendre.

Mais que je te perde, mon maître, si jamais parole imprudente échappe de mes lèvres à son adresse! ou si jamais je relis sans déchirement de cœur ce que tu as écrit du doigt sur le sable! . . .

Elle ne s'est trouvée sur mon chemin que pour le sombre couronnement de sacrifice; mais depuis ce jour, j'écoute ce que mon ombre conte aux orties, et toute pierre, dans le gave solitaire, à mon approche frissonne . . .

Car c'est là la profondeur de la compagne de service d'être gardienne aussi, pour nous qui ne sommes plus ni fils ni époux, de la clef du monde devenu muet.

Elle détacha de sa ceinture—qu'elle porte sous le cœur—cette clef du premier jardin dont elle est toute l'ombre et toute la lumière mais où son amour n'entre plus, n'étant pas de commandement.

Et comme je la prenais de ses mains, elle leva vers moi un regard qui semblait porter tout le poids de l'innocence dont elle est accablée.

C'est ainsi que je pénétrai dans la grotte du secret langage; et ayant été saisi par la pierre et aspiré par le métal, je dus refaire les mille chemins de la captivité à la délivrance.

Et me trouvant aux confins de la lumière, debout sur toutes les îles de la nuit, je répétais de naufrage en naufrage ce mot, le plus terrible de tous: ici.

Mais un jour, dans ces hauteurs où tout devient un jeu, je soufflai au visage de mon dernier désir la bulle colorée de mon âme.

PSALM OF RIPENING

In my youth I failed to find peace beside her, though she offered herself without anguish, obeying her fate that required that she yield herself fully.

Perhaps I hurt her when I asked her only for what, in her eyes, is so little: an understanding and a love of those lower spirits.

Yet I obtained this very thing. And then, terribly armed to face loneliness, I took my leave of her, who had taught me everything, though she could no longer understand me.

Let me lose you, my master, if ever a careless word about her escapes my lips, or if ever I read again, without feeling a pang in my heart, what your finger has scrawled in the sand.

She found herself on my path only for the dark crowning of sacrifice; but ever since that day, I listen to what my shadow tells the nettles, and every pebble, in the lonely mountain torrent's bed, shivers when I approach . . .

For such is the profundity of the acolyte, that she must also be a guardian, for us who are no longer husbands or sons, of the key to a world become speechless.

From her belt that she wears beneath her heart, she loosened this key of the first garden, of which she is all the shadow and the light, but where her love no longer enters, no longer being commanded.

And as I took the key from her hands, she raised towards me a look that seemed to bear the full weight of the innocence that was her load.

And that is how I managed to enter the cave of secret language. Seized by the stone and sucked up by the metal, I had to tread again the thousand paths that lead from captivity to freedom.

Finding myself at the frontiers of light, standing on all the isles of the night, I repeated from shipwreck to shipwreck this one word, the most terrible of all: HERE.

But one day, in those heights where everything becomes a game, I blew into the face of my last desire the many-colored bubble of my soul.

Tu descendis alors, guéri au côté, aux pieds et aux mains, vêtu de je ne sais quel or fluide et joyeux, lavé de toute souillure par la femme.

Et dans un rire de solaires légions, tu me marias à ta conscience et m'armas de la vue médiane.

Et toute l'infinitude de ce que je voyais était d'une seule pièce, et cette enfance du cyclope en moi répétait le nombre UN, et ne pouvait pas compter plus loin.

Et alors tu m'élevas sur ton sein adoré, par l'espace scellé, intérieur, réel,

Jusqu'aux belles portes de plomb de l'humilité, ta patrie et Bethléem de l'or,

Et de là, au pays où l'amour boit doucement, comme un cheval blanc, aux sources de l'étendue et de la durée.

Et toujours plus haut, jusqu'à cette voûte enfin où l'éternel instant

Est mesuré à la courbe de projection de l'œuf

Bruissant comme Raphaël et tout à coup, dans la rémission solaire,

Muet comme la seconde naissance.

Then you descended, healed in your flank, your feet and your hands and clothed in some mysteriously fluid and joyful gold, washed by woman's hands of everything that soils,

And in the laughter of solar legions you wedded me to your conscience and armed me with median vision,

And all the infinitude of what I saw was in one piece, and this childhood of the Cyclops within me repeated the one number, ONE, and was unable to count any further,

And then you raised me to your beloved bosom, through the sealed inner and real space,

As far as the beautiful leaden gates of humility, your place of birth and the Bethlehem of gold,

And from there, the land where love drinks gently, like a white horse, at the springs of extension and duration,

Always higher, up to that vaulted ceiling at last where the eternal moment

Is measured by the egg's curve of projection,

Rustling like Raphael and suddenly, in the solar remission,

Speechless like a second birth.

translated by Edouard Roditi

PSAUME DE LA RÉINTÉGRATION

Il m'advient quelquefois, au milieu de la nuit, d'être éveillé par le silence le plus accompli de l'Univers. C'est comme si, tout à coup, les multitudes célestes, apercevant dans ma pensée le terme assigné à leur course, s'arrêtaient au-dessus de ma tête pour me considérer en retenant leur souffle. Ainsi qu'aux lointains jours de mon enfance, toute mon âme se tend alors vers la grande voix qui se prépare à m'appeler du fond des espaces créés. Mais mon attente est vaine. La paix qui m'environne n'est si parfaite que parce qu'elle n'a plus de nom à me donner. Elle est en moi et je suis en elle, et dans ce Lieu comme nous innomé où s'est accomplie notre union, il n'est pas jusqu'au mot le plus universel, Ici, qui n'ait perdu à jamais son sens; car rien n'est demeuré hors de nous où nous puissions encore situer un Là-bas, et l'espace total où respire la pensée nous apparaît non pas comme le contenant, mais comme l'intérieur illuminé du beau cristal Cosmos tombé des mains de Dieu. Jadis, quand l'esprit du silence parfait me saisissait, je levais les yeux vers les soleils; aujourd'hui, ma vue descend avec leur regard dans mon être. Car leur secret est là, et non pas en eux-mêmes. Le lieu d'où ils me contemplent est celui-là même où je me tiens, et au reproche aimant peint sur le visage de l'univers je reconnais la mélancolie de ma propre conscience. L'immensité engendrée par l'infinitude des mouvements circonscrits est impuissante à combler le vide de mon âme; il n'est point de hauteur accessible à l'extension du Nombre dont les instants ne soient comptés par le battement de mon cœur. Que m'importe donc toute cette distance du rien au rien! Certes, je suis tombé d'un lieu fort élevé; mais c'est un *autre espace* qui a mesuré la chute où j'ai entraîné le monde. Le lieu réel, le lieu seul situé est en moi, et voilà pourquoi l'Univers, ma conscience, veille, veille cette nuit, et me regarde. O mon Père! mon mal n'a pas nom ignorance, mais oubli. Reconduis ton enfant aux sources de la

PSALM OF REINTEGRATION

In the middle of the night, I sometimes happen to be awakened by the most perfect silence of the whole universe. It is then as if suddenly the celestial hosts, perceiving in my thought the assigned goal of their course, stopped dead above my head in order to consider me while holding their breath. As in the distant days of my childhood, all my soul reaches out towards the great voice which is preparing to summon me from the depths of created spaces. But I wait in vain, and the peace that surrounds me is so perfect only because it no longer has a name to bestow on me. It is in me and I am in it, and in that Place that is unnamed as we are too and where our union has occurred, even the most universal word, HERE, has lost its meaning for all time, since nothing has subsisted beyond us where we might still place a THERE, and the whole space in which thought breathes appears to us to be no longer something that contains, but the illuminated interior of the Cosmos, a beautiful crystal fallen out of the hands of God. Formerly, when the spirit of perfect silence seized me, I used to raise my eyes towards the suns. Today, together with their gaze, my sight goes down into my own being, for their secret is there and not within their own selves. The place where they contemplate me is the very one where I stand, and I recognize the sorrow of my own conscience in the loving reproach that is depicted on the face of the universe. The immensity engendered by the infinity of circumscribed movements cannot possibly fill the void of my soul: there exists no height that would be accessible to the extension of the Number, the moments of which are not counted by my heartbeats. This distance between Nothing and Nothing, why should I worry about it? True, I fell from a great height, but *another kind of space* measured my fall in which the whole world fell with me. The real place, the only place that is, is in me, and that is why the Universe, my conscience, watches, awakened this night, and watches me. Oh, my Father, the name of my ill is not ignorance but forgetfulness. Lead your child back to

Mémoire. Ordonne-lui de remonter le cours de son propre sang. Le mouvement de ma chute a créé l'espace-temps, cette eau qui dans l'immobile Illimité sur moi s'est refermée et pour laquelle il n'est pas en ma puissance d'imaginer un récipient. Que mon ascension projette donc l'Autre Espace, le vrai, l'originel, le sanctifié, et que l'univers que voici, le Fils de ma Douleur dont le regard nocturne est sur mon âme, avec moi s'élève vers la Patrie, dans le joyeux courant d'influences bruissantes de la béatitude dorée.

the sources of Memory. Tell your child to return, following upstream the course of his own blood. The movement of my fall created time and space, those waters which closed above me in Space that has neither motion nor limits and for which it is beyond my powers to imagine a container. Let my ascension project the Other Space, the true, original and sanctified Space, and let the Universe that is here, the Son of my Pain, whose nocturnal gaze rests on my soul, rise together with me towards the Fatherland, in the joyful stream of babbling influences of golden beatitude.

translated by Edouard Roditi

PSAUME DE L'ÉTOILE DU MATIN

Les torrents de troupeaux   descendent vers
les bergeries   l'ombre est sur An-Dor et
Pau du pays d'Esaü   sur Matred Toled Beith
Aram   sur tout Sparad de Judée   Mémoi-
re étoilée   nuit d'Israël en esprit   espace
projeté par des yeux de brebis   Lá-bas Arti-
zarra déjà brille   au front de notre Mère l'Ibérie
        son   Schouriène-Ieschouroun   s'éloigne
en cachant son visage   sous la bure de brume
        Selah   Assez bêlé au ciel salé de blan-
cheurs   allons mes lécheuses de murs   au
sel du mur des pleurs habituées   dans le che-
min de l'hysope   entre les haies amères
passez brebis du roi sous la houlette   de fer
        Blanches dix-neuf noires quarante   et
toi quarante-quatrième   nombres tracés de
main de pâtre   en bâtonnets   sur certain
mur de Beith lehem   ils sont plus nombreux
que vous là-haut   les chevreaux de la Vivante
                    de la sœur fiancée du cantique nouveau
Selah   Des cèdres de la bénédiction   la
main   est toujours aussi lente   sur nos têtes
surgie du fond des âges   dans le langage de la
mer occidentale   en vain Naphschi cherche à
surprendre   un seul mot nouveau   le même
cœur qu'au temps des pères   bat dans le bois la

The Last Poem
1936

PSALM OF THE MORNING STAR

The torrents of flocks   pour down towards
the sheepfolds   shade covers An-Dor and
Pau of the land of Esau   covers Matred Toled Beith
Aram   and all Spared of Judea   Starred
memory   Israel's night of the soul   space
projected by lambs' eyes   Down yonder Artizarra
is already shining   on the brow of our Mother Iberia
    her   Schourien-Ieschouroun   withdraws
hiding his face   beneath the sackcloth of the fog
    Selah   Enough of your bleating at the sky
salted with white specks   let us go now my wall-lickers
   to the salt of the wall of accustomed tears   on the
hyssop pathway   between the butter hedgerows   pass
lambs of the king beneath the shepherd's crook   of iron
     White nineteen black forty   and
thou forty-fourth   numbers traced by a
herdsman's hand   formed like little sticks   on some
wall of Beith lehem   they are more numerous than are
you up there   goat-kids of the Living one
   of the betrothed sister of the new canticle
Selah   The hand   of the cedars of
benediction   is still as slow   upon our heads
arisen from the depths of the ages   in the language of
the Western sea   in vain does Naphschi try to
intercept   a single new word   the same
heart as in the time of the fathers   beats in wood

pierre et l'eau				rien de tout cela qui revient
n'est nouveau				toutes ces choses dormaient
dans les livres fermés				les livres sous mes
mains se sont ouverts				passez mes belles Ju-
dith passez		bonnes filles		sous la houlette
de fer			Kimah Ksil et vous les Mazaroth
et vous les autres cieux				sans nom sans nom-
bre suspendus tout en haut				dans les grands
brouillards de Dieu				saints vieillards abaissez
vers la terre				vos regards de silex perdus voi-
lés		Aïéleth-haschahar la bergère		descend
vers Guinath Agoz				le vase de lait de lumière
sur l'épaule				elle appelle l'enfant Olel
gardien du pâturage des lions				caressé dans
son sommeil par les vipères		Selah		Voici
les choses sont ce qu'elles sont				buée des cils
	feux de pluie au bord du toit				dans le
sac du semeur poignée d'étoiles				et tes roues
qui entrent l'une dans l'autre
	Iehezkeel les terribles spirales			voici les
choses sont ce qu'elles sont				profond profond
est Cela		devant celui qui se prosterne
on se prosternera

```
stone and water                        of all that returns there is
nothing new                            all those things were sleeping
in closed books                        the books have opened themselves
beneath my hand                             pass my beauties Judith
pass               good girls                      under the iron
crook                            Kimah Ksil and you the Mazaroths
       and you the other skies          nameless innumerable
suspended aloft so high                          in the great
hazes of God                           holy old men cast down
towards the earth                        your gazes of lost and
fractured flint          Aleleth-hascahar the shepherdess
    comes down towards Guinath Agoz              the light's
jug of milk on her shoulder          she calls to the child Olel
    guardian of the lions' pasture              caressed in
his sleep by vipers          Selah            Here things
are what they are                      the eyelashes' steam
    fires of rain at the roof-edge                 in the
sower's sack handful of stars                and thy wheels
entering one into the other
    Iehezkeel the terrible spirals          behold how here
things are what they are              deep profoundly deep
is That    he who bows down low
will be bowed down to
                                    *translated by David Gascoyne*
```

PART TWO

The Metaphysical Works

ARS MAGNA

1924

TRANSLATED BY CZESLAW MILOSZ

to Renaissance

FOREWORD

Epistle to Storge, the first part of *Ars Magna*,[1] was composed in 1916 and published in the January 1917 issue of *La Revue de Hollande*.

At that time the author knew neither of Einstein's theories nor even the great mathematician's name. Yet, by a coincidence which is striking enough to merit the attention of men of science, the *Epistle*, the fruit of essentially metaphysical meditations on movement, contains all the general conclusions which have been drawn from Einstein's theory by its commentators; space, identified with matter, is presented here as a solid, time as its fourth dimension and the Universe as a limitless but finite body, the components of which can be situated only through a relationship binding them to each other.

In the four poems that follow *Epistle to Storge*—*Memoria, Numbers, Turba Magna* and *Lumen*—the author develops his thesis from a biological and mystical point of view, linking it to hermetic doctrines as well as to Pythagorean philosophy.

Notes for *Ars Magna* and *The Arcana* begin on page 401.

1
Epistle to Storge

ONE summer day in the year nineteen hundred and sixteen, as I lay stretched out not far from you, Storge Androgyne,[2] on the dazzling shore of a sea less vast, less perfidious and less multiform than my pain, suddenly, and deep inside myself, I heard your voice questioning me: But what, after all, is all this? What does all this want of us? Then I fell into deep meditation, and truths were revealed to me, and the inner meaning of many an ancient vision offered itself without a veil to the omniscience of my love.

From the first to the last movement of our physical and mental life, Storge, every thing in this natural world, where we are for a few days, may be traced back to a unique necessity to situate. Truly, we bring into nature neither space nor time, but only our body's movement and the knowledge, or rather the awareness and love, of that movement, an awareness and love which we call Thought, and which is at the origin of our first and fundamental ability to situate all things, beginning with ourselves. Space and time seem to have been prepared long in advance to receive us. Yet all our anxieties come from our need to situate this very space and time; and the mental operation by which, for lack of another imaginable place or container, we assign to space and time a place in themselves, multiplying and dividing them endlessly, does not in the least diminish these terrible anxieties—these anxieties of love, Storge, which pursue us to the very confines of the Valley of the Shadow of Death.

The obscure feeling which accompanies our first fearful appearance in Nature can only resemble the one that sometimes seizes us so brutally when we awaken with a start from deep and dreamless afternoon torpors at the height of summer. Oblivion of time and place then throws us into fright and nameless sadness, and the real cause of that indefinable oppression is not the numbness of our perception, but rather this need, the first and most tyrannical of all, to situate everything in a space and in a time.

It could be said of the compulsion to situate all things (including the space and time in which we situate them) that it is the first of our life's mental manifestations. Certainly there is no thought and no emotion which does not derive from this essential activity of being. The first movements of our mind, in becoming aware of the surrounding world, are blindly subject to it. Later, in geometry and the natural sciences, we find it again with the same domineering features; its rule extends to the most extreme abstractions of philosophy, religion, morality and art; good, evil, love, conflicts of truth and falsehood, openness to Revelation, forgetfulness, the state of innocence, inspiration—all our spiritual progeny claim from us their heritage of marvellous lands and receive it; and the same ancient necessity to situate all things extends its sovereignty over those delightful or dismal regions: the East of the Ancients, the Hells, Saana,[3] Armageddon, the Patmos of Boanerges,[4] Lethe, Arcadia, Parnassus—and others, and yet an infinite number of others.

With my first thought I ascertain my movement and, while doing this, I already situate things in space and time; with my second thought, I make an effort to embrace—hence to situate—the very space and time in which I have set all things. And then I notice that my two extreme notions of the natural world, that of the infinitely great and that of the infinitely small, derive directly from this compulsion I am under to situate all things in a safe place. For, since an object can be situated only in relation to another object, my incurable ignorance of a correspondence between space and time leads me to assign them a sort of place in themselves by extending both of them to infinity. And my aversion to stopping at an indivisible unity comes from the same necessity to situate at any cost: for a last divisible thing still needs some place, and it cannot find one except in that divisibility into halves which I assume to be without extension.

My idea of matter, the foundation of all natural ideas, is thus inseparably united with the appearance of situation, which my purely theoretical ability to multiply and divide to infinity permits me to assign to time and space. Take away from my brain this love of movement and this frenzy of rhythm, and you will at the same time take away the idea of matter. For, if I stop multiplying and dividing to infinity, I lose all notion of the place in which I find myself, I no longer situate or imagine the natural world in itself, as I did before, by multiplying and dividing. The result is that once you take away the eternal retreat of limits in the immense and the infinitesimal, you take away everything, including the idea of matter.

But, you say, we have nothing to do here with matter; multiplication and division to infinity apply only to space and time. Certainly, but time, space and matter are given to us not separately, but as a single unit in the law of movement. Many thinkers, undoubtedly in a false spirit of simplification, have attempted to separate the image of the contained from the image of the container, or the idea of limited matter from that of limitless expanse. Some of them have even pushed their childish daring so far as to divide irreducible infinite space into two parts, one of which, in their view, would harbor cosmic matter and the other the "outer darkness" alone. They have left us limitless space and have rationed matter for us, seeming to believe that the infinite of the one is more easily conceivable than the infinite of the other. Great minds and fertile imaginations have run headlong into this trap. I cannot elucidate here the profound reasons for this aberration. They are spiritual and would constitute too long a digression in this letter devoted entirely to matter. I will only remark that the empty space conceived of by those who believe in a finite universe, forms, together with its filled particle of space, but a single, unlimited whole, since any interruption of this expanse, besides being unthinkable, would itself be an additional space. The infinite, however—the most extreme and eternally fleeting result of theoretical multiplications and divisions—remains stable in all operations; for, whatever the multiplier, the product is infinite, and the same applies to the quotient, whatever divisor is chosen; for no specific quotient multiplied by the divisor would restore an infinite dividend. This is to say, generally speaking, that the infinite has no parts, or, to make the terms agree with those of the "Eureka" proposition, that every part of the infinite is infinite in itself. For space, considered as a container and happening to be a particle of infinite, supposedly empty space, is infinite in itself, and thus the world of matter is infinite; or, to speak less presumptuously, our human picture of the universe of matter is indeed the concept of a universe of unlimited matter.

In *Conjugial Love and Its Pure Delights, Divine Love and Wisdom, The True Christian Religion* and *The Apocalypse Revealed*, the father of modern science,[5] the conciliator of reason and faith, indulges in remembering the terrors he experienced in his youth when he considered the creation of space and time; and thereby he seems to recognize that in his mind the creation of time and space preceded that of matter. But the idea of matter does not follow from that of space and time. Everything is given as a whole in Movement; there is absolute simultaneity and identity. And, whenever we meditate on the subject of universal matter, we should be careful to avoid, as far as possible, the troubling image of interstellar spaces. These expanses, considered in relation to the infinity of describable material things, or even in relation to the immensity of the part of the sidereal sky offered to our observation, are nothing but interatomic spaces; and as soon as we situate them in the universal immeasurable, they become pure appearance. In our poor astronomical sky I know of two particularly brilliant stars, two faithful confidantes, beautiful and pure, which I believed to be separated from their friends by unimaginable distances. And yet, the other evening, as a great moth fell from the lamp upon my hand, I had the tender curiosity to question its blazing eyes . . .

The unlimited is the enemy of subterfuge. It calls for the wisdom of total affirmation or the folly of absolute negation. I am free to assign boundaries to matter as long as I situate an object only in relation to another object in a spatial arrangement or orientation. But as soon as I assume an absolute totality of matter, I no longer have an object to place in opposition to another and in a describable space; I must assign it a place in the immeasurable, in what I call pure space; and there, all determination disappears. Once it is assigned mentally to that pure space the most infinitesimal part of matter fills up the infinity of extension.

Now thought or the act by which we situate all things is at its origin only the knowledge or, as we defined it earlier, only the awareness and love of movement; it is therefore indissolubly united to the movement of the universe. Even the fixity of those bodies which we call inanimate is only apparent, since it is closely associated with the movement particular to surrounding objects and worlds; for everything that is a body is a body of universal matter, and that matter is inseparable from the movement of describable space. Owing to the simultaneity of movement and our awareness, an obscure feeling of the universality of that movement should already have filled us during those epochs when, in relation to the sun, the earth was considered as a fixed center; and Copernicus' discoveries, like all other human discoveries, are perhaps only mathematical confirmations of an immemorial, intuitive knowledge delayed by the immutability of appearance, or stifled by some religious scruple, similar to that which, in Christianity, grew out of the literal interpretation of a purely spiritual passage of

Scripture. This prescience of universal movement has undoubtedly also favored the progress of contemporary electrodynamics. When I situate, therefore, in a describable expanse, an object A in relation to an object B, I simply determine the line of a movement A in opposition to that of a movement B. Yet, since we have established the identity of pure space and matter, we now know that this describable expanse or spatial arrangement and orientation is the infinite itself. What remains is to examine the links connecting this infinity of matter with our laws of movement, constantly keeping in mind that what we concluded about space applies with the same accuracy to time; for awareness of movement is the origin of thought, and movement is not only united to time by an indissoluble bond, but to whoever ponders it lovingly, it also appears as the very matter of duration. Movement may also be defined as a point where the two parallel lines of time and space intersect in the limitless; for by recognizing the similarity of limitless matter and limitless expanse we recognize also that the infinite and the eternal are identical.

To situate a body in a describable expanse means to evaluate and circumscribe its movement in relation to the movement of some other body. But we have identified the expanse offered to our experience with the infinity of matter imposed on our reason; hence it would seem to follow most naturally that the same law of movement ought to govern both the unlimited and the describable. And such, in fact, is the case, as long as we apply this law to universal matter considered as an infinity of spatial expanses similar to that expanse in which we situate one body in relation to another. These expanses, at least in our representation of them, are closely joined one with another. But as soon as we abandon this notion of an infinity of spatial arrangements and pass on to the idea of a single infinity, which is therefore unsituated by opposition to another, the law loses its universality and the limitless is revealed to our reason in its terrifying majesty of *absolute repose.* This latter, as far as our argument now goes, should be understood in a double sense, as an infinity of describable things taken together and as the single infinite. For, whether we choose a body within a describable expanse and attempt to situate it in relation to the movement of an infinity of bodies, or whether, instead, we choose a describable space—for example, the sidereal sky as a whole—and attempt to situate it in opposition to the movement of an infinity of other describable spaces, whatever our efforts may be, in either case movement is immediately lost without ever encountering place. As to the infinity of matter considered as a single absolute whole, we cannot in any way imagine it in flux since it is limitless both as the container and as the contained. In short, the movement and the location of matter are purely relative: real, in a human sense, as long as there is a relationship between bodies; unreal, in the absolute sense, as soon as we situate matter in the infinite.

The spiral ENS,[6] the first simple ingredient, the first movement, the first point of nature, genetrix of an infinity of mobile things, is thus, too, only a mental modification, a certain purely internal state of love proper to Divinity, for it breaks the immobility of Essence only to fall back upon the immobility of Manifestation. For the sake of greater clarity, let me then compare the infinity of matter to the immobile image which Beauty, that enemy of "movement which displaces lines,"[7] would lovingly contemplate in a faithful mirror.

And so Movement, this origin and this end of our thought, Movement, this mystical companion in service who has followed us through the infinity of describable moving things, Movement vanishes at the very mention of the Infinite. And what is more natural? For how can we imagine the concerted movement of the totality of matter, which, by definition, already fills an unlimited space, and realizes it in some fashion, or—better still—embodies itself in the infinity of extension? And yet the absolute immobility of the whole of this single and perfect body, composed of an infinity of particles in motion, is martyrdom for thought. Because thought is that act by which we situate all things in a safe place through awareness and love of movement, while immobility means not only a lack of movement but also a negation of place.

We have called thought an awareness and love of movement. To this word, love, the ignorance and coarseness of the epochs which separate us from the Middle Ages have given many puerile or irreverent meanings, and even those minds that are the least false in these horrible times—times of expiation in which we have the misfortune to live—do not seem to wish to express with it anything other than passion, pleasure or curiosity. But such is not the meaning that I attach to this august, enchanting, and terrifying word, I who take pride in writing with the soul of words. For me, love always means the eternal feminine divine of Alighieri and Goethe, angelic sentiment and sexuality, virginal maternity, wherein are blended, as in a fiery crucible, the adramandonic of Swedenborg, the hesperic of Hölderlin, and the elysian of Schiller[8]: the perfect human harmony formed by the attracting wisdom of the bridegroom and the amorous gravitation of the bride, the true spiritual situation of the one with respect to the other, an essential arcanum so terrible and so beautiful that since I have penetrated it I have been unable to speak of it without shedding a torrent of tears—a terrifying and muted tenderness that, from the first note to the last and, perhaps without the composer's knowledge, haunts and enflames all the music of Richard Wagner, so little understood until today. In its most universal meaning, finally, love is the orphic intuition that teaches us to pour out the superabundance of our movement into the fraternal heart of a stone; to animate the most humble body, to put it in its place and time with that delicate tenderness and that loving infallibility which permits us to situate, in a safe place and in its own time, word and sound in a poem, muscle and step in a dance, tone and accent in speech, the governing line of motion and life in sculpture, the first as well as the last vibration of color in painting, and, in architecture, stone and beam in harmonious and logical distribution of effort. Rhythm is the highest earthly expression of what we call thought, that is, of the awareness and love of Movement.

Here, then, fixed in a few rapid strokes, is the spiritual meaning I attach to the essential word love, the eternal word and the first of all cries. But how to reconcile the sublime love of movement which incessantly makes matter, so harmonious and beautiful, run in circles through describable spaces, yes, how to reconcile this immense love, this art, this science and this universal faith, with the unimaginable immobility of infinite pure matter? For our love needs matter in motion and matter extensible to infinity, and reason offers us precisely matter that can be so extended, although animated only with the mental rhythm by which we extend it. Thus, whatever motion it has and, consequently, whatever site it occupies, pure matter—despite its reality as something describable identified with the infinite—possesses nothing but what is given to it by our purely theoretical power of multiplying and dividing without end, and an eternally unsatisfied creation of rhythms.

Over there, I know not where, the immobile Limitless: neither movement nor place; something, I don't know what, which is the totality of everything there is, of everything I know and of everything I have yet to learn; the container of every real or imaginable place and yet a non-situated container; that towards which I go, towards which all the movement of the infinity of describable things rushes. And what is it? what is it, indeed? An absolute of immobility which surpasses my reason and yet not to such a degree that my reason is unable to grasp some attribute of it; and what I can grasp is precisely unimaginable immobility. Over here—but what does it mean, O Storge, this word "here"?—weak reason, unsatisfied and rebellious, and an immense love: a love that nothing can satisfy, that nothing can appease; a pious love of limitless matter in eternal motion, a universal frenzy of Rhythm.

And let us be careful, Storge, not to lose sight of what preoccupies us now. It is neither the spiritual mystery of affinities, nor our mystical and affective life, nor the unknown into whose depth we must all fall tomorrow; for we are discussing only the matter which we are, which surrounds us and which we will be during the long, long years in the grave. This table supporting my elbow, the ink pot into which I dip this pen, propose to my brain, which is all movement, the insoluble problem: Son of man, I have not where to lay my head. No place; and certainly it would be of little avail to know whence I have come and whither I am going, since I do not know where I am, and yet I am, I who love! For all the rest is vanity, smoke, shadow. But you, Storge, you who are for me both movement and place, and I, your bridegroom in this space, in this matter which is already infinity and in this measurable time which is already eternity, we, we are. You, Storge and I, we are; and perhaps it is my folly or my intoxication, but within this indefinite unsituated universe I know one safe place where reason does not sink, and that place is my love; also just one movement, and this movement is an untiring and empty multiplication and division to infinity, an incessant superposition of spaces and times, spiritual sister of endless multiplication, that eternally unsatisfied poem. For science will never determine the real location of any existing body; but each body is situated in a safe place with regard to omniscience, and omniscience is love. However, when considered from our human point of view, this purely mystical determination of place surpasses our understanding and feeling, and it would be folly to look for proofs of the earthly reality of our life other than in the recognition that the matter which clothes us and surrounds us is absolutely identical to that in which all-powerful Love humbled Himself during the years of the Incarnation.

Where nothing is situated, there is no passage from one place to another, only from one state—which is a state of love—to another; and that is why love laughs at life and death. I do not like the adepts' theory of the astral body, nor do I like the concept of spiritual worlds advanced by Swedenborg. All those people who are poor in love know perhaps, obscurely, that nothing is situated; yet they need a movement and a place at any price; and, animating what is not there, they situate in nothing. Try as they may to tell us that their substantial worlds are alien to time and space, and that place is only appearance in them or even that all reality is the instantaneous creation and correspondence of a mental state, nevertheless one feels that, since they are still constrained by the law of movement, they situate their immateriality in a place determined by its opposition to matter. So difficult is it to break completely our habit of situating A in relation to B, a habit ingrained in our most abstract ways of thinking. Spiritualist doctrine, for fear of losing its balance, is careful, even when most hostile to materialism, not to deprive matter of its movement, thereby driving it from its place: for how can one assign a place to a spiritual world, even outside space and time, if one does not situate it in opposition to the idea of an already established matter?

But you, Storge, you know now that this matter which we thought was infinite is an absolute of immobility, and that it is not situated except in regard to omniscient Love. And you know also that our thought, our life in describable space, O Storge, is no more than an awareness and love of movement, and that the supreme expression of that love, in science, is multiplication and division of the infinite by the infinite; and, in art, rhythm that ceaselessly springs forth and is eternally unsatisfied. The moment has then come, O earthly tenderness, to remove this antinomy by unveiling to you the highest arcanum of universal Love, as it was revealed to me, to me your bridegroom, as I meditated with my head against the sand on the sunlit shore.

Where nothing is situated, there is no passage from one place to another, Storge, only from one state—which is a state of love—to another. In the present state of our tenderness we endlessly multiply and divide, and we abandon ourselves to the furious torrent of rhythm, and nothing satisfies us. But we will die, Storge, and we will enter into that blessed state where multiplication, division, and rhythm, constantly unsatisfied, find the supreme absolute number and the immutable perfect ending of every poem. This is the second love, Storge; this is the Elysium of the Master Goethe, the Empyrean of the great Alighieri, the Adramandoni of the good Swedenborg, the Hesperia of unlucky Hölderlin. It is here already—but what does this word "here" mean, O Storge?—yes, and it is spread throughout universal matter, throughout matter which is infinite and hence deprived of movement and place. Happy is he who is endowed with the spirit of affirmation and who discovers, even here, that sure and single reality, the island of Patmos, land of beatitude, where the fulfillment of mental movement corresponds to the immobility of infinite matter! Because another state of love, a third, has been revealed to me, to me with my unfortunate spirit of pride, rebellion and negation. There, multiplication and division to infinity vainly attempt to fill a black and atrocious eternity of terror, and an insatiable, sacrilegious, infernal rhythm carries one off like a piece of straw in the whirl and din of the chaos of expiation. My dear child, I have visited both of these realms, and here is the faithful account of my journey.

On the fourteenth of December, nineteen hundred and fourteen, at about eleven o'clock in the evening, in a state of perfect wakefulness, having said my prayer and meditated my daily verse from the Bible, I suddenly felt, without the slightest amazement, a completely unexpected change occurring in my whole body. At first I noticed that I was granted a power, until that day unknown, of soaring freely through space; and a moment later I found myself near the summit of a mighty mountain shrouded with bluish mists of indescribable fineness and sweetness. From this moment on, I was spared the effort of rising with my own movement. For the mountain, tearing its roots out of the earth, carried me rapidly towards unimaginable heights, towards nebulous regions silent and streaked by immense flashes of lightning. This singular ascent, however, did not last long. Soon all movement ceased and not far from my forehead I saw a very dense and heavy cloud, which, despite its slightly coppery tinge, I compared to the freshly discharged seed of man. Above the top of my skull, a little to the rear, a glow then appeared like that of a torch reflected by still water or an old mirror. During the rapid succession of these images all my senses remained as awake as they are at this moment while I write; but I felt neither dread nor curiosity nor amazement. An instant later, from regions which I knew were far behind me, a sort of gigantic and reddish egg shot forth; hurled with extraordinary force into space, it reached the line of my forehead in an instant; and there, suddenly changing its movement and color, it became round and small, turned into a golden lamp, lowered itself until it brushed my face, climbed again, grew in size, recovered its oval shape of an angelic sun, stopped not far above my forehead and looked deeply into my eyes. And under this seraphic star a plain of vaporous gold, of the gold of Sheba,[9] enrapturing my sight, stretched out to the boundaries of this country of love. Then a perfect, absolute immobility overtook sun and clouds, giving me the inexpressible sensation of a supreme accomplishment, of a definitive calm, of a complete halt to all mental operations, of a superhuman realization, of the final Rhythm. The letter H[10] was added to my name; I tasted peace, yes, Storge, Storge! I tasted—I!—a sacred peace, there was no longer any trace of anxiety or pain in my head, I was a priest of the order of Melchizedek.[11] Alas! this eternal and very brief vision disappeared; I found myself again in my unbearable quarters; but powerful wings, or, to be more exact, invisible elytra, which I guessed to be immense, fanned me with an enchanting rustling, and murmurs fraternal and compassionate, interlaced with the strange sounds of a lute, questioned me in an unknown tongue. My extremely vivid memory of that change of state which occurred in the midst of undisturbed physical life and perfectly clear consciousness is now mixed with an obscure feeling that my moral preparation was not yet adequate to the importance of the phenomenon and that the beautiful sun of Sheba was itself no more than a veil, a last veil, perhaps, which in my unworthiness I did not dare to lift.

Not long afterward I was granted the grace of visiting my true spiritual homeland. This second journey took place under conditions very different from those of the first; for, far from feeling myself, as in the preceding expedition, in perfect command of my physical and mental faculties, as soon as the dangerous influx seized me I found myself plunged into a very profound slumber. Jeremiah, in Chapter XXIII of his book, establishes a most precise distinction between the first state of pure vision or apocalyptic Patmos, and the second, which is that of receptivity in the depths of sleep. A vast expanse of dark lakes,[12] greenish and putrescent, overgrown by a riot of sad yellow pond lilies, opened suddenly to my sight. Over these waters, stagnant and desolate as the eyes of paralytics, an iron bridge had been thrown. It had a hideous shape and a frightening length, and, at one end, after millions of years of travel, there spread before my eyes a landscape whose infernal, deadly melancholy I will not attempt to express. It was an immense, deserted plain enclosed by a hostile, silent circle of high and watchful mountains. Loneliness without escape, immutable condemnation, utter forsakenness, and in all this satanic immensity there was not even an inch of ground not covered, to the point of suffocation, by yellow, ashy, repugnant grass which, though it was as high as a bush, I compared to the rust-colored and diseased moss that eats away old gravestones. Evening fell. Then a universe of terror, billions and billions of times more vast, more crowded and more scintillating than our sidereal sky, lit up above my head, and the movement of these tormented cosmic systems, visible to the naked eye, was accompanied by an odious criminal noise, the enemy of all meditation, of all composure. And the secret meaning of all this movement and of all this din was: you must multiply and divide the infinite by the infinite during an eternity of eternities; neither rest nor remembrance for you, nor love, nor hope; multiply, multiply, divide, divide; these worlds will disintegrate into chaos, and you will replace them by others; but you will always be here, always at this same place, and you will multiply and divide. Eternally you will feel the last number, the supreme sound, the final syllable of this excruciating rhythm at the tip of your tongue and, miserable victim of your own iniquity, ridiculous plaything of your own scientific pride, you will make desperate efforts to throw away the last number, to spit it out, to vomit it up. In vain. It will fade away from your feeble memory and you will fall back into infinite calculating, into the whirlwind of eternal rhythm. Then, in the depths of my dread and at the height of my distress, I exclaimed: "Where is the Master of this land? Where is the King of this horrible Kingdom of Aven? Let him appear! He will understand me, he will shelter me under his black, cold wing, he will love me, he will save me; for if there is a creature touched by love in this infinity of pain, of terror and forsakenness, it can only be the fallen Prince of these Kingdoms!"

Billions of ghastly stellar glances were concentrated on my face. Demonic laughter brightened the face of the eternal Shifter: "The morning star searches for THE MORNING STAR, the son of man calls the SON OF MAN. Everything is fulfilled. Everything is fulfilled." May the Divine, deaf to my black prayers, listen, O Storge, to yours.

2

Memoria

> ... It will fade away from your feeble *Memory* and you will fall back into infinite calculating.   EPISTLE TO STORGE

THIS is born of love for the Abyss, this is the Ars Magna, and it contains all the sacred poetry of Science. You who, in centuries to come, will read these pages with a filial respect for their author and with unspeakable scorn for the epoch which saw their birth, remember that *Memoria* is the key to the *Epistle to Storge,* and that this epistle, wherein ever since the year 1916 the metaphysical secret of Relativity has been unveiled to you, is the new gate to the palace of the union of fountains. Come, then, bring your ear closer to my brow and listen. My head is like the stone of cosmic crossroads and of cosmic torrents. Here, huge, black, hushed chariots of Meditation will pass. Then there will be terror as at the overflowing of primordial waters. And everything will be Silence. And from a place that has never been reached by a message from any earth, I shall fathom this placeless eternity that opens within me in mute cataclysm. For space, time, and matter are enclosed within this unfathomable but tangible unity which our inner Movement, blood and spirit—not to name it at the outset *blood's thinking*—creates within us and projects across our walled-up eye. This language has already revealed to you who I am. Yes, my child, I am the one that I am, I am the one who knows, and I am the one who speaks, subject to a measure. Learn from me, then, O son of a time in which I shall be understood and loved, that from alpha to omega all this poem, Crown of the two Testaments, concerns the approaching dawn of the Sun of Memory. The knowledge of the primordial substance sleeps in us, in the darkness of our pride, like gold under the weight of mountains. Deprived of its median vision, our science is miserly; what it throws to us from outside, like a bone, century after century, is only an obscure correspondence of a teaching whose light fills the inside of our holy house of clay. Something of our first father undoubtedly subsists in us; generations proceed from a single Movement and this Movement is the unalterable matter of space and time. What did Storge teach you? That immobility is not only an absence of movement, but also a negation of place (consequently of space, of time, and of matter). Memoria adds: Everything that is Movement is blood. Movement is One, because it is space and time apprehended in matter; matter is thus One, like that by which it is matter; and by what is it matter, if not by Movement? Now, if matter is unity, in what Movement other than that of blood shall we look for reality, the sole and only place? The entire secret of Manifestation resides in the transmission through blood, the celestial fiat, of a Movement in which space, matter, and time are identical. Physically, the entire cosmos runs in us; but although the primordial sea—the sea which was one of our first habitats and whose breathing still regulates that of our heart—remembers, we, we have forgotten. The roots of our physical being penetrate so far into the illusory mass of the globe, that it is easier to preach the truth to trees and rocks than to make people grasp that matter, space and time are identical in Movement, or to convince them of the need to abandon the childish concept of an eternity of succession, divided into past, present and future, and to adopt instead the concept of simultaneity, or rather instantaneity, whose imperfect image would be rotation at infinite speed. Thus our blood perpetuates the instant of the first emission, and all the consciousness of the spiritual propellent is still in it, always ready to unveil itself progressively to those minds which, armed with the magic weapon of prayer, have regained the absolute place of Affirmation. All cosmic blood is still in the impetus of the first ejaculation; blood, the first mover, teaches us how to situate all spatial things in Movement alone, and all temporal things in instantaneity alone. This is the secret of the Old Masters and the celestial origin of their double concept of the unity of matter and of the identity of the two worlds.[13] Once I had accepted transmutation as a fundamental principle, the progress of my work beyond theirs had to be limited to a simple extension, for after Boehme, Sendivogius, and Paracelsus,[14] all that remained for me was to identify matter with time and space and, having thus caught all three in Movement, to expel Movement itself from its place (which, as I have recently learned and reveal here, is blood) so that everything falls back into that immobile instantaneity of the Sun of Memory. Unfamiliar as I was with mathematics, by publishing in January 1917 my *Epistle to Storge* I was only a metaphysical precursor of the General Theory of Relativity, about which I then knew nothing and which I would welcome, a few years later, less as the corroboration of twenty years of my own thinking on matter, time and space, than as the dawn of a new and marvellous era of the spirit. It is of little importance that I was not understood by the wretched and egoistic mentality of my contemporaries; for, to tell the truth, I so liked the solitude of my promontory, and the Sun of Memory let me know such inner wealth, that I would blush to see in my discovery anything other than a very old hermetic secret inherited, with the movement of blood, from my ancestors, the sovereigns of Lusatia. Question, my dear child, that blood which, because of its consistency and its color, appears to you to be made of such a heavenly substance; enter its spiritual flow, grasp it in its tragic pulsation and come to tell me whether insanity or wisdom compels me to defend its glory here. You will find in it the warmth and the impetus of fathomless instantaneity; it will tell you of what fidelities and of what rebellions it is the magnificent jousting field; it will reveal to you its thousand poisons and its one remedy; it will explain to you the femininity of Manifestation, and how Eve was drawn from Adam, and why, carried by the rhythm of the first emission, every urge of intellectual creativity not sustained by prayer leads to a repudiation of the procreative act. Finally, it will unveil to you the secret of universal transmutation, for it is the Alchemist who hides the bread and wine of the Last Supper under his robe of rubies. The sun of our memory is only darkened, and everything will be restored to us with the secret of blood, as Relativity brings science back to its heavenly sources. For this blood, essence of Movement and universal rhythm, is the container, the foundation, in short is the place of the simultaneity and instantaneity of time, space, and matter. What a pity that I cannot introduce you into the secret chambers, the gynaeceum of virginal Creation! Alas! To talk and to write, what miserable charity! Because talking and writing are not a communion; they only offer a subject for meditation. And meditation itself is only an anxious and feeble effort of our memory; for the most secret place of all is within us, and our crown is that of the three kingdoms. This is why, when the spirit of the earth says: "subconscious," then I, in the only situated place, write: the Sun of Memory. *Memoria*, I repeat, is the golden key of *Storge* and is itself the gate that you will open wide to the rivers of the paradise of times to come. Reread the bountiful *Epistle* and you will know what the human memory contains. For, mystically, what does Storge say? "I, who could never watch a pebble, taken from the road, drop from my hand without something secret in myself breaking, as if two hearts had split apart, I was the first, I, Storge, to have understood this: that the holy pebble of the road is the indivisible and unfathomable unity of space, time and movement. For matter, space, time and movement have fallen from the situated Place in a single stone of testimony. This is the fundamental arcanum, understand it well; because each initial reality asks for the humility of a body and the trial of a life, and this for the purpose of adoration; because the goal of all things is in the act of adoration. Such is the celestial spirit of Movement, the house of time, matter, and space." And what does the confidant of Storge who is speaking to you, add to this discourse? Simply the following: "This Movement, this wind which drives non-situated systems towards the Place, this Movement is within us, it is our blood." Now, my child, be attentive to what is going to follow. When you possess a thing, is it really the thing which you possess or only the inner affirmation by which you represent yourself as possessor? Yet your blood, which you possess in instantaneity as no husband ever possessed his spouse, your blood, my child, which is primordial Movement, space, time, matter, your blood and its secret, you have ceased to possess them in spirit. The initial possession through simultaneity is there; but what help would this be without heroic Affirmation? The folly of pride is to elevate the smallest booty above the whole gift; and, even if liberality is acknowledged, to ascribe it to the unknown rather than to the father. Listen, my child, I shall never tire of saying it again and again: the whole universe runs in you and, with its wonderful aureole, lights up the head of Him who is omnipresent. It is your blood, your blood which is like primordial water; it remembers in submission, it operates in love. Therefore, nourish your blood with the wheat of affirmation, O my son; do not sustain it only with the fruits of your orchard made bitter by the sweat of your brow. What have you done, what have you done, my child, to forget what your blood, that celestial clepsydra, remembers. Come nearer, open to me at least your conscience, so that I may transmute the lead of your humility into gold. And since we have named the Aliment, pronounce aloud with me these words which I prescribe to you: Blessed may You be, O Bread and Wine, children of the earth and heaven, who throw me into a holy and fecund exaltation after each meal that I take, I, a traveller, in this inn. Be blessed, O Bread, O Wine, in the unity of this blood, of this

Movement and of this space, for ever and ever. Amen. But I do not know if you have understood me well. Your blood, your blood I tell you, is the *fiat* that, even before the cosmic blossoming, received the first imprint of movement, for the sole purpose of clothing with a physical container—thus with a simple appearance of place—the indivisible concept of matter-space-time, that is man himself in the perfection of his humility. This beautiful solar humility having been darkened by the volcanic breath of pride—how can it be, you will ask, my child, that this blood of blindness is willing to describe across the immense uselessness of things its two admirable circles, the great and the small? But that, my son, is exactly what men who have created God and the Universe call instinct and the instinct of self-preservation, and what we, in the only situated Place, know as the Sun of Memory. For this cosmic blood, this *fiat* of movement-space-time-matter, is nothing other than the imprint of a Place which exists as the begetter and the sole refuge of all places circumscribed by relationship, not only in the relation between points A and B, but also by its own reality in our power of affirmation. Do you understand, do you feel now to what an extent your blood and you have become strangers to one another? Let me tell you with as much tact as possible. That your own blood, which is the master of your most profound secret, should travel anxiously in atrocious darkness, let us not dwell on it. But, as soon as the blood of your spouse, whom you love with a holy furor, carries you away in its elysian torrent, you feel like a blind man who crosses a bridge and perceives only the scent and the breathing of the river. For your love gathers from the mystical effusion only an external testimony, including some manifestations of touch, which is an illusion, and of speech, which is false; while the perfect union, the alchemical fusion of which the infant himself is only an ephemeral and tangible signature, occurs beyond the reach of your median eye covered with the nocturnal film of pride, the murderer of all that would endure. Most certainly you will leave this world of corrupted stones, your spouse and you, just as you entered it, in Separation, without ever having been the harmonious chord of a harp; there will be sadness and impurity for the couple in the Gardens; and before your own eyes, from the soles of your feet to the top of your skull, there will be red phalli gripped by the quivering of secret gates and consumed by a delight in that false mental fidelity which, even in the sacrament emptied of its light, comes to inflame and torture the beast of betrayal. And yet, if you are a father, bless creation, for your still virgin spouse has perhaps loved her child in you. Here I am revealing to you a terrifying secret, but you are an inhabitant of the solar Future, a century of Relativity has already passed and the reign of the new spirit begins. After all, is there any beauty more tormenting than that of an angel who troubles the waters? The indestructible marriage brings forth movement towards the situated place, *Magnum Compositum*, whose active virtue still struggles through the terrors of spiritual eclipse; and the proof of this is the help given to an impure science by counterpoisons extracted from blood—timid signs of hope, memories and forerunners of spiritual Magnificence. The fire of omniscience smoulders alike in animal blood, in the nutritive sap of our sisters the plants, and, in general, in the three substances of the terrestrial whole which we have carried along in our fall. Imagine then that the star of Memory has risen, its radiance terrible but also kindly, with an almost feminine gold—ah! how we run, you and I, to greet in their holy language a lizard, a stone, and a nettle! Such, my child, is the fundamental Arcanum; but to set your heart at ease I am going to tell you the same things again in gentle images. Movement, Blood—Love, since at last we must name it—does not travel at all as sight does, in a straight line from creature to creature. It describes a marvellous curve like the path of a rainbow and, gushing out from a heart in order to fall back into a heart, it goes through the great balsamic heart of the Master, his feet of Light on snowdrops of paradisiac freshness. The love of a couple, my poor child, is the fruit of two ingrafted prayers. But have I not spoken to you about the femininity of Manifestation? And you yourself, could you remain insensible to the charm of this water strewn with billions of stellar water lilies? My son, O my son! On this misguided earth where stone waits with a holy patience until you tell it that it is alive, but where Adam grows weary of everything, even of the power to be one with God, my child, my child, have you never heard the perfect hour of the universe resounding in yourself? Listen, I invoke very ancient days; matter, space, and time were still like islands scattered on a tempered sea, all the golden galleys of the firmament lay at anchor in the ancient haven of immobility, man's thought floated peacefully in transparence without asking itself where this universal water was situated, and wise men were already disassociating themselves from God, although with a smile, because when God disappeared, a Place and a Haven still remained—my child, my child, I invoke very ancient days, and nevertheless I am seized by the *dread of reality*! That was a scorching night of the second equinox and I was alone in the silence of the total light of the world; for Renaissance, my Spouse, slept at the feet of the throne on terraces suspended between two immense sheets of dew, one above and one below, the stellar and the terrestrial. And as I contemplated her, the Sleeper enveloped in the fire of night, she appeared to me, across the distance of sleep, remote as a constellation. And yet I felt her in myself, more sweetly and more terribly in myself than ever. With the ray of a sun which had set long ago, she was descending into the most silent depths of my life, into that abyss where recollection and premonition are one. And suddenly I felt her completely inside me and my own, and as if transmuted into the beauty of the universe. What compassion then took hold of me at the sight of that entire cosmos below! I lost even the notion of what was external—love became charity again, and I felt my own blood running through all creation, and the manifestation of Being appeared to me in its feminine form and light. Thus the Conjugial Arcanum was unveiled to me. And then, in immense Instantaneity, I was crowned by the glorious Fire, the Sun of Memory, the gate of the only situated Place, the tomb of Numbers, palace of secret encounters with myself. My child, reread the *Epistle to Storge*. And remember that one must cherish beings and things: for all this, from stone to Christ, and from Christ to the Father, all this is your blood. Sun or atom, all movement is life and love, creation of space-time-matter. These are not grains cast there by a sower's hand, not at all! There is only blood, blood which runs by its own movement.

3

Numbers

... Sun of Memory, gate of the only situated place, tomb of Numbers ...   MEMORIA

BLOOD is the standard of metaphysical values. Space, time and matter are given to you in the instantaneity not only of knowledge but also of simple awareness by universal Movement, which is the *fiat*, that is, the projection of your blood beyond the Place. This blood, this cosmos, workman of your flesh, the perfect and only mover, is a sum of manifest energies. Wholly luminous and still smoking with the tint of its sun, attached likewise to the curative gold that it carries, blood surely offers us a living image of the original Unity symbolized on the pectoral by a ruby. In the physical order, however, blood is the act itself of dividing into two and it already needs, as Christ does, two eyes in order to see itself, while mnemonic sight turned towards the Place emits only a single ray. Blood is thus the second person; and if you have followed me attentively through the deductions of *The Epistle of Storge* and of *Memoria*, you will already have grasped the scientific implications of the Master's words—*This is my flesh, this is my blood*—as well as of the hermetic doctrine of the identity of the two spheres; for what we call life and spirit is only the transmutation, in instantaneity, of macrocosm into microcosm, of bread and wine into blood. Your interior Movement is the Word and is nourished by the Word in the instantaneity of the *fiat*. What you eat is yourself, as the divine Hohenheim has demonstrated to you. And that interior movement is equally *Lux*, total consciousness, the sun of Memory. *Fiat* is thus blood, and in its gushing beyond The Place it irresistibly involves the second term, which is *Lux*: and *Lux* is the solar knowledge which was darkened by the moment when man, refusing to recognize himself in the only Place determined by Instantaneity, fell in love with the phantasm of past and future eternity, and conceived of multiplying and dividing the infinite by the infinite, in the mad hope of situating by his own means the infinitude of cosmic points engulfed in relativity. But I have already exhausted this arcanum in the *Epistle to Storge*, gospel of the new knowledge; and I have no desire to dwell at too great a length on these subjects, because the only readers I have in mind, my spiritual sons in the centuries to come, guided in the study of my work by Einstein's mathematical confirmations, will understand my every hint. Adam's fall and the confusion of tongues are only symbols for the division—into space, time, movement and matter—of the unity originally enclosed with its consciousness in blood. Consequently, man lost the notion of single, internal movement, and his thought, even after Harvey and until today, has remained a simple awareness of the non-situated infinitude of external movements. This is so true that the Redeemer had no other aim than to restore the Church—by which we should understand the concept of Creation in its unity—founding it upon a single stone that, as I have shown in *Memoria*, is blood, which gushes from the Place and becomes space-time; for blood and stone or blood and cosmos are one and the same thing, and that is the reason we search for the sacred stone in ourselves. Blood, we have said, is the Word, the *fiat*; its universal and unique movement is a gushing forth in instantaneity, and it was only after we started to divide unity to infinity that we conceived of that movement as circulation in time. The source of blood is in the indivisible unity, the only *alpha* which does not need a *beta* to be determined. By virtue of instantaneity, blood is thus the unfathomable unity itself; as a manifestation, however, it is already a divisible unity, a living sign of the number two, and, consequently, the begetter of an infinity of non-situated points. For if matter possesses a relative reality, it can only be that of number, which is in a way the body; and the number here is two. But, born of Unity, the Place of mercy wherein we delighted in the spectacle of instantaneity, blood already takes us into the tripartite world; because blood, first and only movement, joined to the number two as a shadow is to a body, gives us simultaneously matter, space and time. And in your human thought, which is only awareness and love of this movement, you recognize the number four. Yes, my child, human thought is only an imprint of the number four on the awareness and love of the trinity of space-time-matter, enclosed in the unity of Movement. But here once more, I am compelled to refer you to the divine *Epistle*. When we reach the number four, we fall back into unity; for this fourth term is completely in your blood, which is Manifestation, and in this way the pentagram is given to us, but in its highest and most profound form: we will call it the universal pentagram, because it is a sign of the transmutation of the Bread and Wine of the great World into blood; and because it is, as it were, a path for the descent of the Father into the human. The number six will be given by the reconciliation, in man, of blood and consciousness, and will be represented by the rising of the Sun of Memory. The seventh day, the most marvellous of all, will be that of fulfillment in adoration. You should know, my child, that what is being revealed to you here is the secret brought from Egypt by Pythagoras, but invested for the first time with its living substance. I shall not deal with the three remaining numbers, the celestial trinity, the great arcanum of space-time-matter given to us not by movement but by immobility; these objects, as well as the unity which embraces them, are inaccessible to our reason. Only the omnipotence of the Lord's Prayer and the Hail Mary can extend the dominion of our median sight to the flower-beds of the joyful

Garden. Moreover, although I choose here to associate my young truths with archaic numbers—to pour my new wine into old skins, to join together the future, this word devoid of meaning, and the past, this misleading echo of the scream at our birth—do not infer from this, my child, that I am rambling under the sway of ancient superstition. I have no respect whatsoever for Number. If I ascribe to it some appearance of virtue, it is specifically in the religious sphere alone, and even there with what reservations! For when it comes to what mathematical number really is, a fetish of my barbarous contemporaries, I have long ago expelled it from its imaginary place. To be sure, by providing it with matter as its shadow I have elevated it, as far as its substantiality is concerned, above the sensible universe. However, where the shadow disappears the object itself fades away; and even though the object here is number, that does not make it any more suited to survive matter. For after all, what is number if not a mental yardstick to measure a figure, which is itself a pure form of place? Or else number is an expression of the relations between one figure and another, or between one part and another, but always according to the order of *situation*. Has not the omniscient Storge reduced Thought to a fundamental and most simple necessity of situating all things? Have not the sages of Israel, those sons of Egypt, enclosed their four worlds in *the letters of an alphabet*, which is numerical, and enclosed the ideal world in a sign of punctuation, the Yod? That is why you are perhaps free to maintain that $3 + 2 = 5$, and consequently that $5 = 3 + 2$. But if you venture so far as to define five as equal to five, your assertion would be in a metaphysical sense sheer madness, because by proceeding thus you would be drawing in an absolute place a figure which derives its being exclusively from its relation to a neighboring figure. Now that figure in turn also owes its reality to that of its place, whether the earth, the sky, or the brain; and the reality of place, as we were shown by Storge, is purely relative, being entirely situated in the relation of A to B. Number is only a measure of a line of movement or a sign of the relation between two moving lines; and precisely in that relation the whole of our sensible reality is contained. Number thus is not an invulnerable haven of an infinity of lines of force. Number is this infinitude itself, and with it aspires to immobility, to its deliverance. Bound to its chariot of billions of wheels, in its vertiginous pursuit of Place, number accompanies infinitude. In brief, number is not even a stable expression of relativity, it is this relativity itself, or rather, the demonstration of this relativity. The true name of mathematical number could well be *Mea Culpa*. For it beats its breast in the manner of penitents: I am number, a splendid expression of the Nothing, of the innumerable, universal Nothing, king without realm, whose entire power resides in unfathomable, limitless terror. It beats its ribs in the midst of a vain mirage of eternity and infinity, while simpletons of materialistic epochs count the strokes, and exult in multiplying worlds, as well as in multiplying themselves, in a security that is so lovely and so conveniently established in its place. It is of little consequence that I give to the number three—chosen haphazardly in the phantasm of infinity—a dress or rather a shadow of cosmic matter, that of a flower or of the earth; neither three constellations, nor three gloxinias, nor three grains of sand will ever meet in their movement anywhere except as a relation of one movement to another movement. Consequently it is only logical to affirm that number attains the miserable sum of its reality not at all in the representation of a Copernicus or an Einstein, but rather in the vision of an Ezekiel. Because in this place of light, which itself is also situated only by its relation to the unfathomable unity, the first division is at least provoked by the initial Movement, in other words, the gushing of blood beyond the one real place of instantaneity. And the result of this division gives us a number whose three elements—space, time and matter—enclosed in the unity of Movement, directly correspond to the higher numbers fulfilling the cosmic septenary, that is, the celestial Trinity of Space, Time and

Substance, which is contained no longer in the unity of Movement but in that of immobility in instantaneity, as we tried to illustrate by our image of rotation at infinite speed. It would be superfluous to stress the human and sensory element in this concept of a trinity of Space-Time-Substance, enclosed in immobile and indivisible unity. The concept is obviously no more than a miserable figure, something very similar to the famous hyper-space drawn around the sphere of our solid space which has recently been enriched by mathematics with a fourth dimension and defined since 1916, in the *Epistle to Storge*, as metaphysically inseparable from time and matter in motion. The understanding of unity and instantaneity sleeps in us its obscure sleep. Blood, the primordial movement, gushing forth in the universal instant, travels in darkness but not in cold. The warmth of the Sun of Memory persists; only the light is absent. Even now, the density of this internal night is not impenetrable, and a furtive ray can reach our median eye; for were it impenetrable, we would know neither the pseudo-intuition of genius, nor the illumination of mystics, nor the admirable wisdom of children, who are early taken into confidence by animals, plants and stones. And even the emission of semen, this weak likeness of the initial gushing forth in instantaneity, would occur in complete insensitivity and in a cerebral setting even more infamous and barbarous. But although the recollection of unity is almost extinguished (a condition which the Bible figuratively depicts as the sin of Adam, the expulsion from paradise, the confusion of tongues, the slavery in Egypt and Babylon), the recollection of the first divisible number represented by blood itself has preserved its freshness nearly intact, and it is this which makes possible the present miracle of substituting a direct and unified vision of Movement for the tripartite concept of space-time-matter. It would even be admissible to suggest that the obliteration of the concept of original unity in cosmic consciousness—an obliteration inevitably followed by the spirit's enslavement by the first divisible quantity, the matrix of the numbers two and three—gave rise simultaneously to the tripartite representation of Movement and to the dualizing development of language, as we observe in primitive man and a child.

In this thankless act of writing, how I regret that I am ignorant of the idiom that I heard resound in my room after returning from a holy pilgrimage and which slumbers in this thick melancholy blood where prayer alone liberates the fountains of the sun! However miserable my language may be, receive with love, O my son, O Affirmer, the few rare truths which it transmits to you across the ages. For, seized by a great emotion, I have opened myself to you, just as when touched by love in his declining years a man suddenly feels himself melting, mind and heart—melting in irresistible tenderness—and all around him a breeze from the most beautiful bygone days runs through the youthful sadness of flowers. And tell me, could I speak to you otherwise than as a father, himself eternally a child in the divine instantaneity of the world? Recognize the servant of the Master, O you who since the days of Adam have been using up your life by troubling the waters of your memory with a sounding which never reaches the bottom. Your sight stopped short at the window walled in by stars; I have touched your forehead between the eyebrows. You know now what a spectacle unfolds behind the dazzling partition of your blindness. Your body was immobile and insensible: I gave you back Movement, and look, you are space, time, matter. You were as if separated from the outside world, grasping it only in number; I have had pity on you, I have acted toward you according to the custom of the Masters; for *numbers* I have substituted *objects*. And now, O Hero by the power of thought and science, take flight with me toward Unity, for I have given you back two Prayers—your wings.

4
Turba Magna[15]

> Bound to its chariot of billions of wheels, in the vertiginous pursuit of Place, Number accompanies infinitude. NUMBERS

MOVEMENT is anterior to the thing which moves. Movement, matter-space-time, is already the thing. This is the new basis for the entire metaphysics of tomorrow. Space-time is not the place of movement; it is its creation, its matter. We do not know any matter other than space and time. The universe from alpha to omega is matter. It is matter, not in opposition to spirit—a miserable human concept—but precisely because it is itself thought, that is, movement. What are the elements of thought if not space, time and matter? This space, this time, this matter, where do we find them? In movement. Something moves, therefore something thinks; therefore I am. Here we are far from Descartes. Let us recognize however that the lucid Descartes was quite close to the truth, as was the great Pascal when he spoke of a point impelled with infinite velocity. Honor to France, crystalline country, native land of pure reason! Something moves, therefore something thinks, therefore I am. And yet, no, it is not this. This "something" comes too early. Movement precedes the thing. It is only thanks to movement that the thing is. For the thing is space and time given by movement. Thus, before the thing there is movement. But before the thing there is nothing; and yet movement, which is matter, space and time, is already the thing. And we must understand that movement is, therefore, the thing by *anteriority*, so to speak, in itself. For whatever effort we may make, earthworms that we are, this anteriority of movement remains, in our representation, contemporaneous with the Nothing. Thus, before the thing there is a simultaneity, rather an instantaneity, of *being* and *non-being*, of nothing and of movement, which is already the thing. In this way, thanks to the discovery of a method of physics unknown before our *Epistle to Storge*, twin sister of the General Theory of Relativity, we arrive at an understanding of a primordial state of the thing, of a state anterior to the separation of Yes from No. That initial state dimly foreseen by Kant in his antinomies will be reconstituted mechanically with the help of our *Novum Organum*—the only one deserving that name—and will confirm the validity of an appealing theory, proposed by Lessing in his *Education of the Human Race*, according to which all revealed knowledge, after it has run the prescribed circle of its evolution, is in the end discovered by science. Should I add that the truth I bring here is as old as the world, and that only the road I followed to reach it is new? Have you not already hailed my Movement—which I identify with Blood and which is both pre-existence and coexistence in instantaneity—as an idea you have sensed when reading about Hesed,[16] love building the world, and about the luminous desire in the Nothing of Jakob Boehme,[17] and also about that marvellous "act" which was substituted for the Word by the masterful hand of Goethe in the first part of *Faust*? Movement, the unity of space-time-matter, is thus a thing; and yet because of its anteriority it coexists with the Nothing in the frame of instantaneity. For, after the darkening of the Sun of Memory, man is no more than the recorder of a movement which he cuts automatically into three slices: past, present and future; and this past, this present and this future are a kind of alphabet in relief for his blind thought, a contrivance and a rail for his rigid language, as well as a channel for the circulation of his blood in the tripartite, non-situated world of space, time and matter. In Reality the act is accomplished in a totally different manner: There, everything that was, everything that is and everything that will be happens in the same single instant. That is why the inconceivable, absurd anteriority of movement finds confirmation in new relationships established by the General Theory of Relativity between space-time-matter and fields of gravitation. When movement stops, any container vanishes. Movement is its own (relative) place; whether we deal with yesterday, today or tomorrow, what we call our thought always falls back upon the same preexistence of movement coexisting with the thing in the Nothing. And this Nothing itself, contemporaneous with Movement in instantaneity, offers only pitiful nourishment to our hunger for *immobility,* filled as it appears to us in advance by the very fact of its coexistence with movement, that is, with the thing. The last accessible peak is already under our feet, and what do we perceive if not our own movement? Contemplate, contemplate, my child, this cosmic blood which is yours: eternally it chases itself, attracted by the lure of the Place; but its anteriority runs faster than it does. Everywhere there is only despair and the abyss! For if a point A finds in the infinitude of describable elements—as in our *Epistle*—a semblance of situation in its relation to a point B, it is only because it is movement, as is point B. And the idea of diversity exists solely because things are movement: the sun is a certain movement which we call sun, and the heart is another movement which we call heart; it is the same with grass, a cloud, woman, gold, excrement, in short, with each thing before our senses, be it physical or mental. Likewise it is the flow of blood alone that determines for an animal, whether endowed with language or not, its various characteristics of race or individuality. To drive lead towards gold or Adam toward Christ, what after all does that mean, if not to capture and to lay in its place, by means of a propitiatory science, a movement which circumscribes the thing although it itself remains non-situated? The Great Art is, of all human activities, the only one that is reasonable and natural. Its body travels with its knowledge, while its spirit does not stray from the Father's and Mother's lovely dwelling place, which is built on solid foundations. The Great Art moves like a Balance whose eternal goal is Immobility. The two scales, Love and Truth, are suspended from the hand of the Lord who is our Justice. We have lost this humble and obedient omnipotence by abandoning the firm ground of adoration for the mirage of an infinity of mobile points which, far from being *matter*, are no more than the *language* of the descriptive anatomy of the universe. My child! there is only despair and the abyss. But in this despair, what heroism, and in this abyss, what affirmation!

Do I need to add that the epoch which has seen me suffer as mortal heart has never before suffered is the most foolish and the most vile of all, being an epoch of movement in every domain, in love, art, science, politics? I do not wish to dwell on a subject so little suited to me, so unworthy of my character and my genius. And yet, I love and admire my epoch, and I thank my Master for having thrown me here: for superabundance of movement is putrefaction and the source of *new life.*

I have written these pages for you alone, my son of a distant future. *Ars Magna* is a Pyramid which is wide at its base and grows narrow. I have given to my Great Work the smallest size and the greatest weight possible, without attempting to be heard by the agitated elite of these centuries of Turba, therefore of putrefaction: for our great political and social wars are terrible ploughs, our idea of love is manure and our science is a softened grain which has not yet germinated under the sun of renewal.

O Movement, O Blood gushing outward in the divine *Fiat*, when I cursed you I was myself a heartbeat of the Master! Now my feet are again solidly planted on the earth my mother. I want to live, live and work, for men, my enemies.

Awake, O Cosmos, expand yourself through your veins, through billions of milky ways, O magic Blood gushing forth from the heart of the Master! O life, O holy life, appear, immense and splendid, in the depths of shadow. Blessed hour! The day of the earth, brutal like man and deceptive like woman, closes its eyes of oceans and seas, but the gaze of wisdom falls from myriad eyes on my gold-illumined soul. My nocturnal truth awakens: I am free, free! I am no longer a cowardly creator of illusion; I have finished with the comedy of purifying the earthly thing which, out of weakness, I love. I am free! It is as if I were dead. Hail, universe, my love!

5
Lumen

1   What, my happy son? You have loved madly and with compassion a woman born like you out of anxious clay, and you tell me you do not understand anything of my language?

2   Come, the sacrifice of night is ablaze above our heads. Between me and you ancient suffering will make itself understood by ancient suffering.

3   Beyond the Nothing, object of supreme desire, there is one who is less than nothing, because he is anterior to the anteriority of Movement: that one who is the most alien, the most unknown among outside objects but also terribly inner.

4   He strikes the stone of space-time fallen from the Place, drawing from it great sparks to illuminate the virginal and maternal face of his love.

5   One of these firebrands breathed out by the conflagration of the universe, the sun, toy of our days, has just flown so far into the void of the sky that you no longer see it. The forest and its birds are a single cloud of sleep.

6   What more do we know about the one who is less than the Nothing of your highest desire? This, my son: that he breathed also at the beginning of things—understand by that your true birth.

7   A loving star of your thought, which is Blood, a flaming marriage of fire and water and their conflux, that is, space and duration.

8   And throughout the eternity of your memory an affirmation which is at the depths of your vertigo has been clamoring in you that the diurnal sun, although it is your bread, is only a poor allegory.

9   And that the last solar truth is in us, covered like Raphael with immobile light; thus the only light, which is situated.

10   When, from the sole of your foot to a wisp of a curl of your hair, your whole being resounds with the word *Yes!*—then the firm place of the cosmos emerges from the running waters of thought.

11   What a place of magnificence that is, my child! Fire and water copulate there and melt into a golden immobility: then everything is instantaneity, total Memory!

12   And somebody cries in us—so loudly that space is shattered—I! And that I is no more our shabby pride but the first and only Being, the immobile heart of Lumen. And we do not even know whether that I is engulfed in us or whether we are inhaled by it.

13   Then the black glands of the venom of life empty themselves in our hands and the gaping of the tomb is closed in mirth.

14   Look around you, my child. How good and simple everything is. Everything here, all this matter, why, this is your own blood, and this blood is movement, therefore time and space.

15   Your heart is an anatomical sun, a propellent of your microcosmic blood, just as the great Suns are fathers and shepherds of systems.

16   That is why the Masters, my lovers, have married fire and water in organic heat, binding them with a sweet-centered ring of gold.

17   And if in their tender prattle the brain became the hermetic Moon, it is not only by analogy of color.

18   Thought is only the leaf detached from the tree of sensitivity, the brain is only the satellite of the heart. It receives, filters, and restores the light of affirmation sent to it by the heart in its spiritual radiation.

19   The moon and the brain are receptors and organizers of light. They humanize the superhuman, make accessible to our fragile eyes the blinding god.

20   The silences of the old Masters are changed into speech in my mouth. For the hour of Relativity has struck! And instruments of search are in our hands. The day of symbols is over. Everything is fulfilled.

21   The veins of the crucifixion have dried up, the great work of expiation is fulfilled. We enter a second innocence in reconquered, conscious, well-deserved joy. Mathematics has been sanctified.

22   The trinity Matter-Space-Time, matrix of non-situated multiplicity, has been seized by us in the living unity of Movement.

23   All this, even here under my crazy pen, is still a reflection, brain, moon. But the eternal moment of the Sun of Mem-

ory, washed in the Jordan of humility, is going to seize us, and this divine instantaneity will lead us into the celestial Canaan, the only situated land,

24   The immobile Empyrean of my father Dante, the pure sphere restored to its original unity by the consecration of the number Ten—

25   O my spouse Renaissance with the great face of France and of Egypt! All this science comes to me from you, for you have taught me charity by instructing me how to trust.

26   By making me trustful, though I was contemptuous in this bitter, oh bitter world! So bitter that only the gift of money from a male to a female or from a female to a male bears witness here to the sincerity of half-love and seals with voluptuousness and rancor the act of terrestrial union.

27   *Liber Paramirum* (which you have made known to me, O Woman Companion), *Liber Paramirum* scorches our heart by speaking of death. How pure and merciful this stopping of the brain and heart seems to me, compared to the Turba Magna which is our life, the whistling of the scythe against flint.

28   "Horrible, atrocious life! Sex open to every passerby, open like the bowl of a beggar, and the heart closed to the poor, closed like the Royalty of all times. Black honey of treason curdled into thick wax on a handful of extracted stings.

29   "Fleeting faces seen as if in an immense, brief flapping of wings through the flicker of candlebutts at the end of an orgy and all disfigured with anxiety, erect to bursting in adulterous lechery. O house not of love but of prostitution, a house with rooms by the hour.

30   "My proud passion, so long pursued and stabbed through

and torn to shreds! Ah! let the divine unity, like the rope around a captive, clasp at last these alien members and organs that I am.

31   "Prince of Peace, Affirmer, dripping with sweat under the olive trees! I have searched, I have waited, I have renounced. At the sound of gold the purest and most faithful woman quivers like an adder.

32   "O barren and unfettered sea! The kegs in the hold are empty, my life has remained solitary and without sweet water; I have spread my spirit like the sail of a castaway; but a cloud passes, I do not receive the baptism of nature. And here a night of corrupted worlds is ablaze in empty despair.

33   "Above and below, everywhere multitudes swarming. We are possessed by a rage of Movement; a reign of speed and flurry on the earth, on the sea and in the air; and this thing which they call 'feminism,' the sorrowful and sterile agitation of white and yellow water lilies, rebellion against the husband, master of a science devoid of prayer, and polygamous out of nervous debility.

34   "The teeming of nationalities, hurricane of conscious wars, poetry and art ruled by the rhythm of motors, mental shorthand. This is where you have thrown me, jealous God, in a vomit of furious mercury."

35   Such was my prayer, only yesterday, in the morning, at noon and in the evening. But today a companion in service walks in my shadow to help me, son of the wandering Cosmopolitan. And I know that superabundance of movement is putrefaction from which a young, revived wheat rises.

36   Listen again to this charitable teaching which I have received from Renaissance my Woman Companion. Let the

Spouse, virginal Mother of life, raise it to her knees stained with the blood of Calvary.

37   My brothers of this time, these Cains whom my Master has ordered me to cherish, have never yet risen above our thin atmosphere.

38   Nevertheless they haughtily maintain that to the one who would leave it, the sun would appear neither yellow or red but blue—electrically and glacially blue in a funereal space strewn with pallid universes.

39   If it is really so, what charitable lesson does it give us, this scientific sun which, passing through our atmosphere humanized by our loving and anxious breathing, becomes once more the gentle Sol of the pious laboratories of long ago?

40   For it clothes itself in golden and singing warmth; and, not satisfied with nourishing us with bread and wine, it sends its sharp, secret rays deep into the great childlike heart of the earth.

41   And there it ripens the incorruptible and curative Gold of divine Charity, the honey-metal, secretion of archangelic bees, the gold which, without the help of the *Ave* and of the *Pater*, will never be recovered by any synthetic venture.

THE ARCANA[18]

1927

TRANSLATED BY CZESLAW MILOSZ

to Nicolas Beauduin

WHAT they also say about my reasons, that "many have read them without having been persuaded," can be easily refuted, because there were others who have understood them and have found them satisfactory; for we ought to believe more one man who says, without any intention of lying, that he saw or understood something, than a thousand others who deny it only because they could not see it or understand it. Hence when the antipodes were discovered, people preferred to believe the report of a few sailors who went around the earth rather than the thousands of philosophers who did not believe that it was round. And as for their invoking the Elements of Euclid here, as though they were easily accessible to everyone, I beg them to consider that among those who are thought to be the most learned in the philosophy of the School, there is not one in a hundred who comprehends all the demonstrations of Apollonius or Archimedes, even though they are as evident and as certain as those of Euclid.[19]

Letter from M. Descartes to M. Clerselier

The Poem of the Arcana

1   As the mountain carried me upward in its flight, I suddenly saw, opening before me *into another space*, the golden door of Memory, the exit from the labyrinth.

2   Such was the origin of the doctrine that I presented in the testament *Ars Magna*, the faithful and pious narrative of the events which led me, two years later, in the summer of the year nineteen sixteen, to the discovery and demonstration of the spiritual and physical law of universal relativity.

3   I am entering the twelfth year of supreme knowledge.

4   Yet I shall humble in the dust before you this brow which has received the crown.

5   I shall humble it before you, my son, Hiram, King of the unified world, Architect of the effective Catholic Church of tomorrow, the universal regent of faith, science and art.

6   For if the truth which speaks here had been revealed to me by a creature, as it will be unveiled to you through the organ of a creature such as I am, most certainly I would not have recognized it.

7   At the source of ancient suffering we find erroneous physical concepts, cosmic visions of punishment.

8   As the essence of thinking is sensation, that is, awareness and love of Movement, any psychology not founded upon an analysis of the physical concept of the world sooner or later disintegrates together with other phantoms of the imagination.

9   The language of life is unadorned. Naked is the speech of death. The world's beauty, our mother, looks in the same way on the cradle and the grave. Yet her face inspires us with a holy confidence.

10   Because deep within ourselves we feel very distinctly that all our innumerable questionings, except one, are frivolous and importunate, full of curiosity and alien to love.

11   A single question, O Hiram, makes us worthy of our great sufferings: *Where is space?*

12   The sickness of Hamlet, Faust and Manfred has its origin in a representation of the Cosmos distorted by Adam's prevarication.

13   In this representation, the idea of space, identified with that of the container, appeared as an immense curtain of darkness hanging in an eternity of time. In this night of terror, the worlds of matter and of movement took on the likeness of inexplicable holes of life and light.

14   Such was the vain vision of criminal pride. Man's universal dominion and his memory of origins disappeared at the very instant when the "I", accursed may it be, suggested to our ancestor a monstrous connection between the idea of space and that of the infinite.

15   Man's first thought had been a total perception of his movement: an instantaneous awareness and *love,* a religious ecstasy of rhythm.

16   Before reaching the brain, satellite of the heart, and becoming reflected there, this thought had been the subtle fire, the initial flash, the most profound secret, the life and the very essence of blood.

17   For blood is contemporaneous with the *fiat.* It is the magic substance of the first spiritual impetus, the spontaneous, living movement of myriads of universes.

18   Blood is the sum of spiritual energies manifested in Creation, this immaterial light of the Vision of Beauty and of God's love.

19 Blood is the first relationship, that of the Seer and the Thing seen, consequently the original appearance of movement, of space-time, of situation, of place.

20 Grasped by the inner sense of vision, which is mnemonic and contemporaneous with God's Creative Vision, blood takes on the angelic aspect of gold which illuminates the central depths of the earth.

21 For in the earth, as in man, remembrance of origins slumbers, unpolluted; and when spiritual prevarication reaches its limit, this remembrance will awaken to testify against false science.

22 The first thought of the King of the world was thus an integral perception of his movement.

23 And this first thought included the sum of all knowledge, for movement is a perfect simultaneity, an absolute identity and an indivisible unity of space, matter and time.

24 Be attentive, my son, for here is the cornerstone, the very Stone of space-time-motion itself.

25 When the spirit of purity and of obedience prompted the newborn Adam to rise from the ground so that he might bless the world's beauty, our ancestor *felt he was the Universe.*

26 Because the magic virtue of the first movement opened for him the fundamental notion—single and indivisible—of space-time-matter.

27 Our ancestor's thinking was, then, the thinking of the Universe rather than that of man.

28 By this thinking, by this awareness of Movement, Adam *situated* his movement, his being, in relation to movement, to the being of the sun, the stars and the surrounding objects.

29 For what we call thinking, both in its origin and later at various degrees of its evolution, is only an awareness and love of movement, and thus a pure determination of place.

30 Adam's thinking, the awareness and love of move-

ment, applied itself likewise to situating each part of the Cosmos, the smallest and the greatest, through a relationship between the movement of this part and the movement of another. In this fundamental operation, Place, space inseparable from time-movement, became identical with a dynamic relationship, and the whole, grasped in its perfect simultaneity, its absolute instantaneity, produced Matter, magic substance of the world.

31 In other words, in Adam's thinking, all describable space—that is, all space susceptible to being situated experimentally in the numerical relation between galaxies, systems, worlds and moving bodies in general—that describable space, together with movement-time, formed a single universal Body.

32 Adam's thinking could not imagine this perfect cosmic body, this total space solidified as it were in a unity of matter placed outside any dynamic relationship, in any way other than *situated* in the Nothing, in the Nothing from which both the void and the full, movement and time, are banished.

33 For the concept of a space, of an *exterior void*, by the inevitable association of this void with the already existing material realm, that is, with the mobile pattern of relationship, would only have resulted in a substantial addition, an infinite extension of the single universal body.

34 Adam's thinking also understood that an illusion of immobility, assuming the aspect of the lack of movement in a thing taken as a whole, attaches to a multitude of objects even if, like the stars their fathers, they are endowed with a plurality of movements; for everything is cosmic substance carried by the torrent of universal blood.

35 This appearance of immobility, this impression of nothing in the thing, struck Adam's thinking with respect and awe. And Adam blessed the trees and the stones.

36 But Adam's thinking, being that of the universe, never tried to assign a place to the entirety of the world, or to make a sum of all those movements which are situated through their relationship alone.

37 For the total universe is not a place. As in time there are wakefulness and sleep, so in instantaneity the entirety of the universe is only a *state* situated in its spiritual opposition to the *nothing*, to the *nothing* from which the void and the full, movement and time, are banished. In the mind of the Just, total space, the non-situated universe, total space, which is the pure vision of beauty and of God's love, was *absolutely alien to any intuition of the infinite.* Space, being matter, could not, in the thinking of the Just, be elevated to that archangelic level where the immutable idea of the infinite reigns in insubstantial light.

38 My son, I am coming out of an absurd and terrifying dream.
39 I ran after myself and I could not grasp myself.
40 The two states which I was, my sleep and my wakefulness, my life and my death, pursued each other and could not be joined because there was no *place.*
41 When suddenly, in a paroxysm of universal terror, I felt *I was catching up with my remembrance.* At the same instant, facing the primordial Nothing, I renounced forever all concern for *reality.*

42 Adam's first thought had been an integral perception of movement: in the heart and in the arteries of the King ran the total light of the world.
43 Adam was sovereign memory. Drawn from cosmic substance, he remembered the cry of his magic birth, similar to the solar laughter of lead changed into gold.
44 Every operation of the King opened with the fundamental affirmation: I am in him who is, for what separates me from Being is the Nothing.
45 The holy notion of the Nothing has been given to me so that I might know that only the nothing separates me from him who is and in whom I am.
46 The Nothing is the code word of the Noble Travellers. It is the entrance and the exit of the labyrinth.

47   This notion of the nothing, whence does it come to me, to me who am movement and, consequently, space, time, matter?

48   I, the Thing, how then did I manage to tear the great funereal seal of the black and frozen void off my idea of the nothing?

49   For the corporeal Water of space-time was not poured by the fiat into the receptacle of a prior void. The Stone of space-time was not thrown into a pre-existing void.

50   The void is space. Yet space, even deprived of ether, is matter, inseparable from some kind of movement identical with time. Therefore the void could not appear without the universes' appearing in the same instant.

51   My only place is in the one who has breathed into the nothing the ecstatic mirage of the world's beauty.

52   O Hiram, this Nothing of which the immobility of inorganic matter is the mute hieroglyph, this Nothing, what void would suffice to fill it up?

53   It is a spiritual, insubstantial, primordial water; and precisely in it, transmuted as it is into blood, movement and thought, we perceive total space, pure appearance; we perceive total space, certainly matter, and yet it is more illusory than the inverted image of the limited expanse reflected in corporeal water.

54   It is an ideal mirror that the Spirit puts before itself so that its beauty may appear freely and as if from outside, so that *Love shall be exalted over the Law.*

55   This is the first sacrifice, the one that raised Being—I mean Being that is its own and only law, that of being and nothing more—yes, this is the first sacrifice which raised Being above its own *necessity*.

56   Because for Being there is no freedom except in the surrender of its most secret essence; by this surrender the law becomes love.

57   Thus Beauty, liberated and liberating, appeared so that

the free sacrifice of love might shine above the necessity of the law.

58   Thus, there gushed forth in the instantaneity of the *fiat*, as if brought about by a total transfusion, free beauty, the spiritual place of Benediction, the first relationship, that which exists between Beth and Aleph.

59   Thus in the nothing—in this spiritual water from which the void, the full, action and number were banished—there lit up the archimagic Vision of a universe *whose mobile interior is space and whose container is the nothing, limit of our gravitational fields.*

60   In this act of manifestation, beauty, the Bride, detached herself from the Bridegroom without breaking the indivisible unity; for she detached herself as an image separates itself from its object.

61   This manifestation, this holy, holy Mother of beauty and glory, can it then be that she is an illusion? Not in the least; she is the truth, the very reality of the Lord who is the spirit of Love.

62   For this is so not at all because she is sensorially perceived in a dynamic relationship, but precisely because she is a perfect vision, a supercelestial ecstasy of the Spirit, her lover.

63   The inexhaustible birth-giving power of the spiritual substance of the heavens and of the earth is the sacred sign of the femininity of procreative manifestation.

64   Such is the holy arcanum of Conjugal Love, the subject of Solomon's Song of Songs. I too would like to sing it. But the Legions clad in gold make a sign that I should keep silent.

65   Thus, just as in instantaneity the bride detached herself from the bridegroom like an image from its object, so in the world of time-space, which was created by the luminous *fiat* and is the movement of this reflection, Eve had to be taken from the similarly double polarity of Adam's substance drawn from the very blood of the universe.

66   Of the universe which is the sacrifice of sacrifices, archetype of the blood given by Abel and original mystery of all cults of immolation.

67   And this blood of creation, O Hiram my son, this blood of creation flowed also for the Atonement. For, there again, was it not necessary that the free sacrifice of love should be exalted above the Jewish law itself?

68   Adam's dominion over this *non-situated* universe of free beauty was thus wielded in the freedom of the supreme knowledge which was founded upon the original relationship of aleph to beth, of the seer to his vision, of being to love.

69   Adam was free, for he knew that movement is not the inconceivable translation from a place to a place, but the intelligible metamorphosis from a state to a state. To be free is to move, certainly for the sake of action, but also, far beyond any action, for the sake of rhythm.

70   Through the interplay of dynamic connections, Adam was the consciousness of the universe and the organ of perception of all things. But through the relationship of beth to aleph, of the vision situated in the nothing to the Holy Spirit which alone is real, Adam was the very freedom of beauty.

71   Thus, later, at the moment of the purification of beings and things, Christ was born of a Virgin, the corporeal image of first free beauty.

72   Just as the vision was projected by the spirit into the nothing, and the first Adam was drawn from cosmic substance fecundated by spirit alone—so, too, the second Adam could be born only from a virginal, spiritual, free beauty.

73   The mysterious and chaste passion, the intellectual intoxication, that we all have experienced on emerging from childhood, is but a dim remembrance of the first love, Adam's love for Eve, his terrestrial mate.

74   Woman, taken from the spiritual substance of man, which was that of vision itself—woman found herself with

regard to man in the relationship of beth to aleph, of the vision to the seer, of love to Being.

75 Just like the seer and his vision, the couple in Eden were an indivisible unity. On the level of dynamic connections, their movements and their speech represented the hidden operations uniting the seer and his vision in the great ritual of reciprocity. Eve was the living, spiritual and virginal image of Femininity, of manifestation.

76 Woman's beauty and charity, the intoxication and compassion they inspire, bring us closer even today to our mother, the world's beauty. But Adam, in the wisdom of his submission, recognized in this beauty the very essence and form of his companion in service. He talked to "Arcturus, Orion, the Pleiades, and the chambers of the south" (those true friends of Job) as he talked to Eve: in the universal and invisible quivering of elytra which was of a muted, penetrating and blissful tenderness.

77 I have guided you, Hiram, up to this sacred flagstone where the master mason has carved the image of the labyrinth.

78 It is here, in this place of fulfillment, that I will take leave of you for the entire period of the great transmutation which is beginning.

79 The present attempts at moral, social and political renewal are doomed to failure. Before leading a blind man toward the light, it is proper to heal him of his blindness.

80 A sacrilegious and false concept of the physical universe has dimmed, like a cataract, the intellectual sight of man. It is necessary first to remove with a strong and charitable hand this opaque secretion which conceals from him the real world of vision.

81 Here, in the tool bag, O King of toilers, you will find the cross, the balance, the ointment, the scepter and the crown of the world. But I must tell you once more how the ancient King became blind.

82   The incorporeal light of beauty detached itself from the being which is identical with the law and is the hidden spiritual fire. It detached itself in order that, just as the first relationship was established between this fire and this light, between this bridegroom and this bride, so love should be exalted above the law.

83   In the very instantaneity of the *fiat*, the incorporeal light of the world's beauty took on the aspect of the Cosmos—its interior space-time—which we know. But in Adam, who is its consciousness, its freedom and its organ of perception, it appeared to itself as a vision of a seer in the nothing, the nothing from which the void and the full, movement and time, are banished.

84   There was a seer and a vision, and Adam was the relationship between the one and the other. It was in him, in the man who is a child of necessity and beauty, that love saw itself exalted in its freedom above the law.

85   But the unity of this law, which is identical with being, subsisted undivided in the trinity of Bridegroom, Bride and the first Adam, who was the consciousness of the conjugal arcanum. For the seer and his vision formed but a single spirit with the primordial relationship that was their intelligibility in the cosmic concept of man.

86   On the level of dynamic relations, this undivided unity was represented by the triplicity of space-time-matter, given in the unity of movement.

87   But this movement itself, this *fiat*, the law-generating manifestation, was nothing other than Adam born of the spiritual substance of the vision. On the dynamic level, therefore, Adam was the representation of being that is its own law. And Eve was drawn from his essence only so that he, too, should represent love exalted above the law.

88   Adam's prevarication caused this exalted love to fall back into the rigor of the law. Such, O Hiram, is the origin of the great and severe law of Israel.

89 Eve found herself, then, placed with regard to Man, King of the World, in the relationship of beth to aleph, of the vision to the seer, of love to being, of bride to bridegroom.

90 She represented the femininity of manifestation, whose consciousness, knowledge and prayer Adam was. Eve's consciousness was in Adam, Eve's knowledge was in Adam, Eve's prayer was in Adam.

91 Eve was free, because her consciousness and her knowledge and her prayer were in Adam, and Adam was the freedom of beauty in its primordial relationship, the father of his own law in the interplay of dynamic connections.

92 Eve was free, she was untainted by any submission to man, for man and woman were one flesh, just as the seer and his vision were an indivisible unity.

93 Like the cosmos itself, this flesh was the incorporeal light of beauty, of vision. Fecundated by the holy spirit, as were the cosmos and the earth, like them the flesh gave birth, and its children, who were born for action, went far beyond action in their movement, for the sake of rhythm.

94 What separated Eve from Adam was the same as what came between Adam and God—it was the nothing, for in every word that Adam spoke, Eve spoke too, except for the word with which Adam affirmed that he was in him who is, and that he was separated from him only by the nothing.

95 Because Eve, by her consciousness, her knowledge and her prayer, was in Adam.

96 Eve was in Adam and what came between Adam and God was the nothing; this one and the same nothing thus separated Eve from God; she was in him. But she was also in Adam, and what separated her from Adam was this same nothing whose sacred name she had no reason to pronounce—as long as she was in Adam.

97 Adam's pre-eminence over Eve therefore resided entirely in this spiritual and secret right to pronounce, both for himself and for Eve, the sacred name of the nothing, which is only a name; for the void and the full, time and movement, are banished from it.

98   And this mystical privilege agreed with the situation of a dynamic connection within this primordial relationship between the vision and the seer.

99   Eve, the femininity of manifestation, the prefigure of physical Nature, was perfectly free in Adam and situated with respect to her husband in a dynamic connection of which he was the begetter; she was included in Adam, who was the consciousness of the primordial relationship, just as the dynamic connection is included in that relationship itself.

100   Eve was in Adam, made one with his consciousness, with his knowledge, with his prayer: Adam pronounced the word *nothing* for himself and for Eve, but when he said "I" he thought only of Eve.

101   For on the level of the primordial relationship he did not have an "I"; but he had an "I" in the world of dynamic connections.

102   Now it happened one day that Adam in his "I" heard Eve ask him: "Adam, being of my love, is it not true that what separates me from you is the nothing?"

103   This word "nothing" reverberated sweetly and strangely on the spouse's lips. Adam fell into a profound meditation.

104   He did not close his eyes. He questioned space, the incorporeal light of beauty. The vision was there. He questioned space, the incorporeal light of beauty. The vision was there. Adam raised his head; an eagle was flying toward the sun. Space was there. Two clouds were gliding slowly as if to melt into one: there was an impatience in Adam; the light clouds were gliding slowly in time. And under Adam's feet the stones were warmed by a marvelous noon.

105   Eve repeated her question; it was the same and yet not completely the same: "Adam, being of my love, is it not true that only the nothing separates you from God?"

106   Space was there, the incorporeal light of the vision of the non-situated universe. Space was there, and Adam, whose

"I" no longer wanted to know this nothing which separated him from God, Adam was thinking about the total universe and whispered: Where is space?

107   Then, O my royal son, O Hiram, at the boundaries of this space—which the ancient King had extended beyond any idea of limit in order to situate it in itself, in the receptacle of a void—in the mind of man the nothing suddenly changed into this infinity of darkness which is the blindness of Adam.

Hiram's Prayer [20]

PURE being, so perfectly identical with your necessity that there is no frenzy of negation that does not situate, other than in relation to you, who are the all, its nothingness doomed to be only an inverse form of affirmation; what am I saying! so terrifyingly existent that the thing distinct from you by your will, Creation, can find a container only in your idea of an exterior, a nothing, since you alone are infinite and no exterior circumscribes you; so intimately united with my "I", so inseparable from my freedom that it is you who sustain me even in my work of destruction; and at the extreme limit of my effort, when matter and the void, both identical and opposite, simultaneously fade from my thought, even then an inconceivable non-being, closed from this fullness and this void, at once changes in my mind into something that is being itself, the *yes* from which I am separated by the *no* which it contains, the whole which a pure nothing prevents me from knowing, the immobile place of all that moves and which no movement can attain, the God in whom I am, just as my notion of an exterior, of a separation, of a nothing, is in me . . .

Unique and revealed Reality, you who are the dearer to me since what loves you in me is neither a part of my being, senses, reason, feeling, nor their sum, but being itself—once again this nothing where the sun of my longing for perfection appears to me and crowns me—you who are the one who is, you the law, you wanted to be the one who becomes; you exalted yourself above the law. From your most humble idea, that of a nothing, of an exterior, you made your abode; you put your love there so that it might call you from outside. Truly you are he who gives his light and his blood; Father, Son, Spirit, I hail you. Let me, still adorned as I am with the memory of the summit of my highest thought, soar anew toward you. In my vision of the world as in yours let any notion of relation and of limit be obliterated. Let there no longer be either finite or infinite. Let there remain only love which has become the place.

Exegetic Notes

Verse 1
As the mountain carried me upward in its flight, I suddenly saw, opening before me *into another space*, the golden door of Memory, the exit from the labyrinth.

Another Space

Space, considered either absolutely in its ideal totality, or relatively in its aspect of extension, seems to yearn to liberate itself, in our representation, from its appearance as a container endowed with an existence of its own.

In this first verse the author alludes neither to theories of the ether, by means of which materialistic philosophy has attempted to eschew a spiritual problem by substituting for it the physical concept of continuity, nor to the hypothesis of a fourth dimension other than time.

The space he describes is the very one which surrounds us, but dissociated from any idea of finite or infinite capacity. The question of the infinite or of the finite docs not arise concerning it. It has ceased to be its own container as well as that of things. It is no longer the place in which we situate ourselves even as substance.

We recognize in it only one of the elements of the tripartite concept of movement, which embraces space, time and matter.

This is the same as to say that the trinity of space, time and matter is given to us simultaneously, as a whole, in the unity of movement.

To the man who sees, space is revealed by the movement of light; to the blind man, by the movement of his arm, of any limb or of his whole body; to the blind man and to the man who sees, and also to the paralytic stricken with blindness, by the very notion of movement, which is their basic thought, the point of departure for the most abstract operations, in short, *a spiritual principle linked in an indissoluble manner to the very flow of their blood.*

In the domain of physics, this truth has been intuited by Descartes, Boscovich, Swedenborg, Robert Grosseteste, and Faraday.[21] In the domain of metaphysics, it has been intuited by the author of the *Arcana*, who, as early as 1916, analyzed the new concept in his *Epistle to Storge* and drew from it the first elements of a general philosophy of relativity. Not to mention that we already find it in the unlimited field of knowledge implied by Plato's theory of recollection, as we find it entire also in the primitive *nia, dia* and *mana*—those dim reminiscences of a revealed knowledge—of Africa and Oceania.

In the *Epistle to Storge*, the first part of *Ars Magna*, the author reconstitutes in all its phases the operation which was to result in a metamorphosis of the concept of the cosmos. Here we can retrace only the most essential features. As soon as we have substituted for the erroneous representation of the *pre-existent container* that of a dynamic simultaneity of the three elements of initial perception, we observe the transformation of space into a totality of matter synonymous with energy, the notion of which is inseparable from that of time. *Space, independently of the existence of an ether, has become a solid body, one of whose dimensions is time; and the whole is a simple product, an instantaneous creation of movement.*

Perhaps it is not superfluous to remember here that, when the author wrote and published the *Epistle to Storge* (1916), the work (still unavailable in print) and even the name of Professor Einstein were completely unknown to him.

Generator of what we shall call space-time-matter, and, because of dynamic simultaneity, its contemporary and synonym in the actual world, movement appears on the metaphysical plane to be endowed with an obvious anteriority with respect to the three other elements of the fundamental cosmic notion. This anteriority is the subject of the fourth part of *Ars Magna (Turba Magna)*. The necessity of reconciling this priority of movement with dynamic simultaneity compels us to admit the concept of a first movement, that of an incorporeal light antecedent to a physical light that, according to the medieval philosophic schools of Chartres and Oxford, created the universe. This incorporeal light is absolutely independent of any odic theory.

Perhaps the day is not distant when science will have to recognize the existence of a natural pattern in which a superior phenomenalism, sometimes practiced by such men as Plotinus or Pascal, develops parallel to the highest operations of thought. An experience which we have recounted in the *Epistle to Storge* has taught us that the first spiritual mover may manifest itself to our mnemonic sight (see *Memoria*, the second part of *Ars Magna*), under the guise of a splendid sun of instruction and blessing, as Shekinah, Metatron, the burning bush of Moses, Mikael, and perhaps Aton of Amenophis IV. It is to the perception of that spiritual movement that the words "mountain" and "golden door of Memory" in this first verse of the *Arcana* also refer.

The Mountain and the Golden Door of Memory

The superior phenomenalism which develops in the incorporeal light is not an oneiric reproduction of the world of causality. On the contrary, because it alone is situated, this phenomenalism is the only real archetype of the cosmic mechanism which, similar in this respect to our satellite, always presents the same material and impenetrable face to scientific investigation not sustained by prayer, trust, and humility. The ascension experienced by the author on December 14, 1914, is treated extensively in the *Epistle to Storge*. The mountain which was its setting is the real, absolute place of the terrestrial mountains celebrated by the principal religions. It was neither in remembrance of paleolithic caves, nor for the sake of security, nor, even less, from a childish desire to be closer to heaven, that ancient sages built their sanctuaries on the tops of mountains and high plateaus. Nisir, Ararat, and Himavat, the mountains of the three floods—Babylonian, Hebrew, and Hindu—are not simple landing points, but rather physical correspondences of the holy mountain whose golden summit dominates spiritual tempests. This ideal Horeb which has seen an infinite number of galaxies disappear and which will survive the millions of Milky Ways now in existence, this indestructible Horeb is the culminating point of religious meditation. It is the visible place of illumination and revelation. There the golden door of secret memory opens onto "another space." There the *Fiat*, the first movement, spiritual uncreated light, appears to the epopt. When he returns to the sphere of physical phenomena the seer, like Minos, regenerated for nine years, carries in his blood the image of the holy mountain. From then on, he will cherish it and venerate it in its earthly correspondences; it will be for him Sinai—also the Mount of Olives and Calvary. And we ourselves, exiles stricken with amnesia, we will recognize that image in the mystic sites here on earth: Elbruz and Kazbek, the holy mountains of primitive Dravido-European humanity, "Peaks of the Blessed where, in the midst of the whiteness of eternal snows, the master of the world sits enthroned, the king of the spirits"; the Anatolian mountains of the great god, the creator of the Hittites, Teschub, "the master of the Summits"; Iouktos of Crete, where the King crowned with lilies comes to talk to Zeus Asterios, his father; Mount Ida with its great sacred cavern and its sanctuary of Camares; Mount Dikte with its holy grotto of Zakro the High, dedicated to the divinities of the summits, Zeus and Britomartis-Diktynna, goddess of high places, the Virgin Mother, the most holy Ariadne, Lady of the Mounts. The *aigaion* where Zeus is fed by the goat Arkhalokhori, Skoteino, the dark beloved of Knossos. Contemporary with Minoan Crete, Cynthus, still Pelasgian, appears to us on Delos crowned by a rocky sanctuary. A few centuries pass and Hector, in Achaean Troy, offers sacrifices on the peak of Ida. The youth of Athena shines on the summit of the Acropolis. Let us turn to Egypt: Abydos, one of the rare mountains in that country, is a labyrinth of tombs and sanctuaries, and on Sinai, after it was conquered by the Pharaoh, the Egyptians built, near precious copper mines, chapels honoring Septon, the lord of the East, Hathor, and the king Snefru. It is on a mountain, too, that the Tibetans constructed in Lhassa the mystical Potala. Leaving the ancient continents and approaching distant shores unsuspected by either Kolaios of Samos or by Neshao II, instigator of the long voyage around Africa, the temple Ccoricaucha of the sun Inti raises its imposing mass on the summit of a mountain which bears on its slopes Cuzco, the holy city, the capital of sapa-inca. We could endlessly multiply these examples; the Montsalvat of the Epistle would always remain the Place of all these places.

The Exit from the Labyrinth

The labyrinth alluded to in the first verse is the cosmic secret of which the ancient mazes in Knossos, Etruria and the islands of Moeris and Lemnos are only the architectural forms. An analogous representation served as an emblem in the Temple of Solomon. This is the road of Jerusalem or the road of the League. Most Merovingian and Carolingian churches preserved its image in mosaic. Gothic churches offer us even today its reproduction at Reims, Chartres, Saint-Omer, Bayeux, and Amiens.

Used as a signature of their guild by the builders of cathedrals, those cosmogonic poems of Christianity, the labyrinth is one of the most secret symbols. Its entrance is also its only exit: birth and death are one and the same passage from spiritual movement to physical movement and vice versa. Just as in the theory of the curvature of space, corporeal light traces a circle of eighty-four billion years, so, too, our spiritual light, the prime mover whose transmutation clothes us with matter, seems to complete in every one of us, from the first birth to the last death, an enormous cycle of dynamic phenomenalism, the vehicle of moral evolution. The goal of this operation, which is our very life, will appear more clearly after we explain the verses referring to the prevarication of Adam and to the femininity of Manifestation. Considering the number of our migrations, finite as the physical universe yet countless, we do not believe that our latent memory is able to contain them. The legend which attributes this superhuman gift to the sage of Crotona[22] undoubtedly has its origin in a symbol related to the power each of us possesses of supplanting the dynamic concept of sequence with that of divine instantaneity, which enlightens us concerning our spiritual principle.

Verse 2
Such was the origin of the doctrine that I presented in the Testament *Ars Magna*, faithful and pious narrative of the events which led me, two years later, in the summer of the year nineteen sixteen, to the discovery and demonstration of the spiritual and physical law of universal relativity.

The "Testament" Ars Magna

In the author's mind, the meaning attributed to this word is that of a legacy to a posterity as distant as possible from this fourth age whose death agony we are witnessing. The poet of *Ars Magna* and the *Arcana* does not write for his contemporaries.

Universal Relativity

Universal relativity should not be understood as a purely philosophical theory—which is also so ancient that the Sufis themselves found very little to add to it—but as the discovery that the materiality of space is synonymous with the relations between mobile bodies.

Verse 3
I am entering the twelfth year of supreme knowledge.

Supreme Knowledge

This is knowledge that has prostrated itself, that is to say, knowledge which, having succeeded in admitting, *a priori*, in the midst of unspeakable torments, the absolute identity of the highest concepts of science with Christian dogma, sooner or later finds its recompense in some conclusive phenomenon of the archetypal world.

Verse 4
Yet I shall humble in the dust before you this brow which has received the crown.

The Crown

The revelation of a superior phenomenalism opens with a mystical consecration, archetype of the coronation of regents by divine right in the material world. The various phases of this rite correspond to the principal moments in the regeneration of a mineral. When the ascent through the nebula is finished and the epopt, perfectly awake, rests in a horizontal position, at a small distance from the large cupric cloud which conceals from him the upper luminous level, a light appears, not very high in the vaporous mass behind the top of his skull, in such a way that it seems to be seen through the parietal bone. At the same instant the large cloud vanishes, exposing the upper region which is suddenly crossed, in an elliptical leap of extreme violence and with the noise of a strong wind, by a metallic red-hot egg.

Turning into a golden globe it descends slowly towards the top of the skull, on which it alights like a crown; thereafter, moving up a little, it assumes the appearance of a magnificent golden sun of oval shape, stands still, becomes rounder, and plunges its omniscient stare for a long moment into the deepest thought of the new King. Meanwhile, behind his skull the star of memory is setting; its marvellous ray transmutes into gold the metallic cloud which stretches endlessly before the eye of the adorer. As soon as he returns to the level of physical phenomenalism, murmurs of angelic sweetness interspersed with the strains of a psaltery resound from all sides. To the memory of the occult King, the pschent of the pharaoh, the miters and the tiara offer a sort of physical correspondence to the oval solar Crown. If the origins of terrestrial royalty are magical, it is not in the naturalist sense ascribed to the word magic by Mr. James George Frazer and other scholars. As we stand on the threshold of a new era, it is simply ludicrous to separate the idea of nature from that of God. Alighieri never mentioned the Daughter without giving a thought to the Father. "Every passing thing is only a symbol," said the master Goethe. Behind the symbol there is an immutable *situated* reality. But to reach it one must begin by entering through the door, and not through the windows. (Luz of the Hebrews, Kundali of the Hindus, the "animal" of Leibniz, Shiva's Eye, the pineal gland, the "petite glande" of the *Traité des passions* of Descartes.)

Verse 5
I shall humble it before you, my son, Hiram, King of the unified world, Architect of the effective Catholic Church of tomorrow, the universal regent of faith, science and art.

Hiram, King of the Unified World

The personage who concerns us here is not the symbolic hero of the Templars or of Scottish Freemasonry in England, Germany and Savoy. The "architect" of those brotherhoods was biblical in name only. The legend of his assassination by three rebellious companions and of the discovery of his body by the nine Masters is only a figure for the death of Jacques de Molay[23] and the reprisals demanded by the knights surrounding de Beaujeu, the victim's nephew. The allegory is clearly indicated by the password Nekom (Vengeance), used by the Chapter of Clermont and the Scottish lodge of the Berlin Union. If the author has considered it useful to follow Lessing, Joseph de Maistre, R. Le Forestier and several other historians of the brotherhoods in their research on the origin of an institution which claims to descend from the Essenes and from the Priests of the Holy Sepulchre, it is above all as testimony of veneration for some of its members, particularly for Kadosh Dante Alighieri of the Fede Santa,[24] and to the Rosicrucian Polybius the Cosmopolitan, *alias* René Descartes. Besides, it would be fruitless to deny the psychological interest of the study of these secret orders where vanity, the essential motive of all human actions, has flourished so freely. However tenuous, an obvious link connects their doctrine, more or less adulterated, with the two orphisms—primitive orphism and that of sixth century Greece—as well as with the evolution of philosophy in general.

The future architect mentioned by name in the *Arcana* is the spiritual son of Hiram-Abi, the builder sent by Hiram of Tyre to Solomon. It is he who will establish his temporal dominion over a world unified at first in spirit by the Holy

Catholic Church, the depository of the one divine and human truth confirmed by philosophy and science.

Faith and reason have been fighting each other for centuries. Was it not prescribed to the one to defend the holy letter, which was undecipherable for children, and to the other to rise by the road of suffering towards the serene regions of the Spirit? Today's science still awaits its synthesis and its philosophy. The poem of the *Arcana* offers a first synoptic outline of both.

The founder of the new Monarchy will also be the builder of the Cathedral of Peace, an august temple of religion and science reconciled for an all-powerful cooperation in the two spheres, spiritual and temporal. Universities, observatories, hospitals, administrative and political departments, theaters and museums dedicated to the only art deserving this name, a religious art more conscious, more synthetic, more universal than was that of Egypt and that of Greece—all laboratories of the highest thought will come to group themselves in an immense circle around the future Church of Our Lady, a Virgin-Mother of Knowledge, the Femininity of cosmic Manifestation incarnate in Mary, the mother of Christ. Every year during the two weeks of Easter, feast of the Resurrection, this universal Church founded for eternity upon the absolute identity of scientific concepts and religious dogmas—this central, catholic cathedral of a planet unified spiritually and politically under the Cross and the Scepter, this Martyrium of holiness and genius—will gather, in its precincts, delegates communicating with each other in the spirit of love, of knowledge and of peace, delegates of the United States of our Earth, today a land not of Abel but of Cain.

For the last few years only one question has preoccupied the most realistic political circles: the approaching moment, relatively not distant, when the organization of Europe will be based upon the principles which guided the foundation of the great American federation. The League of Nations already offers us a blueprint for this future edifice, even though the practical and immediate task it now assigns itself is wisely limited to averting the double menace which is gathering over Eastern Europe and the Pacific. The author of the *Arcana* has had an opportunity to follow quite closely, in his capacity as delegate in a rather sad business, the rapid development of this organism which, in its constitution, discipline and methods, is so superior to the national parliaments of our mediocre democracies. The sympathy he feels for the Assembly and the Executive Council compels him not to conceal anything of his thought. Just as the fall of the Egyptian empire and the disintegration of the Roman world seem to be child's play in comparison with the political, economic, and social crisis we are going through, this crisis itself is a small thing beside the moral anguish into which our epoch is sinking. This anguish is universal. Perhaps it is even more pronounced in the rich Americas than in our dilapidated Europe. The subjugated continents are awakening. Where is the authority which would trace the line of their new evolution? What can we tell these mystical children, who are more subtle philosophers than we are? What will we have to offer them, if not some deadly toy? Newborn countries are never peaceful, and it is simply madness to expect any moral regeneration from the progress of the sciences alone. In fifty years, the two leading nations of Western Europe will be in the situation of the Byzantine Empire. Whence will come the guarantees of independence and of equilibrium?

Who remembers the enthusiasm and the hopes of 1789? And, finally, what could be the value of an understanding even between the European nations when we do not know two of them which have the same age, physiologically, historically and above all morally? The two Americas, of the North and of the South, are themselves powerless, alas, to resolve the conflict which opposes the Monroe Doctrine to Pan-Americanism.

All these difficulties would disappear of their own accord, unveiling the secret and beneficial necessity they mask, if human beings were to repudiate once and for all the materialistic theories and the naive scepticism which trouble its existence and threaten to exhaust its sacred sources, as shown by the depopulation of the most noble countries of the world. Salvation can come only from the Spirit, but this will remain unreal and undefinable as long as we hesitate to restore to it its true name, which is the Holy Spirit.

Our epoch—this epoch which is terrible and beautiful, like a resurrection of faith—is characterized by unspeakable metaphysical anxiety. Having reached the confines of the material world, science, with a dread which, in vain, it tries to conceal from its adepts, fathoms the immensity of the mystical realm which opens at every step. The spread of the means of ultra-rapid transport and mechanization in general, both generating artificial needs, presents even to the multitudes the problem of the origins—and above all, the ends—of *Movement*. What is firm in all this, what is immutable, what is real? That is the question one reads under the mask of impassivity fixed upon the face of the modern crowd.

The anxiety which impels this crowd to its tragic questioning attains an unparalleled degree of acuteness when, in our mind, the visible movement provoking it becomes associated with the eternal whirling of electrons and the gravitation of galaxies. And yet, what is simpler than the answer? What is firm, immutable, and real in all that, is both the question itself and the heroic affirmation which it seeks. This affirmation varies in its form depending upon the degree of a twofold—scientific and moral—evolution; yet every epoch nonetheless receives the answer appropriate to its level. When the supreme affirmation was finally pronounced by the lips of God made man, the materialistic philosophy of the Roman world, speaking in the name of the entire physical Cosmos, opposed to it Pontius Pilate's splendid question, "What is truth?" This is because mankind was not mature, science was not ready, war was not dead. Matter always answers, "What is truth?" because truth is not matter. Nothing is as slow as holy operations and the accomplishment of the Great Work. "It is the end which is difficult," Goethe used to reply to those who quoted to him the adage coined by the Germans on the difficulty of beginnings. And here is the reason why the Prince of Peace himself predicts for us spiritual and physical war as the first consequence of his coming.

Today, in the sacred poem of the *Arcana*, the times foreseen by Guillaume Postel,[25] the times of "perfection in the Restitution of Nature," announce their impending appearance. Religion and science, like spirit and matter, like all the continents and all the states of this world, aspire to holy unification. What the Church in the Middle Ages used to be for Christianity, it will be tomorrow for the whole planet. But it would be sacrilegious to pretend one can foresee its hour and its action, for when the Church raises its voice, the Holy Spirit will speak through its mouth.

Verse 6
For if the truth which speaks here had been revealed to me by a creature, as it will be unveiled to you through the organ of a creature such as I am, most certainly I would not have recognized it.

The Truth

The reader's attention has already been drawn repeatedly to the events which, after thirty years of meditation exclusively devoted to the problem of space, *the key to all knowledge*, have revealed, to a mind fundamentally hostile to philosophies not founded upon experience, the existence of a superior phenomenalism which is *absolutely incorporeal and distinct from any parapsychology*. It is childish to maintain that intuition can do without the sovereign confirmation of facts. Theosophy, or rather what has been understood by this word during the last fifty years, is a fairy tale. Science and philosophy have for their object not what is probable but what is true, and there is no fundamental truth, even on the spiritual level, that in our time cannot be demonstrated by means of some physical or mathematical law. Relativity, appearing to the ignorant and to false minds under the guise of a destroyer of the absolute, is, on the contrary, a door opened onto an era of new spirituality. The very fact that it is accused of negation indicates that its detractors commit the glaring error of identifying the *absolute* with *space*. Still the founder of the new Monarchy, a more fervent Catholic than was his master, will draw all his strength from faith and humility, and will not base his convictions upon the consensus of testimonies of science and religion, a consensus good only for unsealing the eyes of sceptics.

Verse 7
At the source of ancient suffering we find erroneous physical concepts, cosmic visions of punishment.

Cosmic Visions of Punishment

Later in the poem, the two problems of love and death, inexhaustible sources of suffering, will appear to be *indissolubly bound to the question of space. Man has only one desire: to live and to love eternally.* Yet in the space which he conceives, that is, pre-existing and containing, everything has a beginning and an end. This *idée fixe* of fallen man found its naive but faithful expression in the search for perpetual motion, for the sages' elixir and for fountains of youth, puerile dreams which, however, should not make us smile, for the same ingenuously materialistic preoccupation dominates the laboratories of our modern rejuvenators. Ever since the first victory of materialism over revealed spiritual truth, our concept of space, and, consequently, of the universe and of life, which space seems to contain, has been absolutely incompatible with the healthy logic surviving intact in the depth of our latent memory. Man, created free, has materialized his secret being and, together with it, Nature in the universal sense of the word. His folly has prompted him to *situate* the containing space to which he has ascribed a real existence; this space, in his sacrilegious thought, became stretched to infinity and became identified with the spiritual absolute. Now, this precisely is Hell . . . The catabolic transfer, a purely psychological phenomenon, will be the subject of a particularly detailed examination later in our exegesis.

Verse 8
As the essence of thinking is sensation, that is, awareness and love of Movement, any psychology not founded upon an analysis of the physical concept of the world sooner or later disintegrates together with other phantoms of the imagination.

Awareness and Love of Movement

This thought is developed at length in the *Epistle to Storge* (*Ars Magna*). The extremely tight structure of this mathematical poem unfortunately prevents us from extracting even the smallest passage. Consequently, we shall have to use an image, a wretched kind of exegetic expedient. The essence of thinking is sensation, that is, a perception of movement in two worlds, inner and outer. To think is first of all to situate and to compare: however, the two operations may be reduced to one, for the initial comparison is the relation of one place to another. Thus, to think is originally to situate oneself in relation to external objects, at first physically, then morally. Later, it is to determine the position of our world in relation to that of surrounding worlds. To be is to be in a place, to cover a series of points which are themselves moving; it is to move as a mind in a body endowed with movement and carried by a world gravitating around other gravitating worlds. Copernicus, Galileo and Newton, long before they made their discoveries prompted by little moving images coming from the external world, already carried all their knowledge in their latent memory. Intuitions are recollections. By reason of the basic universal law, that of *analogy*, the essential operation of the mind extends to the moral sphere: to love and to hate is to obey a movement of attraction or of repulsion. Consequently, thinking is only an awareness and *love* of movement, an esthetic, a science of rhythm, for movement means determination of *place*, and place itself means determination of *being*. Since all our ideas have their origin in our idea of place, that is, in our concept of space, any psychology not grounded upon an analysis of our representation of the physical universe must be subjective and erroneous.

Verse 9
The language of life is unadorned. Naked is the speech of death. The world's beauty, our mother, looks in the same way on the cradle and the grave. Yet her face inspires us with a holy confidence.

Holy Confidence

Shakespeare, in a masterly passage, summed up the teaching of life. Man is a clown who, all of a sudden, appears on the stage, struts and frets his hour, and then disappears backstage. The world's beauty remains unconcerned like the "dream of stone" in the famous sonnet of Baudelaire's *Fleurs du Mal*. And yet, as Schopenhauer pointed out, the survivor pursues his small enterprises with the serenity of an immortal. In this respect nothing is more instructive than snatches of conversation overheard in cemeteries during funerals. It was during one of these moving ceremonies that the author was initiated by the heirs into the mechanical mysteries of safes.

Verse 10
Because deep within ourselves we feel very distinctly that all our innumerable questionings, except one, are frivolous and importunate, full of curiosity and alien to love.

Curiosity and Love

Since all our scientific and philosophical knowledge can be reduced to the concept of *place*, the problem of space is at the origin of our material and moral preoccupations, and at the basis of systems and works of art devoted to the destiny of our race. Only Christian philosophy has clearly defined the principle opposed to Persius' aphorism *ex nihilo nihil*, which summed up the basic concept of all cosmogonies visualizing the organization of chaos within a pre-existing space. The precise representation of an original Nothing anterior to space—bringing honor to the systems of the seventeenth century—could appear only in thought enlightened by Christian doctrine. This original "Nothing" designates, of course, only the absence of space-matter and not the absence of spiritual energy. During the last two centuries the spirit of negation on the one hand and, on the other, materialism, together with the philosophical poverty of the spiritualistic schools, once more drew humanity back into the thick slime of space, whence like fish of the abyss, humanity does not even try to rise to the surface of this universe which is finite but *situated* in the vision of God alone. When the torch of faith dies out, darkness spreads over the world and the vivifying warmth of affirmation gives way to the cold and mediocre speculations of curiosity.

Verse 11
A single question, O Hiram, makes us worthy of our great sufferings: *Where is space?*

Where is Space?

To this question which sums up the innumerable questionings that beset us from the seventh year of our lives till the grave, there is only one logical answer, and no other could satisfy the need we feel to rise, by a heroic affirmation, above our wretched condition: space is situated neither in itself through extension without end, nor, what would amount to the same, in a hyper-space of x dimensions. The question of the infinite and of the finite is irrelevant here. Space is a relationship between moving bodies; it ceases to exist where the gravitational field of milky ways, of universe-islands, ends. Suppose that all the two million universe-islands known to us gravitate around other universe-islands; space will disappear at the boundaries of the gravitational field of these wholes. Space given by movement alone has a fourth dimension—a dimension of movement—time. Movement, a physical light, a unit of velocity, is the generator of space (Grosseteste); the origins of space are thus physical: space is identical with universal matter, *a single and perfect body*. As to the movement creating space, the movement of physical light, it is born as a result of a *transmutation* of the incorporeal light known to Plotinus, Descartes, Swedenborg and the author of the *Arcana* himself, as well as to many others, ancient and modern. This incorporeal light is a link, an intermediary plane between the universe-archetype as thought by Divinity (*Bereshith*)[26] and the world of Manifestation, which presents a spatial, thus physical, appearance to whoever views it from inside, but whose real and only *place* is identical with incorporeal light, mother of physical light and thereby creator of Movement-space-time-matter.

Verse 12

The sickness of Hamlet, Faust and Manfred has its origin in a representation of the Cosmos distorted by Adam's prevarication.

Adam's Prevarication

The picture which we have drawn of creation offers us a representation of the world as it was formed in the thought of *man free in God* before the sacrilegious identification of *space with the infinite*. Man wanted to assert himself as the only master of his destiny in a containing, pre-existing space, extended to infinity by the first mental operation which made this space—and the man thinking it—equal to God, an identification which was to engender a long series of pantheistic doctrines, ancestors of our present sterile disbelief.

This first operation of cosmic black magic has a certain air of innocence because, being performed in what we call "nature," it appears "natural" to our eyes. But the darkness, the cold, the insensibility in this space extended to infinity by presumptuous thought; this darkness, this cold, is Satan himself, son of man, in all the immense and black majesty of his terrors. Holy Reason is a most delicate mechanism. Introduce as much pride as a grain of sand into the mind of a Saint Francis of Assisi, and you will obtain Hamlet-Faust-Manfred and their grandchildren of today, anguished and foolishly jeering.

Verse 13
In this representation, the idea of space, identified with that of the container, appeared as an immense curtain of darkness hanging in an eternity of time. In this night of terror, the worlds of matter and of movement took on the likeness of inexplicable holes of life and light.

Night of Terror

The night of cosmic terrors to which verse 13 alludes has its counterpart on this earth: the nights passed by mortal lovers under the gaze of the nuptial torch. The pernicious idea of the pre-existence of an infinite space which contains the material universe has not only falsified the workings of thought, but, as we shall soon see, it has adulterated the conjugal principle, the highest terrestrial correspondence of the divine sacrifice of Creation, or Hierogamy. The irreparable damage to this principle is at the origin of what we shall call, with your permission, the throes of love and death, masterfully defined by Baudelaire as "the trite canvas of our piteous fates." The conjugal arcanum will be set forth at length later in connection with the corresponding verses. For the moment it is enough to reveal that the Divine, the incorporeal hidden fire, is the Beloved of the Song of Songs and that he projects his spiritual light, mother of the physical light which creates space, in the form of a cosmic Bride-Virgin-Mother, who is the Femininity of Manifestation. Henceforth we must concern ourselves with pointing out the incalculable moral consequences of a prevarication, consequences with regard to which more than one enlightened reader of the poem of the Arcana has reproached me for ascribing only a metaphysical meaning and a purely intellectual importance.

Verse 14
Such was the vain vision of criminal pride. Man's universal dominion and his memory of origins disappeared at the very instant when the "I", accursed may it be, suggested to our ancestor a monstrous connection between the idea of space and that of the infinite.

Man's Universal Dominion

Man created in the image of God enjoyed supreme freedom such as we cannot imagine outside Affirmation, that is, outside the knowledge and the acceptance of a necessity that was identical with the Divine and that the Divine overcame only by means of the first sacrifice, Manifestation. The unique Being who is one with his law, God, in an emission of incorporeal light, exteriorized the archetypal world of his thought so that he could love it no longer inside but somehow outside, his being. The incorporeal light appeared to his view as reflected in the Nothing from which the void and the full were equally banished. (Jakob Boehme in an outburst of holy rapture exclaims: Our Lord is magical!) This incorporeal light is independent of any physical vehicle and yet perceptible from the summits of meditation, and it objectified for the first time the opposition of the idea of an exterior to that of an interior. Projected upon the Nothing which is synonymous with the non-existence of the void and the full, it transmuted itself into the first mathematical point of space-matter and, blazing up, emitted in turn the first ray of physical light, transformable into electricity and creator of the universe through expansion. The universe of matter thus formed took on in its entirety, which can be embraced only by the eye of God, the likeness of a Bride of Glory.

This Universal Nature, procreator because fecundated in the Holy Spirit without the original emission of mineral, vegetable, or animal seed, is the Virgin-Mother whose remembrance was still vivid during the epoch of Asiatic and Aegean matriarchy.

Material, insofar as it is considered as the relationship between moving bodies and when looked at from within, this universe of incorporeal light transmuted into physical light had, for its unique and absolute container, the Nothing, synonym for the *absence* of the void and the full, in which God had placed it; for created space-matter really exists only in the spiritual vision of its Creator. With respect to this space-matter, man, endowed with a perfect memory of origins, had no reason to ask the question of *place*, that is, of the finite and the infinite. Man, the consciousness of the universe, the personification of the amorous reciprocity between the Bridegroom and the Bride, was destined to live eternally, that is to say, in the instantaneity of his affirmation of the engendering Holy Spirit.

Free like omniscience itself, man situated the total universe, the unique and perfect sphere of Movement-Space-Time-Matter, in the Nothing, and in this sphere whose interior space is a pure relation of moving bodies he saw only a *state of spiritual energy*. When venerating the Divine he worshiped his own omniscience. Only one operation was forbidden to him, although it was possible for him because of his absolute freedom: the identification of God with his own knowledge, his "I."

This forbidden operation tempted him. His thought immediately became the demented representation of a pre-existing space, deified, situated in itself through the insane extension to infinity of the container and the contained. Incorporeal light, the sun of Memory, withdrew into the deepest and henceforth most inaccessible region of his being. Man, separated from God, and deprived of his spiritual unity, was split in two; he became his own master and his own slave, and, torn by the agonies of proud negation, reigned miserably over an unnatural mother, earth, plunged into spiritual night without memory.

Verse 15
Man's first thought had been a total perception of his movement: an instantaneous awareness and *love*, a religious ecstasy of rhythm.

A Religious Ecstasy of Rhythm

The child who opens his eyes or, if he is blind, makes any movement, acquires as a whole and in absolute simultaneity, knowledge, which is at first sensible then intellectual, of space-time-matter. Since the spiritual meaning of this verse has been explained more than once, we shall content ourselves by drawing the reader's attention to the role of sacred music and sacred dances in all religions. Music and dance express the acquisition of the highest knowledge through the divine numbers, whose source is in the movement of incorporeal light, mother of physical light. Incorporeal light is an indivisible unit; physical light is a unit of velocity. David dancing before the ark, the bard Demodokos leading Phiakian rondos, Leto's wanderings represented in Delos by the hyporchemata* of the hierodules,** the ritual Minoan dance of the priestesses of the Goddess-Mother, the hymn to Pythian Apollo, the Cretan paean performed on a cithara and punctuated with foot-beats, the magic whirling of dervishes, the sacred mimics of Inca Amauta, the Mexican mitote (a dance performed by a huge crowd moving in a circle around a fixed point and representing the cosmic choruses which gravitate around the spiritual unity of the central mnemonic sun), the ritual dances of primitive tribes today—innumerable examples of a symbolism brought into being in all countries and in all periods by the notion of the simultaneity of space, time and matter in Movement. Christian processions have the same significance and the torches carried depict the transmutation of incorporeal light into physical light.

Verse 16
Before reaching the brain, satellite of the heart, and becoming reflected there, this thought had been the subtle fire, the initial flash, the most profound secret, the life and the very essence of blood.

The Brain, Satellite of the Heart

In the commentary to verse 1 we have already explained that, apart from the movement of light and of the body, the notion of space was closely associated, at the very core of our being, with the circulation of blood, despite the oblivion in which this phenomenon was buried until the time of Michael Servetus and William Harvey.[27] Blood is a close relative of fire and light; to the same degree as they do, it results from an instantaneous transmutation of incorporeal light. Transforming itself into physical radiance, this light also becomes circulation, generating organic space-matter (flesh). Here is the

* choral songs and dances
** a slave attached to the service of a temple.

reason why scientists of the Middle Ages, remembering the spiritual unity of matter and comparing the heart to the sun, based their medicine on the correspondence between the humors and the stars. As the heart was identified with the sun, the brain became a satellite. It is not only its color which earned it, in alchemical language, the name of *luna*. It is a moon because it is there that the sensitive faculty—or rather the sensitive knowledge which has its seat in the heart and in the blood—is reflected like the light of the sun and transformed into *intellectual* knowledge.

Verse 17
For blood is contemporaneous with the *fiat*. It is the magic substance of the first spiritual impetus, the spontaneous, living movement of myriads of universes.

Contemporaneous with the Fiat

The *fiat* is the transmutation of incorporeal light into physical light. We have just disclosed that the appearance of blood should be identified with this operation. Issued, just like the material universe, from the instantaneous metamorphosis of spiritual light, blood is identical with the universe: one is the Macrocosm, the other, the Microcosm. Like blood, the Universe in all its parts moves independently of Newton's law, in a spontaneous manner. That is why some philosophers of the Middle Ages considered the universe to be an "animal," while Saint Justin did not hesitate to liken the act of Creation to the emission of seed. Today the "hypothesis" of the spontaneous movement of worlds is received favorably by many scientists, particularly by M. Langevin.

Blood's kinship with primitive matter, one of the dogmas of homeopathy, has also played a certain role in René Quinton's remarkable intuitions. Heliotherapy and German methods of extracting gold from sea water vigorously stress the spiritual analogies between blood, sun, sea and gold, analogies which modern atomic theory confirms from a general point of view, without, however, mentioning the system of spiritual correspondences which will be used in future alchemical medicine and of which these analogues are but the sensible signature.

Verse 18
Blood is the sum of spiritual energies manifested in Creation, this immaterial light of the Vision of Beauty and of God's love.

Sum of Spiritual Energies

Issued at the same time as the physical light from the transmutation of incorporeal brightness, blood, before it was adulterated by spiritual prevarication, was the sanctuary of the perfect memory of origins and of the unlimited knowledge of the correspondences which exist between the two phenomenal realms, physical and intelligible. We have shown how the notion of movement, which is inseparable from the circulation of blood even when it is disregarded, still today enables us to reconstruct, without the intervention of any exterior movement, the primitive simultaneity of space, time and matter. A truly philosophical idea of the importance of serums will certainly direct future search for a panacea toward the elements and products of blood and other bodily fluids. "Blood is a most particular juice" (*Faust*).

Verse 19
Blood is the first relationship, that of the Seer and the Thing seen, consequently the original appearance of movement, of space-time, of situation, of place.

First Relationship

By the word blood we understand living cosmic matter endowed with spontaneous movement. The commentary to the preceding verses has already established the common origin of blood and of physical light emanating from the same incorporeal brightness. We have said that the projection of this radiance into the Nothing objectified the opposition of the ideas of outside and of inside. The movement of this projection created the first relationship of subject to object, just as the second operation, that of the emission of physical light by a mathematical point of space-matter, created the first relationship of centripetal and centrifugal. All relationships between imaginable moving bodies were already contained in the projection of incorporeal light, the origin of suns and of blood: the first movement comprised the entire law of relativity, an *absolute* space being incompatible with the spirituality of its origin. The seer is the creator and the thing seen is the creation; the movement of blood, contemporaneous with the *fiat* and synonymous with light, is the relationship which situates them with respect to each other.

Verse 20
Grasped by the inner sense of vision, which is mnemonic and contemporaneous with God's Creative Vision, blood takes on the angelic aspect of gold which illuminates the central depths of the earth.

Gold and the Central Regions of the Earth

What is only an image for the poet Friedrich Nietzsche when he asserts, underlining the words, that *"the heart of the earth is of gold"* (Zarathustra) is, on the contrary, for the author of Ars Magna and the Arcana, the result, confirmed by geology, of the theurgic experience described in the *Epistle to Storge*. Calculation of the growing density of matter throughout its strata and layers has given for the central region of the Earth a number identical to that of the density of gold. By consulting the recent works devoted to that subject by Charles Nordmann, the reader will spare us the research necessary to find quotations. This "central gold," whose origins are solar, opens up new vistas on the constitution and evolution of cosmic matter, vistas which the alchemists of old unfortunately merely glimpsed: hence the obscurity of their allusions to the sun's role in transmutation. Nevertheless an attentive study of their marvelous works has enabled me to recognize, in the solar regulation of the philosophical fire, the very principle of their art: "The one who is washed is the serpent Python, who, having taken his being of corruption from the silt of the earth, gathered by the waters of the flood, when all the compounds were water, should be slain and vanquished by the shafts of the God Apollo, by the blond sun, that is, by our fire equal to that of the Sun" (Nicholas Flamel,[28] *Le Livre des Figures Hiéroglyphiques*). And this charming and wise advice of the same author: "The heat then of your fire in this vessel will be, as Hermes and Rosinus say, according to Winter, or else, as Diomedes says, according to the heat of the Bird who starts to fly so gently from the sign of Aries to that of Cancer." But above all it is the Cosmopolitan's *La Lettre Philosophique* which enlightens us in the most precise and affirmative way as to the role the royal Art ascribed to the sun in the regeneration and activity of gold (obviously, the *fourth* gold): ". . . And as God wanted the higher things to have their image in the lower, it happens that we see the image of the sun in gold, which possesses the dilated virtues of the sun, compressed in its body, and if we reduce them from potency to act, they have enough power amply to provide imperfect or sick bodies with the solar and vivifying virtue they lack. By its magnetic virtue the sun attracts the purest spirits and perfects them to send them back through its rays, in order to restore the bodies of particular creatures and to make them grow." The spectroscope has not, hitherto, revealed gold in the sun, undoubtedly because it exists there in that "living, spiritual" state to which modern homeopathy, which attaches great importance to this matter, would like to restore it.

Verse 21

For in the earth, as in man, remembrance of origins slumbers, unpolluted; and when spiritual prevarication reaches its limit, this remembrance will awaken to testify against false science.

False Science

From a psychological point of view, the scientific history of the nineteenth century has been marked by two widespread phenomena, contrary but equally symptomatic: the resistance offered by the partisans of spontaneous generation to the decisive proofs of Pasteur, and the fantastic infatuation with Bergson's thought. It is precisely by the breadth of these reactions that we can measure the narrowness and rigidity of the bounds within which the mediocre *sensibility* of this time moves. What are vulgar superstitions compared with those of an elite bogged down in a physical or mental mechanism? Is not the latter at the origin of the crass and fatal illusion that makes simultaneity and absolute identity of space, time and matter in movement appear as succession and separation? Powerful men and truly great epochs are recognizable by one sure sign: the discovery that a physical law goes contrary to the letter of Scripture never throws their minds into confusion. The teaching of Galileo does not stop Descartes on his road to Loreto, and what the watchful Church is afraid of is not the text, it is the commentary. Fortunately man is so made that not only his own most intimate nature but also the most mechanical aspect of his genius transcends him: he prepares for war in the air, and it is these ideal routes traced in the sky which will make the Earth into one country.

Verse 22

The first thought of the King of the world was thus an integral perception of his movement.

EXEGETIC NOTES

The First Thought

The sublime order observed by the workings of universal and earthly nature, the knowledge and love expressed by the signature and language of all things, this air of knowing where one is, whence one comes and whither one goes, all these admirable signs of wisdom full of confidence made me appear in my own eyes, long ago in the days of my tormented childhood, as a monster begotten by an unknown and horrible mother for whom I endlessly searched and whose trace I could find nowhere. I felt I was placed so low in the hierarchy of beings that my parents of the flesh—though themselves weak, troubled, and devoid of true charity—seemed to condescend toward me, radiantly like powerful and happy deities whom no spiritual bond united with my miserable fate. I do not know what strange curse weighed on my body and soul. What especially surprised me in the spectacle which unfolded as I wandered through the marvelous and wild places of my ancestors' estate, was that all these things could *move* with such ease, such carelessness, such lightness. I, who was splitting myself in two, like Schopenhauer when he was a child, did not try, as he did, to look for the source of my own torment in the heart of things, so strongly did I feel their external mechanism was adjusted to their most secret tendency. All this beautiful mobility, from cloud and river to the bird in the old lane and the ant on the lawn, was free and ran where life called it. With the slowness of eroding mosses whose feet are imbedded in wood and in stone, I alone was creeping toward the haunted city of my desire. Later, in the period of my youthful dissipation, the same amazement and the same envy would seize me at the sight of the naturalness, the spontaneity, the inadvertent mastery of movements of a human body transported by dance, hunting, or combat. It was only toward the end of my youth that I succeeded in penetrating the inner meaning of this eternal questioning which obsessed me. I was the martyr of a second memory established in my body as if in an alien country: day, night, sadness, joy, agitation and rest, excitement and boredom nagged me endlessly with the same question that I could not understand. One evening, stumbling upon a stepladder in the old flower market at the Madeleine, I suddenly, so to speak, entered into myself. What had tormented me in this manner was, under a thousand masks of love, fear, pride and disgust, one and the same problem, the eternal, insoluble problem of space. But it was only much later, in 1916, two years after the events related in the *Epistle*, that I managed, by sensation rather than by thought, to grasp it apart from any sequence, in full simultaneity of the three terms in the fourth, Movement. I was finished with "absolute" space and "psychological" time. The aim of everything which changes place (and where could you find a thing without movement?) is the immutability of supreme love, it is Faith. Mine awaited me at the end of what an arid journey! I had before me, in a single whole filling total space, only universal matter: what destroyer ever lived through a similar moment? I stripped matter of its spontaneous movement—I killed this immense and living thing; not a scrap of this single and perfect Body subsisted. I identified myself with the Nothing whence the void and the full, and time and movement, are banished. And in this Nothing I recognized the Place of holy light, abyss of unfathomable charity and unfathomable beauty, which had been given to me to contemplate in a reality compared to which all the weight of the Cosmos is only an illusion. I was free in my movements: I ceased to be hidden gold imprisoned in the stone of infinite space—I was free in my only Master. That is how the first thought of the King of the world, the consciousness of his first movement, was revealed to me.

Verse 23
And this first thought included the sum of all knowledge, for movement is a perfect simultaneity, an absolute identity and an indivisible unity of space, matter and time.

The Sum of all Knowledge

Man is a triplicity of space, time and matter, grasped instantaneously in the unity of the first movement. This instantaneity of initial perception is what we call thought; it is the foundation of all sciences. The *first* movement is, consequently, the very instantaneity of the world of space-time-matter, the one indivisible body. But the *second* movement, with which appears the notion *of a relation between one moving body and another*—a creative relation of determined or describable space—this second movement succeeding the first becomes identical with *time*, a dimension of determined or describable space. And because movement thus becomes identical with time, some philosophers by a confusion of notions substitute for the idea of movement, creator of space, that of *psychological time* which, in their mind, acquires an absolute character which Relativity denies to space. What they call psychological time is the very movement to which we ascribe a spiritual origin.

Verse 24
Be attentive, my son, for here is the cornerstone, the very Stone of space-time-motion itself.

The Stone-Space

The sacrifice of the Father (spiritual generation) whose temporal correspondence is the Crucifixion and the Blood spilled by the Son (spiritual regeneration), has already been described in the exegesis of the preceding verses. Here we shall limit ourselves to a summary. Incorporeal fire, the only one situated because it is the Place itself before there was space—God—is identical with his law, with his necessity; and he loves himself in this world-archetype which he is, for to be one's own law, one's own necessity, means to be Love. But

Love is what gives itself, what sacrifices its most intimate essence. The incorporeal Fire therefore projects its incorporeal light upon the Nothing, upon what is not a place but simply the idea of an *exterior* (creation *ex nihilo*). This is the *Fiat Lux*: incorporeal light (first vision) transmutes itself by the omnipotence of love (first miracle) into a mathematical point of space, hence, of matter; from this point it pursues its course under the form of physical light (first movement) whose expansion creates space-time-matter, the universe of manifested matter. Spiritual light is the soul of physical light; it is what lends to suns their secret vivifying power. By becoming the movement of physical light, spiritual light also produces the movement of blood: in this blood, the creator of organic space-time-matter (first man), spiritual light is the soul, the Sun of Memory perceptible in the mystical vision, daughter of God's vision. In crowning himself king of an infinite universe-space situated in itself by endless extension (first sin), man threw a veil of darkness upon the sun of his memory; this first sin is represented temporally by the Crucifixion, murder of the Spirit incarnate in Creation, as well as by the darkening of the physical sun which followed. The extinction of latent memory was accompanied by the extinction of the first language by means of which man communicated with the spirit omnipresent in beings and things (Myth-remembrance of Orpheus). This is exactly the language sought in vain by poets and artists in the depths of their being.

The expansion of physical light, daughter of incorporeal light, created space-matter. This physical creation is the Bride of the Song of Songs, the Femininity of Manifestation, of procreating cosmic matter, spiritually fecundated at the origin without the aid of a first seed. This is the universal and terrestrial Nature born of God as Eve was born of Adam.

However, the total Universe created by the expansion of physical light, the total universe of space-time-matter wherein space-time becomes identical in movement with matter and consequently appears as a single and perfect Stone, this total universe has no absolute situation other than that of the first mathematical point from which it proceeds and which the incorporeal light formed in the Nothing.

Verse 25
When the spirit of purity and of obedience prompted the newborn Adam to rise from the ground so that he might bless the world's beauty, our ancestor *felt he was the Universe.*

Our Ancestor Felt He Was the Universe

Rising from the ground and stretching out his arms in a gesture of blessing, Adam, with his first movement of his body, embraced the simultaneity of space, time and matter, in a correspondence and confirmation of that instantaneity whose notion was intimately united with the very flow of his blood; the movement of his blood was a twin of the spontaneous movement of universes, issued alike from incorporeal light.

Verse 26
Because the magic virtue of the first movement opened for him the fundamental notion—single and indivisible—of space-time-matter.

Magic Virtue

In a truthful style, as well as in sound thought and genuine sensation, everything is phenomenon, nothing is image. The literary image is make-up, concealing the inexpressive faces of natural muses.

The divine muse of the Bible does not pronounce a single word that does not correspond to an object or a fact of the three worlds, namely: of the archetypal or celestial world, of the spiritual world of light, creator of the mathematical point, and of the natural world of physical light. All poets of modern times, except Dante, Goethe and two or three others, are blind children of fallen natural muses.

Verse 27
Our Ancestor's thinking was, then, the thinking of the Universe rather than that of man.

Rather Than

These words are used in verse 27 only to hint at a hesitation (of pure courtesy) with which an affirmer is obliged to convey his simplest and most certain truths to the childishly sceptical elite of his time.

Verse 28
By this thinking, by this awareness of Movement, Adam *situated* his movement, his being, in relation to movement, to the being of the sun, the stars and the surrounding objects.

Adam Situated

To situate oneself or to situate any object is to determine how the movement that one is, or that an object is, relates to the movement with which another being or object is identified. Space, *place*, is nothing other than the relation between movement A and movement B. These relations, of incalculable and yet finite number, are the *interior* space of the unique and perfect Body with respect to which there is no conceivable *exterior*, for this exterior is identical with the Nothing from which the void as well as the full is banished. There are only relations between parts: the Whole is a synonym for spirit.

Verse 29
For what we call thinking, both in its origin and later at various degrees of its evolution, is only an awareness and love of movement, and thus a pure determination of place.

Various Degrees of its Evolution

Mathematics, physico-chemistry, astronomy, philosophy, poetry and art in general are only various aspects of one science whose goal is to situate all things by means of their physical and moral relationships. With a pious and charming naïveté, primitive civilizations put these *places* imposed upon human thought into concrete form, as if to stress that mental movement is itself the creator of spaces and forms: to these childish games of unfathomable wisdom we owe the abodes of the blessed and the damned, all forms of Arcadia and Parnassus, of Lethe and the Styx, of Urania and Mnemosyne.

Verse 30
Adam's thinking, the awareness and love of movement, applied itself likewise to situating each part of the Cosmos, the smallest and the greatest, through a relationship between the movement of this part and the movement of another. In this fundamental operation, Place, space inseparable from time-movement, became identical with a dynamic relationship, and the whole, grasped in its perfect simultaneity, its absolute instantaneity, produced Matter, magic substance of the world.

Matter, Magic Substance of the World

The movement of incorporeal light is an indivisible unit. Its transmutation into a movement of physical light gives the first divisible unit, the matrix of multiplicity, which is total finite space, considered from within in the relations between moving bodies. The same numerical law of triplicity in unity rules over our two perceptions of space and of extension:

movement, space, time = matter. Length, breadth, depth = matter. But the reign of the sacred Tetrad also embraces the elements which make up every one of the three components that we distinguish in the notion of space-matter: cause, effect, end = movement; length, breadth, depth = space; past, present, future = time. By adding the constitutive elements we obtain the number Nine, which gives us for universal Matter, single and perfect Body, Pythagoras' Perfect Decad. Obtained by a new calculation this Decad derives from a pure principle of metaphysical thought unrelated to any mysticism and based upon its three elements: space, time and matter fused in the unity of movement. Total space, always considered from within, consequently borrows its three dimensions from extension and, whether full or not, becomes identical with each one of its determined parts and with their entirety. These parts themselves differ from each other only by the numerical relationship between the moving parts which make them *bodies*, their chemical nature being determined exclusively by the number of their electrons.

Verse 31
In other words, in Adam's thinking, all describable space—that is, all space susceptible to being situated experimentally in the numerical relation between galaxies, systems, worlds, and moving bodies in general—that describable space together with movement-time, formed a single universal Body.

A Single Universal Body

Were we able to stand in the center of total space and look around through the universal globe (let us suppose it is transparent), its matter would appear to us as continuous as that of a crystal ball. Modern astronomy no longer likens interplanetary spaces to those spaces which separate atoms, but to the gravitational fields of electrons whirling around the nucleus of the atom itself. An intra-atomic vision of astronomy would, accordingly, lead us from our sun to a neighboring sun, and without exaggeration we may speak of our Milky Way as one block of matter possessing extreme density comparable to that of the components of atoms and proportional to the average velocity of universe-islands, which is a thousand kilometers per second. As to intergalactic distances, they vary from two hundred thousand to one hundred forty million light-years, and so are incredibly modest, since the smallest of them are inferior to the diameter of our Milky Way by a hundred thousand light-years. The total mass of the universe—of a single and perfect Body—is thus infinitely compact. One should not forget, however, that in our theory these intra-atomic spaces are themselves *matter*, by the sole fact of simultaneity as we conceive it and apart from the existence of an ether. To the science of today, whose instruments have explored only a minimal part of space, the density of the universe appears almost nonexistent.

Verse 32
Adam's thinking could not imagine this perfect cosmic body, this total space solidified as it were in a unity of matter placed outside any dynamic relationship, in any way other than *situated* in the Nothing, in the Nothing from which both the void and the full, movement and time, are banished.

Situated in the Nothing

The entirety of what has been drawn from nothingness can only have nothingness as its place, since any determined place is a simple relation between objects. To be situated in the Nothing does not mean to be identical with this Nothing. A thing whose place is the Nothing is as distinct from this Nothing as it is from God. Pantheism, that religiosity of timorous negators, is as far from our thought as atheism is. The poem of the *Arcana* is a new light thrown upon the intangible book of Catholic orthodoxy. A creation of God's incorporeal light, the finite universe can be situated only in this light; considered in its entirety it cannot have any *relationship* to something else, as there are no other universes, and its only relationship is that which binds matter and spirit. But what other, more indisputable reality could we grant to total substance—so elusive in its parts—than to assign it the place of the bride in the unfathomable vision of the bridegroom? The vision exists, and its existence is more certain than any relationship of a part to a part: for did it not have to project itself upon the idea-archetype of an *exterior*, so that Love might overcome Necessity? God speaks to it, and does not the beauty of all human work reside in that language, as does the value of any vow exchanged throughout the ages? The Logos descends into the grave and is reborn. The presence in the Scriptures of a second and a third meaning is obvious, particularly in the colloquy of love in the Song of Songs: the Couple is that of the King and the Queen, of Christ and the Church, of God and Universal Beauty. But what work, even of divine inspiration, what song of Dante or of Simeon ben Yohai whispered in the dead crypt of our ancient memory, will restore this proud and pure language that Wordsworth sought vainly in the voice of childhood and whose alphabet, having also become secret, is still written on the sky and on the meadow?

Verse 33
For the concept of a space, of an exterior void, by the inevitable association of this void with the already existing material realm, that is, with the mobile pattern of relationship, would only have resulted in a substantial addition, an infinite extension of the single universal body.

Infinite Extension

The absurd and criminal identification of the infinite with space, and, consequently, of eternity with time, falsified the faculty of judgment to the point at which it became unable to situate itself in its principle, that is, to think itself. The works of the most renowned writers abound in nonsense such as: "One eternity behind, one eternity ahead." "Beyond Infinity, Infinity begins," "What unknown universes fill the endless Space which follows after Space, as Time follows after Time." Truly, when mentioning our epoch, our great grandchildren will have all the reasons in the world to blush for shame. Lamarck, Darwin, and Haeckel committed a sacrilegious error by ascribing animal origins to our species, but Nietzsche was not completely wrong when he treated his contemporaries as apes. The mystics alone have had a precise and sane notion of space and of time. Emanuel Swedenborg does not visualize the infinite as an eternal succession of spaces; he considers it to be the *spiritual origin* of space. Space and time came into being, like the universe itself, out of immensity and eternity. They were *introduced* into the world *to distinguish one thing from another. In immensity and eternity there is neither time nor space.* (See *The True Christian Religion*, 27, 29, 31.) However, the powerful and pious thought of that universal genius, shamelessly pillaged by scientific celebrities during the last two centuries (consult on this subject a remarkable work by Rodolph-Leonard Tafel)—the thought of the greatest of the theurgists—was not able to rise to the concept of physical simultaneity, the origin of universal relativity. And yet the road leading there is easy and direct. Let us admit for a moment the existence of infinite space. We cannot attempt to conceive it otherwise than by mathematical means. As far as its unity is concerned we manage to grasp it as an ideal image only when we multiply space incessantly by itself. In this way we obtain an infinity of infinites, which we transform into a single infinity not by the power of our thought but by an abdication of our effort. In order to grasp this infinite in its parts, let us move now in reverse and have recourse to division, not multiplication. We know today that the proton itself is divisible: all the more reason to think that the same is true of total space. Let us then divide, and by the first even number: if we obtain half of infinity it will be already a determinate quantity which, added to the other half, will give us a *determinate* infinity, thus finite infinity. Now, let us divide infinity by infinity—we will have a determinate *infinity*, thus a finite infinity. What conclusion may be drawn from these absurd calculations? That infinite space, the usurper of the Throne of Spiritual Unity, *is not divisible. Infinite space has no parts.* Let us fill this infinity with matter: universal matter has no parts, the problem remains the same. Matter becomes indeterminate; yet what we search for is the Place. If infinite space has no parts, how could we imagine within it a universe of finite matter? Will not this universe be a part of that which has no parts? By a logic that is not of our small world, are we not compelled to formulate the following law: every part of the infinite is infinite in itself? Our universe of matter, a part of infinite space, is therefore infinite in itself. In order to find its place it has no need to be extended to infinity by our thought. As a part, it is infinite in itself, it fills the Whole, but this Whole no longer needs to be extended to infinity in thought. We will say, then, that our space of matter is simply limitless and is situated in itself without any container, since the question of the infinite without parts makes no sense. Our limitless universe (and we gave it this name already in 1916, in the *Epistle to Storge,* published January 1, 1917, in *La Revue de Hollande*) is, then, space in itself, without any exterior space containing it, because as a part of the infinite it is infinite in itself, in other words, limitless, *not limited by any exterior space.* Its only place is thus not of a containing but of an immanent nature. *The question of the finite and of the infinite does not arise concerning it*: material so long as it is considered from its divisible interior, describable in the relations of object to object, of movement to movement, it is in itself spiritual; in itself it is God's incorporeal light projected by a pure act of love on the idea-archetype of an *exterior.* The universe is a Vision of beauty and of love seen by the Only Seer—woe to those who make of it a monstrous material deity extending to infinity or situated in an absurd void without end.

Verse 34
Adam's thinking also understood that an illusion of immobility, assuming the aspect of the lack of movement in a thing taken as a whole, attaches to a multitude of objects even if, like the stars their fathers, they are endowed with a plurality of movements; for everything is cosmic substance carried by the torrent of universal blood.

The Torrent of Universal Blood

We have said that the universal, interior and spontaneous movement of the single Body is identical with that of blood. This is the movement of the Macrocosm and the Microcosm, both engendered by the first movement of one and the same incorporeal light. But in the mobile interior of the single Body, which is motionless because it is not surrounded by space, universal movement splits into a series of movements whose numbers vary according to whether they bear upon organized or non-organized bodies. In the present state of our knowledge, the number of movements applicable to man—if we put aside Wegener's still hypothetical theory of continental drift—would be nine: the gravitation of the galaxy, of the solar system, of the planet; the rotation of the planet; the whirling of electrons; the circulation of blood, and organic phenomena related to it, the movement of the body and its limbs; growth; and, finally, the ascertainment of movement or thought. If we add to this number the global movement which leads us from birth to death, we obtain once again the famous decadic triangle. As to inorganic bodies, we are forced to refuse them at least those movements whose absence makes them appear immobile to our eyes, although according to Schopenhauer's theory any *communicated movement is itself the sign of an inner will to movement*. Whatever the case may be with the immobility of inorganic bodies, we intuitively venerate the correspondence to *Immobility in itself,* that is, the immobility of the unique and perfect Body not surrounded by space, in itself *an infinite part of the infinite, no longer having any need to be situated by means of an extension without end.* Various stone cults beginning with the neolithic period, the symbolism of the corner-stone, as well as the adoration of sacred trees, widely spread from Oceania to Dodona and throughout the whole Indo-European world (see Domeni De Rienzi and Chamisso)[29] seem to conceal beneath their innumerable interpretations this reminiscence of a primitive omniscience subsequently lost.

Verse 35
This appearance of immobility, this impression of nothing in the thing, struck Adam's thinking with respect and awe. And Adam blessed the trees and the stones.

Trees and Stones

We are far from ascribing any sort of idolatry to Adam, who understood God's language, now effaced from our memory and, as we have observed before, vainly sought by our poets. Adam blessed not the matter of trees and stones, but the spirituality of Creation, of the single Body, as he saw its mystical imprint in the immobility of trees and stones. Of all beings and all things of this world, only the sacred palm had its pictorial representation on the walls of Solomon's Temple. As for the stones used in building the sanctuary, it was forbidden to expose them to contact with iron, which prohibition should remind us of the Pythagorean prohibition regarding fire.

Verse 36
But Adam's thinking, being that of the universe, never tried to assign a place to the entirety of the world, or to make a sum of all those movements which are situated through their relationship alone.

Adam's Thinking

The commentary to the preceding verses exempts us from dwelling on the spiritual meaning of verse 36. To assign a Place to the entirety of the world is to bring about a projection of incorporeal light onto the idea-type of an exterior. This first movement, to which Faust alludes in the admirable verse: *"Im Anfang war die Tat"* (in the beginning was the act), is identical with divine omnipotence. The secret of the operation is sometimes unveiled to the mystic after years of suffering, meditation, and prayer. However, the projection carried out by a theurgist is only an image of the Act, and although the clarity, the reality, of the image exceeds that of all objects in the sensible world, it cannot be compared with the reality of the Act itself. Adam possessed the secret. The spiritual place of the world was accessible to him without any preparatory trials. The idea of a *physical* situation of the total universe could not therefore in any way be reconciled with first Nature, all wisdom and submission. The explanation of the fall will be given with the corresponding verses. Let us add, however, that a projection carried out theurgically passes through all the essential phases of the regeneration of a mineral and results in the spiritual formation of the feminine gold of Jewish alchemy: here in the world of phenomena is the origin of the "myth" of the Golden Age.

Verse 37
For the total universe is not a place. As in time there are wakefulness and sleep, so in instantaneity the entirety of the universe is only a *state* situated in its spiritual opposition to the

nothing, to the *nothing* from which the void and the full, movement and time, are banished. In the mind of the Just, total space, the non-situated universe, total space which is the pure vision of beauty and of God's love, was *absolutely alien to any intuition of the infinite*. Space, being matter, could not, in the thinking of the Just, be elevated to that archangelic level where the immutable idea of the infinite reigns in insubstantial light.

The Immutable Idea of the Infinite

Our true, unadulterated idea of the infinite is identical with what is deepest and purest in our being and is nothing other than the idea of the knowledge which God has of himself. The idea of the infinite is that of the consciousness of God. What God perceives when he broods over his consciousness is the infinite. True theurgy, that of grace, which prays and waits without searching, without expecting anything from the vain and sacrilegious semblances of analogy, such a theurgy can give us a feeble image of what God sees in us, but it is unable to make us aware of what God sees in God. The burning bush is but God seen by God in Moses, it is not God seen by God in himself. What God sees in God I do not want, I do not want to see, I do not want to know. And even if this cry of my soul turns against my soul like the sword of the guardian of the gate, I do not want, I do not want to see, I do not want to know.—"Respect, Respect, Respect" (*Wilhelm Meister*).

Verse 38
My son, I am coming out of an absurd and terrifying dream.

Absurd and Terrifying Dream

The political, social, scientific and literary history of humanity is a nightmare dominated by an obscure *idée fixe*, a question without answer: "What am I?" The first question of a sleeper liberated from his infernal obsessions will be:

"Where am I?" Compare this with Goethe's scientific principle: "the thing is to know not *why* but *how*."

Verse 39
I ran after myself and I could not grasp myself.

Adam, the Master of our Freedom, has changed the infinite—that is, his idea of the knowledge that God has of himself—into a space without end, an eternally fleeting result of ceaseless multiplication: Adam has lost his way in the universal darkness which followed the extinction of the Sun of Memory.

Verse 40
The two states which I was, my sleep and my wakefulness, my life and my death, pursued each other and could not be joined because there was no *place*.

There was no Place

In a universe of matter extended to infinity there would be room for everything, except for place.

Verse 41
When suddenly, in a paroxysm of universal terror, I felt *I was catching up with my remembrance*. At the same instant, facing the primordial Nothing, I renounced forever all concern for *reality*.

Reality

What is meant here is the reality of the material world situated in itself by extension. For thought that is concerned only with sensible objects, the question of reality arises only in correlation with these objects. The result is an attempt to determine place through endless multiplication. The most striking example of this universal aberration of ideas is offered to us by a prodigious poet but execrable metaphysician, Edgar Allan Poe. The immortal author of *Ulalume*, of *Silence*, of *The Colloquy of Monos and Una*, of *Annie*, of *To Helen*—I stop, for what is more inappropriate than to cite from a body of work which constitutes a unique literary monument, an incomparable paragon of pure poetry—this great Irishman has left us a metaphysical testament, *Eureka*, which is undoubtedly of all the works deserving an *auto da fé* the most false and the most pernicious. This book, however, provides a lesson which we submit to the reflection of our misguided epoch: endless multiplication does not stop at space; it dares to force its way to God in order to present us with a spectacle of unpardonable prevarication:

> I myself feel impelled to the *fancy*—without daring to call it more—that there *does* exist a *limitless* succession of universes, more or less similar to that of which we have cognizance—to that of which *alone* we shall ever have cognizance—at the very least until the return of our own particular Universe into Unity. *If* such clusters of clusters exist, however—*and they do*—it is abundantly clear that, having had no part in our origin, they have no portion of our laws. They neither attract us, nor we them. Their material—their spirit is not ours—is not that which obtains in any part of our Universe. They could not impress our senses or our souls. Among them and us—considering all, for the moment, collectively—there are no influences in common. Each exists, apart and independently, *in the bosom of its proper and particular God*. (EUREKA, the works of Edgar Allan Poe, edited by John H. Ingram, Volume III, London, A. and C. Black, Soho Square, 1901, p. 164.)

What imagination! But what spiritual infamy! Edgar Poe was not a madman. His thought, of nearly superhuman power, was much more sane than that of his detractors. Alas! No. Edgar Poe was not a madman: he was *accursed*, in the full Christian sense of the word. But since he found the worst of Hells in his American native land, peace to his poet's soul.

Verse 42
Adam's first thought had been an integral perception of movement: in the heart and in the arteries of the King ran the total light of the world.

The Total Light of the World

Adam's first thought was an awareness of his movement. The original notion of this movement blended with the very circulation of the blood. But blood, together with physical light, creator of the world, originated in the transmutation of incorporeal light: the total light of the universe ran therefore in the heart and in the arteries of the King.

Verse 43
Adam was sovereign memory. Drawn from cosmic substance, he remembered the cry of his magic birth, similar to the solar laughter of lead changed into gold.

Memory

This total light was an absolute memory of the spiritual origin of the universe, of physical light and of blood, of the Macrocosm and the Microcosm. Blood, struck by the inner mnemonic ray, is transformed into gold. The author of *The Arcana* has witnessed such a transmutation. On this earth there is no desire so pure, so elevated, so ardent, the unhoped-for fulfillment of which could bring a joy like that felt at the simultaneous regeneration of spirit and mineral, the latter standing in this case for "the perfection of the regeneration" of Nature in its entirety.

Verse 44
Every operation of the King opened with the fundamental affirmation: I am in him who is, for what separates me from Being is the Nothing.

The Nothing

I am the King of a world which, together with my blood, issued from the transmutation of incorporeal light; my only place (and that of the world subject to my law) is, then, the nothing into which God has projected this light. *But this nothing is the idea-type of an exterior*: it is only because of this nothing that I am exterior in the idea of God. Nevertheless, the nothing is only the absence of space, time, matter and movement. I am therefore in him who is.

Verse 45
The holy notion of the Nothing has been given to me so that I might know that only the nothing separates me from him who is and in whom I am.

The Holy Notion of the Nothing

Certainly holy, because it separates us from God for the sake of adoration, and identifies us with God for the sake of union. In the commentary to the preceding verse we have already said that the idea of the nothing is what separates and unites.

Verse 46
The Nothing is the code word of the Noble Travellers. It is the entrance and the exit of the labyrinth.

The Noble Travellers[30]

Transmitted by oral tradition to initiates of the Middle Ages and of modern times, Noble Traveller is the secret name of initiates of antiquity. The last time that it was pronounced in public was on May 30, 1786, in Paris, at a session of Parliament devoted to the cross-examination of a famous defendant, victim of a pamphleteer, Theveneau de Morande. Initiates' wanderings did not differ from ordinary travels for study except that their itinerary, though apparently haphazard, rigorously coincided with the adept's most secret aspirations and gifts. The most illustrious examples of these pilgrimages are offered to us by: Democritus, who was initiated into the secrets of alchemy by Egyptian priests and by Ostanes, the magus, and into Asiatic doctrines during his stays not only in Persia but also, according to some historians, in India as well; Thales, instructed in the temples of Egypt and of Chaldea; and Pythagoras, who visited all the countries known to the ancients (and, very probably, India and China), whose sojourns were distinguished—in Persia by conversations with Zaratas the Magus, in Gaul by his cooperation with the Druids, and in Italy by his speeches at the Assembly of the Elders of Crotona. To these examples it would be proper to add Paracelsus' stays in France, Austria, Germany, Spain and Portugal, England, Holland, Denmark, Sweden, Hungary, Poland, Lithuania, Valachia, Carniola, Dalmatia, Russia and Turkey, as well as the travels of Nicolas Flamel to Spain where Maistre Canches taught him how to decipher the famous hieroglyphic figures of the Book of Abraham the Jew. The poet Robert Browning has defined the secret nature of these scholarly pilgrimages in a stanza particularly rich in intuition: "I see my way as birds their trackless way.... In some time, His good time, I shall arrive: He guides me and the bird." Wilhelm Meister's years of travel have the same initiatic meaning.

Verse 47
This notion of the nothing, whence does it come to me, to me who am movement and, consequently, space, time, matter?

The Notion of the Nothing

This notion should not be confused with that of the void, even the "absolute" void. The metaphysical nothing is a total absence of movement, and, consequently, of space, time and matter. The void, on the contrary, is an extreme, ideal density of substance; and it is this intuitive concept that, in the quarrel between the partisans of the void and those of a "subtle matter," governed the minds of both; the former philosophically identified space with matter through a relationship of localization which made space and matter one, while the latter did this in a more scientific way through the simultaneity of their appearance. Basically, all such differences of opinion, in whatever field they become manifest, are psychological testimonies rather than rational indices. The itineraries of all our learning are traced upon the old golden tablets of memory, and any voyage of exterior exploration should start with an act of faith in the consecrated place of the labyrinth; this act, moreover, should never be taken as a sign of possession of faith, but only as showing a desire of faith. That is why there is no excuse for disbelief biased in advance and refusing *the experience* of prayer.

Verse 48
I, the Thing, how then did I manage to tear the great funereal seal of the black and frozen void off my idea of the nothing?

The Thing

The Thing, essentially: since like the Macrocosm itself, I have my origin in incorporeal light, I am the perfect Body created by the movement of blood, just as the universe is the perfect body created by the movement of the physical light. When mentioning the latter, it is advisable never to forget that it is transformable into electricity, and that from this state of matter it returns to the state of light.

Verse 49
For the corporeal Water of space-time was not poured by the fiat into the receptacle of a prior void. The Stone of space-time was not thrown into a pre-existing void.

Water, Stone

The two terms figuratively designate one and the same thing, namely, the total universe, the single and perfect body, all movement in its interior parts of space-matter and all absolute immobility as a whole, situated not in a void but in the incorporeal light that was projected into the Nothing.

Verse 50
The void is space. Yet space, even deprived of ether, is matter, inseparable from some kind of movement identical with time. Therefore the void could not appear without the universes' appearing in the same instant.

Movement Identical with Time

In an abstract mode of thinking, one should, above all, avoid losing sight of the fact that relationship is the fundamental law of all phenomena, and that there is no form of relationship which cannot be reduced to a simple relationship of situation, hence, of movement. Far from limiting the scope of this law by its recent discoveries, science extended it to the molecule, to the atom, to the components of the atom, and, through the fission of the nucleus, to the elements of the components. However logical it seems at first glance, therefore, no hypothesis should be accepted before it is tested by the touchstone of a law which, both on the largest and on the smallest scale, indicates a close relationship between the subject and the object, whether we attach to the latter a concrete or an abstract meaning. Where, then, would be the situation of the void in which vulgar opinion deems it convenient to place the world? Its situation would be determined by the only imaginable opposition: of an infinite void to its filled part, or rather to the movement of this part, that is, to the interior space-time given by the relationships between moving bodies. Our thought, awareness and love of movement would thus inevitably extend this interior pattern of relationship, of space-time, into the exterior void. Yet space-time as a whole goes together with the three dimensions of each of its parts. The exterior void indissolubly associated in our mind with the single Body would acquire, as a result, the three dimensions of this Body which is, moreover, situated in it: now, as the three dimensions are identical with *extension* (which is matter for Descartes), our exterior void would inevitably force us to imagine a Body extended to infinity, and would throw us into the abyss of melancholy where there is only multiplying and extending, the true origin of all the misfortunes of mankind and of universal Nature. The categorical imperative has no part in the development of our ideas. Rather, we are inclined to admit that the goals of science and those of morality are absolutely identical. The idea of the "invariable" and the preoccupation with "the immobile" constantly bring the former closer to the latter: from there to their meeting in the concept of a purely spiritual origin of movement, the distance is not great. The day when it is crossed, we will breathe freely at last in a universe whose necessary material appearances will not have undergone the slightest change, but whose *reality*, so much desired, will be given to us by its Place, unimaginable except in the incorporeal light and in the divine fire which spreads it: for there is nothing aside from the Seer and the Vision: this is what verse 51 seeks to express.

Verse 51
My only place is in the one who has breathed into the nothing the ecstatic mirage of the world's beauty.

Verse 52
O Hiram, this Nothing of which the immobility of inorganic matter is the mute hieroglyph, this Nothing, what void would suffice to fill it up?

Again the Nothing

The idea-type of an "exterior" into which the ineffable fire projects its incorporeal light, the nothing that became, through a transmutation of this light into the first physical movement, a mathematical point generative of total space-time-movement, the nothing whose seal is upon every immobile object *in its aggregate*, the nothing, what infinity of void could fill it up?

Verse 53
It is a spiritual, insubstantial, primordial water; and precisely in it, transmuted as it is into blood, movement and thought, we perceive total space, pure appearance; we perceive total space, certainly matter, and yet it is more illusory than the inverted image of the limited expanse reflected in corporeal water.

An Image Reflected Upside-Down in Corporeal Water

The thought and the image (alas, one must have recourse to the latter!) are quite clear here. What is more real than the reflection in limpid water of a scene with its sky, its clouds, its expanse, its trees and its ground? There, aerial height is a twin of aqueous depth and becomes compact. And yet the image is less real than the object. Let us now take this object itself, this real scene and, by extension, all the scenes of the universe, that is the whole universe, total space. To be sure, it is real, it is matter itself; but in the nothing, in the idea-type of an "exterior" this matter is only a reflection of incorporeal light, the only reality which transmutes itself there, as we have said, into two ponderable appearances: physical light and blood. "Ponderable" seems to be the proper term, since our planet receives fifty-eight thousand tons of light per year.

Verse 54
It is an ideal mirror that the Spirit puts before itself so that its beauty may appear freely and as if from outside, so that *Love shall be exalted over the Law.*

Exaltation

The knowledge that God has of himself, this inner confirmation of the Divine of which neither the vision of Ezekiel nor the Universal Form of *the Bhagavad-Gita* gives a slightest idea, contains in the ideal archetypal state the non-manifested Universe. As long as the universe remains in this state, God is identical with the law of his own necessity: he is not bound to that law, he is that law, for a law constraining God would have its origin in a necessity which would be the true God. Identical with the law of his own necessity and bearing the non-manifested universe in his bosom, God, source of all ideas, is also the seat of the idea of an archetypal "exterior." It is in this idea of an exterior, an idea which, because of its anteriority and from the point of view of material existence, is the Nothing, that God, inconceivable spiritual fire, projects incorporeal light, creator of the mathematical point, space-time. The universe, in its form of Beauty, of Bride, appears to the Divine as if from outside in its clothing of physical light transformable into electricity, that essence of bodies. In this way, through the first act of renouncing his indivisible perfect

Unity, the God of omniscience transmutes himself into the God of universal sacrifice and inexpressible love. I dare even say that by this first act God strives toward perfection, a perfection of his indivisible and spiritual Unity; for the law is devoid of any finality, while love pursues itself without respite . . . But in order to understand these things, one has to give oneself up to the madness of love, which happens precisely at the moment when Man, either out of pity or out of passion, speaks to the four walls.

Verse 55
This is the first sacrifice, the one that raised Being—I mean Being that is its own and only law, that of being and nothing more—yes, this is the first sacrifice which raised Being above its own *necessity.*

First Sacrifice

First, second, last, eternal—so many words without meaning. Reality is beyond time and space—beyond "space-time." It is in the identity of the object and the image, of fire and of the reflection of its light in the nothing. The "first" sacrifice becomes one, in instantaneity, with the "second," that of Our Lord Jesus Christ, the eternal Word.

Verse 56
Because for Being there is no freedom except in the surrender of its most secret essence; by this surrender the law becomes love.

Freedom

Among humans: for the barbarian, freedom is taking and above all destroying; for the civilized, creating and giving. In the social order it is the search for an organization securing a mutual exchange of gifts: a communism that, for civilized men, is inseparable from Monarchy by divine right. For instance: the system of the Quechua with its obligatory cultivation of lands belonging to the Sun, to widows, orphans, invalids, and to some other individuals, as well as to the estates of the Inca; the Egyptian system of the New Empire in which the government reserved for itself international trade, leaving to individuals only internal trade; the Persian experiment of Mazdek, under King Kavadh, in 488—community of land and of women, abolition of all privileges. We mention these political and social attempts only in connection with our theory of memory dimmed after the golden age of Revelation, an epoch that was probably characterized by a social structure based upon both a communism and a theocratic monarchy whose emblem was the Bee (the Queen, and at the same time a kind of Goddess-Mother, until today the living image of the natural Matriarchy and of the Femininity of Manifestation) and, under the name *"biti,"* continued to be borne also by the King of Lower Egypt during the archaic period. Thus the historical King of Egypt five thousand two hundred years ago still had the title Biti, Bee, and this insect for his emblem. As the analogy extends to Monarchy itself, we obtain the matriarchal communism of the bee-hive. Let us add that it was probably through an association of the lily-like plant of Upper Egypt with the bee of the gardens, friend of the Delta and of the contemporary monarchy, that the Aegean civilization of the Minoan period chose the Lily for its emblem of royalty, and it was adopted later on by the Capetians, just as the bee was taken over the the Merovingians.

Verse 57
Thus Beauty, liberated and liberating, appeared so that the free sacrifice of love might shine above the necessity of the law.

The Free Sacrifice

Do we know any freedom other than that of sacrifice? The Father creates the universe so that the law of necessity which he is should be transmuted into love, so that holy beauty should call him from outside. The Son gives his *blood* just as the Father spilled his *light*, so that the descendants of the guilty man might return to the possession of their rights, so that the regenerated Adam would renounce infinite space, his kingdom of darkness, and, grasping the identity of blood and of physical light in the first movement of incorporeal brightness, would situate the universe in this brightness alone. Every truly great destiny in this life is a sacrifice. People speak foolishly of Bonaparte's egoism, of Caesar's thirst for power, of Alexander's madness for conquest. Ambition was indeed one of the goads of their activity. But the greatness of their sacrifice, underscored by the tragedy of their ends, calls for love rather than for reprobation, and, without allowing ourselves to imitate Carlyle or Auguste Comte, we would act wisely if we dedicate in our labyrinth a modest altar to the heroes and martyrs of the unification of continents and of the world, a unification that has been so nobly, so magnificently and sublimely exalted by Lamartine in his *"Marseillaise de la Paix."*

Verse 58
Thus, there gushed forth in the instantaneity of the *fiat*, as if brought about by a total transfusion, free beauty, the spiritual place of Benediction, the first relationship, that which exists between Beth and Aleph.

The Relationship between Beth and Aleph

In the *Creative Letter* of the Jew Simeon ben Yohai[31] (the most beautiful poem of this world), God creates the world by means of the letter beth, because it is the initial of the word which is used to bless Him (*Barukh*, be blessed). Indeed, the first letter of the Scripture is beth, the initial of *Bereshith*. But the letter aleph, the first in the alphabet and the one that under the circumstances *sacrifices* itself and submits itself to beth (that is, to manifestation) is addressed by the Holy One, blessed be He, in the following divine words: "Oh Aleph, Aleph, although I will make use of the letter Beth to create the world, you will be the first among all the letters and I shall have no unity save in you; you will be the root of all calculations and of all acts done in the world, and nowhere would unity be found if not in the letter Aleph." The relationship between Beth and Aleph is that between Light and Fire, Love and the Law.

Verse 59
Thus in the nothing—in this spiritual water from which the void, the full, action and number were banished—there lit up the archimagic Vision of a universe *whose mobile interior is space and whose container is the nothing, limit of our gravitational fields.*

Limit of Our Gravitational Fields

Since the author of the *Arcana*, while composing his poem, has received the order to put an end to his literary activity (his mission of humble initiator having been accomplished), he has striven to give to this last work as poetic a form as the abstract nature of the subject permitted. Hence a certain obscurity of expression, inseparable from an art whose aesthetic essence is *mystery* (Goethe). What he understands by "limit of our gravitational fields" is the periphery traversed by the light of the most distant milky ways, universe-islands at the uttermost boundaries of space-time.

Verse 60
In this act of manifestation, beauty, the Bride, detached herself from the Bridegroom without breaking the indivisible unity; for she detached herself as an image separates itself from its object.

The Indivisible Unity

The indivisible unity—we cannot stress it too much—is that of incorporeal light projected into the nothing, into the idea-type of an exterior. In this nothing the light transmutes itself into a mathematical point of space-matter, whence it pursues its course as light that is already physical, creator of space through expansion. Transformable into electricity, it becomes the essence of bodies. The transmutation occurs in instantaneity, and blood, made of electrons, is born from spiritual light at the same time as its sister, physical light. The *place* of the "sensible" world is therefore in the spiritual light; but the latter does not separate itself from the fire that sheds it forth: Bridegroom and Bride, Creator and Creation remain an indivisible unity in spirit, though they are clearly distinct in manifestation. Nor do we tire of insisting upon the Christian purity of our doctrine, which reproves with utmost severity any inclination to pantheism. The metaphysical reasons for our repulsion no longer need to be presented. As to the moral reasons, it would be superfluous to point them out to those who are aware of the inferiority in this respect of all Asiatic doctrines, from Sankara's *Mâyâvadin*, to Japanese Amidism, passing through all forms of Buddhism, Taoism and Confucianism. Let them, with all these old systems emptied of substance since the Fulfillment, leave us alone, in our Mediterranean West nourished by Egyptian, Jewish and Greek thought, and by Christian truth. All of them end with the same *social amorality* because they are poor in love and have never understood either the transmutation of the law or the Judeo-Christian conjugal principle. Spiritual unification, the condition *sine qua non* of social unification, can be accomplished only under the aegis of the Catholic, Apostolic, and Roman Church, the supreme spiritual and political truth.

Verse 61

This manifestation, this holy, holy Mother of beauty and glory, can it then be that she is an illusion? Not in the least; she is the truth, the very reality of the Lord who is the spirit of Love.

Manifestation

An illusion, and the most dangerous of all, as long as one situates her either in a container extended to infinity, or in herself through direct multiplication, manifestation is one with the supreme reality of the incorporeal light, perceptible to the eyes of those who have asked and received, searched and found, knocked and *seen the door opening*. For the core of all philosophy and of the entire art of life is in Luke 11.9.

Verse 62

For this is so not at all because she is sensorially perceived in a dynamic relationship, but precisely because she is a perfect vision, a supercelestial ecstasy of the Spirit, her lover.

Perfect Vision

Everything that can be grasped by our senses is pure relationship between moving bodies. The extension of this relationship to an infinity of expanses, that is, of bodies, far from determining their place, will inevitably lead to the disappearance of this. The real situation of limitless space can therefore be given only by the assimilation of this space as a vision independent of any opposition of the finite to the infinite.

Verse 63
The inexhaustible birth-giving power of the spiritual substance of the heavens and of the earth is the sacred sign of the femininity of procreative manifestation.

The Femininity of Procreative Manifestation

The history of religions teaches us that all primitive societies have looked upon nature as a fecund woman, as a mother. At first the analogy seems to be too obvious for it to be necessary to associate the physical observation with the intuition of a spiritual identity of the two childbearing powers, cosmic and human. A study of the least developed religious systems of Africa, of America and of Oceania proves, however, that we should mistrust purely naturalistic interpretations. An exaggeration in the opposite direction looks less dangerous if we consider certain facts well established by observers as competent as Frazer or Durkheim. What could be more direct, more evident, than the link between intercourse and childbearing? And yet it is not to his carnal relations with his spouse that a savage ascribes his paternity. In primitive man, a hunter, a fisherman, a warrior, who is above all a *body in action* and whose thought, in spite of its undoubtedly having degenerated, is not as far removed as ours from the awareness and love of movement, the *spiritual* origins of the latter and its spontaneity have left a deeper mark in the latent memory. In many respects it is we—with our egoism, our machines and enslaved movement, our brutal and sacrilegious pride, our four vices, and the vulgar dandyism of exhibiting them, our demonic inventions and, above all, our physical notion of courage and of honor—it is we, men of the age of poison gas, who are the true savages, and Chamisso deserves to be applauded for having understood all this long before we did during his voyage to Oceania in 1815. If primitive man brings a spiritual principle into a process as corporeal as that of generation, and excludes other factors, I do not see what should authorize us to ascribe to a purely physical analogy the nearly universal cult of the Goddess-Mother and its social derivative, Matriarchy. The problem of the original germ, which played such a considerable role in the intellectual development of Pasteur, must have been posed intuitively and logically at the dawn of thought. It is even very probable that we owe all magic concepts of life and of the world to the attempts at finding its solution. The hypothesis is strengthened by the close kinship of this problem with that of movement. We have just alluded to the appearance of "magic concepts." But the question of the original germ and of the original movement already comprises the entire cycle of the most evolved religious thought. The first civilization, probably Lemurian or Gondvanic Predravidian, endowed with a cosmic memory which we can no longer claim, undoubtedly resolved the problem of origins in conformity with the basic principles of Revelation, by ascribing a purely spiritual nature to the first germ, source of universal movement and of life. In this concept the first maternity becomes a virginal maternity: indeed, all known Goddess-Mothers are Virgins and nearly all gods are children of miracles. The Sumero-Akkadian Ishtar, the Phrygian deities Mâ or Cybele, and Nana, the Goddess-Mother, were, it is true, associated with a male principle, Ningiru, Shara, Enlil, Attis. Nevertheless, this principle also coexists, in the form of the Minotaur in Crete, with the Goddess-Mother Britomartis-Dictynna, which did not hinder the latter from being "the most saintly Virgin Ariadne." The conjugal bond that unites Goddess-Mothers with the gods is thus purely spiritual, as befits a terrestrial correspondence of the bond that Manifestation created between the divine Fire and its incorporeal Light transmuted into the universe, into virgin and procreative cosmic matter. Matriarchy has the same spiritual origin. A naturalistic interpretation is as insufficient in this case as in that of the Goddess-Mothers. The admiration of primitive man is directed toward strength rather than tenderness or even fecundity. The Mother was venerated and feared because of her analogy with the first miraculous Mother,

Manifestation, free of any physical act, or any emission of seed—the Virginal Beauty of the Universe who has exalted Love above the Law. The cults of Goddess-Mothers and of Matriarchy are extremely ancient, much older than Sumer and Akkad, than the Aegean civilization and Egypt. They appear with the paleolithic civilization, for we find a striking analogy, not to say an absolute identity, between the steatopygic figurines of the Aurignacian grottoes in Meudon, in Willendorf, in Laussel, in Bassempouy, and the already historical Goddess-Mothers—separated by about twenty thousand years from the first—that have been unearthed in Susa, in Chaldea, in pre-pharaonic Egypt. We notice also that Goddess-Mother-Virgins everywhere start to reign alone, that gods have been added to them only in relatively recent periods, and moreover, that priestesses, too, have everywhere preceded priests, the most ancient of whom used to wear at the performance of rites the sacerdotal costume of women, a skirt of spotted skin with an animal tail, a vestige of the feminine paleolithic costume. Let us note finally that Egyptian art of the Thynite period always represents woman as larger than man, and that matriarchy still reigned in all its power in Libya at the time of Herodotus. In the political domain, the Queen confirmed the authority of the King or of the founder of a dynasty. Matriarchy and the cult of the Goddess-Mother were symbols of the virginal femininity of Manifestation. Later, we will describe the close relationship which exists between this ancient revealed truth and the most holy, most logical dogma of the Immaculate Conception, as well as between it and the mystery of the Incarnation.

Verse 64
Such is the holy arcanum of Conjugal Love, the subject of Solomon's Song of Songs. I too would like to sing it. But the Legions clad in gold make a sign that I should keep silent.

Solomon's Song of Songs

Swedenborg, who has left us a sublime code of conjugal Love, nevertheless banished the Song of Songs from his Canon. This lack of consistency on the part of the celestial husband of the Countess of Gyllenborg would astonish us had he not been the son of Jesper Swedberg, intendant of Swedish congregations in Pennsylvania and bishop of Skara in Westrogothia. Our opinion of the Reformation is the same as that held by Descartes, the first master of Swedenborg, at the time of his tragicomic wranglings with Voetius. This does not prevent us, obviously, from revering virtue and knowledge wherever we meet them and from recognizing the beneficial character of the influence that the great Swede exerted upon Claude de Saint-Martin and his school.[32] The "audacities" of the divine Song cannot startle one whose thought has been nourished with spiritual and physical analogies, nor can the boldness of Juan de Yepes.[33] The song of David's son is a dialogue between the Father and the Beauty of the Universe born from the incorporeal light and fecundated in the Holy Spirit, between the Son and his beloved Catholicity, the entire future Humanity, finally between the mortal husband and the mortal wife, procreators—they, too—in the spirit. As did the poet, the commentator would like to lay his thought open. But here again the legions clad in gold impose silence on him. R.C.

Verse 65
Just as in instantaneity, therefore, the bride detached herself from the bridegroom, like an image from its object, so in the world of time-space, which was created by the luminous *fiat* and is the movement of this reflection, Eve had to be taken from the similarly double polarity of Adam's substance drawn from the very blood of the universe.

Eve

The great book of life, as soon as it is stripped of the seven seals which prevent us from reading it and are only our own moral imperfections, unveils its secret so graciously that, owing to an opposite inconsistency, we manage to convince ourselves that it is we who have written it and who are the authors of cosmic masterpieces whose precision and beauty nevertheless contrast ludicrously with the miseries of our condition. Those two movements, one of which manifests itself by all the marks of despair, the other by all the signs of the most childish presumption (since it is true that we draw no less vanity from our weakness than from our strength) have the same origin. The immensity of creation terrifies us until the moment when we notice that the marvelous identity of the two worlds is hidden from our sight only by disproportions we observe in the order of size. For this truth to reach us, it is enough that she find the two sinister guardians, mistrust and pride, asleep on the threshold of our abode, and that the nuptial chamber offer her a mirror which does not deform her image. The omnipotent words prescribed by the Son restore of themselves order to the house. Truth then enters deliberately and what she has to teach us may be expressed in a few words. Real things are the great sisters of the things here, that which is below is like that which is above, and if I laugh at seeing the celestial wisdom of love taking on in my poor fussy words the likeness of madness, at least I am not the first to laugh; and long before I, others—the greatest— amused themselves by composing stories of jack-asses, whales, and pumpkins, or by praising the *importunity* that obtains what love has failed to receive. Of those things similar in the sensible and in the intelligible domain, the first is the conjugal arcanum, foundation of the great and of the small cosmos. Did not Goethe in his *Elective Affinities* compare chemical marriages to human alliances? Incorporeal light, mother of physical light transformable into electricity, that is, into the very essence of bodies, having been shed by the secret fire, formed the beauty of the universe; by an operation perfectly similar in its mystery, the bride of man has been drawn from his blood, so that the *light* of woman might guide the husband on the roads of thought and of action—since the motive of thought and action is love, inseparable from any creation. The mystical position of man with respect to woman is thus that of God with respect to Creation; it is by pure reminiscence that the language of lovers even today employs certain images which are laughable because of their primitive simplicity: "you are *everything* to me, you are my *universe*, my sun, my life, etc." And it is exactly these commonplaces, translated into a more noble language, which become Faust's speeches addressed to the fair Trojan woman and Hölderlin's elegies written to Diotima of Frankfurt. Man is a harsh Law, that of movement, action, and nothing more—and it is in the beauty and the charity of woman that the Law transmutes itself into Love. Certainly, all this has but a remote resemblance to Stendhal's theory of crystallization. But we will deal with literary psychology and with dandyism another time. Not here. At the very source of thought and of action, of action-thought (for thought is only awareness and love of movement), we find the conjugal Arcanum, the mystery of spiritual creation and procreation.

Verse 66
Of the universe which is the sacrifice of sacrifices, archetype of the blood given by Abel and original mystery of all cults of immolation.

Sacrifice of Sacrifices

To exalt Love above the law (of necessity), divine Fire sheds forth its incorporeal light; this changes itself into physical light which is transformable into electricity (the Cosmos), and into blood (Man). Such is spiritual creation through generation without seed, a result of celestial love fecundating in the Spirit. Just as the single and perfect Body of Beauty is drawn from physical light, so the body of woman is shaped from the blood of man, who is a brother of material light because of the identity of their origin. This is the first act of spiritual procreation; and this procreation, apart from any copulation, was the very law of life. Man and woman were destined to a purely spiritual manner of existence in a world alien to any idea of the finite and of the infinite, in a world situated solely in the incorporeal light of divine Vision; they were Spirit in the guise of bodies. They were immortal. Man did not know physical toil, nor did woman know the labors of childbirth, for matter was still that of God's vision, the unique place of everything. The sweat of the brow and the wails of childbirth came much later, after woman had materialized love and man had done the same to space by extending it to infinity; hence it was no longer situated in the spiritual light but in itself, that is, in matter and in darkness. Abel is the figure of Our Lord: like Him he gives his blood because God had shed forth His light. This is the sacrifice of Atonement, the movement of return of matter to spirit. Such is the origin of Abraham's sacrifice and of all immolation cults. Cain, on the contrary, affirms the materiality of the world, as his father Adam did before him and, later on, Herod the Jew and Pilate the Roman; he is the instrument of temporal domination and the murderer of the Spirit. This is the never-ceasing struggle of materialism and spirituality, the origin of all terrestrial calamities and of the great confusion, which added the martyrology of science to that of faith.

Verse 67
And this blood of creation, O Hiram my son, this blood of creation flowed also for the Atonement. For, there again, was it not necessary that the free sacrifice of love should be exalted above the Jewish law itself?

The Jewish Law

All the main characters of the Old Testament, along with their most remarkable deeds, are prefigurations of the divine operation destined to enable the earth and its inhabitants—who became lost in the infernal labyrinth of endless darkness created by Adam—to rediscover their place of light. In his fall Adam carried with him beings and things: moreover, the spiritual Kings, illuminated by their consecration and guided by light, were not the only witnesses of the mystery in the manger. The ox and the ass are in a place of honor and with their pure and childlike breath they warm the Prince of inner Peace. The latter raises his arm to bless the regenerated creation. His first movement is that of the incorporeal light which, even before the appearance of time-space, had been shed by the Father, the celestial Bridegroom, into the original nothingness. As Adam once did, so Christ the King raises his arms: in this first thought, which again becomes awareness and love of movement, all its ancient knowledge is restored to the sensible world. Sin is taken away; henceforth the spirit will illuminate man's seed. Question the essence of your thought on a fine July night, streaming with myriads of universes. There is within you a knowledge which will tell you why God, who can do everything, could not, yes, *could not* fail to come among us. Understood in temporal terms, these things happened here. In instantaneity, God's incorporeal light alone was their stage. God could not but create the world, because His law had to be transmuted into love; God could not do otherwise than be born into this world to suffer, because the Jewish law, the harsh law of man, had to be succeeded by Love exalted in Woman, in Mary, in nature glorified once again through its original virginal maternity.

Verse 68
Adam's dominion over this *non-situated* universe of free beauty was thus wielded in the freedom of the supreme knowledge which was founded upon the original relationship of aleph to beth, of the seer to his vision, of being to love.

Free Beauty

Man, the creature, is as free as God. The *only* thing of importance in this world—in this total Universe—is prayer. It is prayer which gives knowledge and charity. Here is the reason why it was of the utmost necessity that man be *free to pray or not to pray*. Prayer was given to him as a golden key and the universe as a box full of diamonds and stellar rubies. The key was *unique*. Your pride rebelled against the idea of using the only key invented by someone other than you. You threw the key into a well and you kept the indestructible box, a night-colored box, hermetically closed forever. But the golden key has been found; its image—the only image in the whole book—drawn by the Master Wolfgang Goethe himself, decorates page 883 of *Wilhelm Meister*, the edition of Grand Duke Wilhelm Ernest, Leipzig, 1906, Im Inselverlag. God is King. He is not a tyrant. He does not force any of his gifts upon us. He wants to be importuned (Luke 11,9). One cannot be more liberal. I, who pray, am free. You, gentlemen, who tomorrow will split atoms and yet will not strut about in the milky ways that are two hundred thousand light-years away, you, gentlemen, who do not pray, are free too. But it is I who am the master of the treasure.

Verse 69
Adam was free, for he knew that movement is not the inconceivable translation from a place to a place, but the intelligible metamorphosis from a state to a state. To be free is to move, certainly for the sake of action, but also, far beyond any action, for the sake of rhythm.

Again Rhythm

In a space that vainly searches for its place lost in the darkness of the infinite, that is, in a universe of multiplication without end and without place, the smallest movement from one point to another passes through the entire infinity of division. A traveller who imagines that he changes place by going from point A to point B is therefore a most ludicrous dupe, because one cannot cross an infinite distance. Physical light itself, with its meager three hundred thousand kilometers per second, is, all things considered, immobile. There is only one means of escaping the illusion which presents a diversity of places to our immobile course through the *non-situated*: to entrust ourselves to a *mental rhythm*, which transports us to the only real place of *original light*.

Verse 70
Through the interplay of dynamic connections, Adam was the consciousness of the universe and the organ of perception of all things. But through the relationship of beth to aleph, of the vision situated in the nothing to the Holy Spirit which alone is real, Adam was the very freedom of beauty.

Consciousness of the Universe

It is in Adam's thinking—*the awareness of movement*—that the relationship between moving bodies, between moving body 1 and moving body 2, the only determinant of relative space-time, became *conscious of itself*. But Adam avoided this illusion of matter (indispensable for the transmutation of the law) by obtaining from prayer a higher knowledge of spiritual reality, that is, of the relationship between the Bride Beth and the Bridegroom Alpha.

Verse 71
Thus, later, at the moment of the purification of beings and things, Christ was born of a Virgin, the corporeal image of first free beauty.

First Free Beauty

This is beauty of the universe born of the first movement, that of incorporeal light. Of this first free beauty, the Immaculate Conception is the temporal correspondence. The birth of Mary is spiritual, as is the birth of primeval nature, brought forth without seed. From Mary, fecundated by the incorporeal light of vision, our Lord Jesus Christ is born, and this birth corresponds to the birth of the first Adam drawn from virgin cosmic matter. This is what Verse 72 tries to convey.

Verse 72
Just as the vision was projected by the spirit into the nothing, and the first Adam was drawn from cosmic substance fecundated by spirit alone—so, too, the second Adam could be born only from a virginal, spiritual, free beauty.

Verse 73
The mysterious and chaste passion, the intellectual intoxication, that we all have experienced on emerging from childhood, is but a dim remembrance of the first love, Adam's love for Eve, his terrestrial mate.

The Mysterious and Chaste Passion

The mediocre poet Wordsworth, in his "Ode on Intimations of Immortality, from Recollections of early Childhood," makes a sort of poetic discourse on the doctrine of Swedenborg without, obviously, naming the latter. The spirituality of the first age of man, still illuminated by the remembrance of

the Place, has great importance there. The execrable metaphysician, E. A. Poe, dedicates to these mysteries a few truly inspired lines in his *Eureka*, a work which we have just treated with too much forbearance. In *Aus Meinem Leben*, Goethe amuses himself by retracing in a few pages the theosophical system of his adolescence: the conclusion, though maliciously disguised, authorizes us to see in this supposed nonsense an expression of the Master's most secret thought. The father of so many beauties who have died in the odor of sanctity and who have been preserved from corruption by their suffering and love (Sperata in *Wilhelm Meister*, Ottilie in *Elective Affinities*) has never been understood either in Germany or abroad. Eckermann, whom Heinrich Heine used to call "the poodle," has bequeathed to us the worst caricature of the Master, a portrait idealized by a half-witted pupil. Beatrice was only nine years old when Dante, himself very young, was led to meet her. Byron lived and died under the spell of the first love of his childhood for a little country girl named Mary, if I remember correctly. The author of *The Arcana* recalls how strong his feelings were, in his fourth spring, for a Laura whose six winters inspired him (fortunately) with a profound respect. These little stories, trifling as they are, may one day profitably be compared to the learned theories of Professor Freud.

Verse 74
Woman, taken from the spiritual substance of man, which was that of vision itself—woman found herself with regard to man in the relationship of beth to aleph, of the vision to the seer, of love to Being.

Of Love to Being

Because in her the harsh law of man was changed into love, just as, in the beauty of the universe born from incorporeal brightness, the sublime law of necessity also transmuted itself into love.

Verse 75
Just like the seer and his vision, the couple in Eden were an indivisible unity. On the level of dynamic connections their movements and their speech represented the hidden operations uniting the seer and his vision in the great ritual of reciprocity. Eve was the living, spiritual and virginal image of Femininity, of manifestation.

The Great Ritual of Reciprocity

At the very instant when the eyelids of the King were being closed, the Dauphin was acclaimed King. But it was the consecration in Reims that conferred on him supreme mystical powers. Similarly, the celestial King was King before he received the Consecration from the creature, as if from outside: nevertheless, only Benediction has the power to transmute the law of necessity into love. It was with the purpose of receiving Benediction that God chose the Beth (Barukh) as a tool of his creation. For God to be loved is not enough. When one loves, one wants to be importuned. Importunity ends by exhausting time. Importunity is always new in the eyes of instantaneity. Only in it does one truly love, and only love enables us to seize the instant. Love blinks its eyes; that is what Eternity is. On the level of relationship between moving bodies, that is, in interior space-time, the movements of Adam and his spouse, situated physically with respect to each other, represented the hidden operations of the great ritual in which the Creator gives his benediction to the Creation and, conversely, reciprocally receives it. In these ceremonies Adam represented the law and fire; Eve, love and light.

Verse 76
Woman's beauty and charity, the intoxication and compassion they inspire, bring us closer even today to our mother, the world's beauty. But Adam, in the wisdom of his submission, recognized in this beauty the very essence and form of his companion in service. He talked to "Arcturus, Orion, the Pleiades, and the chambers of the south" (those true friends of Job) as he talked to Eve: in the universal and invisible quivering of elytra which was of a muted, penetrating and blissful tenderness.

This verse tells us that the spiritual King had the power to fashion for himself an image of the total universe, and to recognize in it the Queen.

Our Mother, the World's Beauty

The conjugal arcanum has remained the daily bread and also the wine of poetry and of science, despite the innumerable adulterations of these spiritual aliments. To this mystery I devoted one of my early works, *L'Amoureuse Initiation*, and I am perhaps ready to repudiate its somewhat extravagant language, but not its immutable philosophy. It is to love that we owe the immortal masterpieces of Byron and Chateaubriand; even when they are poisoned, tenderness and passion awaken a dim echo in the depths of the dense Eden of our second memory. Scientists are less communicative than poets; and yet what an eminent though secret role love has played in the history of great discoveries and in the evolution of philosophy. I never open my small old copy of *Ethics* in the modest popular German "Reclam" edition without calling to mind the image of Spinoza in love, letting his silver spurs ring on the pavement of the Hague and the enormous black plume of his hat fly in the wind. Was it not also love which, in the shape of a very young woman, initiated solemn Auguste Comte into the one-eyed metaphysics of old Kant, so skillful at splitting hairs but always the less essential, never the right ones? And was it not love which was to furnish the essential subject of conversation for those two famous pessimists, Schopenhauer and Byron, during their odd meeting, so little known, in Venice?

Verse 77
I have guided you, Hiram, up to this sacred flagstone where the master mason has carved the image of the labyrinth.

The Place of Action

The poem of the *Arcana* is a Mystery Play which has for its setting the ruins of the Cathedral of Reims, built by the French and destroyed by the Goths.

Verse 78
It is here, in this place of fulfillment, that I will take leave of you for the entire period of the great transmutation which is beginning.

The Great Transmutation

In the evolution of Christian thought and Christian sensibility, our epoch corresponds to the most dismal period of night, that which directly precedes the first ray of dawn. I address here a reader who is already initiated by his insomnia into the horrors of that hour when darkness disintegrates. The sudden melting of a glacier would produce less mire than what rises in one's heart from the rotting deposits of the past. Ah, how everything is old, and unrelenting, and empty! Days lost, summits not reached, and all those acts of cowardice, suddenly reconstructed. Oh tears, tears! But it is only later, in the full light of day, that we weep and never at this instant. The dissolution of matter goes through a similar stage: alchemists called it the Raven's Head. Much will be forgiven to those who have explored the catacombs of Time. Every grain passes through this sweat of death before it germinates.

Verse 79
The present attempts at moral, social and political renewal are doomed to failure. Before leading a blind man toward the light, it is proper to heal him of his blindness.

The Present Attempts

Never has there been so much talk about spirit as at the end of the last century and at the beginning of this new century. I ardently desired to be acquainted with this "spirit" which preoccupied everybody around me. My long stays in Germany, a land where people are even too proud to know what they really want and what they are talking about, could never provide me with information on that subject; and yet hardly a day passed without my hearing some verbose eulogy of *"Geist."* But no one—either in Germanic lands, or in France, Italy, England, Russia, Spain or in any country of Europe or Africa where I travelled—could ever tell me what sort of "spirit" was meant. A guide in Goethe's house in Frankfurt, probably offended by some liberties that I took with a girl of my age, excusable in a very young man, thanked me for my *"trinkgeld"* and addressed me with a long lecture that began with the words: "the great Goethe, too, had reprehensible beginnings . . . but he was soon to know the real value of *Geist. Ja, der Geist, der Geist."* I reached the point where I could not pronounce or even hear that word, no matter in what language or in what place, without laughing in the speaker's face in the most impertinent fashion. Nothing less than the events of 1914 enlightened me on the true meaning of this prestigious word. Alas! the meaning attached to it today is still the same. What do I say, a "meaning"? A multitude, an infinity of meanings: mechanical progress (war in the air), chemical progress (threat of the destruction of entire cities by gas), transformation of the world into an oil-refinery and a number of other improvements of this kind. All this, today as yesterday, is part of current thought and language, part of the heritage of civilization. Add to this lovely picture the "spiritual" renewal which in Africa and Asia, as in Europe, confronts us with the joyous spectacle of an "awakening of nationalities," and tell me, please, whether you do not believe it would be expedient, without delay and without false shame, to adjoin to this word "spirit" a determinative which would at last enable us *to situate* it. Beyond the spirit of wood, the spirit of wine, and the spirit of salt, all three material, I know only one spirit of superior essence. It descends in the incorporeal regenerating light and its name is the Holy Spirit. The way we obtain it conforms perfectly to our worst habits, for it loves and desires our *importunity*.

Verse 80
A sacrilegious and false concept of the physical universe has dimmed, like a cataract, the intellectual sight of man. It is necessary first to remove with a strong and charitable hand this opaque secretion which conceals from him the real world of vision.

The Real World of Vision

The hypothesis of future communication between the earth and spiral nebulae, even the most distant from our milky way, has nothing improbable about it. For a metaphysician there is no "beyond" in the material realm, however far it may extend. His thought is correct only if it contains the entirety of space in the word "here." But even if our research opened up a path to the boundaries of the universe, the space explored in that fashion would not at all cease to appear—to people communicating across its immensity—as a simple relation of one moving body to another body. The conquest of the universe would bring us only a confirmation of universal law, and our thought condemned to be haunted by a physical infinite would feel as cramped in the prison-yard as in the prison itself. Had I, who detest curiosity, been forced to put a question to some thinking reed from the nebula of Canes Venatici, I would have muttered as I have done all my life: Where is space? And it is possible that I would have left without waiting for an answer. Because either he would situate it in an endless multiplication of relations between moving bodies, or he would draw it back to a simple relation of the movement of physical light to incorporeal light; and, things being so, I would have as little to learn from his wisdom as from his folly.

Verse 81
Here, in this tool bag, O King of toilers, you will find the cross, the balance, the ointment, the scepter and the crown of the world. But I must tell you once more how the ancient King became blind.

The Tool Bag

I read the human face with the same emotion as the stars; but now that I know where I am, these things are not so distant nor so secret as they used to be. I am tempted, above all, to search for the humble light of those stars which demand some effort to be perceived, and for the eyes of those among my brothers whose lives may teach me the most. Thus, on winter mornings, in the vaporous haze of the crowded metro, from my corner I like to observe the workers of Paris, those children of the oldest and the only authentic civilization. Frail in appearance yet most robust, they go to a factory or construction site, tool bags across their shoulders. Under the surface banter what an air of men who appraise the real value of beings, of institutions, of products, of ideas. And never that sinister glimmer, that something humble and cruel, shifty and on the watch, which lurks in the corner of the eye of a proletarian in the countries of Northern and Central Europe. What a horrible thing is resentment not purified by anger!

And those peoples forced to keep silent, how much they seem to know, how seriously they seem to take existence! Nevertheless, long observation has taught me to reduce to nearly nothing the role of material interests in life generally, and especially in revolutions. Man would have borne with difficulty the burden of these centuries without faith, had all this absurd action not taken place on the puppet stage of our vanities. Shame even unto the grave on those regimes where the interplay of vanities, exacerbated by too vivid contrasts, degenerates into so-called conflicts of interest, all the more violent because nothing in them is real except the self-love of some men. Then the extremist groups, one occupying the highest, the other the lowest rung of the social hierarchy, often both equally alien to the economy and to the evolution of the masses, exert themselves, each in its own way, to entice the people into an alliance in which they will be only a blind instrument in extremists' hands. So it was, when out of a desperate rivalry of two minorities—one composed of several million persecuted, embittered Jews and intellectuals, the other of a few thousand high officials, past masters in the art of arrogance and plunder—there issued the enormous Russian revolution whose premonitory symptoms, between 1904 and 1906, I saw with my own eyes. And yet the crisis had no other real and legitimate object than the liberation of a few oppressed peoples and an agrarian reform analogous to the one accomplished in France in 1789. It would have been enough for the ruling Muscovite circles to offer, around 1915, to the countries of the Baltic and of the East, as well as to the rural population of Russia, a few examples not even of generosity but simply of understanding, and the Jews would have been spared from pogroms, the nobility and the middle-class from extinction, the nation as a whole from long years of famine and disorder. In a few decades what will remain of this so-called Marxist revolution? Only an agrarian reform, accomplished under conditions and by means absolutely out of proportion to the intended goal. Under the guise of the rise of power of the urban proletariat, so insignificant in Russia, the crisis of 1917 was a political and agrarian revolution. True social reform is still a thing of the future and can be accomplished in an industrialized, educated Russia, just as in the rest of the world, by stages, without ruin and without bloodshed. Nevertheless, let us not forget that a crisis is approaching. In order to stop it, would it not be essential first of all to halt the irresistible expansion of an industrialism which has become necessary because it satisfies vulgar appetites fostered by the spread of materialistic doctrines? What dam would resist such a current? Even dictatorships can do no more than maintain some sort of discipline on the galley which the current carries along. The only imaginable way of tapping this new force would be to link it with intense and hard labor for the unification of Europe and of the world; but this unification in its turn is possible only if the ground is prepared by a spiritual renaissance through the combined effort of science and of religion. These two have ceased to be irreconcilable enemies. Our concept of matter evolves every day. The imperceptible lies in wait for us both within and without. Reality is no more than an elusive movement of numbers. Something moves, therefore something thinks itself. But what matter will be able to tell me what this moving thing is?

The very idea of plurality fades away; in this thing which moves and thinks itself, I myself appear and it is in me that it becomes conscious of itself. That thing and I, we are those moving numbers whose relationships create space-time. We are one and the same blood, one and the same light. But is this knowledge sufficient for me? Once again, I identify myself with total space. What am I? An immense thing, a perfect thing, a unique thing. The universe. Where am I? The whole abyss of natural light cannot tell me this.

In the commentary to verse 56 we have mentioned one of the most peculiar events of antiquity, the Persian communist revolution of Mazdek, a disciple of Mani. The Medes and the Persians were Indo-Europeans. Their native country was neither the Susiana of the Achaemenids, nor the mountainous region of the Parthians. Before they invaded these areas and founded their empires there, they had, for thousands of years, led a nomadic existence on the steppes of mysterious southern Russia, a land which in the night of prehistory seems to have influenced decisively the destiny of the Aryan race. Only one word from the language of the Medes has been transmitted to us by the Greeks of Anatolia: *spako*, dog. It is somewhat curious that nobody has noticed the similarity of this word to the Russian name of the same animal, *sobaka*, which is pronounced s'baka. Around 1700 B.C. (when Phrygia was invaded by the Thracians), did not the famous Scythians, a nation shrouded in impenetrable mystery, speak a language related to Slavic? Were they not direct ancestors to the Slavs? We find the same linguistic analogies in Asiatic countries and even in Egypt. The Thrako-Phrygians adored a lunar divinity callen Mên. Even today, *Menuo* is the Lithuanian name of the moon. Were the "mushki" of Asia Minor simply Muzhiki? But here is something even more extraordinary. Ancient Egypt, around 3300 B.C., was divided into two kingdoms, one in the South and the other in the North. In the latter, the emblem of royalty was the bee *(Biti)*, and this bee gave its name to the King himself, the Biti of Northern Egypt. And the Lithuanian name of the bee is *Bité*. The oldest Egyptian dynasties of the Delta, before the two crowns, red and white, were united under one "pschent," seem, then, to have been Indo-European. This lends special interest to a daring theory (daring—and so most probably the product of genius) advanced by Mr. A. de Paniagua, about the Dravidian "Minns." To come back to Mazdek and his communism, could it not be simply an attempt to return to the natural system of the Scythians, a system which, under the form of "mir," has survived until the present throughout the entire Muscovite empire, offering prepared ground for the Bolsheviks' social reform? Russian Communism is as old as Russia itself. Western Communism, a new and perhaps temporary form of theocratic Monarchy whose universal rule seems to us inevitable, certainly will be very different from Scythian bolshevism characterized by a double, Mongolian and Orthodox, imprint, as well as by a centuries-old tradition of groveling before German pedantry.

The East no longer has anything to offer us. The future belongs to Europe and to the New World. Already the scientific presumption of the last century makes us smile. Within a few years, the disorder and the hesitations of modern knowledge will be laughed at.

The theory of original revelation finds credit in the most circumspect milieus. The knowledge of ancient Egypt and of the Middle Ages provides our popularizers with sensational titles for their huge volumes. To be sure, one should not expect much from our contemporaries. But when the Holy Spirit makes itself heard in Rome, the necessary men will be present to answer the summons.

The society they will create will rest upon the alliance of faith, science and beauty, that is, upon individual and collective freedom acquired at the price of surrendering one's most intimate essence, of a total sacrifice, of a transmutation of law into love. The everlasting vanity of the mediocre, purged of its present materialistic barbarity, will undergo the most severe moral discipline. The utilization of this inexhaustible force will no longer devolve upon schemers, but upon a council of psychologists nominated by a Congregation of Initiates, placed on the summit of the hierarchy and at the base of the spiritual Monarchy. It will rule over the United States of the World. Nevertheless, each State will possess its own dynasty, rooted as much as possible in old national traditions. Scientific, esthetic, and moral competition will open to the instinct of combativeness a field embracing all the world. Nationalities will wage against each other a magnificent all-out war in the realm of intellect. The commandments of the Church will be observed with utmost rigor, and the Catholic holy days celebrated with indescribable splendor, both of them recognized as symbolizing the highest truths of science and of philosophy. The first day of the universal Reign will be marked by conversion of the ancient Elected people to Christianity: but the noble Jewish race will be carefully preserved in its purity without intermixture. The last vestiges of old aristocracies will be honored, too, because a democracy, even monarchic and theocratic, always has something to learn from people who know their origins and respect their traditions.

Such are a few of my dreams, inspired at an early hour on the street or in the metro, by a worker's tool bag, a moving emblem of the future guilds.

Verse 82
The incorporeal light of beauty detached itself from the being which is identical with the law and is the hidden spiritual fire. It detached itself in order that just as the first relationship was established between this fire and this light, between this bridegroom and this bride, so love should be exalted above the law.

First Relationship

The gift of the most secret essence, total sacrifice, transmutation of the law into love, finds adequate expression in the language of physics. In the moral order, affective phenomena constitute a correspondence to the relations between mobile bodies. Boredom, that feeling of emptiness caused by the absence of love, is only the desire to receive a support for a *self* which we cannot find in ourselves. A simple necessity to *situate* ourselves ideally, to know our determinative relation to a spiritual *place*, rules over our affective life just as, in the form of a double electricity, it penetrates the minutest elements of bodies. Physical light, transformable into this electricity, contains the signs *plus* and *minus*—the initial determinatives of place—and we find these (attached to the magnetic poles) also in blood. Since the advent of material light we are thus confronted with a relation of one moving body to another moving body, which relation later on divides itself into an infinity of relationships, making it possible for us to determine the position of all things, from electrons to milky ways. As bodies do, spiritual beings find their ideal place in a gravitation which we name love. This latter is our only reality and when it transports us into the incorporeal light which it makes visible, the whole universe is restored to its place, a place determined by the relation of this light to the divine hidden Fire.

Verse 83
In the very instantaneity of the *fiat*, the incorporeal light of the world's beauty took on the aspect of the Cosmos—its interior space-time—which we know. But in Adam, who is its consciousness, its freedom and its organ of perception, it appeared to itself as a vision of a seer in the nothing, the nothing from which the void and the full, movement and time, are banished.

The Instantaneity of the Fiat

The metamorphosis of water into wine, the first miracle of Our Lord Jesus Christ, is a demonstration analogous to the transmutation into the physical light of an incorporeal brightness reflected by the Nothing. (Alchemy compared the Nothing to primordial water, *hyle*.) Projected into the Nothing, into the archetypal idea of an exterior, as if into water which makes this light appear to God so to speak from outside, incorporeal light transforms itself into physical light, into the universe of beauty and of love, the Macrocosm. Similarly, in the mystical operation of our Lord, water (or the reflecting Nothing) is changed into wine, that is, into blood, the Microcosm. This is a terrestrial correspondence to the divine conjugal arcanum, to the transmutation of the law, to the creation of the bride by the bridegroom, and, in order to make the analogy more obvious, the miracle is accomplished at the wedding of Cana. In this operation the Son becomes one with the Father, and, abolishing for an instant every distinction between persons, ceases to be the Son. Here is the reason why, following a mystical logic superior to any human feeling, he pronounces those terrible and sublime words: "Woman, what have I to do with thee?" At the instant when Love is exalted, Mary is no longer his mother.

Verse 84
There was a seer and a vision, and Adam was the relationship between the one and the other. It was in him, in the man who is a child of necessity and beauty, that love saw itself exalted in its freedom above the law.

Child of Necessity and Beauty

There is no need here to take the word necessity in the Kabbalistic sense which relates it to Rigor, the consequence of sin. The verse speaks of an Adam still rich in the wisdom of submission. But the King of the World, as we shall soon see, was the representation of Being which is its own law of necessity, that of being and nothing more. Adam is this representation as opposed to Eve, who corresponds to the beauty which liberates the universe. An image of necessity, Adam is also an image of freedom conquered by the exaltation of love, since, with Eve, he forms but one flesh, a symbol of the unity of the object and the image, of the Bridegroom and the Bride. This double character of man asserts itself in a most vivid manner in literary works of all times. Long before the Hebrew Job, the Babylonian "Just Man" brings out the contrast between the rigorous law ruling human destinies on the one hand, and the perfect beauty of the universe on the other.

Verse 85

But the unity of this law, which is identical with being, subsisted undivided in the trinity of Bridegroom, Bride and the first Adam, who was the consciousness of the conjugal arcanum. For the seer and his vision formed but a single spirit with the primordial relationship that was their intelligibility in the cosmic concept of man.

The Primordial Relationship

The primordial relationship is one which situates incorporeal light with respect to the hidden Fire, and the Bride Beth with respect to the Bridegroom Alpha. Adam is the consciousness of this relationship, the intelligence of the Arcanum. The hidden Fire is the Father; incorporeal light, source of physical light or of the universe, is the Spirit; Adam, the understanding of the initial relation between them, co-eternal in the archetypal world anterior to Manifestation, is the created figure of the Son. At the very instant when the intelligence of the Arcanum grows dim because of sin, the cosmic concept of man changes into a material representation of darkness without end.

Verse 86

On the level of dynamic relations, this undivided unity was represented by the triplicity of space-time-matter, given in the unity of movement.

Triplicity

The first elements of thought, which are awareness and love of movement, consist in a triplicity of space, time, and matter. But this triplicity is movement itself. Similarly, the Father, the Son and the Spirit are a trinity, but a trinity dissolved in divine unity. In order to penetrate the arcanum which is protected against human pride by the angel's sword, it is enough to begin modestly with the beginning.

Verse 87
But this movement itself, this *fiat*, the law generating manifestation, was nothing other than Adam born of the spiritual substance of the vision. On the dynamic level, therefore, Adam was the representation of being that is its own law. And Eve was drawn from his essence only so that he, too, should represent love exalted above the law.

Law Generating Manifestation

The *Fiat Lux* is the emission of incorporeal light, the first movement. This engenders the movement of physical light or the universe. But we know that physical light and blood are one and the same thing. Adam's blood was, therefore, already in the movement of incorporeal light before its transmutation into physical light. At that very instant, consequently, Adam participated in Being and in the Law. After the transmutation of incorporeal light into physical light and blood, Adam remained in spirit a representation of Being that is its own Law. By his tenderness for Eve, however, he identified himself with Love exalted above the Law.

Verse 88
Adam's prevarication caused this exalted love to fall back into the rigor of the law. Such, O Hiram, is the origin of the great and severe law of Israel.

Law of Israel

The Law of Israel is the universal law of propitiatory sacrifice, of blood or sap offered to the light, with the peculiarity, however, that Judaic sacrifice was offered not to the sun, as by the pagans, but to the incorporeal light of the divine hidden Fire. This sacrifice, of which the paschal Lamb was the supreme expression, prefigured the Redemption. Contrary to the naive opinion maintained on this subject by historians and even by several specialists in exegesis, the messianic role of the Jewish nation concerned mankind as a whole. Israel, even guilty, and Judah, even shaken in its fidelity, conserved the holy treasure of the original Revelation in all its purity and through innumerable trials, for the sole purpose of the future regeneration of the world. The sufferings endured by the Jewish people have exerted their pacifying influence not only upon the sons of Abraham, but upon everything which has the breath of life and partakes of the generosity of the Creator. The Egyptian exile and the Babylonian exile, though their crushing burden was borne only by the Jewish nation, were punishments inflicted on the whole of fallen humanity, and were especially rigorous for the Hebraic race as it had fallen from a more prominent place. The hour has come to leave to barbarians the crass desire to minimize anything which bears a mark of predestination. Is not the position of the French people most tragic, too, in the midst of a Europe and a world which have barely emerged from their primitive savagery? As for myself, and despite the maleficent influence the Jewish race has exerted on my life, I have succeeded in erasing from my memory the abjection attached to its name since the Middle Ages, and in keeping in mind, as did Pascal in *Les Pensées* and Goethe in the *Divan, Wilhelm Meister* and the *Memoirs*, only its innate wisdom and innate purity. The Jews occupied the first place in the task of the spiritual unification of the ancient world. For reasons which belong to a realm very different from that of intelligence, they had to repudiate their mission at the very time it received its final consecration from the Son of David. But as they have, since the days of Herod, preserved a fidelity to the oneness of the Universal God, they will soon receive a double recompense. They will participate fervently in the great Christian task of religious, social and political unification and will obtain an eminent moral position in the future Catholic, Apostolic, and Roman Empire.

Verse 89
Eve found herself, then, placed with regard to Man, King of the World, in the relationship of beth to aleph, of the vision to the seer, of love to being, of bride to bridegroom.

The Relation of Beth to Aleph

The hidden Fire, warmth of the primeval Water of the Nothing (the moment has come to unveil this new figure of the Work), projects its incorporeal light into that Water with the aim of making it an archetypal idea of an "exterior" and of inducing the Law to transmute itself into Love. Incorporeal light condenses into space-matter in a fiery mathematical point; the fictitious distance of any star reminds us of its original image. This mathematical point of fiery space-matter is already virtually the whole universe. Only the energy of the atom could give us a feeble idea of the magic power contained in this point. Transmuted into physical light, this first emission, changing into electricity, appears in the guise of a multiplicity of bodies in movement whose relationships engender the concept of space-time, while the total Body remains pure spiritual vision in the Nothing. Blood, corresponding to the spiritual marriage of Fire and Water, is born from the first emission at the same time as the physical light. In the beginning it is Adam, the law of necessity and fire. In Eve, it is transmuted into light and love.

Ecstasy alone—the unique reality—allows us to relive the entire operation in instantaneity. Ecstasy is the Crowning of Faith. As far as Faith is concerned, it is obvious that it can be obtained only by means of prayer. To wait for faith in order to pray is to put the cart before the horse. Our road leads from the physical to the spiritual: it is proper therefore to start with the physical, that is, with the prescribed words of the *Pater*. The child prays mechanically; that is why it is written: Suffer little children, and forbid them not to come unto me (those who are not discouraged by the ridicule of mechanical prayer).

"And yet, if by chance someone overhears? Would he not say: This man who has no faith and who prays, what a hypocrite! And what a nuisance!" No, not at all. Nothing is more enchanting to one who really loves than importunity. And Eternity, what is it, after all, if not the first endless instant of a first love?

Verse 90

She represented the femininity of manifestation, whose consciousness, knowledge and prayer Adam was. Eve's consciousness was in Adam, Eve's knowledge was in Adam, Eve's prayer was in Adam.

Eve's Prayer was in Adam

Though descended from the original and revealed knowledge of the femininity of virginal, procreative Manifestation, the Asianic and Aegean cult of the Goddess-Mother, universal matriarchy and the feminine priesthood were, soon after the fall of mankind, transformed into an idolatry of Nature and of fecundity, characteristic of the conjugal arcanum when it is adulterated. Among the Thrako-Phrygians this arcanum became an incestuous union between Nana (*niania*, a nurse, in Slavic), the earth, and her son Attis (*Atietz*, father, in the same idiom), god of vegetation; among the Phoenicians, between Ashtoreth and Adonis; among the Cretans, between Dictynna and Asterios. The Goddess-Mothers, at the very time when their cult was dedicated to the femininity of the universe, already indicated a pagan tendency to abandon the fundamental dogma of unity, and their fecundity was confused with multiplicity. Among the Jews, on the contrary, as among the Christians later on, femininity remains purely spiritual and is subordinated to the Law of Being, even though it is an instrument of its Exaltation. This is the reason why, among the Jews and also among the Christians, women have never been admitted to the priesthood. In the system of Swedenborg, man is wisdom and woman is love of this wisdom. Adam is the law, woman is the benediction. It is this cult of inconceivable unity which constitutes the greatness and the power of Judeo-Christianity.

Verse 91
Eve was free, because her consciousness and her knowledge and her prayer were in Adam, and Adam was the freedom of beauty in its primordial relationship, the father of his own law in the interplay of dynamic connections.

Father of his own Law

The freedom of woman, as well as that of man, consists in knowledge of and fidelity to the Law. All creatures who ignore their origins may well proclaim themselves sovereigns of billions of milky ways, absolute masters of their destinies, forever delivered from the fear of death; in short, although they may adorn themselves with all possible virtues and arrogate to themselves all kinds of imaginary powers, they will not escape the obsession of the word blotted out of their memory. To be free is to have the strength to recognize that the greater we are, the less we belong to ourselves, and that we give only because first we have received. To be free is to assimilate thoroughly the idea that although mediocre results may be due to our ingenuity, truly great and durable conquests are never the fruit of our individual power. Because works of genius come from afar, from beyond man, the vulgar will always prefer the essentially personal qualities which appear as talents. To make woman free, it would be enough for men to have knowledge of the spiritual bond uniting nature to God. Any other freedom of woman leads to the depopulation of the few, rare countries truly deserving to live, and to the adulteration of the conjugal principle, source of the universe and foundation of the future Catholic Empire. The Law transmuted into Love gives life to the beauty of the universe and to that of woman; the one and the other are inseparable from Benediction and from Charity. However, the law, the pure and terrible law of being, of necessity and of sacrifice, the law to which is addressed the prayer on the Mount of Olives—and which, as soon as we raise our brutal hand against the veil of love softening its unbearable glare, appears to us in all its majesty and rigor, affirmation of affirmation—the law claims first place in our mind, and woe to whoever refuses it: to rebel against the law means to lose love. Open the Gospels, meditate upon some of the Master's rebuffs: after what has been said, you will understand why so many harsh words have been pronounced by the Law behind the veil of Love.

Adam is father of his own Law, that is, identical to his necessity, or to the first movement, that of blood born with physical light from the metamorphosis of the initial emission. To put it differently, Adam is the law itself according to which the relations between moving bodies engender an appearance of space-time-matter.

Verse 92
Eve was free, she was untainted by any submission to man, for man and woman were one flesh just as the seer and his vision were an indivisible unity.

Eve was Free

The daughters of Eve lost this beautiful freedom precisely at the very instant when the infernal operation of the first King transformed the spiritual world of vision into a universe of matter situated in itself. I do not reprove the modern aspirations of women, and least of all those which are inextricably linked with the legitimate claims of the proletariat. I only wonder why they should have as their objective precisely the buffooneries and vices which make the present condition of the strong sex so despicable; women go their own way only to imitate men more freely and to confess by such behavior that the ancient prestige of the male has not lost any of its previous force. I do not, however, condemn this attitude; it seems to me in perfect conformity with the law. I simply deplore that this law has been altered to such a profound extent by man. What disturbs me is not the reversal of roles; it does not matter where the spirit comes from. But one is nauseated when one witnesses a masquerade dragging its cheap tinsel and finery in the mud and blood of butchery. The mother has the word; thus the end of parliaments approaches. Compared with the femininity of manifestation, how insignificant "feminism" is. The mother has the floor—the mother of men: even today maternity is still virginal and spiritual, for it is the beloved man who is the first child. If a feeling of Exalted Love does not awaken in the heart of woman, if she does not help us to raise a man truly worthy of his ancient name, father of the law, tomorrow we shall all be drawn, inevitably, into the dance of cannibals which already circles this mediocre planet. May the new Queen prepare herself to confirm the statute of the new King.

Verse 93
Like the cosmos itself, this flesh was the incorporeal light of beauty, of vision. Fecundated by the holy spirit, as were the cosmos and the earth, like them the flesh gave birth, and its children, who were born for action, went far beyond action in their movement, for the sake of rhythm.

She gave Birth

In his *Traité de la Réintégration des Etres*,[34] Martinez de Pasqually, in other respects so bizarre and so obscure, gives us a particularly touching picture of the materialization of the world in its various phases. The doctrine of the Portuguese Jew contains many an excellent article of faith, and this explains the patience which the Unknown Philosopher and some other disciples have shown for him. But the methods of Jehovah are infinitely simpler than those of his worshippers. If the comprehension of God had limits, some of our psychic and mental complications—not to mention our infinite and containing space—undoubtedly would be unintelligible to him. The entire divine system is founded upon freedom. Alas! I doubt whether in future society Hiram, and even the apostolic Church itself, would ever be able to give so much free play to their liberality. Yet the saintliness of love demands that the rigors of the law be proportional to so extensive a freedom. The rebellion of the angels indicates that the archetypal idea of resistance and of sin against the Spirit already existed in the non-manifested world, together with the idea of an "exterior," of a nothing. So that it would not be possible to conceive of a freedom equal in magnitude and perfection to man's without immediately losing one's way in speculations—contrary to any true philosophy—on the supreme perfection of some impossible non-being. Created in order that he might vividly express the love of the seer for his vision and of the vision for its seer, spiritual in his blood and his flesh, son and husband of a virgin: such was Adam, the King of the world. His descendants were called to rule over the three realms in a perfect communion of essence and of language, as nothing could remain alien to a being formed from the blood of a book written by light. The desire to learn where space is engenders the desire to learn what love is. But the ceremony of consecration unveiled to Kings the movement of incorporeal light: their thought was an awareness and love of this movement in which an affective state and place were joined together once more. By perceiving this movement man learned to desire a state which opens to the intelligence, beyond the summit assigned for its meetings with Metatron, a path of return from the exterior to the ever-faithful interior, since, obviously, these contraries signify only two ideal aspects of the unique and only situated place. To faith, light is separated and inseparable from fire. The emission is continuous, and yet light travels: physical, it covers in eighty-four billion years the curvature of space in order to come back to its point of departure; spiritual, it describes the entire circle of evolution and returns to Dante's Empyrean of secret fire, to the tenth immobile heaven. The course of the two lights is inconceivable and, nevertheless, real; in all its points it embraces the marvellous sphere of Vision, of total space, of material appearance, projected into the Nothing. Exactly by this the resurrection of the dead is explained: for after the Last Judgment, the spiritual light of blood and its sister, physical light, the essence of bodies, melt and blend through a reverse transmutation into a single incorporeal light, the same which was shed at the instant of creation. Together with all the bodies of which physical light, transformable into electricity, was the essence, this reinstated light returns to the divine source. Caution should be taken here as such deliberations can be justified only by love and the intense desire for faith; curiosity that wanders alone into this maze is doomed in advance; as the thread slips out of its fingers, it ends miserably in the darkness of insanity; for it should be known that madness is the punishment for curiosity devoid of charity and of faith, just as it is the outcome of fornication without love—one of the most horrible forms of our curiosity. Adam's prevarication resulted not only in transforming, in our representation of it, the sphere of the divine luminous vision of light into a world of matter situated in its own endless darkness; it also dimmed the spiritual brightness of the sun of memory, thus identifying our blood, subjugated by passions, with physical fire which also became pure matter situated in a false infinite space: when that blood refuses to reabsorb, through prayer, the spiritual light which is its true essence, it is doomed to endless torments, for its own fire, falsely imagined to be physical, is then situated in a false space determinable only by endless multiplication.

Before, as well as after, manifestation, this abominable fire of internal pseudo-freedom, following the transmutation of the return, remains as an archetypal idea of resistance, of materialism's rebellion and false freedom.

There, as well as here, punishment consists of being in God and of not knowing it. This punishment is eternal because God measures it by the minimal effort he demands from us: to pronounce, as a beginning, in our solitude between four walls, to pronounce a few prescribed words which under their trite, external meaning comprise all the wisdom and all the charity of God. The miserable end of Friedrich Nietzsche should put us on guard against materialistic interpretations of eternity ("Because I love you, O Eternity") which the great poet—by pure intuition—daringly compared to the rotation of light mentioned above, but of physical light alone, the creator of space-time and of extension-bodies, rotation which he called eternal return, in remembrance, perhaps, of Vico[35] and Grosseteste.

As the world, material in appearance, is only a spiritual vision of the Divine, its true nature is what man makes of it in his representation. Before the prevarication, beings and things were related to each other as they are today and looked exactly the same. But they were *pure* in the thought of the King, who did not yet situate them in their matter. Nature, conceived of the Holy Spirit in incorporeal light, without seed and by transmutation, had received as its fundamental law a similarly spiritual procreation. In its higher, purely logical sense the word "natural" can apply only to the Immaculate Conception of the Virgin and to the birth of her divine Son.

Verse 94

What separated Eve from Adam was the same as what came between Adam and God—it was the nothing, for in every word that Adam spoke, Eve spoke too, except for the word with which Adam affirmed that he was in him who is, and that he was separated from him only by the nothing.

The Nothing

Since we are close to the end and since "the incorporeal light" plays a pre-eminent role in the last verses, allow the author to swear on his honor as a servant of Christ the King—the only honor which counts in his eyes, all others being founded upon barbaric traditions where strength and physical courage occupy the first rank—allow then the author, considering the exceptional solemnity of the occasion, to swear on his honor as a servant of the King that the appearance of the incorporeal sun and the ceremony of Benediction and Consecration, such as they have been described in the present work and in *Ars Magna*, have taken place in truth and reality, amidst an unfolding of inexpressible splendor, during spiritual meditation, without any accompaniment of fear or even amazement but, on the contrary, with a feeling of confidence born of silent prayer in response to the miracle of natural beauty and the immensity of the universe; that the mystical operation took place on the fourteenth day of December, in the year nineteen hundred and fourteen, at about eleven o'clock in the evening; that the author, restrained by religious respect from knocking at the door which altogether unexpectedly had opened, has never again, since that memorable night, seen any of these things that he sometimes regrets having unveiled, for the sake of the future, to the intellects of this time of transition in which God has ordered that he live and act; finally, that this spiritual phenomenon has, for nearly thirteen years, exerted a commanding influence upon his thought, as the works that he has published since then testify.

In the verse which concerns us it is written that what separated Eve from Adam, just like what came between Adam and God, was the Nothing. Indeed, as God is the spiritual infinite, that is, the only intelligible infinite, no exterior exists with respect to him, so that before manifestation the ideal archetypal world had for its container the fundamental concept of an "interior," that is, of an indivisible unity; the inhabitants of this world, spiritual ancestors of the Chosen People, represented it by means of the letter aleph, in opposition to beth, which stood for the idea of the exterior, of the negative, of the nothing, of unity divisible into non-situated multiplicity. Insofar as God is an interior and is designated as aleph, God is the law, or, a being identical with its necessity, the inconceivable fire. For men of the archetypal world He was the place, in other words the immobility in which the metamorphosis of one state into another occurred, a metamorphosis which was the idea-type of movement, of the future creator of space-time-matter. Those purely spiritual men lived in the divine fire or inner illumination and instantaneity. Inasmuch as the higher reality of all present, past and future things of our material universe has for its place the archetypal world and the notion of an "interior," it was absolutely necessary that the first transgression prefiguring that of Adam should be committed by the angels, according to the eternal concepts of resistance and of freedom. Then the Divine, in whom love of the first humanity had been subordinated to the law, resolved, through an initial sacrifice which typifies all others, to exalt this love above the law. To this end he had recourse to the Beth, idea of the exterior, of the nothing. In this exterior, this nothing, God, the inconceivable fire, spilled his incorporeal light as later Our Lord spilled his blood. Incorporeal light transmuted itself into the first mathematical point of fiery space-matter, whence it continued its way in the form of physical light transformable into electricity, the essence of bodies. Made of this light, blood, especially man's blood, is its spiritual perfection. Such at least was its original nature in Adam, the man whose heart and brain recorded in unison the flow of the double current of life, physical and spiritual; the first, creator of space-time-matter, the second, seat of the total memory of origins. The reason why Eve was drawn from Adam is identical with that which determined the projection of incorporeal light into the idea of an exterior, of a nothing: it had to happen so that above the law engraved in Adam's heart, man's love for his bride, the femininity of manifestation, should be exalted. Adam, who represents the law, was the priest in the temple of the universe founded, as it is, upon the divine concept of the exterior, of the negative, of the nothing. This nothing which alone came between Adam and God was also the only obstacle to a return to the unity of the positive and the negative, since, in Adam, woman lived in the idea of the exterior, of the nothing, just as the universe had been created through the archetypal concept of the negative.

As to the guilty segment of the first humanity, after manifestation they preserved their notion of a locked interior, the angels of fidelity remaining the only masters of the real Place of all things, the paradise of unity and instantaneity. And yet the exaltation of love resulted in subordinating this paradise itself to the idea of an "exterior," of the negative, of the nothing where God had placed his Bride so that she might adore him as if from outside. The Divine concentrated the best of his love upon this "exterior" which is the home of Adam's humanity. The condemned part of the "interior" fell into absolute oblivion. Its angelic humanity, the victim of a false freedom, was abandoned to the supreme torment of living in God and of not knowing it, of participating in the mystery of the sacred fire, yet perceiving only darkness and the cold of loneliness. The perfection of divine thought embraced this loneliness too, yet only negation was to fathom its unspeakable horror. So when Adam pronounced the word Nothing, this word, in the mind of Eve, could mean only a division of the single flesh into two poles, one positive, the other negative. The Nothing which came between Adam and God was alien to the spiritual realm of woman, for her knowledge was in man. All this having been explained several times, we shall limit ourselves to reproducing verse 95 without commentary.

Verse 95

Because Eve, by her consciousness, her knowledge and her prayer, was in Adam.

Verse 96

Eve was in Adam and what came between Adam and God was the nothing; this one and the same nothing thus separated Eve from God; she was in him. But she was also in Adam, and what separated her from Adam was this same nothing whose sacred name she had no reason to pronounce—as long as she was in Adam.

The Sacred Name

Space is contained in the nothing; it is thanks to the nothing that space, pure vision, is neither finite nor infinite. Let us suppress the nothing, the negative, the exterior; we return immediately not to the paradisal and unique Place of the angels of fidelity, but on the contrary, to the concept of that part of the interior which God has made similar to the idea-types of resistance, of false freedom, and of oblivion. When we deny God's love for the nothing-universe, we relapse into the darkness of the infernal world. In other words, by suppressing the nothing which alone allows us to conceive a universe-vision and to escape the absurd and sacrilegious dilemma of the finite and the infinite (of matter with inconceivable limits, and of matter ungraspable as a whole in eternal expansion)—by suppressing, I repeat, the nothing, we have the illusion of situating the universe in its own matter and of proclaiming ourselves its absolute kings, but in reality we leave the illuminated sphere of love exalted in the divine idea of an exterior, and we return to this interior circle of ignorance and oblivion, governed by the terrible law, the law which is necessity for God and freedom for man. This third meaning of our doctrine will be unveiled to the reader by his personal mystical experience, the source of which is in the

Catholic obligatory prayers. It is not in our power to do anything more than to light the way which should lead him to the abode where his true life awaits him. We shall limit ourselves to a very simple instruction derived from the foregoing. Perfection offers itself to him who searches for the Divine not in direct *inner* union and the hope of premature grace, but in *external* manifestation, that is, in beauty and in charity. It is a crime to forget the latter when one speaks of "the esthetic sense." The most miserable of human creatures is more beautiful than the light of a billion milky ways—to say nothing of our tiny terrestrial mountains and oceans.

Verse 97
Adam's pre-eminence over Eve therefore resided entirely in this spiritual and secret right to pronounce, both for himself and for Eve, the sacred name of the nothing, which is only a name; for the void and the full, time and movement, are banished from it.

For Himself and for Eve

Adam was the total consciousness of the relationship between beth and aleph, between the vision and the seer, between the bride and the bridegroom, between love and the law. From cosmic matter he had received his body; it is *in him* that the exterior, the nothing, was situated with respect to God who, in the exaltation of love, had condemned one part of the interior, and had created moral man in the image of his own sacrifice and his own charity. Adam alone, thanks to his integral memory of origins and to his knowledge of the ritual of reciprocity, therefore had the right to pronounce the sacred name of the nothing. For Eve, bound to Adam by a secondary relationship of one moving body to another, the Nothing was a concept which separated her not from God but from her husband, as he and she were one flesh. This is why it is said in verse 98:

Verse 98
And this mystical privilege agreed with the situation of a dynamic connection within the primordial relationship between the vision and the seer.

Verse 99
Eve, the femininity of manifestation, the prefigure of physical Nature, was perfectly free of Adam and situated with respect to her husband in a dynamic connection of which he was the begetter; she was included in Adam, who was the consciousness of the primordial relationship, just as the dynamic connection is included in that relationship itself.

Prefigure of Physical Nature

It has already been explained how, at the instant of prevarication, the original, purely spiritual universe was transformed in human thought into a universe of matter, into physical Nature. Eve was free in Adam only because, as she prefigured physical Nature through the complete independence of her movements, she was in no way compelled to undergo this possible but not predetermined transmutation. God wanted woman, as well as man, to be free in the miracle of prayer and of spiritual love. But in order that this freedom might exist, was it not necessary that the choice between the archetypes of the true and the false should be left to us? Man doubts his freedom only because he ignores the immense power of love.

Verse 100
Eve was in Adam, made one with his consciousness, with his knowledge, with his prayer: Adam pronounced the word *nothing* for himself and for Eve, but when he said "I" he thought only of Eve.

"I"

The law transmuted itself into love through the separation of the positive and the negative, through the split of original man into husband and wife. This operation corresponds to the initial transmutation of the pre-eminence of the interior into a pre-eminence of the exterior. Thanks to it, Adam could leave behind his "I." The third phase of the sacrificial mystery arrived when our Lord, the new Adam, abandoned his celestial essence and his human saintliness, that is, when he identified himself absolutely with guilty humanity. This third phase will not become accessible to our intelligence until we have paid the prescribed tribute of tears. Adam's self thus resided in Eve, and because the spouse was the true self of the husband, temptation had to speak through her mouth; for Eve prefigured the physical Nature over which Adam's pride sought to extend the dominion of his false freedom. Identical with the spiritual universe, with God's vision, man wanted to become a physical universe no longer situated in the Nothing, in the light of vision, but in its own matter, that is, in the dilemma of the incomprehensible finite and the ungraspable infinite.

Verse 101
For on the level of the primordial relationship he did not have an "I"; but he had an "I" in the world of dynamic connections.

"I"

On the level of the primordial relationship, Adam's "I" was identical with the love of Creation for its Creator, with the love of beth for aleph, of the bride for the bridegroom, identical also with love for the law, of the negative for the positive, of the vision for the seer. Thus the "I" belonged to Adam only in the world of dynamic connections. Man's thought, the awareness and love of movement, situated this movement with respect to the movement of woman. To want to know the "I" is to search for a place, because in the realm of phenomena everything can be reduced to the fundamental need to situate beings and things. For Adam, Eve was the place, in accordance with the subordination of all things to the archetype of the exterior.

Verse 102

Now it happened one day that Adam in his "I" heard Eve ask him: "Adam, being of my love, is it not true that what separates me from you is the nothing?"

In his "I"

Eve, a figure of physical nature which is possible but not predetermined, lends her voice here to a remembrance preserved by her husband in his perfect memory of how one part of ideal humanity had rebelled. The fallen angels had tried to identify themselves with the inconceivable divine fire which was their abode but from which they nevertheless knew they were separated by the notion of a nothing, of an exterior, that is, by the supreme idea of sacrifice. In this idea, before as well as after manifestation, resided the unfathomable mystery of divinity. The absolute freedom of man—the consciousness of the universe created by the Sacrifice in this nothing, this exterior—required that to his intelligence and his will there should be offered a possibility of overcoming the temptation which, in physical Nature, that is, in a universe of matter situated in itself, promised him a way toward an absolute scientific possession of the universe. The question, "Is it not true that what separates me from you is the nothing?" already contains, in an allusion to unity ("You will be but one flesh"), the infernal affirmation of the existence of an external and *real* body. The Nothing whose name Eve pronounces here is still the one which separates her from Adam and whose meaning is accessible to her. But already the Nothing which was destined *to unite* man to God in submission to the inconceivable tends to metamorphose itself into a Nothing which *separates* him from Divinity by suggesting to him the forbidden effort of intellection which as a substitute for the concept of the universe-vision proposes an idolatry of matter as such. The instantaneity of vision, whose place was beyond the dilemma of the finite and the infinite, is changed into space-time in infinity-eternity, since infinity of space and eternity of time, in the form of addition, multiplication, and extension without respite, necessarily accompany the infernal work of materialization.

Verse 103
This word nothing reverberated sweetly and strangely on the spouse's lips. Adam fell into a profound meditation.

Meditation

For the first time the word Nothing resounded in Adam's ear: it came to him not from his thought, but from outside. The Nothing which separated him from Eve now appeared to him measurable and tangible; it invested with a sudden reality that relation between one moving body and another, which creates space-time and which his intelligence, until then, had considered as no more than the pure appearance of the "interior" of a universe-vision placed in the Nothing. Eve has just materialized love.

Verse 104
He did not close his eyes. He questioned space, the incorporeal light of beauty. The vision was there. He questioned space, the incorporeal light of beauty. The vision was there. Adam raised his head; an eagle was flying toward the sun. Space was there. Two

clouds were gliding slowly as if to melt into one: there was an impatience in Adam; the light clouds were gliding slowly in time. And under Adam's feet the stones were warmed by a marvelous noon.

He did not Close his Eyes, He Questioned Space

This space is still the simple dynamic relationship which enables man to determine his position among beings and things, to assign to his movement a place circumscribed by external movements. Adam, whose memory of origins begins to grow dark in the struggle between wisdom and pride, still hesitates to transmute in his thought this space which is neither finite nor infinite, this pure light of vision, into a universe of matter whose limit will be as inconceivable as its eternal extension. This is the reason for the repetitions with which the verse opens. On the brink of the cosmic precipice of eternity and infinity, which madness opens up before him, Adam hesitates. Unfortunately Eve, physical Nature, is there, and on her lips trembles a word prompted by the fallen angels, foes of this incomprehensible Nothing where the initial Sacrifice had to be fulfilled. She hears this word in the hiss of a creature whose body blends with the earth, whose stare seems to come from the sand, whose sudden stone-like immobility resembles the imprint of the unfathomable Nothing, source of all sacrilegious curiosity and of all the evils that result from it. Beginning with this instant, the whole history of mankind will be an incessant battle between the idea of infinite, eternal matter[*] on the one hand, and that of the Nothing on the other; the Nothing which, from a holy and logical notion, will transmute itself into a deification of man, which in its turn will soon give rise to a cowardly and unrealizable desire for physical and spiritual annihilation. (In order to escape the dilemma of the finite and the infinite, man, instead of praying, will invoke Nothingness.) Adam raises his head—a heroic

---

[*] A doctrine of which the philosophy of Averroes is the compendium.

affirmation is going to come from his mouth—no, an eagle flies toward the sun. Space is there, in all its magnificent and brutal reality. Could this be a simple vision of God, a world of love drawn from the Nothing and suspended in the pure idea of an exterior, that is, in a Nothing? Or could it not be that God is a dream? This nocturnal Consecration, this incorporeal sun endowed with the intelligence and will of an Archangel, this golden cloud loaded with royal benedictions, all these things of an instant, are they worth the measurable, tangible, ponderable reality which surrounds me, suffuses me, swallows me and recognizes me as its highest consciousness? A cloud seen in a dream similar to all dreams, did it have the dazzling vividness of these clouds whose course I measure with my eyes, my breath, my heart? When then will they melt into a single vapor? Never has my body felt so free, so powerful. I am the stone palace of time, all ablaze with a marvelous noon.

Verse 105
Eve repeated her question; it was the same and yet not completely the same: "Adam, being of my love, is it not true that only the nothing separates you from God?"

Only the Nothing separates you from God

The Nothing of submission and of wisdom is this divine archetype of an exterior, of a negative, in which the law transmutes itself into love and world-thought changes into universe-vision. The Nothing of submission and of wisdom is the spiritual place where creation blesses and worships the creator. The Nothing of madness and pride is the one which the fallen Legions have vainly tried to submit to reason; they use it as a lure in their attempt to incite the Just to make himself equal to God through an absolute intellectual domination which, by means of extension without end, strains to embrace a universe of which matter itself is the place.

Verse 106

Space was there, the incorporeal light of the vision of the nonsituated universe. Space was there, and Adam, whose "I" no longer wanted to know this nothing which separated him from God, Adam was thinking about the total universe and whispered: Where is space?

The Nothing

The Great Ritual of Reciprocity is a perfect code of human freedom. Love creates truly liberated people, compared to whom political anarchists look like pitiable slaves. Giovanni dei Gioachini, Francesco di Bernadone, Pope Fra Pietro,[36] you free men are guardian spirits of the future Apostolic Church. I who sometimes flatter myself on having broken many shackles, beside you I feel that I am a weakling who still pronounces with anger the holy name of freedom. I have seen what no imagination in this naive and brutal century would dare to dream about, and yet I cannot make up my mind to abandon my solitude and to raise my voice among human beings. I know well that such is the will of him who made me what I am; but true mastery does not so easily adapt to the limits assigned to love by God himself. Had I been free, I would have accepted as much human respect as was my due: now I appear very small because I scorn souls who are too ostensibly mediocre and who, perhaps without knowing it, want to better themselves. Charity, an inexhaustible source of freedom, is not satisfied with giving; it resigns itself to receiving what is necessary for its action without examining too closely the hands which stretch toward it. Every day I have some occasion to measure the distance which original Sin has created between myself and my original condition. One trembles when evoking the most abominable crime. What is easier than to imagine the motives which have armed the hand of a parricide, of a traitor, or of a man tormented by jealousy? But how are we to explain a crime committed by a creature whose mind is open to all the wisdom of the suns and of blood, if not by the miracle of absolute freedom and by a divine trust prepared in advance for the supreme sacrifice? Why was man so perverse as to prefer, to the truth of revealed knowledge, the illusion of an acquired science, and, to the concept of the sacred Nothing in which affection and place are one, the false notion of nothingness so that he might proclaim himself sovereign for a day of a lump of matter sentenced to slow decay in the darkness of death, without beginning or end?

Verse 107
Then, O my royal son, O Hiram, at the boundaries of this space—which the ancient King had extended beyond any idea of limit in order to situate it in itself, in the receptacle of a void—in the mind of man the nothing suddenly changed into this infinity of darkness which is the blindness of Adam.

The Author's Prayer

The Nothing, only intelligible container of a universe which is as free and pure as God's thought, the Nothing superior to any notion of the finite and of the infinite, was repudiated by man. Horrified by the spectacle of the Crucifixion, the sun of the memory of origins dies out together with the physical star. Adam's consciousness of the primordial relationship grows dim. The human spirit is driven from the paradisal light, the transmutation of which occurs in the holy, holy idea of an exterior, lucid region of exaltation, of sacrifice, of charity, and of freedom; of freedom, blessed may it be. The

King whispers: Where is space? And his blindness answers him: Space is in me, in my darkness without beginning or end. Then the numbers of knowledge, of beauty and of peace, the celestial One, marvelous, marvelous, *hosanna in excelsis;* the spiritual Two, which transmutes itself into light and blood, *in unitate Spiritus Sancti;* the Three, Master of the great ritual of reciprocity, *per omnia secula seculorum;* all the great and merciful Numbers, up to the Ten of the return of the prodigal son to the Father's House, Amen; the Numbers of the wisdom of Love, one after another, gird the sword of the Law and return to the sun of suns, where the indestructible Thrones await them. The pitiful King of the World puts his right hand on the head of his spouse, as a sign of harsh dominion over corporeal Nature. In his left hand he raises the universal Apple, fruit of the tree of knowledge of good and evil, emblem of the miserable royalty which feeds on earth and forgets that it is itself devoured by time. In this imperial orb the Lord, one day, will set the Cross. In Adam's thought, instead of the sacred Numbers, there surge forth infernal and corporeal signs of Division and Multiplication without end. It is in the Lord, it is in His peace, that I want to sleep and to rest.

A Few Notes

WHEN Czeslaw Milosz, C.M., wrote most of these notes for an edition of *Ars Magna* and *The Arcana* that was never published, he intended to place them ahead of the text and to introduce them as follows:

> We are confronted with hermetic writings. Perhaps the translator should at least provide footnotes whenever the author expects of us an uncommon amount of encyclopedic learning. Unfortunately, footnotes look pedantic and would not harmonize with the tone of the whole. So perhaps it is better to prepare the reader by listing in advance some terms and titles of literary works and names and by explaining them briefly.

To these notes, all indicated by Czeslaw Milosz' initials, the editor of the present volume has added a few more.

1 ARS MAGNA   There is reason for leaving the title in its original form: the Latin has wider connotations than its literal equivalent, the Great Art. *Ars Magna, seu Ars compendiosa inveniendi veritatem* (*The Great Art, or a concisely presented Art of discovering truth*), 1277, is the most famous work of Raimon Lull (1235-1315), a Catalan poet and philosopher from Majorca. Alchemical treatises often invoked his authority and praised his "science of sciences" with which they identified their own Great Art, i.e., alchemy.   C.M.

2 STORGE   Storge is an allegorical person. The Greek word means love, but especially in one of its varieties, love of parents for their children. In this sense, it is used by Emanuel Swedenborg in his book *Conjugial Love* ("conjugial" instead of "conjugal" was introduced into English by Swedenborg's translators). Storge is androgynous because it represents both paternal and maternal love.   C.M.

In *Conjugial Love* Swedenborg writes: "There are indications which show clearly that conjugial love and the love of infants, which is called *storge*, are conjoined." Among the ensuing propositions that Swedenborg then attempts to demonstrate are the following:

I   That from the Lord proceed two universal spheres for the preservation of the universe in the state created, of which one is the sphere of procreating, and the other of protecting the sphere of things procreated.
II That these two universal spheres make one with the sphere of conjugial love and the sphere of the love of infants.
III That these two spheres flow, universally and singly, into all things of heaven and all things of the world, from the first of them to the last.
IV That the sphere of the love of infants is a sphere of protection and support of those who cannot protect themselves. . . .

Confirming this, in his great work *The Pillar and Foundation of the Truth* (written in 1912, and published in 1914 in Moscow), Father Pavel Florensky writes:

Stergein does not signify a passionate love of someone or something, but a calm and constant feeling, such that whoever loves in this way recognizes that the object of their love belongs to them and is intimately bound to them; by this avowal it acquires inner peace. *Stergein* refers then to the organic bond, that of the species, and, because of this connection, is indissoluble even by evil. Such is the calm, tender and sure love of parents for their children, of the husband for his wife, of the citizen for his country. . . .

EDITOR

3   SAANA   Saana is the name of the capital of Yemen and is always taken in the sense of "Garden," place of repose and contemplation. According to Jean Richer it is the place of First Love. EDITOR

4   PATMOS OF BOANERGES   Boanerges is the name of John the Evangelist (Mark 3, 17: *He surnamed them Boanerges, which is, "The sons of thunder . . .*) who, according to the majority of Biblical scholars, is also the author of *The Book of Revelation*, written on the Island of Patmos.   C.M.

According to Jean Richer, Milosz means by Patmos the only Situated Place, the place of Revelation and of Vision, in conformity with the etymology *Path-Mouses*, the way or path of the Muse, of Inspiration." EDITOR

5   THE FATHER OF MODERN SCIENCE   As a geologist, physicist and religious thinker, Emanuel Swedenborg (1688-1722) inspired many writers and men of science throughout the eighteenth and nineteenth centuries; however, the scope of his influence was rarely acknowledged by those concerned, and today it is known only to specialists.   C.M.

6 ENS   *Ens* in Latin means thing or entity, being—a thing that is. The *"Primum Ens"* of a thing is its first beginning, hence, by implication, its cause or principle *(arche)*. Paracelsus speaks of the *Primum Ens* as "the source of all life." Hence it is related to the *archaeus*, the principle of life.
EDITOR

7 "MOVEMENT WHICH DISPLACES LINES."   From Baudelaire's poem, *La Beauté* (Beauty).
EDITOR

8 THE ADRAMANDONIC OF SWEDENBORG, THE HESPERIC OF HÖLDERLIN, AND THE ELYSIAN OF SCHILLER   The word "Adramandoni" occurs only once in Swedenborg, in one of the Memorable Relations (section 183) of *Conjugial Love*:

> Seen by me in the eastern quarter was a grove of palm trees and laurels arranged in a spiral gyre. I approached it and entering walked on its paths which wound around in several spirals. At the end of the windings, I saw a garden which formed the center of the grove. Separating the two was a small bridge, and on it, a gate on the grove side and another on the garden side. I drew nearer, and the gates were opened by a guard. To my question, "What is the name of this garden?" he answered, "Adramandoni," which means the delight of conjugial love. . . .

In Hölderlin's work two references to "Hesperides" stand out. The first occurs in the last stanza of "Bread and Wine." Ancient poets had spoken of the return of the Golden Age when all men should become children of God. Hölderlin sees this moment as about to be fulfilled, and writes:

> What of the children of God was foretold in the songs of the ancients,
> Look, we are it, ourselves; fruit of Hesperia it is!

and then again, at the close of "Celebration of Peace," he writes:

> For now all things are pleasing
> But most of all the
> Ingenuous, because the long-sought,
> The golden fruit . . .

In *Hölderlin's Major Poetry*, Richard Unger comments: "The vague promise of the earlier poem is here enunciated in greater detail. The golden fruit is 'the form of the Heavenly Ones,' the visible activity of the gods' presence. . . ."

"The Elysian of Schiller" refers to Schiller's poem, "Elysium":

Here the true spouse the lost-beloved regains,
And on the enamelled couch of summer plains
Mingles sweet kisses with the zephyr's breath.
Here, crowned at last, love never knows decay,
Living through ages its one bridal day
Safe from the stroke of death.

EDITOR

9   GOLD OF SHEBA   The meeting of King Solomon and the Queen of Sheba often appears in medieval art where it is interpreted symbolically. The source is II Chronicles, 9.1:

And when the Queen of Sheba heard of the fame of Solomon, she came to prove Solomon with hard questions at Jerusalem, with a very great company, and camels that bore spices, and gold in abundance, and precious stones; and when she was come to Solomon, she communed with him of all that was in her heart.

C.M.

From the alchemical point of view, Sheba is the primordial human soul, Adam Kadmon. "It is he," Jung writes in *Mysterium Conjunctionis*, "who laments in the 'prisons' of the darkness and who is personified by the black Shulamite of the Song of Songs." Jung quotes Johannes Grasseus, who writes of the white dove hidden in lead: "This is the chaste, wise and rich Queen of Sheba, veiled in white, who was willing to give herself to none but King Solomon." Jung also quotes Penotus: "You have the virgin earth. . . . She is the queen of Sheba, hence there is need of a King crowned with a diadem—where shall we find him?"

The "gold of Sheba" thus implies human nature brought to its natural completion in union, marriage or conjunction with its complement.

Sheba, too, is Sophia, Wisdom. Marie Louise von Franz writes:

She is called, further, the "Wisdom of the south" or of the "south wind," and is thus equated with the Biblical Queen of the South, the Queen of Sheba, who in alchemical tradition was, like Solomon, the author of alchemical works, and was identified with Maria the Jewess, "sister of Moses."

EDITOR

10   THE LETTER H ADDED TO ONE'S NAME   The letter H has always been revered in hermetic literature as a sign of spiritual anointing. Swedenborg (in *The True Christian Religion* and in *Apocalypse Revealed*) says that it was added to the names of Sarai and of Abram; and that this signifies that the two became bearers of the infinite and the eternal. The symbolism of Hebrew letters is found as early as the Fathers of the Church (St. Jerome). Dante makes use of symbolic letters in the XXVIth Canto of *Purgatorio*

C.M.

The letter H thus indicates the sealing of a covenant between God and man. In Genesis 17 it is after the Lord has appeared to Abram and said to him, "I will make my covenant between me and thee and will multiply thee exceedingly," and Abram has fallen on his face before the Lord, that the Lord adds, "Neither shall thy name any more be called Abram, but thy name shall be Abraham." EDITOR

11 A PRIEST OF THE ORDER OF MELCHIZEDEK   It is Melchizedek who initiates (invests, blesses) Abram in Genesis 14, giving him bread and wine: "And Melchizedek, King of Salem, brought forth bread and wine: and he was the priest of the most high God. And he blessed him, and said, Blessed be Abram of the most high God, possessor of heaven and earth." Melchizedek is invoked again in Psalm 110,4—"The Lord hath sworn and will not repent, thou art a priest forever after the order of Melchizedek"—and, of course, by St. Paul in the Epistle to the Hebrews, where it is Christ himself who is said to be "a priest forever after the order of Melchizedek," who "without father, without mother, without descent, having neither beginning of days, nor end of life; but made like unto the Son of God, abideth a priest continually."

According to René Guenon (in *Le Roi du Monde*) Melchizedek, whose name means "King of Justice" and who comes from "Peace" (Salem) and who is forever a "Priest-King," is none other than the spiritual King of the World, of Malcuth, the Kingdom of the Presence (Shekinah). In this sense, Melchizedek is related to Metatron (the Angel of the Countenance), the Archangel Michael and also, as Melchizedekian gnostics attest, to the Holy Spirit. Hence in Ismaeli gnosis Melchizedek is a name of the permanent guide or Iman. The priesthood of Aaron or of the Letter is thus to be contrasted with the priesthood of Melchizedek or the Spirit. EDITOR

12 A VAST EXPANSE OF DARK LAKES   Milosz's description may profitably be compared with the Manichean "Realm of Darkness" or matter.

> The Realm of Darkness, so Mani teaches, is cut up by deep gulfs, abysses, pits, quagmires, dikes, fens, and pools, into expanses of land divided and split up by long stretches filled with thick forests interspersed with vents which from region to region and from dike to dike send up a smoky exhalation; while afar off, from region to region and from dike to dike, arise columns of fire and smoky cloud. One part of it lies higher, the other lower. The smoke that goes up from it is the poison of Death. It rises from a pit whose bottom seethes with turbid mud covered over with a layer of dust. . . .

Filhirst, p. 94, quoted, SATAN, Sheed and Ward, New York 1952, p. 130
EDITOR

13 HERMETIC DOCTRINE OF THE IDENTITY OF THE TWO SPHERES   The reference here is probably to the famous alchemical text, the "Emerald Tablet," or *Tabula Smaragdina*, which states:

> In truth certainly and without doubt, whatever is below is like that which is above, and whatever is above is like that which is below, to accomplish the miracles of the one thing . . .

(see, *Alchemy*, Titus Burckhart, p. 196). See also, Milosz's *Memoria:*

> All cosmic blood is still in the impetus of the first ejaculation. . . . This is the secret of the Old Masters and the celestial origin of their double concept of the unity of matter and of the identity of the two worlds.
>
> EDITOR

14 BOEHME, SENDIVOGIUS AND PARACELSUS   Jakob Boehme (1575-1624), a German mystical writer, was, as historians of alchemy assert, related and indebted to the entire esoteric movement of the Renaissance, a period when Christian philosophers discovered the Kabbalah and when secret Rosicrucian confraternities were active. A similar indebtedness applies to Sendivogius—the latinized name of Michal Sedziwoj (1556-1636), a Polish alchemist, and to Paracelsus, i.e., Theophrast Bombast von Hohenheim (1493-1541), a Swiss physician and alchemist. In another passage Milosz refers to the latter as "divine Hohenheim."   C.M.

15 TURBA MAGNA   The archaic "turb" for crowd and the modern "turbid," "turbulence," testify to the vacillation of the English language as to which of the two meanings to choose. The Latin *turba* implies both. Upon reflection, I have decided to leave the titles of chapters in Latin, and to translate only those which are in French.   C.M.

16 HESED   *Hesed* is a Hebrew word for "love constructing the world." It is one of the ten Sephiroth of the Kabbalah.   C.M.

17 THE NOTHING OF JAKOB BOEHME   Some idea of Jakob Boehme's understanding of the nothing may be gleaned from the following quotations from his works:

> We understand that without nature there is an eternal stillness and rest, viz, the Nothing; and then we understand that an eternal will arises in the nothing, to introduce the nothing into something, that the will might find, feel and behold itself. . . .
>
> SIGNATURA RERUM, II, 8

We give you to understand this of the divine essence; without nature God is a mystery, understand in the nothing, for without nature is the nothing, which is an eye of eternity, an abyssmal eye, that stands or sees in the nothing, for it is the abyss; and this same eye is a will, understand a longing after manifestation, to find the nothing; but now there is nothing before the will, where it might find something, where it might have a place to rest, therefore it enters into itself, and finds itself through nature . . .

SIGNATURA RERUM, III, 2

Seeing then the first will is an ungroundedness, to be regarded as an eternal nothing, we recognize it to be like a mirror, wherein one sees his own image; like a life, and yet it is not life, but a figure of life and of the image belonging to life . . .

SEXPUNCTA, 1.7
EDITOR

18 THE ARCANA   Works bearing in their titles the word *arcanum* or, in the plural, *arcana*, abound in the sixteenth and seventeenth centuries. Later Swedenborg, not without alluding to his predecessors, entitled his many volumes of Biblical exegesis *Arcana Coelestia*, which has been rendered in English as *The Heavenly Arcana*.

C.M.

19 QUOTATION FROM DESCARTES   Rene Descartes (1596-1650) is known as the originator of modern philosophy and as a major force in the scientific revolution of the seventeenth century; "the Cartesian spirit" became synonymous with French rationalism. The truth is, however, that philosophers, up to this day, have not reached agreement as to the implications of his thought, each drawing Descartes to his own side. Neither has the rich amount of literature on Descartes elucidated certain aspects of his life, for instance, his night of "enthusiasm," his constant travels while he lived in Holland, his Protestant connections and the way he combined his rationalistic method with a model Roman Catholic piety. He remained "a man walking in a mask," but what the man was and what the mask was are matters of conjecture. According to some of his biographers, he was admitted to a secret Rosicrucian confraternity during his stay in Germany. Upon his return to Paris persistent rumors caused him to deny this affiliation, but it is possible that he is the author of a work entitled *Polybii Cosmopolitani thesaurus mathematicus* which is sympathetic to the Rosicrucian Brethren. Because of Descartes' striving for the unity of science and religion, Milosz linked him to the hermetic Renaissance movement and chose him as one of his masters. His own doctrine identifies thought with movement and thus interprets Descartes' *cogito ergo sum*: Under his pen "I think therefore I am" changes into "I move therefore I am." Milosz applies to Descartes what he believed was his name as an initiate: Polybius the Cosmopolitan. When he speaks of himself as a "son of the Cosmopolitan" it should be read: "son of Descartes."

C.M.

20 HIRAM   The name belongs to Rosicrucian and, subsequently, freemasonic lore. The *Dictionary of Mythology, Folklore and Symbols* by Gertrude Jobes (New York: The Scarecrow Press, 1961) gives the following:

> *Hiram*—Masculine name from the Hebrew, meaning noble, noble born.
> *Hiramite*—A Freemason, specifically a master mason; literally a descendant of Hiram, King of Tyre, who furnished cedar, fir trees and workmen to Solomon for the building of the temple.

However, there are two legendary Hirams: one, the King, the other, his craftsman. In Milosz's text, the Hiram whom he addresses is a "spiritual son of Hiram-Abi, a builder sent by Hiram of Tyre to Solomon."   C.M.

21 BOSCOVICH, . . . ROBERT GROSSETESTE AND FARADAY, VERSE 1
   Roger Joseph Boscovich (1711-1787), a Croatian mathematician, a Jesuit, born in Dalmatia, professor in Rome and Pavia.
   Robert Grosseteste (c. 1175-1253), a bishop of Lincoln, Chancellor of Oxford Schools, philosopher and mathematician.
   Michael Faraday (1791-1867), British chemist and physicist.   C.M.

22 THE SAGE OF CROTONA, VERSE 1   Pythagoras (sixth c. B.C.) has been for centuries considered a possessor of hermetic knowledge. A native of the island of Samos, he settled, after many voyages, in Crotona, in the south of Italy, where he formed a brotherhood of initiates.   C.M.

23 JACQUES DE MOLAY, VERSE 5   The order of the Templars, founded in the twelfth century in the Holy Land by knights participating in the Crusades, remains till today a historical enigma. Suspected of heresy (and their fascination with esoteric doctrines of Islam seems to be beyond doubt), they flourished nevertheless through the thirteenth century and were able to amass enormous riches, which became one of the causes of their destruction. The famous trial of their leaders, instigated by King Philippe le Bel of France with the hesitant connivance of Pope Clement V, took place in the years 1307-1314. As a result, the order ceased to exist, and its possessions were confiscated. Jacques de Molay and another commander were burned at the stake in Paris.   C.M.

24 KADOSH DANTE ALIGHIERI DE LA FEDE SANTA, VERSE 5   The symbolism of Dante's *Divine Comedy* has been subject to many contradictory interpretations. Attempts have been made to decipher it as an alchemical poem (cf. Jacques Breyer, *Dante Alchimiste*, Paris: La Colombe, 1957). A supposition that Dante was a Templar and belonged to a secret confraternity calling themselves *Kadosh* is based upon two medals pre-

served in Vienna. One portrays Dante, the other, the painter Pietro of Piza; both bear on their reverse sides the same letters: F. S. K. I. P. F. T. René Guenon *(L'ésoterisme de Dante*, Paris: Gallimard, 1957) interprets them as: *Fedei Sanctae Kadosh, Imperialis Principatus, Frater Templarius.*   C.M.

25   GUILLAUME POSTEL, VERSE 5   Postel was a mystical and hermetic author of the sixteenth century.   C.M.

26   BERESHITH, VERSE 11   The first word of the Bible in Hebrew: "In the beginning."   C.M.

27   MICHEL SERVET AND WILLIAM HARVEY, VERSE 16   It seems that the discovery of the circulation of blood was made not only by William Harvey (1578-1657) but also and earlier by Michel Servet, in the latinized form Servetus, in fact, Miguel Serveto (c. 1511-1553), a Spanish physician and theologian living in France. A heretic (Antitrinitarian), Servet, fleeing persecution in France, took refuge in Calvinist Geneva, where, at the order of Calvin, he was brought to trial, sentenced to death and burned alive at the stake.   C.M.

28   NICOLAS FLAMEL, VERSE 20   Nicolas Flamel (1330-1413) was a French alchemist of legendary fame.   C.M.

29   DOMENI DE RIENZI AND CHAMISSO, VERSE 34   For the name of Domeni de Rienzi a reader would search in vain through encyclopedias. To my knowledge Gregoire Louis Domeni de Rienzy is the author of only one book: *Oceanie, ou cinquieme partie du monde. Revue geographique et ethnographique de la Malaisie, de la Micronesie, de la Polynesie et de la Melanaisie*, Paris, 1876-1878.

Adalbert de Chamisso, a German romantic poet of French origin (1781-1838), made a voyage around the world aboard the sailship "Rurik," as a member of a Russian scientific expedition. His observations on the nature and population of various continents and islands were subsequently gathered in a book: *Reise um die Welt mit der Romanzoffischen Entdeckungs-Expedition*, 1821. Milosz valued this book highly and saw in it anthropological intuitions of genius.   C.M.

30   THE NOBLE TRAVELLERS, VERSE 46   The author is hardly lavish in providing us with clues when he says that "the last time [this name] was pronounced in public was on May 30, 1786, at a session of the Parliament, devoted to the cross-examination of a famous defendant, victim of a pam-

phleteer Theveneau de Morande." Few readers, if any, can guess what the French parliament was doing at that date. Here is the solution to the riddle: it was busy with the case of that wonder of all European capitals, Count de Cagliostro. What to make of Cagliostro we do not know even today. He is sometimes described as a true initiate, sometimes as a charlatan, most often as both. Joseph Balsamo, who assumed the name of Cagliostro, was born in Palermo in 1743, died in 1795. He charmed the cosmopolitan aristocracy of many European countries. In France he was a protegé of Cardinal de Rohan and a founder of the Egyptian Lodge. Accused by Countess de la Motte of the theft of her diamond necklace, he spent nine and a half months in the Bastille. But on May 30, 1786, defended by a famous lawyer as a "Noble Traveller," he was acquitted. As to Theveneau de Morande—he was a journalist, a pamphleteer and a master in the craft of blackmail. In fact, he chose Cagliostro for his target only later, after the latter had met him in London. Whether Theveneau had contributed to the imprisonment of Cagliostro in the Bastille, I was not able to find out.   C.M.

31   SIMEON BEN YOHAI, VERSE 58   Milosz places him on an equal footing with Dante. For the kabbalists, Simeon ben Yohai, a mystical teacher who lived in Palestine in the second century A.D., is the author of cosmological poetry presented in one of the most important books of the Kabbalah, the book of *Zohar*. Sceptics recognize only the authorship of the Spanish kabbalist Moses de Leon, who edited the Zohar shortly before his death in 1305. According to them, Simeon ben Yohai is an invented character and does not necessarily resemble his prototype.   C.M.

32   CLAUDE DE SAINT-MARTIN AND HIS SCHOOL, VERSE 64   Louis Claude de Saint-Martin (1743-1803) played an eminent role in the French "mystical lodges" of the eighteenth century. His works, which he signed as "The Unknown Philosopher," exerted great influence upon many of his contemporaries and upon the Romantic movement in Europe.   C.M.

33   JUAN DE YEPES, VERSE 64   Juan de Yepes (1542-1591), a Carmelite monk and Spanish mystic, is known in literature as Saint John of the Cross.
    C.M.

34   TRAITÉ DE LA RÉINTÉGRATION DES ETRES OF MARTINEZ DE PASQUALLY, VERSE 93   Martinez de Pasqually or Martinez Pasqualis, a Portuguese Jew by origin, was born in Grenoble, France, in 1710 (or in 1727, unless the latter is the date of his baptism). In 1761, he founded in Bordeaux an esoteric lodge of "Elus Coens" (the Elected Cohens). One of his disciples

was Claude de Saint-Martin, "The Anonymous Philosopher." The name "Martinists" sometimes denotes the followers of Martinez, sometimes those of Claude de Saint-Martin. The full title of Martinez' book in which he exposed his doctrine is: *Traité de la réintégration des Etres dans leur premières propriétés, vertus et puissances spirituelles.* C.M.

35 VICO, VERSE 93   Giambattista Vico (1668-1744), Italian philosopher of law and historian, the originator of a historical method applied to the study of ideas and institutions. C.M.

36 GIOVANNI DEI GIOACHINI, FRANCESCO DI BERNADONE, POPE FRA PIETRO, VERSE 106   Among many Giovannis in the history of the Church of Italy no one is listed as Giovanni the Joachimite. After all, the Joachimites were regarded as little better than heretics. They were followers of Joachim of Fiore (c. 1130-c.1201), at first a Cistercian monk in Corazzo, who founded a more austere branch of the order in Fiore and whose teachings about the three epochs of history—the epoch of the Father, of the Son and of the Holy Spirit—were not looked upon favorably by the Church. However, Dante placed him in Paradise. Milosz probably had in mind Giovanni of Parma (c. 1209-1289), a superior of the Franciscan order. Accused of having embraced the doctrine of Joachim of Fiore, he was condemned as a heretic and sentenced to a long term in prison. Thanks to Pope Adrian V his term was commuted to confinement in a remote monastery, where Giovanni spent thirty-two years. The persistent and popular legend of his saintliness led to his canonization in 1877.

Francesco di Bernadone (1181/2-1226), i.e., St. Francis of Assisi.

Pope Fra Pietro, or Pietro of Morone (1215-1296) was elected Pope in July 1294, and took the name of Celestine V. His goodness and naivete exposed him to many reproaches from the hierarchy of the Church, and he resigned in December of the same year. In 1313, shortly after his death, he was canonized. C.M.

Appendices

A Few Words on Poetry

Milosz and Symbolism

A Note

Bio-Chronology with Photographs

Bibliography

Notes on the Translators

Index

A FEW WORDS ON POETRY

1   Companion to the magic rituals of Piltdown Man; keeper, along with every pseudo-primitive religion, of the cloudy recollection of "life under Cronos"; illustrated from the time of Sumer and the Thinite dynasties by works such as "The Righteous Man of Babylon" or "Hymn to the Sun"; and closely allied, finally, with the great illusion of evolution, Poetry, the passionate pursuit of the Real, seems called upon, as the organizer of archetypes, to survive not only our industrial civilization but also Space-Time itself.

2   This sacred art of the Word, however, just because it springs from the hidden depths of Universal Being, appears to us to be tied more rigorously than any other mode of expression to the spiritual and physical Movement of which it is both generator and guide. And precisely for that reason it separated itself from music, a primarily affective language since the dawn of Panhellenism, and, thus distinct, it has taken part in the ceaseless transformations of religious, political, and social thought, while dominating them. Priestly in prehistoric times, epic at the moment of Greek colonial expansion, psychological and tragic at the decline of the Dionysiac festivals, Christian, theological, and sentimental during the Middle Ages, neoclassical at the outset of the first spiritual-political revolution, the Renaissance, and finally romantic, that is, both mystical and social before and after 1789, poetry has always followed, fully conscious of its terrible responsibilities, the mysterious movements of the great soul of the people.

"Quelques mots sur la poésie," as Czeslaw Milosz says, is "dated somewhere between 1930 and 1937 and published in France many years later, after the death of its author. It presents in concise form the views that may be found in his other books as well" (*The Witness of Poetry*, Harvard University Press, Cambridge, 1983, p. 25). In his second chapter Czeslaw Milosz comments on the essay and translates eight of its fourteen paragraphs. In the last paragraph, the verses quoted at the end come from the seventh chapter of *Ezekiel*. (note by John Peck)

3   After Goethe and Lamartine—the great, very great Lamartine of "The Death of Socrates"—and under the influence of charming minor German romantics as well as Edgar Poe, Baudelaire, and Mallarmé, poetry suffered a kind of impoverishment and narrowing which turned it, within the domain of the unconscious, towards interesting and sometimes quite noteworthy pursuits that were tainted, however, with aesthetic concerns of an almost exclusively individual order. Besides, for nine hundred and ninety-nine poets out of a thousand this solitary little exercise resulted in nothing more than purely verbal finds made from the unforeseen associations of words, none of them rendering the inner workings of either the mind or the spirit.

4   This unfortunate deviation led to a split and a misunderstanding between the poet and the greater human family which continue to this day and will not end until the coming of some great, inspired figure, a modern Homer, Shakespeare, or Dante, whose renunciation of the mere ego, often empty and always scanty, will initiate him into the most profound secret of the working masses, more than ever alive, vibrant, and tormented.

5   And so, for nearly a century now, literati working in verse or rhythmic prose have set their efforts almost entirely under the sign of a search for "pure poetry." These two terms, betraying a somewhat childish preoccupation as soon as they are brought together, call for precise treatment. Unfortunately, they become more or less intelligible only after a long process of elimination. If they have any meaning, they can only name a poetry that would eliminate religion, philosophy, science, and politics from its sphere, and even those influences that might work on the poet through the methods and tendencies of all other branches of art. "Pure poetry," then, would be a poetry of spontaneity, of the most profound and the most direct kind.

6   We may be told that pure poetry, although seeming to be indefinable, in fact exists, and that in order to discover it one need only have the necessary faculty. We should then ask, humbly, where they look for it and in what works they find it, those aristocratic spirits and elite souls who presumably do not get drunk on Homer with the

stevedores of Naucratis or Miletus, on Dante with the workers of Florence or the gondoliers of Venice, and on Shakespeare with his audience of London street Arabs. Pure poetry: is it the slaughter of the suitors by Ulysses, the descent into the underworld by Aeneas, the Heaven of *The Divine Comedy, Ballade et Oraison, A Midsummer-night's Dream*, the fifth act of *Bérénice*, the end of *Faust*? Is it "Ullalume," "Elegy for Diotima," "The Afternoon of a Faun"? Or, more simply, is it the poetry of our time, which has no audience, the poetry of "the unrecognized," the work of those mediocrities which all of us are without exception, and who do not even read each other?

7   It is possible to say, without any prejudice or indulgence of paradox, that for nearly a hundred years the world has produced not one single poet, by which I mean a true poet worthy of comparison with one of those great rivers that extend equal welcome to barges and gilded galleys, and that splendidly carry within their impetuous and deep waters both the good and the bad, both fertilizing silts and sand, offering in a sovereign rhythm and flow at the same time an image of the permanence of divine things and of the passing of generations. What kind of stuff are the Parnassians and the Symbolists made of? What will remain, within twenty years, of the huge and hollow poetic production of our time?

8   At bottom, the search for pure poetry derives directly from the mannerism of the "aesthetic" schools. Under different names it was already the subject of our discussions around 1895 at the Kalissaya, the first American bar in Paris, which numbered among its regulars my friends Oscar Wilde and Moréas. And I shall never forget the look of disapproval which I earned one day from the Irish poet, when, in the middle of a conversation about Shelley, the great ancestor of aestheticism, I indicated my preference for that disciple of the classical Pope, the hasty workman Byron, who in his sublime *Manfred*, that most human and least romantic of poems, did not hesitate to take on again the great, eternal Promethean theme and to treat it in his own way.

9   But the moment has come to ask ourselves what the poetry of tomorrow will be like. We can say right away that certainly it will

not be the child of today's poetry, which is so anxious that it addresses neither humanity at large nor even an aristocracy, being the offspring of a world-wide bourgeoisie in decline.

10   The poetry of tomorrow will be born out of the scientific and social transmutation taking place under our very eyes. The Great War, the last or next-to-last leap of capitalism and imperialism, is still waiting for its bard. So let poetry quietly arm itself with patience. It is the spiritual consequences of events and not the events themselves that arouse the inspired. The Russian revolution would like to fabricate its minstrel from the ground up. But it is not through the mechanical application of a materialistic doctrine that one calls to life a new social order, and still less so a poet.

11   This poetry—which of course will be the opposite of a didactic art—will contribute in large measure to realizing an inner synthesis of the great discoveries in physical chemistry, astronomy, and also prehistory and archaic history. The world of Egypt, Sumer, and Asia is coming forth slowly from the grave. We have begun to decipher Iberian, Minoan, and Etruscan texts. The lands of the West now confront the venerable prestige of the East with a past that stretches from the Sargasso Sea to the Hamitic, Ionian, and Hebrew shores of the Mediterranean. The mythical unity of the world more and more takes on the shape of a reality that is called on to exercise an immeasurable influence over the religious and political unification of the small planet Earth.

12   A new mysticism is elaborating itself which, setting out from proven scientific foundations, seems bound, through a new metaphysics, to join up with ancient teachings and there, imbued with Cartesian intuition (for Descartes the "rationalist" is one of the forerunners of modern intuitionism), to discover at once the alpha and the omega of Pure Reason.

13   The form of the new poetry will be, in all likelihood, that of the Bible: a spacious prose hammered into verses.

14   It may also be that none of this will come to pass, and that the puny, emaciated poetry of the present is the drivel of final exhaus-

tion and senility. But that would signal not the drying up of an art but the end of humanity. Who knows? Perhaps we are much older, much more blasé, and much farther removed from God than we think, than Plato's Timaeus himself thought. If that is so, nothing more remains to us than to wish that at the least a new Ezekiel will appear and that he will know as well as the old one how to yell through flashes of lightning: The end is here! The End has come upon the four quarters of the land! Now the end is upon you.

translated by John Peck

MILOSZ AND SYMBOLISM

Other parts of this book deal with Milosz the mystic, profoundly reoriented in his life by the illuminating experience of the night of the fourteenth of December 1914. As one of Milosz's most perceptive critics has shown,[1] it was this experience which brought religion, for the first time, to his life. He was then thirty-seven years old and had been writing and publishing poetry for well over fifteen years. I should like to try to show what Milosz's early experience with poetry was, and how that experience led to the final, mystical philosophy discussed by Czeslaw Milosz in his Introduction. What I am saying may be disturbing to some readers for I believe that the pre-1914 poetry indicates a psychological and intellectual predisposition which should in no way leave us surprised by the post-1914 poetry and its religious basis. There may have been an "illumination" and Milosz may, as he has said, "have seen the spiritual sun" but one can make a case for saying that his activity previous to that date made of him a man who had long been seeking what, in a brief revelation, he finally experienced.

The predominant literary, poetic school in France, at the end of the nineteenth century, when Milosz was young and preparing to write poems of his own, was, of course, Symbolism. It is perhaps better called a movement and not a school for, although it had permanent qualities throughout its history, it is primarily an outgrowth of certain aspects of Romanticism which continued to evolve until the avant-garde movements of the beginning of the twentieth century—traces of which one would seek in vain in the poems of Milosz—put an abrupt end to Symbolism, at least in France.

Romanticism can be defined as a reaction against the rational philosophy which stemmed from Descartes in the early seventeenth century and which dominated thought in France up to, and to some extent beyond, the French Revolution. Descartes had rejected sense experience as a possible source of truth and had postulated reason, a faculty of mind he claimed was independent of the senses, as the sole means by which man could find truth in the world around him. As Euclid did not describe spatial relations in his geometry by observing triangles, parallelograms and the like in the empirical world but rather by thinking out, by reasoning, what spatial relations must be, so the rational thinker, said Descartes, finds in the proper use of his reason the universal laws governing the behavior of phenomena. An entire culture was built up, in France and the rest of Europe, on the basis of these "truths" valid for all men at all times. One of the major problems created by this attitude was, however, that of the mind-matter dualism inherent in this philosophy. Reality was conceived of as being "out there" in the world exterior to man. It was an objective reality and, because one obviously cannot be an object to oneself, it was necessary to think of man as something else, a subject, viewing the world of objects. The distrust of the affective and sensuous and their modes of apprehension implicit in this approach not only prolonged the medieval distrust of nature as a place where man could so very easily forget himself to the point of losing his soul but also separated man quite neatly from the chaos of the phenomenal world.

From Germany, beginning at the time of the "Sturm und Drang" movement, the Romantics challenged the very basis of the rational tradition across all of Europe. It was, in fact, to use Hegel's terminology, the antithetical phase of a dialectical process; a deep reaction to all the values, social, literary, artistic and philosophical, which had preceded. A revolution. Indeed, Romanticism emphasized a close relationship between man and nature, all of which indicated a breakdown of the mind-matter dualism in Cartesian philosophy. Reality was no longer viewed as phenomena "out there" which could only be understood fully by the proper use of that quality of mind Descartes called "reason." In fact, this development made it very difficult to distinguish between things as data perceived by the senses and the ideas we have of them as things in themselves. A philosopher whom we know Milosz read and knew quite well, Emmanuel Kant, gave a philosophical justification for the attitude toward reality which was felt so strongly by the early Romantics. Kant recognized that the thing in itself, what he called "das Ding an sich," was forever beyond the intellectual grasp of man. Man does have, however, a mind which is so structured that he is able to arrive at similar notions, at a certain consensus about the world, which he shares with his fellow man. There are modes of perception, temporal and spatial, that are common to all men, as well as categories, all of which make us see the exterior world in somewhat the same way. This leads to a "synthesis of apprehension," in Kantian terminology, which makes it possible for us to have an understanding of the exterior world, in our individual minds, which we can agree upon. The question is, of course, far more complex, but it is important to note that the breakdown of the rational philosophy brought about a concomitant breakdown of the entire culture which this philosophy supported. Perhaps the most important thing to say about post-Kantian idealism and the early Romantics is that they displaced the locus of knowledge and, instead of its being in the objective world "out there," they placed it in the mind. Henceforth it became essential to understand not so much the outer world as the mind which perceives the outer world. Knowledge was, therefore, posited as a function of mind, and Schelling, Fichte and the Romantics ushered in a century of psychologism or study of the deep workings of the mind.

In practice, particularly amongst artists and writers, the move toward nature and the imaginative conceptualization of the experience of nature in mind led quite rapidly and inevitably to what is called the dilemma of radical individualism approaching solipsism. In other words, reality created in mind could not be the same for each and every one. The ideal of the seventeenth and eighteenth centuries of rational truth valid for all men at all times collapsed. Other qualities of mind such as memory and will affected what was perceived and conceived in the mind. It was this aspect of Romanticism which led directly to what, in the second half of the nineteenth century, was called Symbolism. Man's imagination creates the world by a process of unification of sense experience which, in art, is the privilege of the genius. The "symbol" is the work of art itself and is part of what Kant called the "second nature" built out of what our senses bring to us from the world we perceive and which we are able to give form to through creative genius. Coleridge's concept of "coalescence of subject and object" is an example of this creative process whereby men and nature are united, reconciled, in the mind of the artist. The extreme form of this process, and one which is close to Milosz's view, rejects nature as such and either implies, as did Oscar Wilde, that nature is inferior to what man's imagination can create or, as William Blake did, that nature must be perceived by the "visionary eye," imagination, in order for man to find true unity with it. This attitude, so characteristic of late Symbolism, forms, I believe, the intellectual climate in which Milosz began to write poetry and which created for him a propitious environment of ideas, a psychological predisposition, leading directly if not inevitably to the experience of December 14, 1914 when, as one of the post-Kantian psychologists, Carl Jung, might have put it, Milosz found at the center of his mind, of his psyche, the imago dei.

One of the most salient themes of Milosz's early poetry is the solitude which quite naturally accompanies the Symbolist aesthetic. Exterior nature and the things of the world leave him indifferent or, in some cases, disgusted. One of his poems not in this anthology has the line: "Ah! Disgust! disgust, terrible disgust with all things!"[2] Reinforcing his determination to live in the mind, this attitude leads him to say: ". . . I know the confines of solitude."[3] In "September Symphony"[4] the poet refers several times to "solitude, my mother" in a way that shows he thought of solitude as the warm, comfortable, sympathetic state in which the past of his life would become clear to him and would allow him to give form and permanence to that life through his poetry. I have often felt that the greatest, the most ambitious of all the Symbolists was Marcel Proust, and, although it would have been impossible for the young Milosz to know anything but, perhaps, the first volume of his oeuvre, it is certainly true that occasionally he does remind us of the author of *A La Recherche du temps perdu*. This, not only because both of them attempted to restructure past life in a work of art, but also in detail in the way that the past is rediscovered by what Proust called "involuntary memory." The single piece of extensive prose by Milosz was his novel *L'Amoureuse initiation*. Some call it a long prose poem. At one point the protagonist, speaking of the effect on him of "the mossy and sleepy odor of old houses," says: ". . . in the course of my solitary pilgrimages to the sacred places of memory and of nostalgia, I only needed to close my eyes in some old dwelling place to be instantly carried back to the dark home of my Danish ancestors and thereby live, in the space of an instant, all the joys and all the sadnesses of childhood. . . ."[5] Needless to say, this novel, written in the first person, is most often considered to be highly autobiographical.

Another theme, this one showing Milosz's determined seeking

after some sort of transcendance, another form of escape from the solipsistic confines of his own mind, is the emphasis on neo-Platonic philosophy. The immortal soul, prisoner of the body here on earth, is constantly reminded, by the presence of various forms of beauty in the phenomenal world, of the perfection of the domain of the absolute from which it has been exiled. In "The Confession of Lemuel," the Chorus says to the Man: "Speak. Tell/Unsparingly what your soul has seen/In the blind, wandering and forsaken cosmos."[6] Further on in the same poem he refers to these memories of the soul as those "that are no more a gauge of time." Even "the humblest of things has its silent truth" says the Chorus, and, in another poem, "Vacant Lots,"[7] he apostrophizes his soul in a way reminiscent of Du Bellay's "L'Olive" and asks where is the love of the "nameless man and woman" and suggests that his soul alone, outside the contingencies of human time and space, will be able to remember. And, finally, in "The Psalm of the King of Beauty"[8] the poet states most clearly his neo-Platonist position: "For the motionless Absolute is the secret desire of that which moves." That indefinable yet ever so real sense of self which Milosz already felt to be the core of his existence was obviously oriented toward the suprahuman.

Baudelaire, in the very poem in which he states for the first time a poetics of Symbolism,[9] makes extended use of the device known as synesthesia. The mind as the locus of reality brings together the diverse elements of sense experience and, by means of the imagination, makes of them a meaningful synthesis. The synthesis is not to be construed as a mere total of the sense data but, remembering that Kant spoke of the imagination, "die Einbildung," as a necessary component in understanding, rather as a product of the imagination working upon the multiplicity of sense percepts. In our Western analytic epistemology we tend to think of sense experience as made up of discrete components, derived from the five senses, and consequently do not see them primarily as constituents of an irreducible whole and complex experience. In this respect the Symbolist poet, and to a somewhat lesser extent the Romantic poet as well, can be seen as significant precursors of that aspect of the phenomenology of Edmund Husserl where "intentionality" means the focusing on the object as an indivisible totality which is not made up, for example, of separate qualities as in Lockean psychology. In his mind the Symbolist poet often experiences sense data as confused, in the etymological meaning of the word, where the usual distinctions our language tends to impose are lost. In "Correspondances," Baudelaire speaks of "long and drawn out echoes which mingle in a deep and mysterious unity."[10] These "echoes" are the sense experiences which come back to man as reverberative responses to his contacts with things and which he, through imagination, unifies in mind. Synesthesia is an expression of the complex interrelationships the "confusion" of sense experience in mind inevitably leads to. It is a clever use of our usually analytic, discursive language to emphasize creative synthesis. It plays a very important role in the poetry of Milosz. In "Unfinished Symphony"[11] we read that "The smell of that silence was just like that of corn." Such a juxtaposition of what is, by implication, a visual sense datum or possibly a gustatory one with what is obviously an olfactory one is both disturbing and suggestive of how the poet's mind responds to silence in this context. We are getting very close to that period in modern poetry when many readers, conditioned by a rigorously rational use of language and thought processes, will back off from poetry and accuse it of not making "sense." In a later poem, "H",[12] the sound of a harpsichord is described as being yellow in color, and we cannot help but think of Rimbaud's curious use of color in the famous "Sonnet of the Vowels." In "Insomnia"[13] Milosz speaks of "tales full of the smell of old islands," and one could go on citing other examples, but the important thing here is that the apparent separation of sense data in direct perception has given way to a unity which only the mind can create when it, and it alone, is the force which makes what we call reality. In other words, Milosz is ready to recognize the primacy of mind, his mind, in the creation of what he will later call the "Rien." This is a major step towards the readiness required to experience and find meaning in the mystical event of December 1914. It is a still further break from the scientific, positivistic, rationalistic attitudes still so prevalent in French and European thought in Milosz's day and a move toward true freedom of mind.

The branch of Symbolism we associate with Milosz is not that of Rimbaud, who attempts to achieve a kind of phenomenological purity of sense experience, what is immediately and immanently presented to consciousness, after having rejected his intellectual heritage, but rather that of Mallarmé who, like Milosz, sought a transcendence, an escape from the world of appearances into one of pure being. There is, however, no religious element in Mallarmé's poetry but there is the same reliance on mind and imagination to force, as Mallarmé put it, "the words of the tribe," the vocabulary of everyday, to give access to the pure world of essence. There are, in fact, many indications in the poetry and other writings to show that Milosz did read and assimilate much of Mallarmé. Sometimes it takes the form of a suggestion, subtle but nonetheless certain, that Milosz has remembered a characteristic rhythmic pattern of the French poet, as in "When She Comes,"[14] but, unfortunately and understandably, not captured by the otherwise excellent rendering in English. In the original French the line goes: "Le vieux, le stérile, le sec moment présent," and it follows rhythmically the famous first line of Mallarmé's sonnet about the swan: "Le vierge, le vivace, et le bel aujourd'hui." Both lines, too, are about time. Milosz refers to the present moment as being old and sterile while Mallarmé sees it as virginal and living. Parenthetically it is interesting to note also that in Mallarmé's sonnet the swan, who is to be interpreted as its homonym in French (le cygne meaning swan and le signe meaning word are homonyms), escapes from the spatial and temporal contingencies of our world and becomes pure essence. In other words, le cygne (le signe) has been transformed by the creative imagination of the poet into an element within what Milosz will call "le Rien."[15] It seems to me that, in this line, Milosz was suggesting a homage to the great master of Symbolist poetry; the similarity in scansion and meaning are too great to permit any other interpretation. The use of such references is a very common device in late nineteenth and twentieth century art in general. I think that a possible explanation for this, at least in Milosz's case, is that the subjective reality of mind is made up equally of perception changed into the stuff of mind and of the products of other creative minds. The distinction is slight between these apparently different sources of experience in the Symbolist mind.

Milosz's poems recall also the other great Symbolist poet Paul Verlaine, but these references are less obvious. They are apt to take the form of regular lines of an uneven number of feet as Verlaine suggested in his "Art Poétique." In the original French of "All the Dead are Drunk"[16] we have quatrains of eleven-foot lines. Up to Verlaine's time lines of poetry were even in number of feet and the balanced regularity of their rhythmic progression was one of the most characteristic aspects of French verse. One could find in Milosz, many other examples of this tendency of French writers to dialogue with their own past, but many of them appear to be passing comments rather than indications of real influence.

Perhaps the most obvious way in which Milosz can be related to the Symbolists is in his almost exclusive use of free verse. "Vers libres" were first suggested as appropriate to the Symbolist temperament by Gustave Kahn, shortly after Baudelaire's unsuccessful attempt to find in prose poetry the best form for Symbolist poetry. Free verse was quickly picked up and exploited by all the major writers of the movement. It is a form which allows for the fact that the new poetics must reject the rigid discipline of traditional verse forms in order to allow the creative imagination to seek its own outer form freely. We have already seen Verlaine's advocacy of lines of uneven feet as an example of this but, in the Symbolist movement in general and in Milosz's poetry in particular, this innovation was far less important than that of Gustave Kahn. The very highly individual orientation of the Symbolist mind, its solipsistic quality, required a freedom in matters of form which the "vers libres" best offered. The difference between lines of poetry of unequal length and the kind of prose-poetry which Milosz also wrote, particularly at the end of his career, is not so great as it first appears; the prose poem often seems merely a different way of putting the same sort of poetic material on the page. One thing is certain, the very classical, and some might say very French, idea of inspiration arising out of overcoming the difficulty prescribed forms impose is indeed anathema to the Symbolist aesthetic. T. S. Eliot, however, has reminded us that there often lurks, in free verse, the "ghost of traditional verse," and, in fact, there are twelve-syllable Alexandrines with caesuras hidden in the free verse of Milosz and, in one case at least, there is an entire sonnet (of the typically French type with two quatrains and two tercets) written in alexandrins.[17] This sort of ambivalence towards form, although fairly rare, indicates how strongly rooted the old prosody was in France but should not be construed to mean that there was uncertainty as to which form of metrical structure was best suited to the Symbolist temperament; free verse clearly dominated.

In conclusion, let it be said that Symbolism, the movement which Paul Valéry felt could best be described as primarily a "kind of aesthetic mysticism," was, in truth, just that for Milosz. It was a mysticism without a teleology; one that created in most of its practitioners a sense of frustration because the rejection of the traditional culture did not lead to the discovery of something that could replace this loss. The very basis of the Western rational, scientific way of life had been discarded in this radical form of the Romantic revolt. Symbolism was a seeking which in few cases, of which those of Milosz and Paul Claudel are perhaps the most obvious examples, led to a satisfactory conclusion. The goal sought by Milosz, albeit unconsciously, was the mystical experience of December 1914. His solution was certainly not one valid for the collectivity of which he was part but it was valid for him as an individual.

Mortimer Guiney

Notes

1   André Blanchet, "Le destin bizarre du grand Milosz" in *La Littérature et le spirituel*, volume 2, Aubier, Paris, 1960.
2   In a poem not in this anthology entitled "Le Coup de grâce" from his early volume *Le Poème des décadences*.
3   Translated by David Gascoyne in this anthology.
4   Translated by Christopher Bamford in this anthology.
5   This novel, available in French, has not yet been translated into English. This translation is by the author of this chapter.
6   Translated by David Gascoyne in this anthology.
7   Translated by Kenneth Rexroth in this anthology.
8   Translated by Edouard Roditi in this anthology.
9   "Correspondances" from *Les Fleurs du mal*.
10 My translation.
11 Translated by David Gascoyne in this anthology.
12 Translated by David Gascoyne in this anthology.
13 Translated by David Gascoyne in this anthology.
14 Translated by John Peck in this anthology.
15 For a discussion of this concept of Milosz's mysticism see Jacques Buge, *Milosz en quête du divin*, Nizet, Paris, 1963.
16 Translated by Edouard Roditi in this anthology.
17 "XVII" from *Les Sept solitudes*, not in this anthology.

MORTIMER GUINEY is the author of two books written in French and published by Librairie de l'Université, Georg et Cie in Geneva: *La Poésie de Pierre Reverdy* (1966) and *Cubisme et littérature* (1972). He is the chairman of the comparative literature program at the University of Connecticut at Storrs.

A NOTE

From the age of Malherbe who, in the seventeenth century, assumed the task of purging French poetry of the more exotic and lush Italian influences of the earlier Renaissance, to the middle of the nineteenth century, French poetry remained, by and large, almost immune to foreign influences except, of course, those of the Latin and Greek classics. Among the earlier French Romantics of the first half of the nineteenth century, the influence of Macpherson's pseudonymous *Ossian* and of Byron, but of the latter's life more often than of his works, can sometimes be detected; and the prose of Chateaubriand, in *Le Génie du Christianisme*, proclaims his admiration for Dante, Tasso and Milton, whose works other French Romantics then began to read more assiduously, though generally in none too faithful or inspired French translations. Gérard de Nerval, however, translated Goethe's *Faust* and some ballads of Wieland and other German Romantics, and thus remains quite exceptional among French poets of his age and generation.

Foreign poets began to exert more diversified influences on French poets of the second half of the nineteenth century, when Baudelaire, for instance, translated Edgar Allan Poe and a few other French poets, such as Louis Bouilhet, Leconte de Lisle, Ephraïm Mikhaël or Gustave Kahn, little by little developed an interest in Orientalist themes of the kind that Delacroix, Fromentin and Gérôme had already exploited and popularized in French painting. Around 1870, Lautréamont moreover displayed, in *Les Chants de Maldoror*, a curiously personal interest in the kind of Satanism that he derived from his readings of Byron's *Manfred*, Maturin's *Melmoth the Wanderer* and the French translations of the Polish poet Mickiewicz. A few years later, Jules Laforgue, who lived for a while in Berlin, distinguished himself as a French disciple of the sophisticated ironies of Heinrich Heine. But the foreign influences that one can detect, if at all, in French poetry of the last few decades of the nineteenth century are generally limited to those of a few English or American poets: of the *Sonnets* of Shakespeare, for instance; of Poe, whom Mallarmé also translated; and of Whitman's *Leaves of Grass*, which continued well into the twentieth century to influence variously a number of French poets who practiced *vers libres*, ranging from André Gide in *Les Nourritures terrestres* or Valery Larbaud in his pseudonymous poems of A.O. Barnabooth to Blaise Cendrars, Luc Durtain and the Unanimiste poets and, even later, Drieu La Rochelle in his earlier poetry.

In the second generation of French Symbolist poets of the turn of the century, O. V. de L. Milosz thus proves to be quite exceptional in that much of his early poetry displays a far wider range of foreign influences than that of any other French poet of his age; and this is due, of course, to his own exceptional cultural background, in fact to his knowledge of Russian, Polish, Lithuanian and German literatures. Milosz appears, however, to have been more specifically influenced by a limited number of Romantic lyrical poets of Central and Eastern Europe who were all masters of a very sophisticated kind of nostalgia for a more or less imaginary past, or else of irony, often expressed at the expense of the poet himself. Milosz thus appears, in fact, to have been influenced by Heine, among German poets, rather than by the Olympic serenity or the Dionysiac turbulence of Goethe, and by Lermontov rather than by Pushkin among the Russians. In such early lyrics of Milosz as *Karomama* or *The soft and rusty creaking*, this ironical nostalgia for the past leads the poet to compose pseudo-historical vignettes of a more evocatively Romantic and less historically accurate nature than the reconstructions of episodes of the Greek past of his contemporary, the great Greek poet Constandinos Cavafis.

Milosz was intensely aware, both in his private life and in his writings, of the divided loyalties imposed on him by the cultural background of his own family and of his early upbringing. In the early Thirties, he suddenly declared to me one day, in all seriousness, that he was a Jew according to the *Talmud*, since his mother was the daughter of a Jewish Professor of Hebrew at the University of Warsaw. I used to visit him from time to time, in those years, at the Lithuanian Legation, a charmingly ornate former private home that overlooked, on the Place Malesherbe in Paris, the statues, dispersed in patches of greenery, of Sarah Bernhardt and of three generations of the Dumas family, a Napoleonic general and two popular writers. Milosz was then the diplomatic representative, in Paris, of the recently reborn Lithuanian nation, but found time, in spite of his political responsibilities, to receive in his office a remarkable number of young poets, and it was there too that I met one day Czeslaw Milosz, a very young Polish poet who had come to visit him from Warsaw.

A growing awareness of the implications of his partly Jewish ancestry may indeed have been responsible, under the pressure too of increasing political anti-Semitism in Central and Eastern Europe, for the shift in the writings of O. V. de L. Milosz, from his earlier ironical and very aristocratic nostalgia for the past to a more and more absorbing interest in, of all things, the mystical Jewish traditions of Cabbalah. In his physical appearance and his temperament, there had always been something slightly Quixotic. Many years later, the physical appearance and the temperament of the Polish painter and writer Josef Czapski sometimes reminded me of Milosz. Though Czapski was much taller, he likewise bore a striking resemblance to the Knight of La Mancha in the Gustave Doré illustrations for the great Spanish classic.

Milosz's knowledge of Hebrew and of classical Cabbalist literature and mysticism remained at all times, in spite of his studies, fairly limited, so that the sources of his more esoteric works and his Cabbalistic knowledge were mainly second-hand and, from the point of view of more orthodox Jewish Cabbalists, somewhat heretical. His main source of information and initiation, in this very difficult field of mysticism, remained indeed the pseudonymous writings of Eliphas Lévi, a nineteenth-century French author whose works, in the light of the greater knowledge and understanding of Cabbalah now available thanks to the very scholarly and reliable writings of Gershom Scholem, are entirely discredited. Another source of the Cabbalist speculations of Milosz may well have been the writings of Carlo Suares, an Egyptian-Jewish mystic and follower of Krishnamurti with whom Milosz began to associate occasionally in Paris in the early Thirties.

Be that all as it may, the very personal and, in a way, "heretical" character of the Cabbalistic speculations of Milosz, whether in prose or in verse, does not detract from their literary value, whether as testimony of real mystical experience or as pure literature, always expressed in exemplary and lapidary French. The last time I saw Milosz, in 1935 if I remember right, I asked him if he had been writing any new poems. With exquisite modesty, he replied evasively while an ambiguously nostalgic smile hovered on his lips: "Que voulez-vous? J'aurais voulu avoir écrit la *Bérénice* de Racine." In spite of his very Romantic temperament, his ideals were, in many ways, still those of pure Classicism.

Edouard Roditi

BIO-CHRONOLOGY

This bio-chronology (drawn from all available sources, above all from the letters and documents published in the *Cahiers* of *Les Amis de Milosz*) is not meant to be complete but only to give a sense of the life and times of O. V. de L. Milosz.

1199

On this date, according to family legend, King Leszek of Poland grants to one Budzilas Lubicz the heraldic name of *Bozawola*, meaning "Will of God," together with an appropriate coat-of-arms: an inverted horseshoe upon an azure field in whose center a cross of knighthood stands, a like cross being emblazoned upon the lower rim of the horseshoe itself. The helmet is surmounted with a crown of nobility, embellished by three ostrich feathers . . .

1578

Gregory Milaszewicz Milosz, the first recorded bearer of the patronymic Milosz (Milasius, in Lithuanian), a proprietor of goods and lands in "Labunava, alias Ganusuwiczi and Serbiny," registers an exchange of forests with a neighboring landowner. Milosz writes:

> Documents belonging to this older branch of the family, as well as armour found in the tumuli of Labunava-Serbiny, attests that the Miloszes descend from an ancient Serbian royal family of Lusatia.

(Serbian refers here to the Lusatian Sorbs or Wends, the smallest, westernmost branch of the Slavic nation, isolated in the twelfth century by Germanic tribes.)

1802

Joseph Milosz, the poet's great grandfather, born in Labunava-Serbiny in historical Lithuania, obtains from Prince Sapieha the vast estates of Czereia, and thereby founds the White Russian branch of the Milosz family. Milosz writes:

> Although about a century and a half has passed since the separation of these two branches, Lithuanian and White Russian, intimate relations never ceased to exist between them, and my father, from the first years of my life, took care to foster in me the attachment and respect with which our White Russian branch of the family venerated the ancient stock of the 'Miloszes of Kaunas.'

1811

Birth of the poet's grandfather Arthur Milosz, of whom Milosz writes:

> Officer at the age of nineteen in an Uhlan regiment of the Polish-Lithuanian army, he took part in the whole campaign of 1831 against the Russians. He had his right leg carried off by a cannonball at the battle of Ostrolenka. He married an Italian cantatrice of great beauty and remarkable talent, Natalia Tassistro, daughter of the conductor of La Scala in Milan and descendant of an ancient, impoverished family of Genoa. . . . I have my grandfather's letters, which show a great heart and a most cultivated spirit. He considered his wife to be the very model of all the graces and virtues. My grandfather and grandmother formed an outstandingly beautiful and noble couple. All the affection which, normally, I would have cultivated for my mother and my father, was transferred to my grandparents by a curious enough combination of circumstances and psychological complications. . . . My love for my grandparents is reflected in my person: beauty excepted, I am a sort of physical and moral amalgam of Arthur Milosz and Natalia Tassistro.

1838

SEPTEMBER 11TH: birth of the poet's father, Vladislas Milosz, in Vilnius.

1858

MARCH 16TH: birth of the poet's mother, Miriam Rosalia Rosenthal, in Stanszow, Poland, of a poor but honorable Jewish family: Mayer (or Moyer) Rosenthal, teacher of Hebrew, and Gitla Wertzmann (or Weremann). (Another date is given but Milosz says that his father was about forty when he met his mother, which would fit with this date.)

c. 1875-1876

Vladislas Milosz, riding in his carriage in Warsaw, catches sight of a beautiful young Jewish woman. According to the account Milosz gave to Petras Klimas, Vladislas Milosz "stopped his carriage and approached her; without their exchanging a word, she agreed to become his mistress. He took her off to Czereia . . ."

1877

MAY 28TH: birth in Czereia of Oscar Vladislas de Lubicz Milosz, the only child of Vladislas de Lubicz Milosz and Miriam Rosalia Rosenthal.

1880

Marie Weld, from Alsace, becomes Milosz's governess, the warm old heart in a house in which otherwise "madness and coldness roam" ("September Symphony"). As Milosz recalled in a poem called "The Return," it was this 'Marie" who first taught him the meaning of "Mary":

> It is with a throbbing cry of bitter gratitude,
> With such a cry as day's end raises
> That after so much pain and so much loneliness
> I welcome in tears the unlooked-for return

Of her who once in the frozen house
Where the child's soul died of neglect
Took me upon her destitute knees
And breathed on my tears the sigh of her name . . .

Elsewhere Milosz writes:

I have never been able to give free rein to my affection for my parents. My father was violent and ill. My mother's materialistic and uncomprehending solicitude oppressed me so much that very early I had the habit of hiding myself in the most secret parts of the parks and gardens in order to escape from the feelings that her presence aroused in me. I passed my days with my French-Alsatian governess, Marie Wild [sic], and with my tutor, Stanislas Doboszynski who, although of Lithuanian origin, was an ardent Polish patriot.

It was this Doboszynski who taught Milosz the art of reading and writing Polish and the love of Polish literature.

1886

JULY 2ND: baptism and first communion of Oscar Milosz at St. Alexander's Church in Warsaw.

1889

Milosz writes:

I came to Paris in April 1889. My father was treated there by Dr. Charcot for a very serious nervous disorder.

The family lived in the rue de Nicole. It was the year of the Great Exhibition. In her *"Anecdotes-Souvenirs,"* Renée de Brimont writes,

From the top of the Eiffel Tower his father held forth to him on the laws of equilibrium. He snacked on two *brioches* following a visit to the "Machine Hall" and he was a Sunday passenger on the Captive Balloon of celebrated memory. Mr. Vladislas Milosz was interested in aeronautics and believed in the future of "flying ships." He would have liked to orient his son towards the exact sciences. Thus during the flight he would not have missed the opportunity to expound his theory of gravity or of atmospheric currents. Wasted efforts. Milosz confessed to me that he took an aeroplane only once thereafter, and that he vastly preferred God's little aerial models, his friends the birds.

In October, Milosz's parents return to Warsaw and Czereia, leaving the poet behind at the Lycée Janson de Sailly, first as a boarding student, then as a day student living in the household of Edouard Petit.

1889-1890

Milosz writes:

I completed brilliant enough studies at the Lycée Janson de Sailly, first as a boarder, then (beginning May 1890) as a day-student under the direction of Mr. Edouard Petit, the Inspector General and writer specializing in pedagogical questions. Mr. Edouard Petit exerted a most salutary influence on my mind and character.

And again:

My childhood took place in Paris in a unique context and atmosphere. Old Jules de Strada, the great philosopher, the friend of Lamartine; Jean Lombard, the powerful evoker of Byzantium; Edouard Petit, the eminent pedagogue, were my first confidents. Suarez, Albert Jhouney, how many others, frequented the house in which I grew up . . .

According to J. Grinius, "At the age of thirteen [Milosz] was enchanted by Lamartine, the poet of nature and of tenderness. At seventeen he was carried away by Edgar Poe, writer of mystery and imagination; a little later, he adored the mystical, desperate poet Baudelaire. . . ." Roland de Boris, Milosz's classmate and oldest friend, the recipient of the *Cahier Dechiré (Torn Notebook)*,

Milosz's first notebook of poems, writes: "I knew him ... on his arrival in France, and we immediately came mystically together in a 'neo-romantic fanaticism' as he was later pleased to recall...." Jean Bellemin-Noel notes:

> To this spirit of Romanticism re-discovered our poet never ceased for a moment to remain intensely faithful; and nothing forbids us to imagine that in moments of doubt he dreamed nostalgically of having been born among the successors of Goethe, some hundred years earlier, the rival of Novalis and Hölderlin, the contemporary of Byron and Shelley and indeed the companion of his quasi-compatriots Mickiewicz and Slowacki ...

All this notwithstanding, Grinius reports that Milosz complained of "having been brought up in the principles of the most naive and brutal free thought."

c. 1895

Milosz writes:

> Under different names [pure poetry] was already the subject of our discussions around 1895 at the Kalissaya, the first American Bar in Paris, which counted among its regulars my friends Oscar Wilde and Moréas ...

1896-1898

Milosz studies Hebrew and Assyrian under Eugène Ledrain, translator of the Bible, at the École du Louvre and the École des Langues Orientales.

c. 1898

Renée de Brimont writes:

> A Parisian of my acquaintance who, around 1898, frequented the literary cafés of the Left Bank, gave me the following sketch: At a table which brought together Moréas, George Moore, Ernest La-

jeunesse, and a few other friendly night-people, a very young newcomer sat down. He spoke with a singular eloquence. Oscar Wilde, seated at a nearby table, inclined an ear towards him, and recomposed his heavy mask. Then, leaning towards his neighbour, he said: "Do you know them? That is Moréas—the poet. And this is Milosz—poetry itself."

1899

DECEMBER: *Le Poème des Décadences* (*The Poem of Decadences*), Milosz's first volume of poetry, is published by Girard et Villerelle, 59, rue des Mathurins, Paris.

1899-1900

At the literary cafe, the Napolitaine, Milosz meets Christian Gauss, later to become the famous humanist and educator, "Dean Gauss of Princeton."

1900

JANUARY 17TH: A letter by Paul Fort, recognizing Milosz's genius, is published in *Le Journal*, together with a laudatory commentary by Raitif de la Bretonne (Jean Lorrain).

JUNE 23RD: First public reading of a poem by Milosz at the Théâtre Sarah Bernhardt.

NOVEMBER 9TH: Milosz writes to Gauss,

> For some time now I have been—despite the beauty of Parisian life, a beauty so fine from a distance—horribly sad, horribly sad; sad with a sadness that nothing can vanquish. Don't laugh, but nothing, nothing, not even alcohol, not even work can vanquish it. This life is horribly empty with its anxious loneliness surrounded by idiots of the Napolitaine and the Kalissaya . . .

He adds:

In two or three months at the latest I expect to leave for my own sad country which must be a little like yours. My father is worse than ever, and I think that the hour of my return must soon sound. I have worked a great deal since you left. I have written more than a thousand lines of verse, and I think I shall be ready to publish in February or March. . . .

1901

JANUARY 1ST: Milosz attempts to commit suicide.
FEBRUARY 12TH, he writes to Gauss:

You know how repugnant life is to me: this hatred—reasonable because without reason—led me to make an attempt on my life, so useful to the world and to humanity. On the first of January of this year, towards eleven o'clock in the evening—with perfect calm, a cigarette at my lips,—the human soul is, after all, a strange thing,— I shot myself in the region of the heart with a revolver. As you see, I missed. Alas, when life attaches herself to a prey she does not easily let go. But the indulgence of fate is truly worse than death; I suffered horribly. The next day, the doctor,—the leading Parisian surgeon, Marchand,—did not want to operate, saying that I was too weak and would not live till evening. My heart and left lung were so swollen and filled with blood from internal bleeding that I had no room to breathe: I was, from one moment to the next, about to die of suffocation. A priest came to administer the last rites. But, by evening, I had taken a turn for the better to the great astonishment of the doctors . . .

1902

Milosz returns to Czereia, "recalled to Lithuania by a business of ancestors"—most probably the death of his father.
OCTOBER: Publication of the first important article on Milosz by Francis de Miomandre, *"Un Poète de l'Évocation"* ("A Poet of Evocation") in the journal, *L'Ermitage*.

1904

Apart from short trips, Milosz remains in Czereia, restoring the family mansion, reading, and writing. Above all, writing a "don Juan," as he reports to Gauss in January, 1904:

> the son of Byron's don Juan, the great-grandson of Molière's, the great-great-grandson of the Spanish Juan of Tirso de Molina . . . the last representative of this dark dynasty, the don Juan of today, most terrible of the don Juans. The drama is very simple: don Juan IV is a being who seeks for the absolute in this love of love which satisfied his ancestors but which is not enough for him . . .

In the same letter, Milosz adds:

> For a year and a half now I have been quite alone in Lithuania, a Baltic province, in the land of my forefathers, where I have been detained by matters neglected for forty years and whose material weight has fallen upon my fragile shoulders of *Geisterseher*. In summer I ride on horseback and compose verses by the thousands: in winter I travel by sleigh and, puffing on my pipe, re-read Kant, Schopenhauer and Plato. Also, from time to time, I take small trips with two friends—in Spain with Don Quixote* and in Italy with Heinrich Heine. One can get used to everything: the important thing is to live as little as possible in what is called the world of reality . . .

Also at this time Milosz composes his only, and now lost, book of poetry written in Polish. He writes to Gauss (on the 14th of November 1904):

> At the same time as my French book appears, there will appear in Warsaw my book of Polish poems, with which I am quite happy, although the language is not very pure, because too long a stay in Paris has 'frenchified' me a little.

* "Don Quichotte, c'est moi," Milosz used to say.

1905

Milosz witnesses the Russian Revolution (see *The Arcana*, Commentary to Verse 81). While in Russia, Milosz also experiences anti-Semitism. Years later, in 1924, in response to a questionnaire submitted to him by the review *Chalom*, Milosz confessed:

> I have travelled in Arab countries. I have even been taken for a Jew there, doubtless on account of my somewhat aristocratic nose. I was the victim of the same misapprehension in Russia, during the pogroms of 1905.

SUMMER: At the resort of Rigi Kaltbad in Switzerland Milosz meets the sculptor Léon Vogt, with whom he enjoys an intensely mystical moment of prophetic, Nietzschean rapport. The two men recognize in each other "Knights of Love," and Milosz is led to confess his deepest convictions, at which we can only guess from hints contained in later letters. For instance, this one dated March 5th, 1910:

> I am working on the Supreme Book, the Book of Revelation, this final work which I announced to you at Kaltbad five years ago. . . . Do you recall a certain afternoon spent beneath a leprous tree, facing the castle, and on the road to Klösterli on Rigi? We were three then, as the Flesh, the Soul, and the Spirit are three. More and more often I re-live those hours of initiation . . .

And (in letters to Mme. Vogt, in 1925: and again in 1927) Milosz wrote:

> Léon has doubtless spoken to you of the theories I told him about at Rigi, in 1905, theories regarding the role I would be called upon to play one day in the renewal of Christian metaphysics.
>
> My mission here-below is among the most secret, and I already spoke of it to Léon in 1905, in Rigi—defining it as an annunciation of a future Christianity . . .

1905/6

Milosz sells Czereia to a government-sponsored company engaged in parcelling land out to the peasants. From now on he will live on the interest derived from various government bonds so obtained. His mother, whom he will see only infrequently, goes to live in Warsaw.

1906

Publication of *Les Sept Solitudes (The Seven Solitudes)* by Henry Jouve, 15 rue Racine, Paris.

Composition (February 7-8) and publication (September-November in *Vers et Prose*) of the prose poem and fantastic story, *"Très Simple Histoire d'un Monsieur Trix-Trix, Pitre"* ("Very Simple Story of a Mr. Trix-Trix, Clown").

1906-1910

Milosz wanders throughout Europe (Germany, Russia, Poland, England, Italy, Spain) and North Africa. In some sense, these are the poet's years in the desert.

As he writes to Vogt in November 1910:

Sinister and sterile is the life of Zyndramus the Olde.

And yet the hard labor of the dream is always there, as he writes to Gauss in 1906-7:

I trust that, calmer and more confident, you have taken up once more the hard labor of the Dream, the only consolation here-below, more real than Love, more noble than Death, more powerful than Faith. This alone exists: this is Christ Crucified, this is the promised Christ-Consoler. I seek nothing more. I expect nothing more, than the moment of great thrill and tears realised by our suffering— the incorporation, as it were, of whatever we dream that is beautiful, gentle, consoling. And let the devil of the cafés, factories and automobiles take the rest! As long as there remains a feeling to express in musical words, a regret to clothe in the old rust of tears and to garland with russet-red and ancient ivy, suicide, believe me, is a naiveté . . .

And, again, in June 1910:

Do not forget Poetry in your spare moments; here-below, there is still only She; all the rest is but an instrument. She alone is a beautiful thing and true or, better still, She alone is a thing-in-herself.

The poetry of these years expressed itself primarily in the gestating composition of the great confessional novel *L'Amoureuse Initiation (Amorous Initiation)* and in the numerous translations made or planned, chiefly from English (Byron, Coleridge, Shelley and Rosetti) and German (Schiller and Goethe). At this time Milosz also probably planned (or made) other translations (now lost): from Polish (Mickiewicz, Slowacki, Norwid) and Russian (Pushkin, Lermontov), as well as from German (above all, Lenau and Chamisso). Though Goethe was always his favorite, England was the great discovery of this time, as he wrote to Gauss in 1910:

Of the few years of our common silence I have only a few things to say, the most important being about the long stay I had in England, whither I went above all to learn the language of the gods (since English poetry is the most beautiful of all poetries). I know enough English now to follow a literate conversation, and what pleases me most is that I shall soon be able to provide a good translation of the English poets (Byron, Shelley, Coleridge, Tennyson) . . .

Milosz adds:

I go only very rarely into my own country—I have not much to do there. I love no one there and no one is much concerned with me. On the other hand, I often go to England, above all to the county of Kent, whose trees and melancholy enchant me . . .

1909

Milosz meets in Venice Emmy Heine-Geldern, younger daughter of Baron Gustav Heine-Geldern and his wife, Regina, the great-niece of the German poet Heinrich Heine. Emmy was the love of Milosz's life. Born February 21st, 1890 in Vienna, and hence thirteen years younger than he, Emmy was for him the celestial spouse: "child of fate," "the only woman I loved."

1910

Publication of *L'Amoureuse Initiation (Amorous Initiation)* by Bernard Grasset, 61 rue des Saint Pères, Paris.
    MARCH 5TH: Milosz writes to Vogt:

> ... whether wandering or perched in an eagle's nest above a many-coloured and solemn grocer's, I am what I have never ceased to be, to wit, a Zyndramus whom neither the passage of time nor that of light will ever hinder from seeking the Mystical Kingdom wherein to be seated, in a Palace of Love, upon a throne of Glory and Beauty. Priest-King I am, have been and shall be. My power even grows hourly greater; I am the Abode of Love and speak to God face to face.

    SPRING: Milosz begins work on his second novel, which will eventually become *Les Zborowskis (The Zborowskis)*.
    JUNE 6TH: Marriage of Emmy Heine-Geldern and the Baron Leo Salvotti von Eichenkraft und Bindeburg.
    MAY-NOVEMBER: Milosz writes the nineteen poems of *Les Éléments (The Elements)*.
    DECEMBER 14TH: he writes to Vogt:

> One must never love oneself to seek a name, a form, or a place for one's love. Everything which defines a love limits and diminishes it as at the same time: that is why the concept of a God is dangerous, whilst the vague word Nature is just what is needed.

1911

Publication of *Les Éléments (The Elements)* by Bibliothèque de l'Occident, 17, rue Eblé, Paris.

JANUARY 10TH: First meeting of the Society of Polish Artists in Paris, founded by Stanislas Ostrowski; Milosz is one of the sixty-two "founding members."

SPRING: Milosz travels in North Africa; later, on his return to Paris, he spends some time with Christian Gauss, who is passing through town.

SUMMER: Milosz joins his mother in Bohemia. He continues to work on his novel and writes to Vogt:

> As for the translations, they are ready and will appear in Paris on my return.

DECEMBER: Milosz writes in another letter to Vogt:

> The Future is enriched by two very beautiful poems, love poems if you will, full of a strange tenderness.

END OF DECEMBER: sudden inspiration for *Miguel Mañara*, from an article read in *Le Temps* in the bar, Le Fouquet, in the Champs-Élysées.

1912

JANUARY 3RD: Milosz writes to Vogt:

> For eight days now, under the power of a dazzlement of heart, flesh and spirit, I have been plunged into a *Mystery* in 5 acts, of which I have already knocked out 4, (2,000 lines if you please, very free, naturally). It is truly of an *extraordinary beauty*—and I think that I can die without regrets. I write all day and all night—until 5 or 6 in the morning—and at midday I am at my table. I hardly sleep or eat; but in two days all will be finished, and I will be able to rest for months . . .

SEPTEMBER-OCTOBER: publication of *Miguel Mañara* in the *Nouvelle Revue Française*.

OCTOBER 8TH: Milosz writes to Gauss:

> I do not know the literary value (always a little commercial) of my drama; but I do know that it was furiously thrown onto the paper, in the silence of the night, not by my sorry ego, but by someone that every poet worthy of the name carries within himself and whom he hides jealously, with a holy modesty, from the eyes of other men and even his dearest friends . . .

OCTOBER: Milosz's *Chefs d'Oeuvre Lyriques du Nord, Angleterre-Allemagne* (*Lyrical Masterpieces of the North, England-Germany*) is published by Eugène Figuère, Paris. It contains translations of Byron (12), Shelley (3), Coleridge (1), Rosetti (1), Goethe (23), Schiller (11). Clearly Goethe and Byron predominate. Of Goethe, Milosz writes to Gauss:

> Goethe is my god, whom I place well above all that we know to be the greatest and most beautiful . . . he soars in my love even above Shakespeare, Dante, Byron, Edgar Poe.

As for Byron, whose "evil soul" Milosz suspected of having chosen to inhabit his own body, Milosz wrote in his Introduction that he hoped to reveal the "true, profound and much moved soul. . . ."

This year, also, Milosz begins to suffer from xanthoma, a "lepra" of the skin; and the idea of *Méphiboseth*, conceived some time before June, is executed in the fall: for by January 1913 it is "finished long ago, and even recopied twice," while it was only the previous June that Milosz announced to Vogt,

> I have an idea for a "David and Bathsheba, Wife of Uriah the Hittite," likewise a mystery. There the flutes and silver trumpets of Mañara will be replaced by the Organ, the dark, terrible organ of the purest Love, the great love of the Father: Jehovah himself, surrounded by archangels, will speak at the end of the play; can you feel that, isn't it true?

1913

Publication of *Miguel Mañara* by Éditions de la Nouvelle Revue Française, 35 and 37 rue Madame, Paris.

MARCH 3RD: Milosz sends a postcard to Vogt from Rome:

> Mañara and Méphiboseth will soon be followed by a Saint Paul (Saul of Tarsus) which I am carrying completely written in my head and only needs to be thrown onto paper . . .

SPRING: Milosz becomes acquainted (probably in Theosophical circles) with Carlos Larronde, founder of the *Théâtre Idéaliste.* Larronde would later produce Milosz's plays and be one of the group who, with René Schwaller, would form the cultural, spiritual and esoteric association behind *L'Affranchi* and *Les Veilleurs* ("The Liberated," "The Watchers"). At their first meal together, Milosz told Larronde: "I am on the threshold of serenity."

JUNE: Milosz's skin ailment and the treatment for it grow severe. He writes to Vogt (June 3rd):

> You will see me appear with a brow ransacked by iron and fire; the treatment which I am undergoing has become extremely severe, and the doctor will not let me leave for more than fifteen days at a time . . .

On June 9th he notes the "worrisome state of my forehead which could well, one day or another, condemn me to absolute reclusion." He adds that he has become "interested" again in his "old novel."

SEPTEMBER 1ST-16TH: Munich, composition of *"Symphonie de Septembre"* ("September Symphony"). On September 15th, he writes to Vogt:

> I have never breathed a word . . . about a sad story which began four years ago in Venice, continued in Austria and, thanks to the pernicious interference of my mother, terminated "abruptly," as the English say, with marriage of the Lady of my Thoughts to a young man crowned with artificial gold. . . . For three weeks I have been listening here to Wagner at the Prince Regent's Theater and to Beethoven and Bruckner at the Tonhalle, under the direction of Löwe. Doubtless you are asking yourself what Venice four years ago

has to do with Munich in 1913. A little patience, Walvater Wotan. Under the influence no doubt of Bruckner's admirable Vth Symphony, She who broke my heart and whose image has pursued me night and day for four long years, the Lady, I say, appeared to me in a dream—exactly fifteen days ago—in the night of Sunday to Monday. I still shudder at the terrible and enchanting reality, or rather, truth, of this dream. I must tell you that a very deep sympathy still reigns between this lady and the Chevalier Zyndramus: a purely seraphic sympathy, devoid of all lust and sentimental ardor, that neither time nor absence can lessen. The word frightens me a little because of his high majesty, nevertheless I do not hesitate to use it: the word is Love. . . . I saw her again in the dream in the form of a young woman who was sick, and it was in a desolate voice that she gave me the order to sing, in a single poem, my whole life . . .

This same letter announced the completion of his novel, *Les Zborowskis*. It must have been during this visit too that Milosz discovered Hölderlin, whose "pure poetry" immediately became his "bedside reading."

OCTOBER-DECEMBER: *Méphiboseth* appears in *Vers et Prose*.

About this time Milosz is introduced to Natalie Clifford Barney, probably by F. de Miomandre, and becomes an intimate of her circle.

1914

FEBRUARY: *Méphiboseth* published by Eugène Figuière, 7 rue Corneille, Paris; *Miguel Mañara* produced privately.

MAY: Translation of two poems by Hölderlin, "The Sun God," and "Sappho's Last Song"; manuscript of *Saul de Tarse* (*Saul of Tarsus*) sent to Éditions de la Bibliothèque de l'Occident; manuscript of *Les Zborowskis* (*The Zborowskis*) sent to Figuière.

About this time, the second volume of *Chefs d'Oeuvre Lyriques du Nord*, containing translations from Russian and Polish, is sent to the *Nouvelle Revue Française*.

AUGUST: World War I begins. In the subsequent confusion, the manuscript of *Chefs d'Oeuvre Lyriques du Nord Vol. II* is lost.

DECEMBER 14TH: Night of Illumination. Carlos Larronde writes:

Milosz, aged 4, with his mother.
DOUCET COLLECTION

Milosz, aged 12, with his mother.
DOUCET COLLECTION

Milosz, aged 19.
DOUCET COLLECTION

Symphonie de Septembre.

I

Soyez la bienvenue, Vous qui venez à ma rencontre
Dans l'écho de mes propres pas. Du fond du corridor obscur et froid du Temps.
Soyez la bienvenue, Solitude, ma mère.
Quand la joie marchait dans mon ombre, quand les oiseaux

Du rire se heurtaient aux miroirs de la nuit, quand les fleurs.
Quand les terribles fleurs de la jeune pitié étouffaient mon amour
Et quand la jalousie baissait la tête et se regardait dans le vin
Je pensais à Vous, Solitude, je pensais à Vous, délaissée.

Vous m'avez nourri d'humble pain noir et de lait et de miel sauvage,
Il était doux de manger dans votre main, comme le passereau.
Car je n'ai jamais eu, ô Nourrice, ni père ni mère
Et la folie et la froideur erraient sans but dans la maison.

Quelquefois, Vous m'apparaissiez sous les traits d'une femme
Dans la belle clarté menteuse du sommeil. Votre robe
Avait la couleur des semailles; et dans mon cœur perdu,
Muet, hostile et froid comme le caillou du chemin,

Une belle tendresse se réveille aujourd'hui encore
A la vue d'une femme vêtue de ce brun pauvre
Chagrin et pardonnant: la première hirondelle
Vole, vole sur les labours, dans le soleil clair de l'enfance!

Manuscript page of "September Symphony," 1913.
CHAPON COLLECTION

Certain jour d'été de l'année mil neuf cent seize, comme j'étais étendu, à quelque distance de Vaux, Storge, ~~...~~ Androgyne ~~...~~ sur le rivage éblouissant d'une mer moins vaste que ma douleur, soudain, tout au fond de moi, j'entendis Votre voix qui m'interrogeait : ~~...~~ mais ~~...~~ ? ~~...~~ que nous veut ~~...~~ tout ceci ? Alors je tombai dans une méditation si profonde, et des vérités me furent révélées, et le sens intérieur de mainte vision ancienne s'offrit sans voile à l'omniscience de mon amour.

Du premier au dernier mouvement de notre vie physique et mentale, Storge, ~~toutes~~ chose de ce monde naturel où nous sommes pour quelques ~~...~~ jours, se laisse ramener à une nécessité unique de situer. Nous n'apportons, à la vérité, ni le temps ni l'espace dans la nature, mais bien le mouvement de notre corps et la connaissance ou, plus exactement, la constatation et l'amour de ce mouvement que nous appelons pensée et qui est la science première et fondamentale de situer toutes choses, en commençant par nous-mêmes. L'espace et le temps semblent avoir été préparés de toute main pour nous recevoir; cependant, toutes nos inquiétudes nous viennent du besoin de situer cet espace même et ce temps, et l'opération mentale par laquelle, faute d'un autre lieu ou contenant imaginable, nous ~~...~~ rapportons une place en eux-mêmes, en les multipliant et divisant à l'infini, n'ôte rien de ces terribles angoisses, — de ces angoisses d'amour, Storge, qui nous poursuivront jusqu'aux confins de la Vallée de l'ombre de la Mort.

Le sentiment obscur qui accompagne notre première apparition éperdue dans la nature ne peut que ressembler fort à celui qui se saisit parfois si brutalement de nos réveils en sursaut, après ces torpeurs d'après-midi profondes et sans rêves, au fort de l'été. L'oubli du temps et du lieu nous jette alors dans une épouvante et une tristesse sans nom, et c'est moins dans l'engourdissement

constatation et amour

Manuscript page of *Epistle to Storge*, 1916.
DOUCET COLLECTION

Milosz by Henry de Groux, 1917.
DOUCET COLLECTION

Milosz at the League of Nations, September 1921.
BACKIS COLLECTION

Manuscript of *Memoria*, c.1922.
DOUCET COLLECTION

Psaume du Roi de Beauté

Des îles de la Séparation, de l'empire des profondeurs, entends monter la voix des harpes de soleil. Sur nos têtes coule la paix. Le lieu où nous sommes, Malchut, est le milieu de la Hauteur.

Les pleurs féconds versés dans une pensée à mon Père, les mondes d'or éclairent de beauté l'abîme. Royale tête qui pourtant reposes sur mon cœur, quel effroi de nombres tu lis dans la mémoire de la nuit. Reine, sois femme vraiment par la compassion suprême. Toute blanche d'une pitié de la grandeur, songe au plus solitaire, au Créateur! Le lieu où nous sommes, Malchut, est le milieu de la Hauteur.

Devant le saint labeur des constellations, ne sens-tu pas ton cœur se déchirer? Malchut, Malchut épouse! mère des générations! L'espace, essaim d'abeilles sacrées, vole vers l'adramand d'extatiques odeurs. Le lieu où nous sommes, Malchut, est le milieu de la Hauteur.

Car de la chose en mouvement l'immobile absolu est le secret désir. Régent solaire, pieux semeur de ce qui doit naître et mourir, je n'aime que ce qui demeure. Moi-même, moi Microprosope! je brûle de me transmuer.

Manuscript of "Psalm of the King of Beauty," 1923.
DOUCET COLLECTION

Ici ou dans la profondeur, rien n'est situé ! Rien n'est situé ! Toute réalité est dans l'amour du Père. Le lieu où nous sommes, Malchut, est le milieu de la Hauteur.

Paix sur la terre, ô mon Épouse, ô femme ! paix dans tout l'empire irréel, aux âmes de douceur pour qui tu fais chanter les sept cordes de l'arc-en-ciel ! Quand je contemple, Épouse, ta face renversée, j'ai le cher sentiment que toutes mes pensées naissent dans ton suave cœur ! Le lieu où nous sommes, Malchut, est le milieu de la Hauteur.

Et pourtant, et pourtant je voudrais m'endormir sur ce trône du Temps ! tomber de bas en haut dans l'abîme divin ! m'asseoir à jamais immobile parmi les sages, oublier que le mot Ici était absent de mon langage. Car moi qui crée sans cesse pour mériter le Rien, je suis le désir de la fin, Malchut, de la fin, de la fin des fins ! Oh, te coucher, Épouse morte, dans mon cœur, et te ressusciter pour le jour éternel du Père ! Le lieu où nous sommes, Malchut, est le milieu de la Hauteur.

Cimiez, 12-16 Mars 1923.

A R. de B., Solveg de France.

I. S. S.

O. V. de L. Milosz, Prince de Lusace.

Lithuanian Diplomatic Representatives, Kaunas, 1923.
BACKIS COLLECTION

* * *

Or, il advint qu'un jour Adam entendit en son moi Ève qui l'interrogeait: « Adam, Être de mon Amour, n'est-il pas vrai que ce qui me sépare de toi est le Rien? »

Ce mot Rien résonnait doucement et étrangement dans la bouche de l'épouse. Adam tomba dans une profonde méditation.

Il ne ferma pas les yeux. Il interrogeait l'espace; l'incorporelle lumière de la Beauté. La Vision était là. Il interrogeait l'espace, l'incorporelle lumière de la Vision Beauté. La Vision était là. Adam leva la tête: un aigle volait vers le soleil. L'espace était là. Deux nuages légers glissaient lentement comme pour se fondre en un seul: il y avait comme une impatience en Adam: les nuages glissaient lentement dans le temps. Et sous les pieds d'Adam, les pierres étaient chaudes du merveilleux midi.

Ève répéta son interrogation; c'était bien la même, et cependant ce n'était pas tout-à-fait la même: « Adam, Être de mon Amour, n'est-il pas vrai que le seul Rien te sépare de Dieu? »

L'espace était là, incorporelle lumière de la beauté de la Vision de l'Univers non-situé. L'espace était là, et Adam, dont le Moi ne voulait plus connaître ce Rien qui le séparait de Dieu, [pensait à l'univers total et] Adam murmurait : où est l'Espace ?

Alors, ô mon fils royal, ô Hiram, aux confins de cet espace que l'ancien Roi étendait par delà toute idée de limite afin de la situer en lui-même, dans le récipient d'un Vide, le Rien se mua tout-à-coup dans l'esprit de l'homme en cet Infini de ténèbres qui est la cécité d'Adam.

Manuscript page of the "Poem of the Arcana," 1926.
DOUCET COLLECTION

Milosz by Aron Bilis, Paris, 1930.

Milosz on vacation, c.1930(?).
DOUCET COLLECTION

Staff of the Lithuanian Legation, Paris, 1931.
BACKIS COLLECTION

Milosz and Jean de Boschère, Fontainebleau, c.1935.
DOUCET COLLECTION

Milosz and the Baronne de Tinan, Maggie de Lauris and Renée de Brimont, by the feeder, Fontainebleau, 1938.
DOUCET COLLECTION

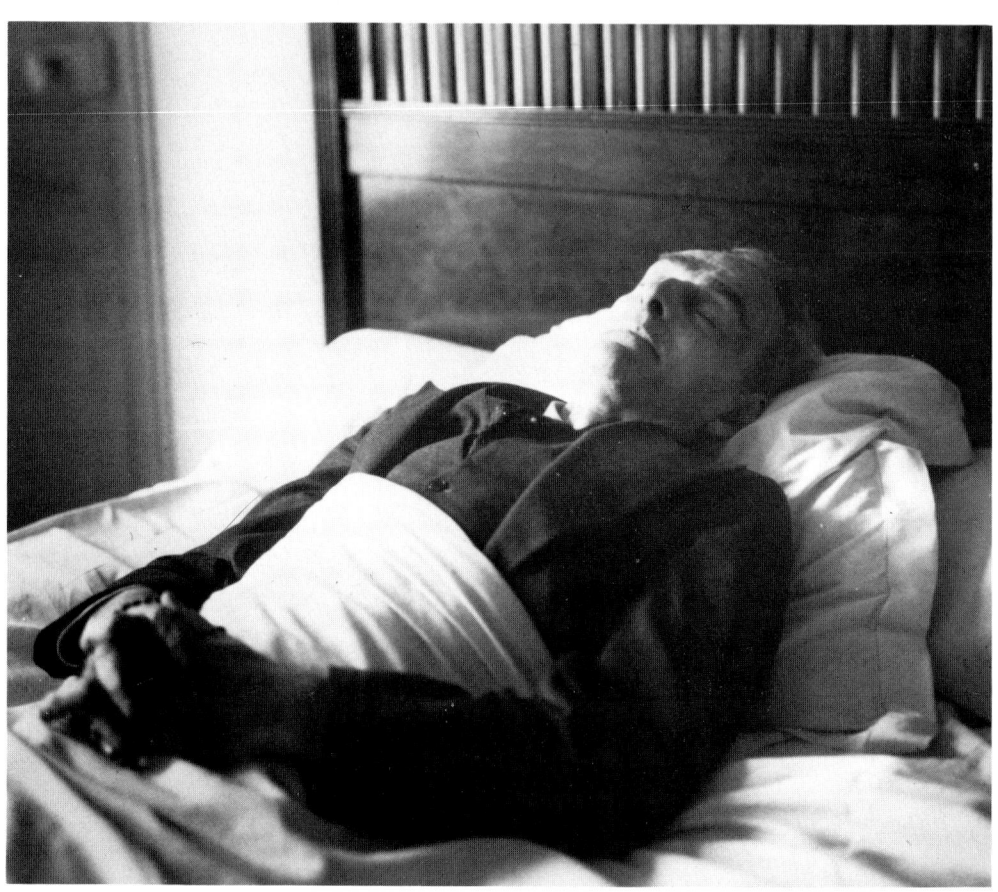

Milosz on his deathbed.
DOUCET COLLECTION

Milosz was suffering a tragic crisis of health at the time. For weeks no one saw him. He isolated himself in his apartment, opening his door only to rare friends, possessors of an agreed-upon sign. One sinister winter's morning in 1914 I presented myself at his door. Milosz welcomed me fraternally, detained me in the hallway, and I shall always hear him saying to me, as he leaned his tall silhouette against the wall: "I have seen the spiritual sun."

1915

At the beginning of the year, Milosz meets the Baroness Renée de Brimont, "Renaissance," who was to become one of his most faithful friends, his "companion in service," and, under the penname of René de Prat, was to write several important studies of his works. At this time also Milosz writes *"Nihumim."*

Publication of *Poèmes (Poems)* by Figuière. This was Milosz's first "collected" poems, and it included, in addition to the first three books: the *"Symphonies"* ("Symphonies"), *"Insomnie"* ("Insomnia") and *"Nihumim,"* as well as *Miguel Mañara* and *Méphiboseth*.

SEPTEMBER 19TH: Milosz writes (probably with reference to "Nihumim") to Gauss from Dinard:

Last winter I wrote some poems which satisfy me,—one, among others, which was given to me in a vision inspired by reading all Swedenborg's works . . .

At this time, too, Milosz begins the serious study of Hermetic literature, probably pursued concurrently with an active involvement in various esoteric milieux.

1916

Mobilized in the Russian Division of the French Army, Milosz is assigned to the *Maison de la Presse* in Paris (the Office of Diplomatic Studies, attached to the Office of the Minister for Foreign Affairs).

JULY (Paris)-SEPTEMBER (Dinard): Composition of *"Épître à Storge"* ("Epistle to Storge").

SEPTEMBER 25TH: Milosz writes to Gauss of the forthcoming appearance in *Revue de Hollande* of:

> a metaphysical study, an introduction, in the form of a letter to a wife (whom I have never met and of whom I have been thinking for twenty years—how many glasses of Black & White have been emptied in that time?) . . . an introduction, I say, to my philosophy of Affirmation. I wrote the piece here, and I think it is quite good; for one can draw from it a new theory of space, time and movement. Despite everything, I am not too miserable—In the evening I am seventy years old and in the morning I have the feelings and illusions of a whippersnapper escaped from school—hence I am my own grandfather and my own grandson.

1917

JANUARY: *"Épître à Storge"* ("Epistle to Storge") appears in the *Revue de Hollande*.

Milosz works at the Maison de la Presse, composes poems (e.g., *"La Charrette"* ("The Cart")), and continues his esoteric association and reading, as well as his friendship with Natalie Clifford Barney, who not only welcomes the little group of initiates (*"Les Veilleurs"*) at her salon, but also shows her appreciation for Milosz by sponsoring a book of his poems, *Adramandoni*.

An unexpected glimpse of Milosz at this time is afforded by Ilya Ehrenburg in his autobiography, *People and Life (1891-1921)*:

> At the Maison de la Presse I met a man who attracted my attention at once. It was O. Milosz. He had a northern face and a faintly foreign accent; he had been born in Lithuania, but wrote poetry in French. Max Jacob had told me of him. . . . Occasionally I talked to Milosz, not about journalistic matters, but about poetry and the future. He would gaze at me with his pale, faded eyes and say, very calmly and quietly, that soon someone would invent a machine which would write poetry, and then some little boy of genius, still in short trousers, would hang himself with his father's tie when he

realized that he could never move anyone with words. It was strange to hear this from a man whose job was to brief me . . .

NOVEMBER: Russian Revolution. Milosz loses his source of income.

1918

JANUARY: *"Quelques Verités sur la Révolution Russe"* ("Some Truths Concerning The Russian Revolution") appears in the journal *L'Affranchi*, signed "L. de Labunow, Lithuanian." Indeed, at this historic juncture, the esoteric group of *Les Veilleurs* (Milosz, René Schwaller, Carlos Larronde, etc.) begin to contribute heavily to the journal *L'Affranchi*, while at the same time starting two new journals equally dedicated to spiritual and cultural renewal: *L'Art* (edited by Carlos Larronde) and *Revue Baltique* (edited by Arthur Toupine). For all these three journals (the first two bearing beneath their title the device, *"Hiérachie-Fraternité-Liberté"*), Milosz wrote frequently.

FEBRUARY: Proclamation in Vilnius of the independent Republic of Lithuania. Milosz chooses to become a Lithuanian citizen. Czeslaw Milosz notes:

After the Russian Revolution of 1917, as the holder of a Russian passport, Oskar Milosz found himself juridically a Russian emigré. He had to opt for one of the new states formerly occupied by Russia and now aspiring to independence: for Poland or for Lithuania . . .

In *L'Affranchi*, Milosz writes the first of four articles on *"L'Emprise Allemande sur la Russie"* ("The German Ascendancy over Russia").

MARCH: The second article of *"L'Emprise . . ."* appears in *L'Affranchi*, together with an article entitled *"La Patrie"* ("The Homeland"), signed O. W. Milosz, and another entitled *"Pologne Lithuanie"* ("Poland Lithuania"), signed Labunowo. Also: publication of *Adramandoni* by Menalkas Duncan, brother of Isadora Duncan, 14 rue Visconti, Paris. Published with the help of Natalie Clifford Barney, each of the six poems in this volume is dedicated appropriately: *"Symphonie de Novembre"* to Mme. la Duchesse O.

de Clermont-Tonnerre; *"H"* to Miss Natalie Clifford Barney; *"La Charrette"* to Mme. la Baronne A. de Brimont; *"La Gamme"* to Mme. la Baronne M. Clauzel; *"Les Terrains Vagues"* to Mme. F. de Miomandre; *"Le Pont"* to Miss Natalie Clifford Barney.

APRIL: The third article of *"L'Emprise . . ."* together with an article, *"Les Droits des Peuples d'un point de vue Polono-Lithuanien"* ("The Rights of Peoples from a Polish-Lithuanian Point of View") appears in *L'Affranchi.*

MAY: Conclusion of *"L'Emprise . . ."* and an article entitled *"Lithuanie"* ("Lithuania") appear in *L'Affranchi.*

JUNE: In *L'Affranchi* Milosz introduces and begins the publication of his translation of Arthur Toupine's novel *La Guerre et la Verité (War and Truth).* This work by the Latvian author and Rosicrucian sympathizer will continue to be serialized in the July, August and September issues of *L'Affranchi.*

AUGUST 2ND TO AUGUST 24TH, composition of *"Cantique de la Connaissance"* ("Canticle of Knowledge"); *"Elmiro Celli, Un Paysagiste Mystique"* ("Elmiro Celli, a Mystical Landscapist") and *"La Charrette"* appear in *L'Art.* Celli, with his wife Rosa Celli, was a friend of the *Veilleurs.*

About this time Milosz also writes to Natalie Clifford Barney, referring to the poems in *Adramandoni:*

> Will I ever be able to forgive my poems their infidelity to you, to me? My Muse has committed the sin of Lot's wife: behind her an infernal city, full of beautiful damned youth was burning. She turned around. Now she is solidly rooted. Yes, but as a statue. Besides, in art, as in love, politics and religion, the end justifies the means, and one must have the courage to treat a book as one treats a people, or one's own heart. And then again, there is no salvation except in Unity. A dispersed and chaotic work is not even worth the honor of repudiating it. I have legalized my union with my work only in order to render our separation more irremediable. For it happens that I have something else to do . . .

SEPTEMBER AND OCTOBER: Milosz begins contributing to the *Revue Baltique* (edited by Arthur Toupine and announced in *L'Affranchi* as being "devoted to the particular defense of the Baltic countries which are the key to world peace") articles such as *"Au Seuil d'un Monde Nouveau"* ("On the Threshold of a New World") and *"La Défaite Allemande et le Conseil National de Lituanie"* ("The German Defeat and the National Council of Lithuania"). In *"Au Seuil..."* Milosz writes that Lithuania and Latvia offer

> the final vestiges of a high spiritual culture in the midst of a world ruled by the absurd cult of domination and of matter, the crude heritage of Rome.

And he adds:

> Lithuania, Latvia, you are the mothers of this Indo-European race, the spiritual center of the modern Aryan world.

OCTOBER: In *L'Affranchi* Milosz writes an article entitled *"Les Valeurs Nouvelles"* ("New Values"), signed Labunowo.

> New values are here! Let us create new words ... Yesterday's values have been transmuted—and where are the names of today's values, of tomorrow's? Where are the new words? How shall we say what is happening, what has happened? More than a political and social terminology has disappeared: the very spirit has flown from the words of our current language. Theocracy, monarchy, republic: all is being deformed, transformed, fused.... What will emerge? A sterile cinder or a precious amalgam? Or perhaps matter drenched in spirit ... a great philosophical, political, social, and moral *magistery*, one worthy of the most beautiful, the purest amongst us: hierarchy, now applied for the first time to the interior order of a nation, of a continent—of a world? ... The new values are here, but even the most prepared amongst us do not yet have words with which to designate them. The very collapse of great empires seems like a purely local accident in the midst of the tornado which is carrying away the planet. What geological catastrophe, what universal material shock could engender such a disarray? Something greater, something more mysterious than a physical revolution is occurring.... After an absence of more than twenty centuries spirit is redescending into matter. The control of events escapes us. Things happen by themselves. The crowd, this inert mass of matter, blind and deaf beast, the least accomplished beast in the world, brings us into the presence of deeds whose meaning surpasses the limits imposed on the most conscious mind.... What chaos! What

delirium! What mystical transmutation! Nothing that still seems to belong to the world of 1913 will continue to exist . . .

DECEMBER: *"Cantique de la Connaissance"* ("Canticle of Knowledge") appears in *L'Affranchi*, dedicated to René Schwaller.

At this time, Milosz made his first true Lithuanian contact. P. Klimas recalls:

> It seems that the first Lithuanian that Milosz met in Paris must have been Father Vilimavicius, a man of lively character who was later to be a member of the Lithuanian Parliament. He came from the United States to Paris at the end of the year 1918. In a journal he found an article signed Milosz about Lithuania. He asked some questions and having learned that the latter worked in the office of diplomatic studies at the *Maison de la Presse*, he went there and asked to see him. Once in his presence, he greeted him and addressed him in Lithuanian. Milosz remained impassive and said not a word. Father Vilimavicius then realized that Milosz did not speak the language. Since he himself did not speak French, they ended by talking in Polish. Returning to the office of our delegation, Father Vilimavicius told us how he had discovered in Paris this providential man. And so, with the priest as intermediary, we asked Milosz to come to work as secretary to our Delegation. Milosz immediately accepted this proposal . . .

1919

JANUARY 1ST: Milosz becomes Diplomatic Writer to the Lithuanian Delegation to the Versailles Peace Conference.

JANUARY 10TH: Milosz receives René Schwaller into his "clan," thereby giving him the name, *Lubicz*:

> Availing myself of a right belonging to my ancestors, I am pleased to give to my brother René Schwaller a mark of my esteem and a witness to my love by receiving him into the clan to which my family belongs and by conferring upon him the right to bear the coat-of-arms denominated Lubicz, with the variant *Bozawola* or 'Will of God.'

On the same day *Méphiboseth* is performed by Carlos Larronde's *Théâtre Idéaliste* at the Odeon Theater.

JANUARY 28TH: Milosz gives a lecture on *"La Fédération Letto-Lithuanien"* ("The Latvian-Lithuanian Federation"). This month, too, he contributed to the *Revue Baltique* an article entitled *"Les Républiques unies de Lituanie et de Lettonie"* ("The United Republics of Lithuania and Latvia"), signed Lubicz de Labonovas.

FEBRUARY: Speech by Milosz at the opening of the *Centre Apostolique, Hiérarchie-Liberté-Fraternité.* The Apostolic Center was the "exoteric" form of *Les Veilleurs,* whose "esoteric" center was named *Tala,* Hebrew for "Place." In his speech Milosz spoke of the role of the artist and the poet in "the formidable era opening before us":

> I do not know what his song will be—I only know one thing: that it will be the continuation, and as it were, the crowning, for many centuries to come, of the New Testament, as this last was itself the fulfillment of the Old Testament. It is not a book, it is not books that we are waiting for; we are waiting for the continuation and fulfillment of the only Book. The epoch in which we have the good fortune to live is one of those which is given to man—and, what is rarer still, to poets—to research the supreme joy of pride in the humbling which announces and prepares a renewal of *adoration.*

At this time Milosz translated P. Klimas's *"Der Werdegang des Litauschen Staates"* ("The Development of the Lithuanian State"), making it available for delegates to the Versailles conference.

FEBRUARY-MARCH: Milosz's translation of Arthur Toupine's *"Au Bord de la Mer Baltique"* ("At the Edge of the Baltic Sea") appeared in the *Revue Baltique.*

MARCH 29TH: Lecture on Lithuania given by Milosz in the rooms of the Geographical Society:

> Come, I will lead you in spirit towards a strange, misty, veiled, murmuring land. A beat of our wings, and we shall fly over a country where all things bear the dull colour of memory. An odor of lilies, a mist of mouldering forest surrounds us. It is Lietuva, the land of Gediminas and Jogaila. The pale, indifferent sky of the pensive country that opens before us has all the brightness of the gaze

of primitive peoples; it knows nothing of the sumptuous sadness of ripening. After seven winter months' lethargy, it awakens with a bound to the sudden beauty of Spring; and from the middle of September onwards, this fertile renewal, which never gave birth to Summer, already begins to recall, with the voices of crows, the seven long months of Winter. Then, the Lithuanian summer scent of honey gives way to the odor of Autumn which is like the soul of Lithuania. A bittersweet scent, like an old tree overturned and buried beneath moss; like a ruin after the downpour of summer's end. A wan light covers the plain; a sulphurous fog sleeps on the forests; the pallor of the *idée fixe* swamps the sun's silent force. Although there is not yet any snow, the sleigh replaces the cart on flooded roads. The odor of flax rotting on the river spreads across the countryside. Then finally the November snow appears, and the watch-dogs take up their interminable colloquies with the wolves of ancient forests lost in the fog.

MAY-JUNE: Lecture by Milosz in the rooms of the Geographical Society, *"Les Relations Actuelles entre la Lituanie et la Pologne"* ("Present Relations between Lithuania and Poland").

I am a Lithuanian poet in the French language who, after a stay of more than thirty years on the hospitable soil of France, his second homeland, had the joy, three weeks ago, of seeing his Lithuanian homeland again, and who, for the last three days, has breathed with great joy the air of his French homeland.

AUGUST 5TH-23RD: Composition of *"Talita Cumi."*
SEPTEMBER: *"La Cloche du Matin"* ("The Morning Bell"), Milosz's translation from the Lithuanian of Vincas Kudirka, appears in the *Revue Baltique*. Also, unsigned, in the same publication is his article, *"L'Art et la Pensée des Peuples Baltiques"* ("Art and Thought of the Baltic Peoples").
OCTOBER-NOVEMBER: *"L'Alliance des États Baltiques"* ("The Alliance of Baltic States") appears in the *Revue Baltique*, and then serves as the introduction to a booklet of the same title, published at the author's expense, by Desmoineaux et Brisset.
DECEMBER: Milosz is officially appointed Lithuanian Delegate to the French Government. At the same time *"La Langue Lituanienne"* ("The Lithuanian Language"), signed Lietuvis, and *"Le Sol-*

stice d'Été en Lituanie" ("The Summer Solstice in Lithuania") appear in the *Revue Baltique.* In the latter Milosz writes:

The whole soul of the primitive Aryan world still breathes in the freshness of the *dainos.*

In the former:

The soul of the world is troubled, the very foundations of Aryan civilization are shaken. The white race has lost all direction. In this anxious period of waiting for new values, one's gaze turns towards a land which has been long forgotten but where the spirit of the race still survives.

And again:

The Lithuanian language seems to us to be called upon to play a very great role not only in the literature of the future but even in the general evolution of the Indo-European race, beginning with the Russian nation, to which independent Lithuania, a land of ancient culture, ardent labor and wise organization, could well serve as a model or as some kind of spiritual guide during the period of reconstruction, so full of dangers, that lies ahead.

1920

JANUARY: *"Chants populaires lituaniens"* ("Lithuanian Folk Songs"), three *dainos* translated by Milosz, appears in the same issue of the *Revue Baltique* as does *"La Situation Politique de la Lituanie"* ("The Political Situation of Lithuania") and *"Les Bolcheviks et le Printemps"* ("The Bolsheviks and the Spring").

FEBRUARY-MARCH: *"Les 'Dainos', chants populaires lituaniens"* ("'Dainos', Lithuanian Folk Songs"), including translations of five *dainos, "La Situation Politique et Économique de la Lituanie"* ("The Political and Economic Situation of Lithuania") and *"L'Affaire de Kovno"* ("The Affair of Kaunas") appear in the *Revue Baltique* and the *Revue Parlementaire,* many of Milosz's articles of this time being reprinted in the latter.

MARCH 11TH: *de facto* recognition by the French Government of the Republic of Lithuania.

APRIL: *"Les 'Dainos', chants popularies lituaniens"* ("'Dainos', Lithuanian Folk Songs"), signed L. de Labunovas, and *"Vilna, capitale de la Lituanie"* ("Vilnius, Capital of Lithuania") appear in the *Revue Baltique* and the *Revue Parlementaire*, the latter also containing an article entitled *"Clergé Polonais et Clergé Lithuanien"* ("Polish Clergy and Lithuanian Clergy").

As for the *Dainos*, Milosz drew on the same source that Goethe, Lessing, Ruhing, Schiller and Chamisso had: the eighty-five *dainos* published in Berlin, first in 1825, then in 1843, by L. J. Rhesa, the director of the Lithuanian Seminar at the University of Koenigsberg. For instance:

O Sun, son of God,
In what regions have you tarried?
Where have you been all this time
Passed since our last farewell?

Over there, in the land beyond the sea,
I have watched over orphans
I have warmed up shepherds,
My gifts are innumerable.

O Sun, son of God,
Who lit your morning fire for you
Over there?
In the evening who made your bed?

The Morning Star and the Evening Star.
The Morning Star lit the fire,
The Evening Star made the bed.
Who will count my faithful, my servants?

DECEMBER 1ST: The French Government having recognized the Republic of Lithuania, Milosz is officially named Lithuanian *Chargé d'Affaires* and assumes his post at the Lithuanian Legation.

1921

MAY: Milosz attends an international conference in Brussels to resolve the question of Vilnius.

AUGUST-SEPTEMBER: *"La Confession de Lemuel"* ("The Confession of Lemuel") appears, in a version slightly different from that later published, in the journal *Les Écrits Nouveaux*.

SEPTEMBER: Milosz goes to Geneva for the admission of Lithuania to the League of Nations.

OCTOBER: Milosz writes to Count Prozor:

Diplomat by day and, in a more and more maddening fashion, thanks to the rapid chain of events set in motion by Poland's unbelievable politics, by night a poet, I think I shall soon be able to send you a long poem, which I am re-reading with surprise and which, I think, will interest you particularly, insofar as it is the expression of a state far removed from earthly existence. A bit of an alchemist by heredity as by personal taste, I have finally come to realize my life's dream—the creation of a poetic language which transcends even music and directly reflects, by means of the soul of words, inexpressible modes of existence. Formerly Mallarmé and, more recently, the futurists and the cubists, seem to have pursued the same objective; but, unfortunately, in French poetry, research of this kind always has a purely mechanical character. In my new style, which seems to me to be definitive and, as it were, the crowning of twenty-five years of effort, the concern for external organization hardly appears: a whole part of our human language remains unexplored; and it is this spiritual country, still so obscure, that I have reached in my pilgrimage. The world of spirits is not closed—Goethe says in his Faust;—but unfortunately he, too, thought in terms of time and space. I have developed in myself the sense for pure spiritual reality and I observe that it can be perfectly expressed by means of our purely earthly human language, on the condition that this calls down, very regularly and in perfect humility, the directing influx by means of prayer. Today my rhythm is already an imposed rhythm; my words already express something other than thoughts and feelings: they are hardly mine (what a horrible thing, to believe oneself a creator!), they do not issue from me, they are almost terrifying in their impersonality. I am, rather, in the spiritual state of a man who, under his very own eyes, sees himself realizing the Work.... Please forgive this horrible scrawl. I have just passed through an infernal period of work and anxiety, and the spiritual effort of these last nights has so enfeebled me that I have all the trouble in the world in forming a phrase and pushing my pen. The notes, memos, letters and other technical labors of the last six weeks, marked by the stay in Paris of a legion of Lithuanian politicians, would fill a library...

NOVEMBER: Milosz is named Lithuanian *Chargé d'Affaires* in Brussels.

1922

JANUARY: Milosz in Geneva for a Council Meeting of the League of Nations.

FEBRUARY: Milosz writes to Count Prozor:

I have just sent to Kaunas by special courier a long report containing the account of more than 15 conferences held with the gentlemen from the Quai and the Embassies...

P. Klimas recalls:

Milosz was an experienced stylist and had a remarkable ability to formulate in clear and precise fashion his thinking on all subjects. This fact made him an invaluable collaborator at the Legation, where he wrote diplomatic texts, letters and memoranda. In the beginning Milosz was buried by translation work and writing—he did not even have a typewriter at his disposal. He often worked all night. Both at the delegation and later at the Legation he did his work carefully and punctually and never handed a translation in late. From this point of view he was of exemplary meticulousness. One day an official at the Quai d'Orsay told me that the entire [French] ministry was astounded at the remarkable literary style of the correspondence emerging from the Lithuanian Legation: "Never have we seen notes written in so perfect a style," he told me, "and for a long time we asked ourselves what this Lithuania could be from which even the most banal notes were written in so remarkable a style. When we knew that it was Milosz, we understood."

APRIL-MAY: Milosz attends an important international conference at Genoa.

AUGUST: Milosz travels to Lithuania with Count Prozor and his daughter, the actress, Greta Prozor; publication of *La Confession de Lemuel* (*The Confession of Lemuel*) by La Connaissance, 9, Gallerie de la Madeleine, Paris. Dedicated to Léon Vogt, the volume contained: *"Épître à Storge," "H", "La Charrette," "La Gamme," "Les Terrains Vagues," "Le Pont," "La Berline Arrêtée dans la Nuit," "Talita Cumi," "Cantique de la Connaissance," "La Confession de Lemuel."*

SEPTEMBER 12TH: Milosz writes to Gauss:

> The great question which now particularly causes me not a little confusion in the unravelling is to have us recognized by the *Entente* and to obtain the port and the territory of Memel (Klaipeda) and also of Vilnius, our ancient capital, annexed with the territory of the same name by Poland. Between Poland and Lithuania, which are united by an undeniable comunity of political and economic interests, I would like to see reigning the most friendly relations because in the future the two countries will find themselves with regard to their powerful neighbors in an analogous—even identical—position. But to arrive at such an alliance based upon mutual confidence and respect, the United States, France, and the other great democracies must make Poland understand that its own interests demand a restitution of Vilnius to Lithuania and the amicable settlement of all the other questions of interest to both countries. . . . Dear friend, do you want me to reveal my state in a single word? I no longer belong to myself. I have given myself totally. And I only love them for Him, to obey Him; to please Him. For one can only love Reality, and Reality is an absolute of Abstraction. . . . Thus I live, as little the superman as possible, but with the terrible and dear feeling that the day approaches when I shall begin to talk to God as no one, not even Dante, not even Goethe, has spoken to him yet. And I do not mean to say by that that I shall write a poem more beautiful or even as beautiful as the Divine Comedy or Faust; but only that I am certain of creating something equally and perhaps even *more sincere* . . .

DECEMBER: *"Psaume de la Maturation"* ("Psalm of Ripening") appears in the review *Intentions*.

1923

EARLY SPRING: Milosz in Lithuania (Kaunas), then in the South of France.

APRIL: *"La Nuit de Noël de 1922 de l'Adepte"* ("1922: The Initiate's Christmas Eve") appears in *Revue Européenne*.

JUNE: *"Psaume du Roi de Beauté"* ("Psalm to the King of Beauty"), written while travelling earlier in the year, appears in *Intentions*. Milosz writes to Pierre Andre-Mai, its editor:

> ... I have two delegations (Memel/Klaipeda and Kaunas) and endless negotiations at the Quai. I must reread Boehme, Sendivogius and Paracelsus to wash me of all this.

SEPTEMBER 28TH: Milosz writes to Count Prozor:

> Just today I have sent in to M. de Fouquières the instrument for the ratification of the Convention of Memel (Klaipeda). Our diplomatic situation (whose settlement was subordinate to the submission of these papers) therefore becomes completely regular: a French Minister will be installed without delay in Kaunas and a Lithuanian Minister here. Thus, dear friend, I have the feeling of having worked well for my country without ever having striven for personal success. I have arranged everything (and for a long time) at the Quai without consulting our Government: they now know this in Kaunas, and doubtless they are surprised to have had in their service for six years, without the least suspicion of it, a disciple—not in words, but in action—of the Master.

NOVEMBER: Milosz in Kaunas, Lithuania, for a meeting of Lithuanian diplomatic representatives.

1924

JANUARY: Publication of *Ars Magna* by Éditions Alice Sauerwein, Paris; death of Léon Vogt. In his last letter to Vogt, which arrived the day after the latter's death, Milosz wrote:

Alas, everywhere we see the same spectacle: marvellous nature—a setting of strength, love and joy—and within this setting an ancient, tormented, sickly, abject human drama . . . I do not accuse only our age, for Aegean Pre-Hellenic civilization, and even the Egyptian world, must already have known this contrast, this disequilibrium between what joyfully accepts the law—tree, water, flower, stone, animal—and what rebels, and seeks a foul pleasure in a kind of existence that is condemned by its own reason, for—and this is a truly extraordinary thing—all those lost souls whose picture you painted for me know as well as you or I the path to happiness and physical and moral health because *the law of life is written in the very movement of their blood*—but they are children of Adam and do not believe themselves to be *free* except in *losing Paradise*. We shall read, if you like, my next book *Ars Magna* together. With a little patience . . . you will, I am sure, infer from my abstractions of a spiritual alchemist the great practical lesson. But there we are, *I have not been sent for everybody*, but for the salvation of a few only, and the obscurity of my Testament has been *commanded* me (as it was, besides, to Goethe, and to all those who have held in their hands the heart of life . . .).

FEBRUARY: Milosz in Geneva for the settlement of the Memel/Klaipeda question.

MAY: Milosz in Kaunas, as Secretary-General, for a conference of Representatives of Estonia, Latvia and Lithuania.

SEPTEMBER: Milosz in Geneva for the League of Nations. He writes to Mme. Vogt:

I have just spent three weeks in Geneva at the Lithuanian Delegation to the League of Nations—three weeks of overwhelming work.

OCTOBER 2ND: Milosz writes to Gauss:

My situation, dear Gauss, becomes more and more singular. Having assumed the defense of the young Lithuanian democracy's interests in Paris, I severed all ties with imperialist Poland. For six years, as the delegated diplomatic representative of a country at war with France's ally, I played a role in Paris that no one else could have done. The French Government wishes to hear from my mouth certain truths which would have cost any other Lithuanian, and perhaps even Lithuania herself, dear. But there you are, great difficulties are smoothed over, the State is recognized *de jure*, the business of Memel (Klaipeda) is settled to Lithuania's advantage, and I am needed much less. What I have done for the young democracy is therefore forgotten, and they remember only one thing: my aristocratic birth, from the heart of an old, Polonized family (a little bit Jewish, too).... Your colleague, Mr. Cous, spoke to me concerning lectures in America on new French literature and on Lithuania. Knowing the contemporary literary movement but a little, I would prefer to give a series of lectures on Lithuania, and on another subject that I know thoroughly: hermetic metaphysics and doctrines, from Egypt up to today, passing through the Pre-Socratic, Plato, the School of Alexandria, the Neo-Platonists of the Middle Ages, Swedenborg, the mystical eighteenth century. Do you think that such a subject could interest your compatriots, and could give me the means whereby to live modestly for a year or two...?

In the May and the December issues of the Jewish review *Chalom*, Milosz's replies to a questionnaire are published. In response to the question of the influence of Semitic thought generally Milosz writes:

I can admit to only two forms of expression for Jewish thought, which is the apex of a spiritual pyramid of which Hindu, Egyptian, Aramean, Greek and Neo-Platonic philosophies form the base and the four sides. These two forms of expression are: biblical poetry, the mother of the eumolpic poetry of Orpheus and Pythagoras, and what I call in *Ars Magna* the philosophy of heroic affirmation, entirely contained in the *Bereshit*, the first word of the *Sepher*.... In order for an intellectual Jew to fulfil his mission nobly, he needs something more precious to my mind than the genius of a Heine or even of a Spinoza. As soon as a Jew steps aside from the way of Knowledge—which is also that of sacrifice—he is trapped by matter, into which he descends not in order to vivify it but in order to dissolve it. A folly of movement—true decomposition—has taken hold both of our contemporary spirit, nourished as it is by relativity, and of our body, deprived forever as it is of the support of an absolute place. Jewish thought is no stranger to catastrophe. Given, nevertheless, that it has provoked it in the domain of pure science, but that, on the other hand, the spiritual consequences of recent physical discoveries have many surprises yet in store for us, it would be a crying injustice to refuse to relent towards it. Let the Hebrews not forget, however, that it is easier for them to rediscover the path of the immutable: does not the kingdom of the spirit, the only fixed thing, the last "situation," wholly illumine itself in a single letter of their alphabet, the Yod?

As to the influence of the Bible upon him, Milosz writes:

The best years of my life I have spent in my solitude, getting drunk on the Holy Scriptures and nourishing myself on them, first with my teacher Eugène Ledrain, then with some of my spiritual guides: Goethe, Swedenborg, Martinez de Pasqually, Claude de Saint Martin. These writings—and also Jewish exegesis—exerted a decisive influence upon Blaise Pascal, the disciple of the Kabbalist Raymond Martini. The Rosicrucian Polybius the Cosmopolitan, alias René Descartes, sought in them peace of spirit. Corneille and Racine drew their most serious inspiration from them . . .

1925

MARCH 13TH: Milosz writes to Mme. Vogt:

After a stay—brief enough, in truth but very tiring—in Kaunas, small misty, muddy and rainy capital of Lithuania, here I am again amidst the snows and ice of Geneva, whither I have followed my delegation to the League of Nations. I spend my days—and also a good part of my nights—scratching paper, with the feeling of expending my last energies in a labor without joy or glory. But, after all, it is perhaps something more interesting than glory or joy—for it is life itself, in all its ugliness and mystic uselessness.

MAY 27TH: Milosz writes to Mme. Vogt:

The new minister has already been admitted, the presentation of his credentials will occur soon; and doubtless this successor will bring news of my fate. It is possible that I shall be left here for a while in my new functions; nevertheless, an immediate dispatch to Rome to the Vatican is not excluded, and I would be happy to know your opinion as to the attitude it would be appropriate to adopt in such a circumstance.

As for my functions as Honorary Councillor in Paris, I don't think that they will last long. I find myself therefore, at the end of an exciting enough existence, in the situation of a young man forever threatened with having to take up a new career. But do not believe, dear friend, that this state of affairs could for a moment trouble my perfect interior serenity. I have never believed for a single instant in the reality of this life, and earthly existence has never been for me anything but a more or less boring and happily transitory stay in a room of a not very clean inn.

JUNE 10TH: Milosz writes *"Psaume de la Réintégration"* ("Psalm of Reintegration").

JULY 1ST: Milosz is relieved, at his own request, of his functions as *Chargé d'Affaires* and is named Honorary Councillor with the title of Resident Minister.

AUGUST: *"Vilna et la Civilisation Européenne"* ("Vilnius and European Civilization") appears in *Le Monde Slave*.

SEPTEMBER: *"Un Précurseur: O. V. de L. Milosz"* ("A Precursor: O. V. de L. Milosz"), an article by René de Prat (pseudonym of Renée de Brimont), appears in the *Revue Européenne*, followed by *"Psaume de la Réintégration."*

NOVEMBER: Milosz's mother has a stroke in Warsaw. Milosz sends money, but is unable, for political reasons, to pay his respects in person.

1926

JANUARY: Milosz writes *"Le Poème des Arcanes"* ("The Poem of the Arcana").

FEBRUARY 11TH: he writes to Mme. Vogt:

> I am very pleased with my latest poem—a formidable elucubration of thirteen pages which, from more than one point of view, merits being considered as the crown of my work.

APRIL: *"Le Poème des Arcanes"* appears in *La Vie des Lettres et des Arts* with an introduction by René de Prat (Renée de Brimont).

JUNE: Death of Milosz's mother—"after six months of paralysis and almost total unconsciousness."

SUMMER: Milosz begins his contacts with the birds of Fontainebleau:

> The death of a parrot of marvellous sagacity having inspired me to love only birds at liberty, I took the opportunity of a summer vacation at Fontainebleau to try to establish a contact between so-called civilized man and the wild birds . . .

JULY 5TH: Milosz writes to James Chauvet:

> . . . I would be embarrassed to indicate to you the sources of my doctrine. At the risk of being accused (by others than you) of charlatanism or megalomania, I find myself constrained to confide in you that the knowledge came to me by way of revelation—after twenty years consecrated to passionate and uninterrupted meditation, of which time, space and movement furnished the subject. It was not until after having felt open within me the interior vision, which I call mnemonic, that I abandoned myself to the curiosity of learning more about the doctrines of my predecessors in sacred science. These studies only taught me that which they could teach me, to wit, that truth is one, and it needs only a little respect and love to discover it within the depths of one's consciousness. There exist only two kinds of men: the negators with irreconcilable systems, and the modest affirmers who, since Plato and Pythagoras, through the initiates of Alexandria and the Christian mystics up to Claude de St. Martin, Swedenborg, etc., have all said the same thing to him who can listen.

NOVEMBER-DECEMBER: Milosz writes the exegetic notes to his poem, "The Arcana."

About this time, too, Milosz returns to the Roman Catholic Church and takes a spiritual director. As Renée de Brimont reports in a letter to Armand Godoy:

In 1925 or 1926 Milosz went to find the Reverend Father Clavé de Otaola, who was of Spanish origin and a Missionary of the Congregation of Mary Immaculate. . . . The Father was old, subtle, and of great distinction and culture. The two of them saw each other often, and spoke openly. Milosz liked the Father very much.

Years later, in a letter to a Belgian monk, Father Louis Hardy, Milosz wrote:

I wrote [Les Arcanes] almost without wishing to; its only merit is that of having irresistibly and definitively showed me a path which led at once to Reason and to the Lord's Table. Ah, if only our unfortunate contemporaries knew to what point these things are inseparable . . .

1928

MAY: A copy of the bust of Milosz done by Leon Vogt is requested by Natalie Clifford Barney for her "Temple of Friendship."

SUMMER: Publication of Les Arcanes (The Arcana) by Librairie Teillon, 83, rue des Saints-Pères, Paris.

NOVEMBER: Milosz writes to Mme. Vogt:

The book, which is a commentary on Ars Magna, brings to humanity a new conception of the universe and a demonstration of Christian dogmas: it opens an absolutely virgin era of human evolution for the human spirit—but the doctrine will not be understood until after my death. My mission here-below is among the most secret—and I already spoke of it to Leon in Righi in 1905—defining it as the annunciation of future Christianity.

1929

FEBRUARY: A translation by Milosz of Konstantine Balmont's "Contes Populaires Lithuaniens" ("Lithuanian Folk Tales") appears in the Revue Européenne.

APRIL: His translation of Balmont's "La Lithuanie et la Chanson" ("Lithuania and Song") appears in the Mercure de France.

MAY 14TH: Milosz writes to James Chauvet:

... One of my most devoted friends, Carlos Larronde, originally from Bordeaux, critical poet, mystical sociologist, and glazier involved in the repair of Cathedral stained glass, is in Paris and is actively, passionately busy grouping around me some common friends, worthy of our confidence and capable of exercising a salutary influence in all sorts of domains in the evolution of our terrible and admirable epoch.

I have decided to undertake the direction (purely spiritual, it goes without saying) of this fine movement which, thanks to a very symptomatic conjunction of circumstances seems to announce itself as susceptible of embracing very wide spheres—among others, that of the proletarian masons whose G[rand] M[aster] is one of our friends....

The hour of Apostleship has sounded. Dress for meeting: the robes will be of black silk, with a white collar. The Master alone will wear a red cap. These are the three colors of the great work (spiritual and physical). The fundamental teaching will be that of the *Arcana*. I am the enemy of exteriorization, but our modern attire is truly incompatible with all effort toward the Good, moral or social. Our group will have no more than twelve members.

AUGUST: His translation of Mickiewicz's "*Switez*" appears in the Nietzschean review *Zarathoustra*.

SEPTEMBER: Milosz publishes translations of twenty-six *dainos* in the *Revue de France* and then in an off-print edition by Corbeil. In his introduction, Milosz wrote:

Apart from the features which have earned it the precious homage of Goethe, popular Lithuanian poetry would merit a place of honor in European folklore by the fact alone that the idiom in which it is clothed is closely related to Sanskrit and constitutes, in the opinion of philologists, the most living and precise vestige of the Indo-European mother-tongue.

And he adds:

Destined to safeguard the physical and moral qualities of the mother-race, the Lithuanian nation, although small in population, has never bowed beneath the heavy burdens which the mysterious decrees of Providence, sometimes from the East, at other times from the West, have laid upon her. . . . Never has she bowed her head before Slav or before Teuton. Pagan until the fourteenth century, since her conversion she has known how to reconcile the sanctity of Christian dogmas with the purity of her immemorial doctrines. Faithful guardian of the treasure of primitive revelation, she did not hesitate to submit to the religion of universal love, without, for all that, repudiating in her heart the ancient cult of the creative power manifest in nature . . .

OCTOBER 24TH: Milosz writes to Mme. Vogt:

Unfortunately my health, which must, more and more, be taken into account, does not allow me to go out in the evening. Then again the success of the labors I have undertaken for some years and which must occupy the last phase of my life demands an absolutely ascetical lifestyle and the setting aside of all preoccupations alien to religion and knowledge. The very name of poetry, music or painting makes me shudder with an unspeakable horror.

He adds,

My confessor, Reverend Father de Otaola, died towards the end of August; but happily for me his spiritual son, Reverend Father Huriet, also an oblate of Mary Immaculate, has been willing to undertake my direction. We are doing excellent work together . . .

DECEMBER: Publication of *Poèmes, 1895-1927* (*Poems, 1895-1927*) by J. O. Fourcade, 22, rue de Condé, Paris. Milosz writes to Mme. Vogt:

As far as my book is concerned, Fourcade the Publisher and Cassou are a little late, but it has returned from the printers and will make its appearance with a great to-do in French and foreign bookshops in about ten days. . . . You know, dear friend, that it has not been from foolish modesty that for 32 years I have condemned my work to relative obscurity, but only because in my youth (youth is always a little vain) the glory it won hindered me from seeking the conquest of the supreme truths accessible to man. These divine arcana I possess today: my knowledge surpasses that of a Dante. Therefore I no longer have any reason to dread, for my work or my spirit, the solar glory of which they are worthy. That is why I consent that Fourcade, whose *Poems, 1895-1927* (such is the title of my book) is after all their property, should make such colossal publicity about them.

And he adds:

I am just emerging from a period of intense work and am putting the finishing touches to a large collection of Lithuanian tales and fables translated, or rather recreated, by me. I am handing in the manuscript to Cassou and Fourcade next week. It will be my debut in the comic or even burlesque genre . . .

1930

Publication of *Contes et Fabliaux de la vieille Lithuanie* (*Tales and Fables of Old Lithuania*) by J. O. Fourcade, 22, rue de Condé, Paris.

JUNE: A translation by Milosz of Mickiewicz's *"Les Lys"* ("The Lilies") appears in *Les Lettres*.

JUNE 10TH: Milosz submits his letter of application to become a French citizen.

JUNE 12TH: Milosz writes to James Chauvet:

I have seen Gary de Lacroze, present head of Josephin Peladan's old Rose-Cross at his home in Sceaux-Robinson. . . . All I can tell you is that Gary has followed the same road as I to end in an absolutely identical affirmation, namely, that one can discover nothing in the hodgepodge of philosophies and doctrines which is comparable to the eternal and most simple truths contained in the two Testaments. I am presently re-reading these for the fourth time since 1914 and I notice in my development a progress I could not have hoped for that allows me to accept the letter in all its clarity and nakedness, safe from the confusion that the search for a spiritual meaning formerly occasioned. . . . Truth is one, it has its beginning in a primordial Revelation and its end in the religion, founded by the Son of God, Spiritual Light Incarnate.

The expectation of the Consoler, whose coming He announced to us, is the only hope which is allowed us. All other doctrines are either infinitely obsolete or heretical. All that derives from man alone should be held as suspect and dangerous. The mages whom I have met in this life were all charlatans without talent and without real knowledge . . .

AUGUST-SEPTEMBER: Milosz spends a month at the Aigle Noire, a small hotel which will become a second home, in Fontainebleau.

1931

JANUARY: *Miguel Mañara* is performed in Brussels before the Queen of Belgium.

MARCH: Milosz is made a Chevalier of the Legion of Honor; the honor being conferred at a dinner on March 11th, honoring the fifteen years that Milosz has dedicated to Franco-Lithuanian relations. Also this month: *"Deux Contes Lithuaniens de ma Mère l'Oye"* ("Two Lithuanian Mother Goose Tales"), dedicated to his "colleagues of 'The French League for the Protection of Birds,'" appears in the *Mercure de France*.

MAY: Milosz becomes a naturalized French citizen. Though officially ceasing diplomatic activity, Milosz continues to fulfill his old functions at the legation.

SUMMER: Milosz meets his distant cousin, Czeslaw Milosz.

> I had the pleasure this summer of making the acquaintance of my nephew as he would formerly have been called, a direct descendant of my great-grandfather. I expected a horror to appear, a monster worthy of the rest of my family. . . . How surprised I was to find myself before a physically attractive young man of 19, a poet at once most zealous and well-balanced, moved with feelings of respect for my work, very attached to the intelligent and venerable side of monarchist, catholic and aristocratic tradition, and a little communist—just what is needed to do useful work in our unbelievable epoch—in a word, a young gentleman whom I consider a little as my son . . . (Letter to Mme. Vogt, November 11th.)

1932

APRIL: Another *"Un Conte Lithuanien de ma Mère l'Oye"* ("A Lithuanian Mother Goose Tale") appears in *Cahiers du Sud*.

SUMMER: Milosz uncovers "the key to the Apocalypse" and begins his inspired exegesis of its hidden meaning. He writes to Caffe de Broquery in July:

> I have re-read at least 50 times in the past fortnight the Apocalypse of Saint John.

Also in July a partial version of *"Les Origines Ibériques du Peuple Juif"* ("The Iberian Origins of the Jewish People") appears in the *Nouvelles Littéraires*.

DECEMBER: *"Les Origines Ibériques du Peuple Juif"* appears in a first full version in the *Revue des Vivants:*

> The present study, the fruit of thirty-seven years research, in some sense constitutes the prologemena to a long and exacting work which is in preparation. The gathering of the elements which compose it began around 1895, at the time when, under the direction of my late teacher Eugène Ledrain, I undertook the study of Palestine Mesopotamian antiquities at the School of the Louvre . . .

1933

Publication of Milosz's *L'Apocalypse de Saint-Jean Déchiffrée* (*The Apocalypse of Saint John Deciphered*), privately printed at the author's expense in Paris. In his foreword he wrote:

> One will be doubtless surprised to see in the following pages the code of David applied not only to Eskualda and Hebrew words, but also to French and Polish. But can one refuse Divine Omniscience, endowed—as our version of the Apocalypse irrefutably proves it to be—with a point of view freed from space and time, can one refuse it, I say, the pre-knowledge of the languages whose archetypes it carries in itself. . . ?

APRIL 26TH: Milosz writes to Caffe de Broquery:

Certain natures receive from youth to old age the nourishment necessary for their inextinguishable passion: at first poetry, then metaphysics, and finally science—but true science, the passionate and loving science of the Divine.

Publication of *"Les Origines Ibériques du Peuple Juif"* ("The Iberian Origins of the Jewish People") by Éditions des Vivants, 14, rue de Condé, Paris.

Publication of *Contes Lithuaniens de ma Mère l'Oye* (*Lithuanian Tales of Mother Goose*), dedicated to "My Colleagues of the French League for the Protection of Birds," by E. Chiron, 40, rue de Seine, Paris.

1934

SEPTEMBER 12TH: Treaty of Agreement is signed between Lithuania, Latvia and Estonia by foreign ministers of the three countries in Geneva.

DECEMBER 8TH: Milosz installs an "official feeder" for the lawn birds of the Palace of Fontainebleau.

DECEMBER 16TH: Milosz writes to James Chauvet:

The broad way opening before us is that which the very hands of our Lord Jesus Christ and His Angels have traced through the darkness and undergrowth of our lives. However veiled to our human eyes may be the truth to which it leads, we must in our humility recognize that we neither can nor ought to know anything else of it. Any discovery of our reason that does not conform to the prudent and carefully weighed teaching of the Holy Church can only be, even if it rests upon the most rigorous mathematical and physical evidence, an illusion of our senses and of our tiny and arrogant insect reason. The Holy Church, founded upon a revelation which comes to us directly from God and the period of the earthly Paradise by means of the Holy Jewish People—the Holy Church, I say, is always right compared to science whose most imperative 'truths' rest only upon trust in a 'Divinity which cannot deceive' and which, contrary to the science of Descartes, our infamous and blind contemporary science which is powerless where anything is concerned that is not lucre or murder, seeks any means to dethrone. The apparent humility of our savants is itself but a confession of their attachment to Reason alone (as they understand it).

Their abominable reasoning is the following: "Let us be humble because only our human reason exists, and this reason does not go very far." This is monstrous, iniquitous. Man was not created for such humility, he was made to know God, *to glorify himself in Him*. Created in God, he wished to be free in himself, in his *little I*. This is Adam's sin. Immense sin, because it was to save a feeble remnant that the Holy Creative Light made himself man and suffered nailed to the wood.

Still today, on the eve of the terrible punishment promised by St. John, still today, my dear Chauvet, the door of salvation is open: *Pater, Ave Maria*, and genuflection. It is because the greatest number refuse their Creator, their Saviour, this feeble tribute, this poor gesture of love and faith, that the heaven of heavens will foam with a holy fury, the fury of the Lamb.

Genuflection: It is the touchstone of all doctrine and any life. Far be it from me to judge the good Jew, the good Muslim, the good Buddhist! Their goodness only interests God. But it behooves me, a Christian, to judge, not according to the intention, but according to their attitude of pride or humility, my brother Christian, how much the science of Guénon and the others is worth.

1935

SEPTEMBER 14TH: Milosz writes to Armand Godoy:

I thought much of you and yours in Lourdes, whither I went three weeks ago for my annual pilgrimage.

The other sacred site to which Milosz was in the habit of making annual pilgrimage was the Cathedral of Auxerre, the "Apocalyptic Church" as he called it, one of whose Chapels contained a statue of the Virgin who carried just above her heart the Book with the Seven Seals Broken; Milosz called her the Morning Star.

OCTOBER: Milosz writes *"Le Nourrissage Hivernal dans le Parc du Château de Fontainebleau"* ("Winter Feeding in the Park of the Palace of Fontainebleau"):

> In gratitude towards these representatives of a First Nature, all-penetrated by love and spirituality but corrupted by the hardening of the human heart, after eight years of monthly visits I resolved to endow my small companions with an official "feeder". . . . The apparatus was admirably received by the birds. . . . Last winter, an indisposition having condemned me to a three months' absence, I returned to Fontainebleau with the fear of having been a little forgotten there. Vain fear! As soon as I arrived paths, woods and bushes resounded with calls, and I was greeted with a light-headed joy by all kinds of species. This incident is one of the three or four dearest and most moving memories that I shall carry with me from this hard planet Earth.

1936

"Le Nourrissage Hivernal dans le Parc du Château de Fontainebleau" ("Winter Feeding in the Park of the Palace of Fontainebleau") appears in the *Bulletin de la Fédération des Groupements Français pour la Protection des Oiseaux* and *La Phalange.*

NOVEMBER: Milosz writes *"Les Origines de la Nation Lithuanienne"* ("The Origins of the Lithuanian Nation"):

> The soils of Lithuania, Palestine and Spain must have locked within them inestimable and related scientific treasures. The exploration of these illustrious lands has hardly begun. And yet it is in their depths and not in the dust of the distant East that the keys of our past and our future await us . . .

DECEMBER: Milosz, after nine years of silence as a poet, writes his last poem, *"Psaume de l'Étoile du Matin"* ("Psalm of the Morning Star").

1937

"Psaume de l'Étoile du Matin" ("Psalm of the Morning Star") published in *Dix-Sept Poèmes de Milosz* (*Seventeen Poems by Milosz*) by Éditions de Mirages, 46, rue de Naples, Tunis.

SEPTEMBER 20TH: Milosz buys a small house in Fontainebleau.

DECEMBER 25TH: Milosz faints and almost dies. On January 4th, he writes to Armand Godoy:

> Ten days ago at Fontainebleau, carrying a case of seeds and suet for my birds, I almost failed to wake up from a spell caused by the combined attack of the cold and the sympathetic nerve.

On the same day he wrote to René de Berval:

> I have returned from Fontainebleau where I spent the Feast Days with my birds. I almost fell into an eternal sleep under my celebrated feeder in the French snow . . .

1938

"La Clef de l'Apocalypse" ("The Key to the Apocalypse"), dated February, 1938, is privately printed at the author's expense:

> The universal conflagration with which the unchaining of the various imperialisms and the basest political appetites threaten us must inevitably unleash, well before 1944, the immense catastrophe foreseen as a punishment by the Prophets and the Evangelists. We know that our appeal will not be heard. But we owe it to ourselves to address this last warning to the blind and rebellious Powers which rule the world.

Retiring from the Lithuanian Legation, Milosz moves permanently to the little house he has bought in Fontainebleau.

1939

FEBRUARY 16TH: Milosz receives notice from Kaunas that the President of the Lithuanian Republic has granted him a monthly pension.
MARCH 2ND: 6:30 p.m., death of Milosz, struck down by a pulmonary embolism in his house in Fontainebleau.

Canon Petiot describes those final moments:

Milosz had a song bird of whom he was particularly fond. The bird remained free in a room reserved for it but in the evening was put into a cage for the night. Now on this particular night the bird did not want to return to his cage. Milosz had to keep running after it. Each time that he was on the point of catching him, the bird escaped. In the end, Milosz got his hands on the bird, but, frantic, exhausted, and panting, he suddenly collapsed. He was dead.

MARCH 7TH: Milosz is buried in the cemetery at Fontainebleau. Petras Klimas, the Lithuanian Minister, and René Bruyez, poet, speak at the graveside.

BIBLIOGRAPHY

The complete works of Oscar Milosz are being published by Éditions André Silvaire, 20, rue Domat, Paris (v). So far, twelve volumes have appeared:

Tome I. Poésies I: *Le Poème des Décadences—Les Sept Solitudes.*
Tome II. Poésies II: *Les Éléments—Autres Poèmes—Symphonies—Nihumim—Adramandoni—La Confession de Lemuel—Derniers Poèmes.*
Tome III. Théâtre I: *Miguel Mañara*—Traduction fragmentaire de *Faust.*
Tome IV. Théâtre II: *Méphiboseth—Scènes de "Don Juan."*
Tome V. Roman I: *L'Amoureuse Initiation.*
Tome VI. *Contes et Fabliaux de la Vielle Lithuanie.*
Tome VII. Philosophie I: *Ars Magna—Les Origines Ibériques du Peuple Juif—L'Apocalypse de Saint-Jean déchiffrée—La Clef de l'Apocalypse.*
Tome VIII. Philosophie II: *Les Arcanes.*
Tome IX. *Contes lithuaniens de ma Mère l'Oye—Daïnos—Les Origines de la Nation lithuanienne.*
Tome X. *Chefs-d'œuvre Lyriques du Nord.*
Tome XI. Théâtre III: *Saul de Tarse—Daïnos—Diverses traductions.*
Tome XII. Roman II: *Les Zborowski—Très simple histoire d'un Monsieur Trix-Trix, pitre—Le Cahier déchiré—Poèmes inédits ou retrouvés.*

André Silvaire also publishes:

Connaissez-vous Milosz?—an introductory selection of texts, edited by Jacques Buge
Soixante-quinze lettres inédites
Lettres inédites à Christian Gauss

Buge (J.) et Silvaire (A.), *O.V. de L. Milosz (1877-1939)*
Godoy (Armand), *Milosz, le Poète de l'Amour*
and the *Cahiers de l'association Les Amis de Milosz*, the Journal of the Association of the Friends of Milosz, of which twenty-one issues have already appeared.

The secondary literature includes the following:

Barney (Natalie Clifford), *Souvenirs Indiscrets*, Flammarion, Paris, 1960

Bellemin-Noel (Jean), *Le texte et l'avante-texte, les brouillons d'un poème de Milosz* (A study of the mss. of the poem *La Charrette*), Libraire Larousse, Paris, 1972, *La Poésie-Philosophie de Milosz*, Klincksieck, Paris, 1977

Blanchet (André), *La Littérature et le Spirituel, II, La Nuit de Feu*, Aubier, Paris, 1960

Buge (Jacques), *Milosz en Quête du Divin*, Libraire Nizet, Paris, 1963

Cassou (Jean), *Trois Poètes: Rilke, Milosz, Machado*, Plon, Paris, 1955

Lebois (André), *L'Oeuvre de Milosz*, Éditions Denoel, Paris, 1960

Miomandre (Francis de), *Le Pavillon du Mandarin*, Émile-Paul, Paris, 1921

Richer (Jean), *Aspects ésotériques de l'oeuvre Littéraire*, Dervy, Paris, 1980

Zidonis (Geneviève-Irène) *O. V. de L. Milosz, Sa vie, son oeuvre, son rayonnement*, Olivier Perrin, Paris, 1954

Note should also be taken of:

the unpublished dissertation of Stanley M. Guise, *La Sensibilité ésotérique de Milosz*, available for consultation in typescript from the library of the Sorbonne; and

Hommage à O. V. de L. Milosz, "Les Cahiers Blancs", no. 4, 1939

Le Goéland, Feuille de Poésie et d'Art, no. 45, 1939

Cahiers consacrés à Oscar Venceslas de Lubicz Milosz, poète, no. 1, 1939; nos. 2-3, 1940; no. 4, 1941.

Poésie 42, n.d. (1942).

Also:

Dix-Sept lettres de Milosz à Armand Guibert, G.L.M., 1958

and

Place (Georges G.), *O. V. de L. Milosz* (a bibliography), Éditions de la Chronique des Lettres Françaises, Paris, 1971.

NOTES ON THE TRANSLATORS

CZESLAW MILOSZ (1911-   ) is the author of numerous books in Polish of which some have been translated and published in English. These include: *The Captive Mind* (1953), *The Seizure of Power* (1955), *Native Realm* (1958), *The History of Polish Literature* (1969), *Selected Poems* (1973), *The Emperor of Earth* (1977), *Bells in Winter* (1978), *The Issa Valley* (1981), *Visions from San Francisco Bay* (1982), *The Witness of Poetry* (1983), *The Separate Notebooks* (1984), *The Land of Ulro* (1984). Czeslaw Milosz has also translated the poetry of Zbigniew Herbert and Aleksander Wat into English, and has translated Simone Weil, as well as several books of the Old and New Testaments, into Polish. In 1978, Milosz was awarded the Neustadt International Prize for Literature; in 1980, he received the Nobel Prize for Literature; and in 1982 he was invested as a Member of the American Academy and Institute of Arts and Letters.

DAVID GASCOYNE (1916-   ) published a volume of poetry, *Roman Balcony and other poems* (1932), and a novel, *Opening Day* (1933), before he was eighteen. In 1935, before he was twenty, *A Short Survey of Surrealism* was published. Since then he has published: *Man's Life is this Meat* (1936), *Hölderlin's Madness* (1938), *Poems 1937-1942* (1943), *A Vagrant and other poems* (1950), *Night Thoughts* (1956), *Collected Poems* (1965), *The Sun at Midnight* (1970), *Collected Verse Translations* (1970), *Journal 1937-39* (1978), *Journal 1936-7* (1980). David Gascoyne, a distinguished poet, has been the recipient recently of the Biella (Italy) European Poetry Award for 1982.

KENNETH REXROTH (1905-1982) was one of the best known American men of letters of his time. A poet, an essayist and autobiographer, Rexroth was also an important translator of poetry from the French, the Chinese and the Japanese.

EDOUARD RODITI (1910-   ) lives and works in Paris. His published works include: *Poem for F* (1934), *Prison within Prison: Three Hebrew Elegies* (1941), *Oscar Wilde* (1947), *Poems 1924-1948* (1949), *Dialogues on Art* (1960), *New Hieroglyphic Tales* (1968), *Magellan of the Pacific* (1978), *Emperor of Midnight* (1974), *The Disorderly Poet* (1975), *Thrice Chosen* (1981), *More Dialogues on Art* (1984), and *The Wandering Fool* (1984). In 1981 Mr. Roditi received the Margery Peabody Waite Award of the American Academy and Institute of Arts and Letters for "continued effort and integrity in his art."

JOHN PECK (1941-   ) is the author of two volumes of poetry: *Shagbark* (1972) and *The Broken Blockhouse Wall* (1978). He has taught at Princeton University and Mount Holyoke College. In 1975 he received the award of the National Institute of Arts and Letters; in 1978, the Rome Prize Fellowship; and in 1981 a Guggenheim Fellowship. At present John Peck is a freelance editor and teacher in Europe.

CHRISTOPHER BAMFORD (1943-   ) is President of the Lindisfarne Association.

A NOTE ON
THE LINDISFARNE PRESS

The Lindisfarne Press publishes books in many fields, including history, literature, philosophy, science, sacred science, religion and art. It also publishes the *Lindisfarne Letter*, the journal of the Lindisfarne Association, recent issues of which include such themes as: *Celtic Christianity, Homage to Pythagoras, The New Biology* and *The Evolution of Consciousness*. The Lindisfarne Press also provides an extensive mail order catalogue service in order to make available not only its own books and tapes but also hard-to-find publications and 'tools for cultural renewal' in many different areas. For further information, please write:

THE LINDISFARNE PRESS
P.O. BOX 127
WEST STOCKBRIDGE
MASSACHUSETTS 01266
U.S.A.